I am with you

ALWAYS

I am with you ALWAYS

STEPHEN SULYK

Pleasant Word
A Division of WINEPRESS PUBLISHING

Printed in the United States of America

Packaged by Pleasant Word, a division of WinePress Publishing, PO Box 428, Enumclaw, WA 98022. The views expressed or implied in this work do not necessarily reflect those of Pleasant Word, a division of WinePress Publishing. Ultimate design, content, and editorial accuracy of this work are the responsibilities of the author.

ISBN 1-4141-0062-0

Library of Congress Catalog Card Number: 2003113579

This book is dedicated in loving memory to my parents, Michael and Mary Sulyk, and my grandfather, Ivan Sulyk, whose love, prayers, and examples of Christian life nurtured the seeds of a priestly vocation deep within my heart.

Table of Contents

Word to the Reader

In the book of the prophet Isaiah, God said to his Chosen People: *"Fear not, for I have redeemed you; I have called you by name: you are mine! When you pass through the water, I will be with you; in the rivers you shall not drown. When you walk through fire, you shall not be burned; the flames shall not consume you"* (Isaiah 43:1–2).

These words of God can be applied in a real way to Metropolitan Archbishop Emeritus of Philadelphia, Stephen Sulyk. His life's journey began in the tiny village of Balnycia, located in the Western Ukraine's region called Lemkivschyna. It continued in Germany, through the hard times of the Second World War, over the ocean to the United States. Here young Stephen, over whom Divine Providence watched, did not drown in the waters of material wealth. The newfound flames of freedom did not burn him, nor did secular society consume him. He maintained a deep spirituality and love for prayer, which he had inherited from his parents and especially his grandfather.

One of his mother's questions to her little son: *"Stephen! Would you like to be a priest?"* evidently inspired him to choose a vocation to the priesthood. He entered a seminary in Germany, then also in the United States of America, which brought him finally to the Metropolitan's throne of Philadelphia. Here he started his episcopal ministry to our Church. He took an active part in the World Synods of Bishops in the Vatican, in the United States of America Conference of Catholic Bishops, and in the Bishops Synods of the Ukrainian Catholic Church. He was elected by our bishops to the Permanent Synod and participated in all solemn celebrations that were marked by joy, and sometimes, by sadness. His life's journey and his service to the Church and to our people, the Metropolitan sincerely and objectively presents in these his memoirs, "I Am With You Always" (Matthew 28:20).

These Memoirs indisputably will become an important source of study and contribute to a proper understanding of the history of the Ukrainian Catholic Church in Ukraine and in the Diaspora during the last forty years of the second millennium. They are interesting especially because they are inspired by faith in God, enriched by quotations from the Scriptures, by spiritual explanations of the liturgical rites—especially of the Holy Mystery of the Sacred Priesthood—about the vocation to priestly and monastic ministries, and about a practical approach to the solution of various pastoral problems.

They are extraordinarily important also in that they competently and objectively present the all-important events of the stormy history of our Ukrainian Catholic Church, which took place during the past forty years. In sum, it will become a unique document in which a reader will be able to get acquainted with major historic events in the life of our Church of this period.

There is no doubt that God chose and called him to the important mission of a metropolitan archbishop's ministry at a time of very complex circumstances, marked by secularism, by the decline of faith, by the difficult situation in which it found itself, as a result of a lack of firm ecclesiastical leadership and a long period of persecution.

Reading these memoirs, a reader will be able to appreciate and gain proper understanding of quite a few important historic events of our Church and people, which caused joy or, at times, anxiety to many of our people. To the major ecclesiastical events of this period, one can include the following: Liberation from Siberian gulags of the confessor of faith, His Beatitude Patriarch Joseph Slipyj; episcopal ordination of many of our bishops; preparations for and celebration of the 1000-Jubilee of the Baptism of Ukraine; the 400th Jubilee of Church unity in Ukraine, known as the Brest Union; resurgence of the Ukrainian Catholic Church in Ukraine from the catacombs and her struggle to find her proper place under the sun; the election of the first Slavic Pope John Paul II and his favorable attitude toward our Church; events concerning the normalization of the life of our Church in Ukraine after her resurgence from the half-century long catacomb existence; the decisions of several Synods of Bishops of our Church; the exposition of various covert intrigues relating to the leadership of our Church in Ukraine and the resolution of the question of only one approved text of the Liturgy, etc.

Divine Providence used diverse ways to guide young Stephen to his destiny. The Lord always protected him by His grace in order to finally lead him to the Holy Priesthood and to the Episcopal ministry as our Metropolitan Archbishop. Indeed, he proved himself to be a judicious leader among our bishops during the last two decades of the second Millennium of Christianity.

The readers of these unique memoirs will have an opportunity to recall many emotional experiences, find answers to many questions concerning the contemporary history of our Church, or for the first time become acquainted with them without necessary and difficult search in the archival documents inaccessible to most readers. By these memoirs Metropolitan Stephen leaves to future generations unquestionable proof of his sincere service to God, to his Church, to his people, and especially service to the truth.

Father Basil Cembalista, editor of *Svitlo*.

My Birthplace

I was born in 1924 in the village called Balnycia, a very small village, located in Lemkivschyna, Western Ukraine. The village is located in the Carpathian Mountains, on the boundary with Sub Carpathian Ukraine. In 1549 Sianik County chairman Petro Zborovsky, using his regal rights, gave the territory of Balnycia to Ivan Stechev from the village of Vola Myhova. He is considered to be the first settler in Balnycia. Thick forests then covered Balnycia. In the year 1561 there were already seven settlers. The settlers deforested and cleared the land, plowed, and sowed grain. By 1661 there were already 17 settlers. But in 1657, Hungarian Rakoczy's bandits attacked and burned the village so that there remained only one house. Again in 1686 some bandits from Hungary attacked the village, ransacked, and destroyed it, causing a great deal of damage.[1]

West of Balnycia flows a small brook named Oslava, which emerges from a small underground source in the upper end of the village. It flows into the river Sian near the town of Zahirya. Oslava marks the eastern boundary of Lemkivschyna. In Balnycia were

---

[1] *Bieszczady, Przewodnik, czwarte Wydanie aktualizowane, Pruszkow-Olszanica, 1995 pp. 45–48 Bieszczadow (W X-XVII.) & zasiedlenia Historia "Balnica p. 240."*

seventy-eight Ukrainian, two Jewish, and two Polish families, not taking into account the members of the Border Police, who were not permanent residents of the village. In the village from the 1880s there was a four-grade elementary school. In 1856 a new Ukrainian Catholic Church, St. Michael's, was erected, (a previous church building was located some distance away on a tract of land belonging to the church). The pastor resided in a nearby village called Maniv, and from there served Balnycia and Shcherbanivka.

In Balnycia were the barracks housing the Border Police. Down on the village end was a mill and a sawmill. Below the mill on a thickly-wooded hill was a small chapel built of stone. In front of it was an underground source of constantly flowing water believed to have curative powers. Once a year, on Pentecost Sunday, people with their priest went in a procession with a cross and banners from the church to this chapel, where the Divine Liturgy was served and the water was blessed.

Highland tillage was not fertile, for it was stony, and the climate was cold. Winters were long, and summers short. Only potatoes, oats, winter rye, barley, and various vegetables could be cultivated there. Wheat was not a crop. This is why the daily bread was normally made of oat flour, and only on special occasions from rye. The peasants worked from dawn to night at their village, and young boys and girls shepherded the cattle on hilly pastures, covered with a short dry grass that was insufficient feed for the cows, which gave very little milk.

In Balnycia thatched roofs covered most of the peasant houses. Both local Jewish families had small shops and a tavern. The residents of Balnycia normally shopped in Vola Myhova, four kilometers away. For more variety of goods, one had to go to the town of Balyhorod, about 20 kilometers away. Before World War I, when there were no state borders, our people went shopping as far south as the town of Snyna and Humenne in the Carpatho Ukraine. On the east side of Balnycia a narrow gauge railroad line connected the railroad station town of Novey (New) Lupkiv on the West with the town of Tisna on the East. This railway usually transported huge trunks of trees and lumber harvested in the Carpathian forests. At the end of such a train was one passenger car. One could take this car to get to Novey Lupkiv and connect to the regular train. Otherwise, it was necessary to ride on the horse-drawn cart to reach Novey Lupkiv fourteen kilometers away.

The roads were not paved. They had ditches on both sides. One had to expect frequent bumpy and uneven surfaces with mud holes here and there. There were no automobiles there at all in my time. An unusual event happened when the first car appeared. Everyone stopped working and looked toward the new horseless carriage with a noisy motor on the road. The barefoot children ran toward the road to see what was happening. Even greater admiration was given the first airplane that appeared in the skies above. There was no electricity in the village and, therefore, no indoor plumbing. We used a kerosene lamp to light the house, and the outhouse was located across the courtyard near the stable. A deep well was outside near the house where the water was always cold and very good for drinking. To get the water out of the well, we used a bucket suspended on a pole equal to the depth of the well, connected to a crane. The only radio in the village was owned by the schoolteacher. The only telephones were at the railroad station and the border police barracks. The advancement in technology that took place in my lifetime is bewildering. I lived through the experiences of horse and buggy transportation to the supersonic jet airplanes, rockets and space travel; from primitive dwellings to skyscrapers; from no telephone to television, cell phones, computer technology, Internet, and e-mail. Indeed, it is amazing and mind-boggling! *All of this in one lifetime.*

My Family

My parents were Michael Sulyk and Maria nee Denys. My father was born in Balnycia September 4, 1889, and died in Sambir, October 19, 1974. My mother Maria was born in Balnycia February 10, 1895, and died in Sambir June 15, 1969. They had seven children: Ivan (born September 15, 1919, died May 1, 1930); Vasyl (born January 18, 1922—died June 17, 2002). Vasyl was married to Olena Dunda. They have two children: Jaroslav and Orysia. Jaroslav is divorced, has a daughter. Orysia is married to Ihor Soluk and has one son, Roman.

I was the third child born to my parents. I was born on Wednesday, October 1, 1924); Dmytro (born August 18, 1927, died September 26, 1944); Anna (born October 3, 1929); Nicholas (born October 28, 1931, died in 1944); Ivan, Jr. (born October 4, 1936). A Soviet army shell killed Dmytro, when Balnycia found itself in the middle between the advancing Red Army and the retreating German army in World War II. Nicholas died from a loss of blood when he stepped on a mine and lost his leg. Anna and Ivan Jr. now live in the city of Sambir, Ukraine, with their families.

A son was born to Sulyk's neighbor in Balnycia on October 2, 1924. His father went to the priest to baptize his son. A zealous priest immediately recorded all the necessary information into the

Baptismal Register. The following day, Michael Sulyk, father of the newly born son Stephen, born October 1, 1924, went also to see the priest with the same request. The priest, Father Nicholas Bachynsky, consented, but said, that the birth date will have to be "October 2" because he will not record "October 1," below "October 2" in his Baptismal Register. And so to this day my official birthday is "October 2." I received the Sacraments of Baptism and Chrismation (Confirmation) the following Sunday, October 5, 1924, in St. Nicholas Church, Maniv. My godparents were Ignatius Stec and Anna Hoblak.

My grandfather, Ivan Sulyk, (born February 1, 1863, and died April 13, 1942) was an extraordinarily honest and virtuous person. He was deeply religious and devout. He was appointed to be the sacristan in the local church, and this duty he performed with special devotion, dignity, respect, and zeal. He was the first to enter the church, and the last one to leave it.

While a small boy, I remember falling asleep at night to the whisper of the evening prayers of my grandfather, which he recited on his knees in front of the holy icons on the wall in the next room. In the morning I would wake up to the low whisper of my grandfather's morning prayers. When he became old and frail and could no longer go to church on Sunday, he would read the Holy Bible, the Lives of the Saints, or recite other church services or the Divine Liturgy at home. He was a holy man, balanced, golden-hearted and calm. For each one he met, he had a kind word. He would greet the passers by and wish them well. Anger or hatred could not be found in his heart. Nobody ever heard from his mouth an untruth, complaint, quarrel, curse, obscenity, or slander. He treated me and other children in a loving way and was our good friend and advisor. When he passed away I was not home but in school in the city of Sambir. When after a week or two I received a letter from my father informing me of the sad event, I cried tears of deep grief, for I loved my grandfather very much. But the communications were not like today. There were no telephones, and the mail was the only way of communication.

My paternal grandmother, Parascevia, nee Stec (born September 16, 1869, and died January 8, 1956 in Sambir), although devout, was of a different temperament. She was quite talkative and argumentative. She bore thirteen children. I remember only three of them. The other ten died before my time either in childhood or in World War I. The eldest was my father Michael, and then my uncle Nicholas (born November 11, 1896, and died February 24, 1990, in Trzebiatow, in Northwestern Poland). The youngest child was my aunt Sophie, (born August 11, 1912, and died February 11, 1994 in Dearborn, Michigan). After my birth my parents were deciding what name to give me. Young Sophie was present there and insisted that I be named Stephen. She wanted Stephen and insisted upon it. Her will was done. I will always be grateful to her for the noble name of Stephen, first deacon and first martyr

My mother Maria was of a gentle temperament, quiet, hard working, and very tolerant. She treated her children with sensitivity and love. Her warm maternal embrace, in which she held me, while kneeling by my bedside teaching me to make the proper sign of the cross or to say my prayers, will forever remain with me. Even when the children became noisy and quarrelsome, she would patiently, but resolutely, remind them to be good. But in her voice one could feel the indulgent love of a mother. Both of her parents died before I was born.

My father Michael was a quiet but decisive man. He had great life experiences and was able to give his children the best advice and guidance. While only seventeen years old in 1907 he went to the United States of America, to earn some money and thus help his parents. He was employed at first in a machine shop in Wilkes-Barre, Pa., and afterward as a lumberjack in the state of Delaware. After a three-year stay in the United States, he returned home. A short time after his return, he was drafted into the Austro-Hungarian army. He served in the town called Braunau am Inn in Northwestern Austria. Having served for four years, he was about to be released, when World War I, began. So he spent two more years fighting in the front lines. While in a battle near the city of Peremyshl he was wounded and lost his right leg just above the knee. He and other disabled soldiers were released from the army in 1917 and were given special half-year long courses to prepare them for the transition into civilian life.

As a disabled war veteran, father received a monthly pension from the state, which was a big help for the family. In 1931 he had a new house constructed and nearby also a large barn, a stable, and other structures needed by a farmer. The old house was covered by a thatched roof, as were most of the houses in the village. The new house was more modern with a porch in the back, kitchen, family room, and three bedrooms. It had a basement and a tin roof.

As his children grew up, he endeavored to give them a better education, sending them to school in the city. God's Providence ordered so that father's misfortune in war became for me a source of good fortune. From his monthly veteran's pension he was able to send me to high school and later on to college, enabling me to become a priest and later on a bishop. *"You are great, O Lord, and you do wondrous deeds"* (Psalms 86:10).

My Father's handicap did not prevent him from performing his normal daily chores on his farm. He was able to do as much as a man with two healthy legs. He was likewise active in the community's public life. For many years he performed the duties of the town secretary, and would participate in the annual county meetings in the county seat of Lisko. He loved to sing and taught his children to sing church and Ukrainian folk songs. He would tell his children stories of his life's adventures, his journey to the United States of America, his war experiences, and about the struggle of Ukraine to gain her independence.

He read Ukrainian newspapers and told us about contemporary events. At first, he was an aid to the local church cantor. When the cantor died, he became the cantor, while his brother Nicholas was a cantor in the neighboring village of Solynka.

Coat of Arms

The Elementary School

To be admitted to the first grade a child would have to be six years old. I was not yet six in September of that year. But since my older brother was going to school, I followed him. The teacher refused to register me and told me to go home and to come back next year. I refused. I went outside and sat on the front door steps. After few days of such demonstration, the teacher relented and registered me in the first grade.

Young Stephen while in the Sambir School in 1936

In the elementary school in my native village the teacher was a Polish lady named Victoria Czajkowska. She obstinately called the pupils "rusiny," i.e., ruthenians. Ruthenians was our old name, while the land was known as the Kievan Rus', and present-day Russia was then known as Moscovia. When in 1709 a Ukrainian leader, Ivan Mazepa, lost the battle near the city of Poltava, Russian Tsar Peter I occupied Ukraine. In 1715 he issued en edict by which he changed the name of Moscovia to Russia and called Ukraine the Small Russia. Ukrainian leaders rejected this change and slowly changed their name from Ruthenians to Ukrainians. But our Polish teacher refused to acknowledge the change. As soon as she would leave the classroom for a while, one of the boys would write on the blackboard the name "Ukrainian." She would get really angry and scream at us, saying, "There is no Ukraine." When she would find out who wrote on the blackboard, she would punish him by making him kneel in the corner of the classroom. But this did not resolve the argument. As long as she continued to call us by that name, the boys would continue to play their tricks on her.

In 1935 the local parish received a new pastor, a zealous, energetic young man named Peter Wesolovsky; (he died in the city of Lviv, April 2, 1995). Every Tuesday he would come to our school to teach us catechism. One Sunday after our first class with him, he asked my father, "The small boy, Stephen in the fourth grade, is he your son? Father said: "Yes, he is!" "He is wasting his time in this school, the priest replied. Send him away to a city school or at least to Father Warecha in the next town of Vola Myhova who has a private tutor teaching his two daughters at home. The idea pleased my father. Soon he went to Father Warecha and asked him whether it would be possible for his young son, Stephen, to take lessons of the fifth grade in his house. Father Warecha gladly consented. I was very happy with the idea and gladly changed schools. I took the lessons with Oksana, the elder daughter of Father Warecha. I resided in the neighborhood of the rectory with my aunt and attended daily classes at Father Warecha's rectory. Saturdays I would go home.

Father Warecha was a highly-educated man, very cultured and very active in his parish. He was fond of his people. He was the first pastor to organize his parishioners. Under his leadership a cultural center was built. In it was a public library, a reading room, and cooperative store. He taught the people to support their own enterprise by shopping in their own small shop. With the help of his hired teacher, he organized a small theater, and the local amateur dramatic group presented stage plays.

In the early spring of 1936 the diocesan bishop, Josaphat Kocylowsky transferred Father Warecha to another parish in the town of Voroblevychi, some twelve kilometers northeast from the city of Drohobych. Father Warecha took with him his private teacher and me as well. I lived in the rectory and continued to take classes in the fifth grade. At the end of school year, I successfully passed the exams.

Voroblevychi is a large settlement with two churches. I was then only ten years old. To be away for the first time from my home and parents was quite an experience. Father Warecha used to ask me, "Stephen, aren't you lonely for your home and parents?" I would not admit that I was lonely, and said, "No, I am not. I feel at home here with you!" And truly, he and his family treated me as their own, and I learned much by just observing their behavior and listening to their conversations.

The School in Sambir

spent summer vacations at home helping my parents in what ever needed to be done. On Father Vesolovky's advice, father made proper arrangements for me to continue my schooling in the city of Sambir, 140 kilometers East from home. So in the autumn of 1936 my father and I departed by train to Sambir. There he found a small boarding house for students. There were only 15 boys there. A priest's widow, Mrs. Konstantynovich, a kind and sympathetic lady, was in charge of it. Her son, Erastus, lived with her. He likewise was a student, a senior in high school.

Mrs. Konstantynovich appointed every year a senior high school boy to be the prefect of the boarding house. He, in turn, selected older students to be instructors to the younger ones. Life in the house was regulated by a daily schedule. The ringing of a bell in the morning woke us up to wash, dress, and make up our beds. Then at the sound of the second bell we had to gather in the dining room and under the prefect's leadership recite aloud our morning prayers. After common breakfast, each of us went to his school. Classes started at 8:00 A.M. Lunch and dinner were served to us at the appointed time. After lunch there was free time for recreation or leisure. Some would like to play soccer or basketball. Whoever wished go to town to purchase something had to have the prefect's permission. At the appointed time, the bell rang again and everyone had to gather in the study room with his books. At that time no loud talking was allowed.

After supper at 6:00 P.M. there was again leisure time. At 7:00 P.M. the bell rang again and all of us had to go back to the study room. The instructor checked our homework and questioned his pupils individually to see if they learned their lessons correctly. If need be he would explain the subject matter and try to teach them. This system was very helpful, especially to the new boys.

The school system at that time in Poland required the completion of six grades of elementary school before one could pass an entrance exam and be admitted to a high school, called a gymnasium. The high school had only four years and ended with a test called the "maturity exam." Before one could be admitted to a university he had to have two-year-long lyceum studies of select specialization. In Sambir, by autumn of 1936, I was admitted to the sixth grade of the elementary school. By autumn of following year I took an entrance exam and was admitted to the first year of the local high school. There I studied for two years, 1937–38 and 1938–39. High school students had to use prescribed uniforms of navy blue with a light-blue stripe down the trouser seams and on the jacket sleeves, as well as a special cap. School started daily at 8:00 A.M. and ended at 1:30 P.M. On Sundays all of the pupils had to come to school for a special talk by the school catechist. The priest-catechist and a teacher were present. Afterward they escorted all the pupils to the church for Divine Liturgy.

At Home on Christmas

For Christmas and Easter holydays I always went home to be with my parents and the family. The family observed rich traditions inherited from their ancestors. For Christmas Eve supper, called "the Holy Supper," a wheat sheaf, preserved especially from the harvest, was placed in the corner of the dining room symbolizing God's gifts to the family. The table was covered with two tablecloths, one for the ancestors of the family, the second for the living members. Under the table as well as under the table cloths some hay was spread to remind us that Christ was born under such conditions. The table had one extra place setting for the absent members of the family or for the deceased members, whose souls, according to belief, came on Christmas Eve to partake of the food.

A loaf of bread braided into a ring, with three such rings placed one on top of the other, was placed in the center of the table with a candle, which my mother lit, in the center of the top ring. The three rings symbolize the Trinity, and the circular form represents eternity. A candle used for the Holy Supper was blessed by a priest on the Feast of the Presentation of Our Lord in the Temple, to remind the family that the Christ Child is with us in the temple of our hearts. With the appearance of the first star, which is believed to be the Star of Bethlehem, the family gathered to begin the supper.

After all the preparations were done, the father offered each member of the family a piece of bread dipped in honey, which had been previously blessed in church, extending his wishes to everyone with the greeting, *"Christ is born!"* He then led the family in prayer. After the prayer, the family sat down to a twelve-course meatless Christmas Eve Supper.

There are twelve courses in the Supper, because according to tradition, each course is dedicated to one of Christ's apostles.

The first course is always *kutia*. It is the main dish of the whole supper. Then comes *borshch* (beet soup) with boiled dumplings filled with chopped mushrooms and onions. This is followed by a variety of fish—baked, broiled, fried, cold in aspic, fish balls, marinated herring, and so on. After the supper the family usually sang Christmas carols.

One trip home for Christmas will always remain in my memory. I arrived by train at the New Lupkiv railroad station about midnight. No one was there to pick me up, and the narrow gauge railroad was not running because of the snow. So I decided to go home by foot. The road was covered by frozen snow, and the storm raged. The snow under my feet crunched at each step, and the cold made me shiver. The wind blew the snow over the road so that in the darkness of the night it was hard to see where the road was. The air was very cold, so I took my handkerchief and tied it over my mouth and nose. In about half an hour I noticed that a long icicle hung down from my handkerchief. As soon as I broke it off, a new one started to grow. I reached my home about six o'clock in the morning.

It was one of those long January evenings during the Christmas holydays. Only one petroleum lamp burned in the house. After the evening meal, the family was seated in the warm house and sang Christmas carols. My mother, having finished her dishes, sat down next to me. As we finished one of the Christmas carols, she asked me quietly: "Stephen, would you like to be a priest someday?"

I was surprised by such a straightforward question by my dear mother. Not considering her heartfelt feelings, I simply replied: "Who me, a priest? I never gave it a thought. Besides, I do not know that I am capable of being one." A lot of time passed, and much water went under the bridge. But I never forgot that magical evening at home and my mother's quiet question. Her words would come back to me many years later when I was far away from my parents and my home, or when in my solitude I knelt by my bedside for my evening prayers. Sometimes I recalled her question when I was in a church for the Eucharistic Liturgy. But in those days it had no influence on my plans and dreams. Her question ripened in my heart much later when I was struggling with myself as to my vocation to the priesthood.

In the late summer of 1939 I was packing my suitcase and preparing to return to the high school in Sambir, when on September 1, World War II started.

The War Years

I will never forget those terrible days. Few events are so deeply engraved in my memory as are those days. A year or two before the war, the Polish government withheld my father's two-month pension for the war reparations. He received a bond in which it was stated that my father gave the government a certain amount of money. In the early summer of 1939 the government informed my father that he could cash the bond by purchasing some items in designated stores.

While traveling on some business in the city of Sianik, my father bought me a bicycle, something I had long wanted and asked for; he made me really happy. I rode that bicycle everywhere, anywhere my heart desired. But my joy was short lived. As soon as the war began, a Polish policeman came to our house and confiscated the bicycle for military needs. I think I should be forgiven the sin of wishing in my heart that the Poles would lose the war.

It was a beautiful sunny day that first Sunday of September 1939. Everyone was getting ready to go to church when I ran inside the house and told my father who was shaving: "Daddy, look outside and see those strange soldiers with guns running and then hiding behind bushes. Could they be German soldiers?" Everyone in the house ran to the windows to see what was going on. My father said: "No, these are not German uniforms. They might be Slovak soldiers." A few minutes later, a low-ranking officer and two soldiers entered our house, greeted us, and said that they were Slovak army men helping Hitler conquer Poland. Then the officer asked my father: "Would you, Ukrainians, like to belong to Slovakia?" My father replied: "I really don't know if that would be possible. How many millions of people are there in Slovakia?" The officer replied: "Two and one half million." My father retorted: "There are over forty two million Ukrainians. So I really don't know if that would work." My mother offered each of them a glass of milk and some bread. They thanked us and departed to further pursue the glories of the war.

Polish border guards and the police left our town the first days of the war, and the German "blitz krieg" conquered Poland in just two or three weeks. Germans occupied Western Poland, including our town. East of us the river Sian marked the border of the Soviet occupation. Since the city of Sambir was East of the river Sian, I could not go back to school. The borders were closed.

Soon German border guards came to our town. They not only guarded the state border, but also would kidnap young men and women and send them to Germany as forced labor. One night they arrested eight men in our town and sent them to the concentration camps. No one ever heard of them again. Not long afterward they arrested the two Jewish families and killed them. When my older brother, Vasyl, was going to work on the farm, he was captured by the German border guards and sent to a concentration camp near the Polish city of Krakow. He was kept there for one-and-a-half years, got very sick and almost died. He was then released and sent home. When he entered our house, my father did not recognize him. Thinking that he was a beggar, he asked him, "What can I do for you?"

Forced Laborer in Germany

I was not able to escape my destiny to become like many others a forced laborer in Germany. One nice morning in early spring of 1940, the local German border guards compelled me to go with them, placing me on a train to Germany. In my naivete, I was not too upset by the fact that I could not continue my high school education. I even thought somewhat positively about this forced journey into Germany. This, I thought, will give me a chance to see more of the world; to learn how the people live there; what their customs are, and learn to speak German.

Stephen at forced labor in Germany

More and more such forced young men and women were added at each station to the railroad train on which I was traveling to Germany. The train reached its destination in the city of Leitmeritz in Sudetenland, which was then part of Germany. (After the war, the territory of Sudetenland was returned to Czechoslovakia.) All the passengers were gathered into one spacious hall where German farmers were already waiting to select for themselves workers whom they preferred. This reminded me of the slave labor market of old. I was dressed somewhat better than the others and attracted the attention of a certain middle-aged man who pointed his finger at me. Immediately I was called to the registration table, where they found my name, and told me to go with the man, whose name was Josef Matzke from the nearby town of Mirschowitz.

Matzke was married but had no children. He was the owner of a restaurant with a bar and a spacious dance hall. The restaurant and the bar were seldom used during the war years. Behind his buildings he had a large orchard, and some distance away, five acres of a fruit tree orchard. Between the long rows of trees he cultivated strawberries. The whole orchard was kept meticulously in perfect order.

As soon as we arrived at his house, he put me to work. My daily toil was mostly in the orchard, pruning the fruit trees, weeding and cultivating the soil, harvesting the strawberries, and, in the fall, picking fruit from the trees. The work was not too difficult, and I became used to it.

Matzke had a full time employee in the large orchard. He was an elderly Czech. He liked me and would teach me many of the skills of gardening, pruning, etc. He spoke to me in his native Czech language, and that gave me an opportunity to learn at least conversational Czech. My German improved so that in a few months I was speaking so well that my employer was very pleased.

On Sundays I was free and was able to go to the city. There I found out that we had a priest, Father Nicholas Wojakowsky, who celebrated Divine Liturgy for our people every Sunday in a local Roman Catholic Church. There I found my nephew Michael Senko and many others. From them I learned that there were several Ukrainian families who migrated to the then Czechoslovakia after Word War I, when Ukraine lost its short-lived independence. The territory of Sudetenland at that time belonged to Czechoslovakia until Hitler annexed it in 1938. On my trips on Sundays to the church and other social events I got to know the priest. Several families became my friends and helped me in many ways.

When in June of 1941 Germany attacked the Soviet Union, I knew I had go home and go back to school. Joseph Matzke was drafted into the German armed forces and his wife was alone. She asked her sister to live with her. I asked her permission to take a short vacation in order to visit my parents and relatives at home. She liked me and valued my solid work. She was able to get permission from German officials who gave me a permit to travel home and back. The only thing she asked of me was to please come back. My homecoming and the family reunion caused all of us a great amount of joy and celebration.

My parents informed me that about a month after my return from Germany, the police inquired of my whereabouts, and why I did not return to Germany. My parents told them that I went back to school in the city of Sambir. When they came to the school for me, the Principal said simply "no" to them because I was now a student, and could not return to Germany. So they left me alone.

Returning to Sambir

The German occupation authorities would not permit the reopening of our high school. Their plans for our future were to keep us as slaves for the German "uebermenschen." They permitted only trade schools and a Teachers College. Very few high schools were permitted. Our Teachers College benefited from this misfortune since many of our university professors had no employment and would teach in our Teachers College. So we had an outstanding faculty.

School commenced in the beginning of September. I was able to pass the entrance exam for the Teachers College. All subjects were taught in Ukrainian. The principal of the school was Ignatius Matrynetz, my former teacher in the prewar high school. The other faculty members were Luke Luciv, a renowned literary critic and author; Alexander Bereznycky, a historian; Vladimir Silecky, professor of the Krakow University; Carl Shumsky, Alexander Orlowsky, Julian Horniatkewych, Ivan Chajkivsky, Panas Martyniak, Vladimir Tretiak, and the catechist, Rev. Vladimir Ivashko. The school was coeducational.

Life in the Residence Hall for Boys

Our school administration, with the cooperation and help of the city fathers, was able to provide separate buildings for girls and for boys as dormitories for the students from out of town. The boys' dormitory was located on Zamijska Street with Alex Bereznycky as its director. I was assigned to a room together with two roommates, Andrew Mycio (who died in Newark, N.J., January 3, 1979), and Vladimir Maslak, now a retired surgeon in Lviv, Ukraine.

Stephen in high school in 1941

High school concert and stage play in 1943.

Life in the residence hall was not dull. Each day was regulated by a strictly controlled program of study, sports, discussion, free time, prayer, and rest. The senior students were appointed as prefects and were in change of the daily program. There was one thing that spoiled the good time in our life in the residence hall. It was wartime, and there was a great shortage of food. The city was not able to supply a sufficient amount of food to satisfy the appetite of young and growing boys. Some boys had their parents or relatives bring them additional food from the farms. My home was too far away from this city to expect my parents to travel the distance. My brother Dmytro, who was in a school in Sambir and resided with me in the boarding house, would alternate with me to go home about once a month and bring some additional dried bread, butter, cheese, and fruit. Traveling by a train during the war was very dangerous and difficult. The railroad cars were overcrowded. Rarely could one find a seat, and you were happy if you just could find standing room, hemmed in on all sides. The German police often checked documents, and arrested anyone who looked suspicious.

Wartime was indeed very difficult and terrible. Ukrainian society in Western Ukraine was divided politically into two competing nationalistic factions, each of which tried to recruit members from among the students. They succeeded in many cases. As a result, in each class, secret party groups were formed that worked under strict conspiratorial rules. This whole movement formed a sick and fanatical atmosphere in the school. If one refused to belong to either party, he was considered unpatriotic. The teachers tried very hard to convince the students that the real patriot is he who loves his country and all Ukrainians, irrespective of his political persuasions. But this did not help much; one cannot reason with fanatics.

A Boy Scout

The scouting movement was founded in Western Ukraine in the beginning of the 20th century. It developed mainly in the cities in high schools and colleges and became very popular. In 1929 Polish authorities issued a prohibition so that this youth organization could not exist publicly. German occupation forces permitted its existence, but under a different name—Ukrainian Educational Youth Organization. In late 1941, special courses were given to educate scoutmasters. Alex Bereznycky took part in these courses. During the summer of 1942 each school selected two students and sent them to a special boy scout camp for a three week long scout instructor's training. I was one of them. The camp was held in wooded terrain near the city of Lviv. There were about thirty participants. Former scoutmasters were our instructors.

In the fall of 1942, Alex Bereznycky began the organizational process of boy and girl scout troops in our school. All the troops formed separate boys' and girls' chapters, and I was appointed our school's first scout leader. Alex Bereznycky and Father Ivashko were the main promoters of the scouting movement in our school. They organized regular meetings, promoted all sorts of activities, and celebrations of national holidays and anniversaries. All of us had to get special scouting uniforms and insignias.

This was my first opportunity to be a leader and put into practice what I had learned in the instructors training camp. I was not accustomed to leading; I would rather follow. But this time I was forced into this unusual position among my classmates. I tried to be decisive, and always stressed gentle equality, friendship, and support of others. This position was good because I learned how to treat other people properly. I found genuine support and encouragement from among my friends and classmates. Special memories remain with me of the multiple field trips our troops made to a variety of places. The best was a weeklong trip into the Carpathian Mountains in the Hutzul region.

Possible Military Service

The news from the Eastern front in 1943 was not good for the Germans in Ukraine. Since they lost to the Soviets at Stalingrad, the tide turned against them and they were retreating. Early in the spring of that year the German authorities turned to Ukrainian leaders asking for help. They offered to train Ukrainian volunteers to form a separate Ukrainian military division or two. Students in our school were not in agreement as to the morality of this move. Some claimed it would give us an opportunity to get arms into our hands and modern military training. This, they said, might become useful if the opportune time comes to free Ukraine. Others had the opposite idea. They warned us—why should we go to war to die in order to save Hitler?

One morning, guests came to our school: an SS colonel, an Austrian by the name of Bizantz, and a Ukrainian representative, Mr. Holowaty. They came to promote the idea of getting volunteers from among our students. The Principal of our school, Mr. Martynetz, called all the senior and junior boys into one large conference room. We formed a semicircle and faced the Principal and his guests. I stood in the center of the semicircle. He introduced them to us and encouraged us to listen to the speakers and to cooperate with them.

Mr. Holowaty, a brilliant speaker, gave a fiery address about twenty minutes long. He said something like this: "The time is ripe. The great opportunity may never come again. We have a chance to form our own army division or two, maybe even a whole army. How many millions of our brothers and sisters in the past gave their lives to free our land from bondage. They failed, not because it was their fault, but because the time was not ripe. The time is ripe now. Let us grasp the opportunity, and you, young and patriotic Ukrainians, raise your hands now and volunteer to enlist into the new Ukrainian army division."

The eyes of all the boys turned to me to see if I would raise my hand and volunteer. I did not, and all but one followed my example. I looked straight into the Principal's eyes and kept silent. When the guests had departed, Mr. Martynetz called me to his office and said, "I always held you in high regard, and hoped that you would give good example to the rest of the students. Why did you not volunteer?" I replied, "You always taught me to honor and respect my parents. I am not a mature person yet, and I think that it is my sacred duty to ask their advice and consent before I make such an important move in my life." The Principal replied, "You are right this time. Go home and get your parents blessings; come back and enlist."

The pressure to enlist in the military division was constant and from all quarters. So I went home, asked my parents' advice as to what I should do? My mother was fiercely opposed to this idea and begged me not to volunteer. My father said, "It is your life. You are still young, and if you could avoid enlisting, then do so. But if you want to go, you have my blessing." When I returned back to school, most of my classmates had already succumbed to the pressure and enlisted. So did I.

Then somebody handed me a small envelope, addressed to me. The message read, "Stephen, come immediately to Lviv to such and such address. I have to talk to you. Your friend Slavko." Slavko had been one my scoutmasters from the instructors' camp. Since then we had become friends and kept in contact. I knew that he would not trouble me to travel to the city of Lviv if it were not important. So I went to Lviv, found the street and the house, and knocked on his door on the third floor. He greeted me warmly and, asked me to take a seat. He said: "I know all about the pressure that was exerted upon you to enlist in the military division. Stephen, you are not cut out to be a soldier. Military service is not for you. They cannot force you, even if you have already enlisted. I have friends in the Ukrainian Central Committee involved in this business, and I will talk to them to leave you alone. God willing, the war will not last too much longer. After the war you will have an opportunity to further your education and achieve something in your life. Now, I will help you to find some employment when school is over." I accepted his wise advice and went home.

On my way home by train, I thought about how God leads me in my life. I felt deeply in my heart that this was a critical decision for the rest of my life. It was probably a turning point. Something like an invisible hand was guiding me. God sent me my friend, Slavko, to show me the way.

My First Employment

Through Slavko's intervention, I received my first employment in October of 1944 at the Ukrainian Relief Committee in the town of Horlyci, which is located 100 kilometers west of my home. It was already inside the Polish ethnic territory. Only a short distance to the South and the East were solid Ukrainian villages. There were only twenty Ukrainians working in the town. My job was mostly office work and typing various things on a Ukrainian typewriter. Sometimes I was sent with matters pertaining to the Committee to various villages to meet with their representatives, the local priest or teacher. This gave me an excellent opportunity to get to know so many good and outstanding people and their way of life.

The head of the Relief Committee was Mr. Osyp Utrysko, a lawyer by profession, and a kind and understanding person. Vasyl Stecyk, a teacher, his wife and their children were acknowledged as outstanding members of the community. They became my friends and advisors.

Later on in the summer my work had changed. All main highways leading west were suddenly filled with long caravans of horse drawn carts and wagons with refugees from central Ukraine. In a great panic they were escaping from the advancing Soviet armies. On their carts they had all their belongings, men, women, and children. It was a pitiful sight. I felt a great sadness and compassion for these poor people.

On one of the main highways outside our town, our Committee established a Relief Station, composed of a warehouse with foodstuff, hay and oats for the horses, a kitchen and two-room apartment. I was appointed to be the head of this station. They gave me three persons, a couple and a woman from among the refugees to help me. The woman was the cook and the couple would feed the horses and help in the kitchen. After about a month of this work at the Relief Station, the refugee caravan stopped, and the station was closed for the time being.

One day in July, the office of our Committee was informed of terrible news: the Soviet armed forces broke through the German defensive lines and were pressing forward. The break took place northeast from us, somewhere near the city of Lviv. Panic overcame the Ukrainians in Horlyci. There were no more passenger trains or buses in operation. There was no way I could go home to my parents. Local authorities informed our Committee that they would provide one closed freight railroad car for our evacuation. Everyone was to be at the railroad station by 4:30 P.M. that day with all their belongings. The Committee supplied the freight car with sacks of flour, potatoes, some other foodstuff, and blankets.

I decided not to be evacuated; not to go to Germany. After I saw the many thousands of refugees fleeing to Germany, I became afraid, and thought to myself, who is going to feed all these thousands of homeless people in Germany which is being bombed daily. So I informed my co-workers in the office that I was remaining behind.

It was about 3:00 P.M. on that memorable day that someone knocked on my door. Amazed and somewhat frightened, I carefully opened the door, and there stood my friend Slavko from Lviv. "What are you doing here in Horlyci?" I asked him. "The same as many thousands of other refugees. I have to go west because for such people as I, there will be no place here when the communists come," he replied. "I met Mr. Stecyk on the street a while ago, and he told me that you decided not to go with them, that you want to stay here. Is this true?" "Yes, I replied. I don't want to go and starve to death in Germany. All the hundreds of thousands of refugees fleeing west to bombed out Germany are destined to starve to death there."

Then Slavko started to talk some sense to me. He said that I could not survive here in this town. There is no way for you to go home, he said, for all transportation lines are down. When the Soviet armies come here, the first thing they do is to force young men to join their army. With very little or no training they will send you right into the fire on the front line. Go to the railroad station and join the others. There will be provisions made for the refugees. You will not starve to death in Germany.

Slavko was older and more experienced in life. He easily convinced me that I should go west with the others. I thanked him and said good-bye. I hurriedly packed my suitcase, leaving behind most of my books, and rushed to the train station. On the way I stopped in the district office to get a permit to enter Germany. A Ukrainian man was in charge of that office, and he too was in a hurry. He typed my name on a ready form, signed and stamped it, and handed it to me. Without looking at it, I put it in my pocket and left for the railroad station. Later on when I compared my permit with that of other persons, they all had "only to Germany," and the word "back" crossed out. On my permit the word "back" was not crossed out. So, this meant that I could go to Germany and back.

The hand of God was evidently present here as well. I would have made the greatest mistake of my life. But God watched over me and sent me a friend to show me the right way.

Leaving My Homeland

About twenty persons were in the closed freight car with a sliding door on each side. There were no beds or chairs there. Everyone sat on his own suitcases or on the floor. We had to wait for several hours before a steam engine arrived. Then we were on the way. However, we stopped at various stations and added new cars to our train until the train was very long.

The sun was setting over the horizon. The landscape of the fields, forests, and mountains was passing as though it were a motion picture. Conversations stopped and everyone was immersed in his own prayers or thoughts. I, too, was praying, asking God to guide and protect me, for I felt the pain of loss for my homeland, my parents, sister, and brothers. Will I ever see them again? I was not able to say goodbye to them or ask my parents' blessing. They did not know nor would they know for a long time what had happened to me. I myself did not know where I was going, what awaited me in a strange land, among strange people. What was my future? But then a thought crossed my mind: *Why am I worried. I am not alone. God is with me. He will guide and lead me. My heavenly Mother, the Most Holy Mother of God, will intercede for me before Her Son.*

"For you are my hope, O Lord; my trust, O God, from my youth. On you I depend from birth; from my mother's womb you are my strength." (Psalms 71:5–6)

A Long and Dull Journey

The rhythmic clicking of the wheels on the railroad track lulled everyone to sleep that first night as we, the new refugees, were leaving our homeland. Someone pushed the doors of the car closed for the night. The travelers, hunched over their bundles, covered by a blanket, slept fully dressed in an uneasy and nervous sleep. The train stopped once or twice. The engine would be unhooked to add some more cars to the train. Each time the new cars were joined, the clash would awaken everyone.

The train was in no hurry. Often we were pushed off to the side and waited there until some military transport passed by. We did not know where we were. Seldom were we able to read the signs over the railroad station. While stopped along the way, we were able to disembark, find some waterspout to wash our face or a shirt. Some filled bottles with drinking water. Others walked to stretch their legs. On one such stop there were two large wooden barrels loaded on a railroad flat car. On the bottom of each barrel was a spigot inviting us to see what it contained. We did so, and found out that it was white wine, cold, fragrant, and very delicious. Making sure that no one saw us, we filled our bottles and glasses and relished the welcome drink.

We never knew where we were. Days were passing slowly. The train attendants never came by our car or spoke to any of us. On several such stops we heard sirens wailing, warning of air raids and bombings. Then, far away, we would hear deep sounds of bomb explosions. The earth would tremble as from an earthquake. The air raids might have been British or American.

This kind of monotonous travel lasted one week, then two and three, and we still did not know where we were going, what our destination would be. We were very uncomfortable and exhausted in the same railroad boxcar, sleeping fully clothed with our bundles serving as pillows. The month was August, hot and humid. There was no way of taking a shower or a bath. But after a month of such tortuous travel the train reached our destination—a huge refugee camp at Strashoff near Vienna, Austria.

Refugee Camp in Strashoff

As soon as the train stopped, a sharp command in German was given by a policeman: "Ausstigen!"—disembark! The railroad station was next to the huge camp. As soon as we came off the train, we were transported to a special barrack where the women were separated from the men and went to another location. We all had to undress, get a hot shower, and our clothing, placed in a separate bag along with our suitcases, was sent through special delousing instruments. It felt good to be able to take a hot shower after the month-long journey in a railroad boxcar. Our group from the town of Horlyci stayed together and did not want to be separated, for we got to know each other really well and became friends during our journey.

After the shower, each found his clothes and suitcases. Then husbands met their wives, and from there we were led into a housing barrack. In one spacious room were about fifty narrow bunk beds with straw mattresses, each with a straw pillow and a bedspread.

It felt good to be able to stretch out on a bed after sleeping on the floor of a boxcar for such a long time. So I climbed into my bed to rest just a bit. In a moment I fell into a deep sleep. But before long I woke up, and jumped out of the bed. My body was in pain from the bites of large fat bed bugs. I uncovered the bedspread and found a whole colony of large fat bed bugs. They were so large that I was stunned, for I had never seen such creatures. I quickly took my suitcase and went out of the barrack. The weather was nice and warm. I went into a rest room, took my shirt off and shook off the bugs. Then I did the same with my trousers and underwear. Then I found a nice spot under a tree far away from the barracks and made my bed there. I stayed there for the few days of our stay in Strashoff.

Transfer to Thuringen

In less than a week's time, we were told to pack and go to the train station. This time we were privileged to ride in old passenger cars. We placed our suitcases on the shelves, took our seats, and enjoyed the luxury of not having to ride in a boxcar. It seemed that the authorities separated the refugees according to their nationality, so in our train were all Ukrainians. Again, no one told us where we were going or how long the trip would last.

It was only a two-day journey. The train stopped in a small town in central Germany called Thuringen. It was a small railroad station located on a main east-west railway line. Soon after our arrival, we were told to climb into trucks, which transported us into a hilly forest. Not too long after that, a huge truck came with a prefabricated barrack. The workers began to prepare the foundation and assemble the barrack. The first night we spent beneath the sky. On the second day the barrack was ready and the beds were delivered. I stayed there with the Stecyk family whom I befriended while in Horlyci.

The following day all of us were taken to the place of our work. I and another young man were selected to go daily seven kilometers away to the main kitchen and deliver food for our workers in two large covered containers placed on a cart with two bicycle wheels. On the way to the kitchen we had to cross a little town the name of which escapes my memory. When the food containers were empty, it was just a pleasant walk. But when they were filled to the brim, it was an effort for one of us to pull and the other to push. This daily trip gave me an opportunity to get to know the town and the surrounding territory. I noticed that no real work was done on the surface. There were underground factories that no one of us was permitted to enter. Huge trucks were always going in and out, but they were covered with canvas so no one could see what they were carrying. Someone noticed that a high chain link fence was being erected all around our encampment. We surmised that some secret weapons were being made underground, maybe even the famous "V-2" rockets.

My Escape to the Sudetenland

I did not like what I was seeing of the surroundings while daily going to and from the main kitchen, especially the new high chain link fence that was going up. So I decided to escape from there and go to the Sudetenland where I was a forced laborer in 1940. To be able to travel by train during the war one had to have a travel permit, and I had one. Besides, in Sudetenland I had my nephew Michael. One day while going to the main kitchen, I stopped at the railroad station and inquired when there was a train leaving for Krakow, Poland. I was told, daily at 5:00 A.M.

The only person I secretly told my plans was to Vasyl Stecyk. Late at night I packed my suitcase, and while everyone was asleep, I got up very early in the morning, left the barrack and went to the station. There were no questions asked of me when I bought a ticket to Krakow. But when on the train and watching the passing landscape, two Gestapo, dressed in their black uniforms, came up to me and demanded my documents. Looking calmly straight into their eyes, I showed them my travel permit; they read it very carefully and gave it back to me, and said, "Thank you!" Thinking back on this one incident in my life, I cannot recall where I gathered so much courage as to look calmly straight into their eyes with full confidence and without any fear at all. People at that time trembled with fear by the very mention of the name "Gestapo."

At about midnight the train stopped in the city of Drezden. I got out, went to the station and inquired about the next train to Sudetenland, to the town of Leitmeritz. I had to wait four hours. I bought a ticket, and when the time came, I got on the train and was on my way.

My Stay In Sudetenlad

The first thing I did when I arrived in Leitmeritz, was to see my nephew Michael Senko who worked for a farmer in a nearby village. He was pleasantly surprised to see me, and kept asking all about the family and the fate of his relatives. We sat and talked until very late at night relating to each other our personal experiences and adventures for the last few years. In the morning Michael obtained permission from his farmer to escort me to the city. I reported to the city's employment office, showing them my travel permit and telling them that I came from Ukraine and would like to have a job. When they inquired about my education, I showed them my diploma from Teachers College. That made a great impression on them, and the fact that I spoke fluent German helped me get a good job.

At once they assigned an apartment to me. It was located on the outskirts of the town in a residential section. The apartment consisted of one spacious room on the third floor with a washroom. Two sisters whose husbands were soldiers in the war occupied the first and the second floors. They had no children. Both of them went daily to work. The apartment was not very luxurious, but it was by far better than the barracks in the woods.

My first job consisted of registering railroad freight cars that were coming to and leaving the local freight station. The work was very easy and not demanding at all. A man by the name of Victor worked with me and taught me all that was needed to be done to do the job well. Victor became interested in me and would spend a lot of time discussing various matters with me.

After about a month or two I was transferred to a job in a factory where aircraft propellers were produced. I worked in the shipping department. There, completed propellers were to be packed into a wooden chest for shipment. My task was to have them first mounted on a special scale and verify that each of the three blades had exactly the same weight. If one of the blades was off, a little spray paint was applied to balance the three. The job was easy and my coworkers were friendly toward me.

There was one difficulty that I was facing there, namely food provisions. During the war all food was sold only to those who had monthly ration cards. Only a limited amount of bread, butter, eggs, potatoes, etc. was allowed to a single person. In the beginning, it was very difficult to manage the allowable food so that it would last to the end of the month. Sometimes I was forced to call on my nephew Michael to bring me a farmer's loaf of bread and some butter. His home-baked bread was much more delicious that the store bread, and the loaf was a large one.

The two sisters in whose house I had my room noticed my difficulty with ration cards and offered to help me. They said that if we put the ration cards together, it would be much easier to manage the food. I gladly agreed to give them my ration cards each month and the necessary amount of money so that they would do the shopping. With that they started to cook for me, and then I had it really good.

My return to Leitmeritz gave me an opportunity to renew my previous social activities with the Ukrainian community in the city. Father Nicholas Wojakowsky was still there, and he sang Liturgy each Sunday for our people. After the war, and the arrest by the Soviets of Rt. Rev. Petro Verhun in Berlin, the Apostolic Administrator for our Church in Germany, Father Wojakowsky became a temporary Apostolic Visitator, residing in the town of Passig near Munich. He was in charge of the many parishes that were formed in each of the Displaced Persons' camp.

One of the first days of the month of May in 1945, as I was going to work early in the morning, I noticed big changes in the city. The streets were empty. There was not a soul to be seen. What happened, I asked myself? Then I noticed a pile of handguns, a machine gun, and lot of ammunition on the sidewalk. It was dangerous to be on the streets at that time, so I turned around and went back home.

Language Translator

Two or three days after I stopped going to work, someone knocked on our door. One of the sisters came up to my room, pale and trembling. She said there is a Soviet soldier and a layman at the front door, asking for me by name. "Now what? Will they force me to go back to Ukraine, the Soviet Union"— was my first thought? What do I do? There was no back door. There is no way I can escape while they are standing at the front door. So I called on the name of God. With fear in my heart, I went down to meet the uninvited guests.

To my big surprise when I opened the front doors, I saw Victor, the man who worked with me on my first job, and a Soviet soldier. Victor greeted me with a friendly smile, and said in Czech, "We came to ask you to help us. We in the Czech district government cannot communicate with our Russian brothers. So our chairman asked me to go and see if you would be so kind as to work for us as a translator."

I replied, "Please understand me, I am not refusing your request, but I never learned the Russian language, and barely understand the Czech language. I speak Ukrainian and German." Then the Soviet soldier stated in Russian, "We are the First Ukrainian Army here, and we do understand Ukrainian. Come on, come with us and be our translator." I had no other choice and could not refuse to go with them or else something worse might happen to me.

So I became a translator of languages unfamiliar to me. I got an office and a typewriter, and there was a secretary in the next room. They gave me a Czech–Russian and Russian–Czech dictionary and I did my best. When there were some letters or documents to be translated, I used the dictionary and then the secretary corrected my Czech. It was much harder when one day some high-ranking officers came to the district chairman, and I was asked to translate. I again stated that I did not know the Russian language. Would you please speak in the Ukrainian language, I asked. They refused and kept speaking in Russian and got really angry with me for not translating correctly. After they left, the district chairman said to me, "Do not worry, you'll stay with us."

All our people who were expatriated to Germany as forced laborers were now again forcibly taken by the Soviet authorities and returned to the Soviet Union. Many of them did not want to go to the Soviet Union, a communist country and dictatorial regime. Some were successful in escaping; some were helped by their German farmers to hide; but the great majority were sent back to the Soviet Union. Those who were suspected by the Soviets of being Ukrainian nationalists were taken directly to Siberia and the Gulags. My nephew Michael was forcibly taken away, not even able to say good-bye to me.

One day some Soviet soldiers came to our office and demanded that I go with them and return to the Soviet Union. But our district chairman protested: "We need him here; he must stay! He is our translator, otherwise we cannot communicate with your authorities." They replied, "Then you have to write a letter to our commanding general, and ask him for a month of relief from this law." The chairman wrote such a letter; I translated it into Russian, and went to see the general. He asked me to sit down and tried to convince me to go back home and to go to school and make something out of myself instead of wasting my time here. I tried to tell him that that is my wish also, but I could not abandon my friends. They really needed me. So the general gave me a one-month's reprieve from his law.

The Hand of God's Providence

I t was late June of 1945 and very hot. There had been no rain for a long time. It was a Sunday afternoon and my room on the third floor was practically unbearable. So I took a towel with me, and walked across town to the shores of the Elbe River. The beach was quite wide and clean. The water was refreshing. There was only a very light breeze. It was much easier to breathe here than in my apartment. So I spread out my towel to sun myself and to rest a bit.

My mind was filled with the events of the recent past in my life. Was it only by chance that a communist, Victor, was the instrument that saved me from being forced to return to the atheistic Soviet Union? Or is it the hand of God that somehow guides my destiny in life. Even from dreadful and dangerous situations, something good comes. But how did I ever deserve such guidance and protection from God?

Engrossed in such thoughts, some children's chatter came to me from afar and awakened me. It seemed to me that they were speaking Ukrainian. I listened more intently, and still I had the same impression. I raised my head up slightly and looked in that direction. I saw about 150 yards away from me a couple with two children sitting in a circle. I got up and started to take a leisurely walk. First I walked to the right, away from them, then I turned back and not even looking in their direction passed them. While I was passing them the man of the family spoke loudly enough for me to hear, and it was perfect Czech language. Then I thought that I might have overheard the children speaking Ukrainian.

The following day I had an appointment at a dentist. I was getting one of my first wisdom teeth filled. The dentist was finished with me, but before I could get up from his chair, someone entered his office. I could not see his face for I was turned away from him in the dentist's chair. The man asked in perfect Czech, "Is my wife's crown ready?" The dentist replied, "And what is her last name?" The man said, "Torbych." The doctor said, "It will be ready tomorrow, come at 11:00 A.M."

When I head the name Torbych, I almost jumped up from the chair. Having turned around I recognized him. He was the man with his wife and children on the beach yesterday. He did not know me, but I know him. When I was in Sambir in the Teachers College, he was the chief of the local city police, and everybody knew him.

Having thanked the dentist and paid my bill, I hurried to catch up with Torbych. I knew that he was a native from Carpatho-Ukraine, which before the war was under Czechoslovakia, and he was an officer in their army, and then in their police force. That is why he spoke perfect Czech. Hearing me walk behind him, he increased his pace, but I caught up with him and greeted him in Ukrainian, "Mr. Torbych, please, I know you and I wish to talk with you." "How do you know me?" "I was in Sambir for years as a student in the Teachers College, and that is how I know you." Then he interrogated me to see if I was lying. "Tell me," he said, "who was the principal of that school? Give me the names of some of your teachers." When I replied correctly, he said, "And what are you doing here? All of our people were already forced to return to the Soviet Union?" "Well, I am here because the Czech leader of the city asked me to be a translator for them and the Russians. I work in the city hall." Then he said, "We have to talk some more but not here on the street. Come to my house tomorrow after work." He then gave me his address.

How to Escape to the American Zone of Czechoslovakia

Mr. Torbych was a mature man, experienced in life and quite knowledgeable. At the time Carpatho Ukraine declared her independence from Czechoslovakia in 1938, he was an officer in their military. When the small independent country was attacked by the huge Hungarian army and was occupied by them, he escaped north over the Carpathian Mountains into Western Ukraine. There he married his wife and started a family; the boy at that time was four years old and the girl was two years old.

The following day after work I found the street and the house and paid a visit to the Torbych family. It was the first time that I was introduced to his wife and two children. George Torbych removed from his drawer a geographic map of Sudetenland and Western Czechoslovakia. He showed it to me and said he had already mapped out his route of escape into the American zone. The route went mainly through forested lands and uninhabited parts of the country. It would have been a very difficult and dangerous journey with his two small children. He said: "There is no future for me here. The Soviets are hunting for every one who was in the Ukrainian Police during the war. They claim that we were collaborators with Hitler while all we did was protect our own people. But how are you going to explain this to the Communists? Now, meeting you, our plans have changed completely. And this is how they have changed. To get legally across the border to the American zone, all we need is a certificate from the local authorities that we are Czechoslovak citizens. Since you work in city hall, you can supply us with such certificates. I presume that you have access to the stationary of the district chairman and to the official stamp." "I do," was my reply. "I will compose in good Czech language the text for each person, and give it to you. You will be able to type the text on to the stationary for each person and place the official stamp on it," he said. I assured him I would be able to do that.

The task did not present me with too many difficulties. I had a typewriter in my office and had the stationary also. I just had to be very careful not to be seen by anyone. When all the certificates were typed, I was able to get the seal from the chairman's desk when he was out, and stamped all the certificates.

I took the prepared documents to Torbych's house that same day. After reading them carefully, he exclaimed, "Excellent, excellent!" He then sat down and carefully signed the name of the district chairman on each of the certificates. Now, he said to me, "Let us not waste too much time, because we do not know the future. Let us go to Prague and from there to Pilzen. However, before I take my family with me to Pilzen in the American zone, I need to know what dangers await us as we cross over there."

"All right, George, tomorrow I will ask my boss for a three-day leave of absence. When I get it, then I will be able to go with you," I said. So the next day I asked the district chairman to give me a leave of absence for three days for I would like to visit the famous capital city of Prague, because I never was there. He was delighted and gladly gave me permission to be absent, and even told me what sights in Prague I should definitely see. "But do not forget to get back here to work on Monday," he added.

I had a classmate, named Anne Wolchansky, living in Prague, and had received a card from her recently. I took her address with me. Torbych was of the opinion that she could be very helpful to us and give us the right advice. Since we had a few hours to wait for the connecting train to Pilzen, we went to see my friend. We found only her elderly mother in her apartment. She told us that her daughter, together with her fiance, Bohdan Kucan, already fled last week for Pilzen and the American zone.

The train from Prague to Pilzen left at about 6:00 P.M. Just before coming to the city of Pilzen the train stopped in an open field. From both sides, two policemen entered the railroad car with machine guns drawn. One of them was a Czech and the other a Soviet policeman. Each passenger had to produce proper documents, or else he was escorted off the train. I was instructed by Mr. Torbych not to get into any conversation with them, just say one word, yes or no. If you talk more, they will immediately recognize that you are not a native Czech. When they came to us, they first asked Mr. Torbych, "Are you a Czechoslovak citizen?" He answered in Czech "ano"—yes, and handed them his certificate. I did the same when I was asked the question. The certificates were good and satisfied them. Even though my heart was in my throat, and my breathing was quick, I tried to look very calmly straight into the policeman's eyes. It took about half an hour to finish monitoring all the passengers. The train started up again, and soon we arrived in Pilzen.

The atmosphere of true freedom in the city of Pilzen in the American zone could be detected immediately. Nobody controls you, checks you, or asks you questions. Everyone is free to come and go wherever one desires to go. We immediately inquired about the location of the nearest American refugee camp. Having received the directions, we went there. Though it was already late, we were received well. The guard at the gate received us politely, gladly answered all our inquiries, and invited us to spend the night there. Next morning we found out that my classmate, Anne Wolchansky, and her companion were sent to one of the camps in Germany.

The following day, both of us bought our train tickets to get back home to Leitmeritz through the capital city of Prague. The train stopped again just outside of Pilzen, and the same rigid monitoring took place. In the face of such brutal police power with machine guns raised as though ready to shoot at you, we were overcome by fear. We sat silently through the trip, for it was impossible to have a conversation that no one would eavesdrop.

Returning home, Torbych proposed that we take one day to pack our belongings, and on the next day plan to leave for Pilzen. He insisted on this proposition because no one knew what changes might be in the works tomorrow. For security purposes we would not board the train on the same station. There were two stations in the city. So I would board at the first station, and he with his family at the second station so as not to raise suspicions.

Without telling the two sisters in my residence anything about my plans and without good-byes, having packed my suitcase the day before, very early in morning I went silently out of the house to the railroad station. I bought a ticket to Pilzen and boarded the train. The next station was only fifteen minutes away. As I sat there by the window and watched the landscape, I was praying in my heart that God would protect Torbych's family and myself and lead us to safety and freedom.

As soon as the train stopped at the following station, I noticed Torbych, his wife, and the children. There were very few passengers boarding the train. So I came down and helped George with his two large suitcases. He then gave a helping hand to his wife who carried the little girl on her left arm, had a big bag hung over her neck, and a suitcase in the other hand. We occupied a separate compartment. The mother laid both of her children on the seat, covered them with a shawl, and they fell asleep with the sleep of innocence. George and I sat opposite them. George told me that he instructed both children not ever to speak loudly or to cry during the whole trip. If they had some need, they should whisper it in their mother's ear. I was amazed how faithfully they observed their father's instructions. Not one of them ever opened his mouth or cried out. They kept perfect silence all throughout the trip. When one of them needed to go to the washroom, he whispered in his mother's ear only.

We arrived in Prague around noontime, and had to wait until 6:00 P.M. for our train to Pilzen. It was not advisable for us to us to sit in the train station for so many hours, drawing attention to us by the secret police who were always present there. George Torbych was familiar with the city and led us out of the station into a nearby city park. There always were people in the park, strolling, resting, or just passing through. Here we would be noticeable to a lesser extent.

As soon as we found a good place in the park, George left us and went into the city to get some provisions, especially for his children. In about half an hour he came back with a bag full of goodies. He bought two bottles of milk for the children, some ham and smoked sausage, bread, butter and two large bottles of soda. I congratulated him for his skillful enterprise, and said, "With you Mr. Torbych, we will not die of starvation."

Just to pass some time, I went for a walk though the large park, delighting in looking at the beautiful flowers, plants, and especially many statutes of famous people from Czech history.

As I was walking through the park and observing its beauty and monuments, I had enough time to pray and meditate on my own life's fortunes. Here was I, a young man, inexperienced and ignorant in the world's affairs, far away from my parents, far away from home and in a strange land. At that particular time I had access neither to the press nor even to a radio. I did not know what was going on in the world. I would have never been able to devise a plan of escape into the American zone. Had I stayed on in Leitmeritz in just a few weeks I would have been forcefully repatriated to the Soviet Union. And yet here I was on the way to freedom. Again and again, the idea that someone was watching over me, that someone was guiding my steps and leading me was utmost in my mind. The incident on the beach on a Sunday afternoon, the meeting in the dentist's office with Mr. Torbych, all this was as plain as the sun that it was our Lord Jesus Christ and His Blessed Mother who took me under their protection and were leading me in my life. It was God who helped me to meet Mr. Torbych and gave him the idea to include me in his plan of escape. *"Was not the hand of the Lord upon him?"* (Luke 1:66). So I prayed also for Mr. Torbych and his family that they, too, would safely reach the American zone in freedom and safety.

About half an hour before the train's departure to Pilzen, we went back to the station, boarded the train, and departed on time for our destination. We passed the border control and arrived in Pilzen according to schedule. Someone informed the refugee camp by phone, and they sent a truck to pick us up and to deliver us to the camp. The watchman at the gate recognized us and welcomed us back. After the registration, we were assigned rooms in the camp and, after a small supper, rested for the night for the first time in freedom. After only two days in the camp, we and many other refugees who were coming in daily were taken to a railroad station, boarded a train, and were taken to the city called Aschaffenburg, southeast from Frankfurt am Main in Germany. The town of Aschaffenburg was in shambles from the bombing. Here and there one could see new buildings being erected. The streets were full of bricks and parts of the walls from the bombed buildings. Only a narrow path was cleared through which the buses with the refugees could barely pass. We could see from the bus that was barely crawling the work that was being done to clear the streets and haul away the rubble. Small and narrow rail lines were laid along the former streets with small metal carts like dumpsters resting on two opposite poles. The volunteer workers, mostly women and old men, worked literally like ants. They filled the carts with the rubbish and then a small engine or horses would haul away the rubbish to some dump. Yes, these hard workers, women and old men, worked without pay, for this was their homeland, their country, conquered and devastated by a madman called Hitler.

The buses took us to a refugee camp that had served as military barracks for the German army. They consisted of solid three story brick and concrete buildings, each about 250 feet long. There were about four such buildings, which we called "blocks." In addition, there was an administration building, a kitchen, meeting rooms or classrooms, an auditorium with a stage, and a large playground. Each block could house a few hundred people. Most rooms were large dormitory type accommodations with two rows of beds, all together about ten beds to a room. The restrooms and showers were communal along each side of a long corridor. Each floor had some small rooms that were given to more outstanding people, like the priest or some doctor, professor, or a family with small children. Some of the beds were bunk beds. Childless couples would separate their bed by hanging a line with a blanket across, so they were able to have some privacy.

There were four such Ukrainian refugee camps in Aschaffenburg. Our camp was called "LaGuarde." Each camp organized its own administration according to democratic principles. Each also had its own police to keep order, promote peace and tranquility, and protect the camp and its inhabitants. Each camp was surrounded by a high iron picket fence with only one entrance gate in the regular military manner.

Each camp had its own church, both Catholic and Orthodox. Our church was located in the spacious attic of the third block. In a short time our artists made an altar and an iconostas with icons that were done well. Father Eustachius Weselowsky was our pastor, and Father Stephen Bachynsky was assistant pastor. Soon a church choir was organized and the parish worked in almost a normal way. A grade and a high school were organized as well, for there were plenty of professional people, former teachers, and even university professors.

It was like living in a small Ukraine. The camps, located all over western Germany, became organized and started publishing newspapers, books, and magazines. Old and new political parties flourished. Youth organizations began to operate normally. Our camp organized a high school students' dormitory. George Fedoriw was appointed the director of the dormitory, and I was appointed his assistant. All this was possible because the United Nations Refugee Relief Association supported all the refugee camps.

In Search of a New
Way of Life

L ife in a dormitory was good especially when the twelve boys were in school. I occupied myself by reading and typing. I brought a small Olympia portable typewriter with me. An Orthodox bishop by the name of Sylvester wrote his memoirs. He approached me and asked if I would type his memoirs on a typewriter so they could be better preserved and maybe someday published. I agreed and he promised to pay me so much per page. The memoirs were very interesting. They described how bishop Sylvester and the other Ukrainian Orthodox bishops were leaving the homeland of Ukraine and how they together were able to escape from the Communists. In his descriptions of mutual cooperation among the bishops, as well as their disagreements, he was quite factual and literal. So, when the boys were in the school I was able to type a number of pages per day. It was very interesting work for me, a young man, to learn that bishops were only human with all human frailties and weaknesses.

The director of the boys' dormitory, George Fedoriw, presently a priest of the Toronto Eparchy, was very congenial and friendly with me. The dormitory was located on the second floor of the first block. It was a very large room, containing twelve beds for the boys and a row of metal lockers, making a separation for the director and his assistant with two beds and a desk. George Fedoriw and I had plenty of opportunity to spend time together, to get to know one another, and to discuss matters of mutual interest. He had been in a German concentration camp in Teresienstatd, near Leitmeritz, so he was thin—as they say, only skin and bones. Conversations with him were always very interesting. I could see that he was a man of great knowledge and experience, one who had suffered much. Because of this, I respected his opinion.

I began to think of my future. In order to be accepted into a university, I needed a diploma from a gymnasium, something more than an American high school. There was a Ukrainian gymnasium in the city of Augsburg that was moved there from the city of Podebrady in Czechoslovakia, near Prague, and had German accreditation. Having consulted with George Fedoriw, he encouraged me to go there, and even volunteered to go with me so that I could take an exam there to get the needed diploma. Our local high school in the refugee camp did not have the accreditation to give such diplomas. So I took all the school diplomas I had from my schools at home, and George and I took a train ride and went to the famous city of Augsburg. The principal of the school was Prof. Augustine Shtefan, a very well-known Ukrainian activist and scholar from Carpatho Ukraine. He set up a board of teachers who were to conduct the examination. At first it was an hour-long written exam. In the afternoon, five teachers conducted an oral exam. Each teacher questioned me about his own subject—Ukrainian literature, history, geography, mathematics, and the Latin language. I passed all the subjects, but Latin was my weakest subject. They passed me and gave me a diploma, but Mr. Shtefan encouraged me to do some more work privately on my Latin.

After our return from Augsburg, some of my friends were planning to go to Frankfurt to register as university students. The state was paying the tuition. It was a golden opportunity for me to join them and see if I, too, could register. I wanted to study medicine, so I went along with the others. Yet, I was not successful because the school of medicine was not yet open. I had to wait a few more months for its opening.

At the Crossroads

After my failure to be accepted into a medical school in Frankfurt, George Fedoriw questioned me as to why I wanted to be a physician. He said it was his impression that I would make a good doctor of souls—a priest. I did not answer him at all for I never gave it a thought. It was not in my plan so far. My idea of a doctor was the opportunity to be able to help others when they were in need and could not help themselves. But my conversation with George Fedoriw started me on thinking about what he had said.

The idea of possibly becoming a priest would not go away. It was following me day and night. I tried hard to get rid of it. I read a lot. I got myself busy to fill my head with other matters, especially in the scout's organization, "Plast." I went out with boys and girls to dances. I started dating a girl. But the more I tried to get rid of the idea of priesthood, the more persistently it clung to me. It was as though that "Hound of Heaven" was after me persistently and without relief.

The world has its attractions, and I, at that time was a child of the world. I had many dear friends in the camp, boys and girls of my age. We got to know each other and liked each other's company, and were attracted to each other. Priesthood seemed to me at that time to be something far away from the real world, a life of seclusion, of separation from what I was enjoying now.

The question my mother once asked me, "Would you like to be a priest?" came back to me again and again. At that time I really missed my parents. I missed someone near and dear to me to whom I could open my heart and confide my thoughts that were torturing me. There was no one I could trust completely. It seemed to me as though I was in a vicious circle, walking and getting nowhere, or lost in a deep forest not knowing which direction to go to get out of it.

George Fedoriw would never volunteer any information concerning his life, his past, or his plans for his future. At first he did not tell me that he was a seminarian, studied theology at the Lviv Theological Academy, and gained a doctorate of philosophy in Prague. When I found out that he was in a seminary, I told him, "Remember when I came back from Frankfurt and told you that I was planning to study medicine, you placed a thought into my head that does not want to leave me. You said it was your impression that I should be a priest. This idea is torturing me, and I can't get rid of it. What should I do?"

"I do not know what you should do. I am not a prophet; I do not know the future. Only God knows. The genuine idea of priesthood comes from God directly. No human being is able to give you the right guidance. If your idea that does not want to leave you comes from God, then you had better talk to Him. Ask His advice in humble and persistent prayer. Ask our Heavenly Mother Mary to guide and protect you. God has a way of letting you know what you should do. When the idea of priesthood is from God, then it is no use opposing it with the risk of offending Him. You must trust God and submit your will to His. Don't tell God what He should do; ask Him to tell you what you should do. If you do what He tells you to do, your future will be safe and happy."

Struggle with an Angel (Genesis 32:29)

I did not have much choice but to listen to the advice of George Fedoriw in order to be able to rid myself of the vicious dilemma. At that time I was not much of a praying man. Oh, I said my morning and evening prayers. I attended Divine Liturgy on Sundays. I did not know any better. But I started to pray the way I knew how to pray. But nothing was happening. Heaven was not opened to me and no voices came down to me from heaven. One night however, when sleep would not come, I laid there and started to talk to God with words that came to my mind:

"My Heavenly Father, You always took care of me, even though I did not deserve it. You took me by the hand, guided and protected me from evil. You know that right now I am lost within my thought as though I was in a deep forest and could not find my way out. I walk in a circle and do not know my way home. Show me the way to get out of this vicious circle. Tell me what I should do in my life, what road should I take to please you." *"Teach me, O Lord, your way that I may walk in your truth."* (Psalms 86:11)

After this short prayer from my heart, I stopped and just listened. Deep in my heart I felt that God was with me and heard me. Then in my heart I heard: "I will help you provided that you will not rely on your own knowledge, skills, and talents, but will rely on me wholeheartedly. Place your life into my hands and say to me: Do with me as you wish!"

I understood then beyond any doubt that the solution to my problem is only one—to do only what God wants me to do, and not what I wish to do. I have to choose what God wishes me to choose. It has to be His way, not mine.

I concluded then with this thought—"O Lord, my God, "You have prevailed." (Genesis 32:29) Without You I am nothing. All my plans and my youthful fantasies are only dreams, smoke, and fog. Should I go against your will, you will not bless my plans and me. All of it will turn into nothing. If you truly are calling me to serve you as your priest, how then can I refuse to obey your most holy will? For to serve you, the Creator of heaven and earth, should be the greatest and the highest honor in this world. But am I worthy of such a great vocation? Will I be able to stand firm in it, and not fall and bring shame and dishonor to your Church? I feel very weak, feeble, and unworthy of such an exalted dignity. Why don't you choose for yourself someone stronger and more capable physically and spiritually, much smarter and more wise than I? They would be able to do much more good for your Church than I can. But, forgive me, O Lord. I should not tell you what to do. I just do not understand why you have chosen me instead of others who are much more worthy of this dignity? This is why, even though I do not understand, I will blindly trust in you and place myself and my whole life into your hands, as did my parents and my grandpa. From now on "I am yours." (Psalms 119:94), do with me as you will."

Only then true peace came into my heart. There were no more struggles, no more indecision and doubts. I knew what I wanted.

Soon I sat down and wrote a letter to the Apostolic Visitator, the Rev. Nicholas Wojakowsky in Passing near Munich, asking him to help me to go to our seminary in Rome to study for the priesthood. His reply was negative. The letter was dated December 3, 1945 (n.972a/45). "His Excellency the Apostolic Visitator asked me to inform you that it is not possible for him to help you to go to Rome since it is very difficult to get an entrance visa to Italy. We are making plans right now to open our own seminary here in Munich of which we will inform you at the right time. (Signed by) Rev. M. Malicky, chancellor."

Only George Fedoriw knew of my plans to study for the priesthood. I kept this intention as my private secret. But somehow the inhabitants of the LaGuarde camp got the news from someone. Yet no one ever said a word of encouragement, friendly advice, support, or good wishes. The only thing I could hear here and there was great amazement that Stephen, such a talented young man, chose the priesthood. From among my friends among the scouts the saying was, "Stephen lost his mind!"

Meditating on this matter now, I've come to the conclusion that the reason for such amazement when I chose to go to the seminary was the lack of spirituality among our new immigrants, which explains why there were so few vocations in those groups.

Hirschberg am Harsee

Holy Spirit Seminary was first opened on the 9th of February, 1946. I was informed about this event by the Apostolic Visitator and immediately left the camp in Aschaffenburg. The seminary was located about forty kilometers east of Munich. The railroad station we used was the town of Waldheim. Then we had to walk north a few kilometers, and there in the woods on a hill was a castle called Hirschberg. A German noble family named Hirschberg-Podewils built it in 1910. On the other side of the castle, about five hundred yards away, was a beautiful lake called Harsee. In 1943 Hitler nationalized it and used it for his purposes. Italy's Mussolini stayed there for some time. Then Hungary's admiral Horty lived there with his staff. In 1945 the American Army took over the castle and used it as a rest home with Horty's staff as cooks.

Our Church was able to get this castle from the American Army for use as our seminary. It was legally organized as a small refugee camp so the United Nations Refugees Relief Association (UNRRA) could supply it with food. I came to the seminary on February 9, 1946. In a few days many other boys arrived. I boarded with Wasyl Martynyk, later on a priest in the Edmonton Ukrainian Diocese in Canada, Franko Kupranec, later on a Basilian Father and an editor of their journal, *The Light*. Both of these men have passed away years ago. There were seventy seminarians all together. Many of the seminarians had been in the Holy Spirit Theological Academy in Lviv, Ukraine. Some were studying philosophy or theology in various Latin Seminaries in Germany, and others such as myself, were here for the first time. The Rector, Rt. Rev. Mitred Archpriest Wasyl Laba, and some of the professors came from the Academy in Lviv. Father Laba, besides being a rector, was also a teacher of Holy Scripture, patrology, and canon law. For the first semester the Vice Rector was Rev. Michael Lewenetz.

About a year later Rev. Alexander Malynowsky came to Germany from Poland. He was appointed rector of the administration and Father Laba remained rector of studies. A Redemptorists priest, Father Vladimir Malanchuk was our spiritual director. A year later, Father Zachary Zolotyj became our spiritual director. Rev. Peter Holynsky—teacher of church history and pedagogy; Father Zenowy Narozniak—liturgics; Father Bohdan Lypsky—moral theology; Father Michael Sopulak—dogmatic theology; Dr. Wasyl Lew—Church Slavonic language; Dr. Wasyl Lencyk—church history; Nicholas Holowaty—Hebrew language; Dr. Ivan Mirchuk—history of Ukrainian culture; Dr. Jaroslav Rudnycky—Ukrainian language, literature and philology; Dr. Michael Sonewycky—Greek language; Vladimir Cisyk—church music and seminary choir. Occasionally other outstanding scholars would come to our seminary and lecture on the subject that was their specialization.

Since we had no library in the castle-seminary, each teacher tried to write his lectures and some of us would type the lectures and then duplicate them on a mimeograph machine. I had my own portable typewriter and did most of the typing.

The subjects were taught on a high scholarly level, and the spiritual life was very satisfactory. The students applied themselves seriously to prayer and study. Yet there was one negative side of this seminary. The UNRRA would supply a sufficient amount of food, but the Hungarian kitchen staff would steal the food, sell it for profit, and the seminarians would go hungry. They did it so proficiently that no one could catch them.

I was trying very hard to be patient with the lack of food, but at times I just could not study or type. The pains of hunger were too much for me to take. So one late afternoon when it was time of silence and study, I got up and went down the stairs from the third floor. Fr Lewenetz saw me and said to me, "Where are you going? You are supposed to study now." I told him that I cannot study because I am hungry, so I am going into the woods to pick some berries. And he said, "I am going with you, for I too am hungry. He was trying to better the situation with the food supplies, but Father Wojakowsky did not give him the necessary support. So after one semester as our very much beloved vice rector, he asked to be transferred away from the seminary.

Hirschberg Castle in Germany where Ukrainian Catholic Seminary was located in 1946 to 1948.

Many of the seminarians were forced to go back on weekends to their refugee camps and bring some additional food back with them. For me it was impossible, for Aschaffenburg was too far away. Others would go to the nearby villages to the farmers and buy food or trade some clothing articles for a loaf of bread. Some students could not take such a shortage of food and quit the seminary, never to return.

1946 Summer Vacations

During the summer vacations, all the seminarians left the seminary and went back, each to his refugee camp. I went back to Aschaffenburg. I tried to be helpful to the pastor and the parish. I took an active part in the Boy Scout troops and went camping with them. At that time, my friend Dmytro Pilecky and I joined the third branch of the senior boys scouts "Plast," who called themselves "The Spirits of the Forest." This group organized a trip into the Alps. Pilecky and I agreed to take part in this trip. We were told to be at the gate of the refugee camp in the town of Berchtesgaden at 6:00 A.M. Our train came on time and we hurried to the appointed place of meeting. However, the guard at the gate told us that the group left half an hour ago to catch the 6:00 A.M. train to Kenigzee.

We decided to follow them hoping we would be able to catch up with them. We took the 7:00 am, train to Kenigzee, and from there took a boat across the lake to St. Bartholomew landing place. We asked for instructions how to get to a restaurant called Funten Zee, way up in the rocky Alps. With our backpacks on, we started to climb to the unknown place without knowing the way to get there. Each of us found a tall staff in the woods and used it for support and as a weapon of defense.

The path had no directional signs at all. Our group did not leave any signs for us to follow. So we were not sure this was the right way to go. The path led us higher and higher into the rocky Alps. After an hour or so there was no more forested landscape, only bare rock. On both sides of our path stood very tall rocks, straight up into the skies, something like Gothic cathedral towers.

The path led higher straight up, higher between the two tall rocks. After three or four hours of climbing, we were very tired, and each step was becoming an effort. We decided not to rest because time was of the essence. We needed to reach the place before nightfall. We finally reached the peak where the path was less sloped, and it was covered with hard snow. There for the first time we found human footprints. We surmised that these were the footprints of our group, but there was no certainty about it. The sun was setting and it was getting darker and colder when we noticed on the horizon smoke from a chimney, and the house. Finally we arrived and our friends were waiting for us with the evening meal. There were twelve of us altogether and we had to introduce ourselves, for it was the first time we met as a group.

After the meal, we spent time discussing various matters pertaining to our branch of "The Spirits of the Forest." Then each of us was asked to tell the rest something about ourselves. Most of the boys were college students studying in various German universities. I was the only seminarian. After a weeklong stay high in the Alpine Mountains, we left for home, each to his refugee camp.

Return to the Seminary

I was happy to return to the seminary, the spiritual life, and the studies. All of us started a new academic year with renewed vigor and intensified prayer life. It was good to see the friendly faces of my buddies, the seminarians, and our teachers.

One of the professors brought a copy of a Ukrainian Daily newspaper *Svoboda* with him from the United States, published in Jersey City, N.J. I got hold of it and wrote a letter to that newspaper, asking them to help me find my uncle, Dmytro Stec, somewhere in the United States. In a few weeks I got a letter from my uncle with a $20.00 bill in it. My Uncle Dmytro was born in Trenton, Pa. October 12, 1907. His parents returned to Ukraine when he was only two years old. He married Sophie Sulyk, my father's sister, May 13, 1928. They had one daughter Mary, born 1929. In 1931 Dmytro returned to the United States in order to find a good job, earn some money, and then get his wife and daughter to join him. He returned to the United States when the Great Depression began. There were no jobs to be had. He washed dishes in a restaurant and could barely make ends meet. We would correspond regularly, and from his letters I learned something about the destiny of my parents and the rest of the family.

Action Wisla

From my uncle's letters and from the newspaper *Svoboda* I learned that in 1946 in communist Poland the barbaric and bloody "Action Wisla" took place. With Stalin's blessings the Polish communist government forcefully resettled 600,000 Ukrainians from their native land occupied now by the new Polish state. Among those who were resettled from my native village Balnycia was my aunt Sophie. In her letters to her husband, my Uncle Dmytro, she described the events.

In the summer of 1946 Polish army units came to our village and ordered all our people to pack their belongings within two hours and be ready to leave. They could take with them only what they could carry or place on their horse drawn carriage. Facing gun barrels, our poor and helpless people had no other choice but to pack whatever they could take with them and leave their homes, belongings, fields, and cattle. The soldiers started from the lower end of the village. Somehow the word came to the people of the upper end. They packed some food into their bags and ran away into the woods. They were forcefully resettled in 1947 into East German territories, which were annexed to Poland after World War II. My Aunt Sophie, her daughter Mary, as well as my Uncle Nicholas with his family were resettled into the territories of western Poland.

The lower part of the village (where our house was) was re-settled in 1946 into what was the Soviet Union of that time. My father placed his whole family and all of his belongings on a small carriage. He left behind our new home, the barn, the stables, the orchard, the cattle, and fields that were almost ripe for harvest. Everything that he and his ancestors were able to earn was being left behind. The soldiers would grab anything that was left behind, and then put the homes on fire.

The poor people were crying bitter tears when they had to part with their homes and property for the last time and go to unknown lands among strange people. As the caravan of horse-drawn carriages was being assembled, my father went up the hill to say good-bye to our church. He knelt before the closed doors of the church and prayed. With bitter tears in his eyes, he was saying goodbye to the place he loved so much, where he was baptized and married, where he as a cantor sang the Liturgies on Sundays and Holydays. He was saying good-bye also to the nearby cemetery where the earthly remains of his father and his three sons were resting, as well as those of his ancestors. Then the soldiers came, picked him up, and compelled him to go back to his carriage.

My parents were resettled into the Soviet Union. At first they were settled much further in the eastern past of Western Ukraine, near the city of Tarnopil, but my father did not like it there. He turned his horses around and went back west to the city of Sambir, which he knew from before the war when he visited me there in high school. About twenty families followed him, and all settled on the suburbs of Sambir.

This forceful resettlement of Ukrainians from their native lands, called "Action Wisla"—Vistula, was a very cruel and unjust action, perpetrated by Stalin with the Polish communists. It did not improve the relationship between these two Christian neighboring peoples. Of course, American President Roosevelt played a part in this as well. At the conference in Yalta, he agreed to this division of Europe, consenting to Stalin's wishes.

To Cross the Atlantic Ocean

Correspondence with my Uncle Dmytro Stec continued. His few dollars in every letter was a great help to me in the seminary, for now I did not have to suffer hunger pains anymore. I was able to afford an extra loaf of bread on a weekly basis. In one of his letters during my summer vacation of 1948, I found the necessary papers to obtain an immigration visa to the United States of America. So I visited the United States Consulate and presented my papers. I was told that the papers were valid and in due time I would be informed of the date of my departure for my new home in the United States. Immediately I wrote to Father Rector of the Seminary and informed him of my plans. He gave me his blessing and informed me that our seminary was moving from Hirschberg to Culemborg in Holland where the local Catholic bishop offered us a seminary building.

While waiting for the information from the Consulate, I started learning English with a German teacher. I would go to his house and have my lessons three times a week.

In late September I was informed by the United States Consulate that my departure for the United States would take place October 22, 1948, from Bremerhafen. I had plenty of time to prepare for my departure across the ocean, to say farewell to all my friends, and to write a letter to my seminary friends as well.

I always thought of myself as an experienced traveler. Since my early youth, as a ten-year-old boy, I was away from home in the city schools. Yet now, facing a trip across the ocean, I experienced certain anxiety that is fear of the unknown. I remember one time before the war, as I was packing my suitcase and getting ready to go back to school in Sambir, my Aunt Sophie and her daughter Mary were in our house. I kissed both of them good-bye. My aunt started to wipe tears from her eyes and said to me, "You are an eternal traveler, always packing your suitcase." Without thinking much, I retorted, "When someday you get to the United Sates with your husband, send me papers and I will come to America and will stop being a vagabond." Neither then nor now do I know why I said that. It might have been a sort of prophecy.

October 21, 1948, arrived and all who were scheduled to go the United States were taken to the railroad station and put on a special train that was to go to Bremerhafen. Many of my friends came to the station with me to say a farewell. Kisses were exchanged and tears wiped from our eyes.

In Bremerhafen the next day our ship was waiting for us. It was a military personnel transport ship, named "General Black." The passengers boarded the ship and each was assigned his hanging canvas bunk bed, a hammock. Women were separated from men in some other compartments but with no more luxury than the men had. The ship was pushed off from the shores by barges the same day. Many passengers stayed on deck and watched the shores slowly disappear on the horizon. The boundless sea received the ship into its arms, and the waves were playing with it as with a toy. Before dusk set in, the ship passed through the Strait of Dover and into the English Channel. Everyone was amazed at the high rocky cliffs of Dover. With each passing hour these shores were getting smaller and smaller, until they disappeared on the horizon. White seagulls accompanied us for a long time. They would sit down on a wave crest, and then fly up again as though they were playing a game.

Among the passengers was Julian Revay from Carpatho Ukraine with his daughter. He was a former member of the Czechoslovak parliament, and then the prime minister of Carpatho Ukraine. I got to know both of them, and we spent a lot of time together in friendly conversations.

The first day of our voyage was very pleasant and easy going. The following day I got seasick with nausea and vomiting. There was no medical aid on board the ship and no one to help or advise me. With each passing day the sickness got worse until I was vomiting blood. I felt the effects of this seasickness for years to come.

The New World

It was Sunday, October 30, 1948 when our ship neared the eastern shores of Connecticut, then Long Island. Two tugboats met the ship and escorted her to New York harbor. High jets of water welcomed her as she passed the Statue of Liberty since ours was the first ship of new immigrants to the United States of America according to a recently passed law.

When our ship got into New York harbor it was getting dark. Many people were welcoming the new immigrants. They must have been relatives and friends, for they were embracing and kissing each other. There was no one to welcome me because my uncle lived in Dearborn, Michigan, and it was just too far for him to travel. Some women from the welcoming committee came to me and escorted me to their car and took me to a hotel for the night. In the morning they came for me, and drove me to a railroad station and put me on a train to Detroit. The trip lasted an entire day, and it was Monday evening, October 31, when we arrived in Detroit. Here again some women put me in their car and drove me to Dearborn to my uncle's house. However, my uncle was not home at that time. The women asked a neighbor to take me in until my uncle returned.

I did not have to wait long. In about ten minutes the lights in my uncle's house went on, so we knew that he had returned. I thanked the neighbor and went across the street to my uncle's house and rang the doorbell. The door opened and my uncle was surprised to see me there. He welcomed me with open arms. "Why didn't someone let me know you were coming? I would have picked you up at the station." As he was talking, he looked into his mailbox, and found a letter announcing my arrival. But the greatest surprise was reserved for me. Right behind my uncle stood Mary, his daughter. We embraced and kissed. She explained that she came from Poland only two weeks ago. I was so happy to see her and immediately asked her, "Where is your mother?" I was told that she was still in Western Poland, but there was hope that she, too, would soon be permitted to come to the United States.

Joy and happiness filled the little house. My uncle wanted to know about my journey; how many days it took to cross the ocean; was there a storm on the ocean; did I get seasick? I was happy to tell him anything he wanted to know, but my curiosity about Mary's arrival and her stay in Poland prompted me to change the subject of our conversation. I wanted to know something more about their forceful resettlement; about their stay in Poland; about any news she had from my parents, brothers, and sister. We talked for hours until my uncle said that was enough for today, and that I must be tired. He then urged me to take a shower and go to bed. We would talk more tomorrow.

The following day was the presidential election day when Harry Truman was elected president. My uncle took his daughter Mary and me, and after he cast his vote, we went shopping. He bought me a new suit of clothes, two shirts, and some underwear. Toward evening my uncle's brother, Nicholas Stec, with his wife Jennie came visiting to welcome me. He had left for the United States when I was still a young boy, and I did not remember him at all. The following Saturday the three of us went across the river from Detroit to Windsor, Canada, to visit my uncle's younger brother, Peter Stec and his family. All three brothers were born in the United States. I remember very well Peter's departure for United States. It was just a year or two before World War II. Mary was very happy, too, for she had not seen her uncle Peter for many years.

The following Sunday all three of us went to St. John's Ukrainian Catholic Church in Detroit. Rev. Stephen Pobutsky was the pastor, and Rev. Ivan Prokopowych was his assistant. My uncle introduced me to both priests as a seminarian. From then on both priests took a very special interest in me. Father Pobutsky urged me to immediately write to the bishop in Philadelphia and ask to be admitted to the seminary in Washington, D.C. I thought that it would be too late now, since it was already November, and the semester had started in September. I thought I would try to get a job somewhere, make a few dollars and learn English better before I would apply for the next academic year. Father Prokopowych agreed with me. He invited me to his house, and so we became good friends, and our friendship lasted for the rest of his life. He died December 13, 1977.

"By the sweat of your face shall you get bread to eat" (Genesis 3:19)

About two weeks after my arrival in America, my uncle took me with him to work. He worked for the Ford Motor Company at the River Rouge plant in Dearborn. I was hired and assigned to work on an assembly line. It was my job to file a joint on the left of the trunk so smoothly that after it was painted the joint was not visible. The assembly line was constantly moving, and I had to walk along with the assembly line as I was filing the joint. There were three men on each side of the assembly line. Every fourth car was mine to do. The assembly line was designed to get the most out of a worker. One had to have not only a sufficient amount of physical strength, but also enough skill to do the job right.

The foreman watched us all the time, inspecting each car. At first he taught me how to do the job. Then he corrected me when something was not just so. When one of us had to leave the assembly line, the foreman would call in a substitute. He reminded us to be back in five minutes. Eight hours of such intensive work would exhaust me physically since I was not used to such physical work. Yet I did not give up. I worked as hard as I could, and the foreman was satisfied with my work. Now I could better see and appreciate how hard it was for so many workers to earn their daily bread, to feed the family, buy a house and pay for it.

During the lunch period the assembly line stopped, everyone took his lunch box, and finding a place to sit, enjoyed his meal. An elderly man came up to me during lunch one day and asked me my name and place of origin. When I named my village, he said that he too came from the same village. He gave me his name, Stephen Hoblak. He knew my parents and grandparents. He came to America forty years earlier and since then had worked for the Ford Motor Company. He was very friendly with my uncle and knew the whole family.

Change of Employment

Due to economic reasons, the Ford Motor Company declared a lay off in accordance with the agreements with the labor unions. Those workers who had the least seniority, were laid off first. All I had at that time was four weeks of seniority, so I was among the first to go.

With the help of my uncle and his friends I got a new job within two weeks. It was in a meatpacking storehouse of the Kroger Company, which has a whole network of food stores. The storehouse was located in Detroit, and I commuted by city bus. The entire storehouse was refrigerated, and some special rooms were large freezers. Thus during work we had to be dressed warmly, over which we wore a white coat and special gloves and a warm cap. The foreman would receive orders written on special forms from various stores, and we had to fill the order by placing various meat products into special crates with a copy of the written order on top.

My work started daily at 10:30 P.M. and ended at 7:00 A.M. At that time, the trucks we had loaded with the orders started moving out, delivering the meat products to the stores before they opened in the morning. The work was not monotonous and was not difficult. I liked it especially after my experience at Ford Motor Company.

My Aunt's Arrival

In March of 1949, my Aunt Sophie arrived by air from Poland at the Detroit airport. My uncle, his daughter Mary and I went to the airport to welcome her to her new home and new country. After seventeen long years of separation, the family was once again together. Their hearts were filled with joy and gratitude to God for having given them the grace to survive the tragedies of World War II and be united again in the family circle. Nicholas and Peter, Dmytro's brothers with their wives, as well as numerous friends soon came to visit and welcome Sophie.

Dmytro was a man of quiet temperament, though sometimes a bit nervous, a characteristic he always tried to hide. He was always honest, a man of his word, and a true gentlemen. His outstanding quality was to be kind, friendly, and helpful toward others. He was a hard worker and very knowledgeable concerning the art of carpentry, plumbing and other related skills. Anything needed in the house was fashioned by himself. He finished the attic of his house, making it two full rooms. The basement he likewise finished by covering the walls with siding, the ceiling with acoustical tile, and the floor with linoleum. In the corner he made a powder room with a shower.

Sophie, as far as her character was concerned, was a perfect copy of her father Ivan Sulyk. She was of a quiet temperament, always with a nice smile and friendly. No one ever saw her angry. She never said a bad word against anyone. Pious and religious, she loved to pray, especially the rosary. When she fell asleep in the Lord, they found her in the morning with the rosary in her hand.

She never missed church on Sundays and holy days. When Father Prokopowych organized a new St. Michael's parish in Dearborn, Sophie was eager to help in the church kitchen by making pirohies or cooking for dinners or banquets. In my aunt and uncle's small house there was no longer room for me. Nicholas, Dmytro's brother, and his wife were childless and happy to take me into their house. From there I commuted daily to my job and on Sundays to the church.

My Struggles and Doubts

After careful deliberation and heartfelt prayers, I decided in March of 1949 to petition Bishop Constantine Bohachevsky in Philadelphia for admission to St. Josaphat Seminary in Washington D.C. in order to continue my education and formation for the priesthood. In my petition I enclosed all the documentation from our Seminary in Hirschberg, Germany. A reply came soon with the following statement: "Philadelphia, Pa., March 14, 1949, Prot. # 62/49. In reply to your letter dated March 12, 1949, please be informed that we received a reply from the Seminary Rector. Your letter of excardination is still missing."

I then wrote a letter to our Seminary in Culemborg, Holland, asking for advice. Rev. Malynowsky replied, "March 21, 1949, In reply to your letter I wish to inform you that a letter of excardination cannot be issued by a rector of the seminary because it is the exclusive competency of an ordinary Bishop. Your Bishop Ordinary presently is behind the iron curtain and no communication with him is possible under these circumstances. Bishop Bohachevsky is making this demand on you, because he apparently does not want to have you as his seminarian . . ."

This reply came as a shock to me. I was not able to do what the bishop demanded of me. I was convinced that Bishop Bohachevsky knew that my bishop, Josaphat Kocylowsky of the Peremyshl

Eparchy, was incarcerated by the communists, sentenced, deported from his eparchy, and imprisoned. Then I read in the Code of Canon Law that such a document of excardination is required only from ordained clerics, and not from seminarians. Based on this information, I came to the conclusion that Bishop Bohachevsky really did not want me to be his seminarian or his priest. The will of the bishop for me is the will of God. So I wrote him another letter, requesting the return of my seminary documents.

This demand by bishop Bohachevsky disturbed me immensely and deprived me of peace of mind. After my arrival in the United States, I had many very serious doubts concerning the priesthood. In Hirschberg Seminary there were no demands on the seminarians concerning a celibate priesthood. Here in the United States only celibate candidates could be ordained priests. This demand I faced for the first time, and it was a very difficult time for me, one of constant doubts, indecision, and outright confusion. It took me months of prayer and meditation, seeking advice of priests and confessors, until with the help of God I decided to be a celibate. And now this obstacle placed in my way by Bishop Bohachevsky recalled all my doubts once again. I was not certain anymore that my decision to be a celibate priest was correct since "the voice of a bishop is the voice of God." Through Bishop Bohachevsky, God informed me of His will.

What do I do now? The idea of studying medicine came back to me. So I went to Wayne University in Detroit in order to inquire whether the study of medicine would be possible for me. They examined my seminary documents and told me that I could apply to premedical school since none of the subjects I studied had anything to do with medicine. But when I was told the amount of school tuition, it became clear to me that it was not for me.

Council of a Good Layman

One Sunday as I was leaving church, I met Mr. Julian Revay, well known to me from our trip together across the ocean. He asked how things were going for me? Would I continue my theology studies, or would I opt for something else as my profession? I trusted him as a man of great experience in life, hoping that he would give me good advice. I told him briefly of my petition to the bishop, of his reply, and of my difficulties, doubts, and indecision. "When I am in church on Sunday, I want to be a priest. When I say my morning or evening prayers, I want to be a priest. At work on Monday, the evil one whispers to my ear, "Why should you become a victim of celibacy?" And thus I change my mind a few times a day. All this is becoming very exhausting to me, and it is my torture. I wanted to study medicine, but financially it is impossible for me."

Revay gave me this advice, In all the history of our nation, priests were actually the teachers and the leaders of our people. They lived with the people and shared with them their good and bad fortunes. Throughout the ages the priest in our village was the counselor, the educator, the judge who settled the misunderstandings among the people and the one who showed them the

119

way to live. Without our dedicated, self-sacrificing and patriotic priests our people would not exist today. Our neighbors would have absorbed them. Our Church and our priests were always that fortress, that spiritual statehood which ruled the souls of our people and which preserved our national identity. With our Byzantine rite, our Church was different from the huge, world-wide Roman Catholic Church, and with our Catholic faith our Church was different from the Russian Orthodox Church and thus protected us from Moscow and russification. Yes, our Church is the one spiritual force that preserved and protected our nation. This is exactly the reason why Moscow, be she white or red, hates our Church so much and has always tried to destroy her. The religious differences are only a cover up. Our Church is the obstacle for Moscow to more speedily russify the whole of Ukraine. You have to abandon all your doubts and not torture yourself. A soldier in a war has no time for doubts. He has to make a decision right then and there or else he is killed or taken prisoner. So should you do, too. Say your prayers, and then make your decision once and for all. Never again go back on your decision.

The Advice of a Missionary

A t St. John's Church in Detroit Rev. Maxim Markiw, OSBM, was preaching a Lenten Mission. I went to him to confession and then asked if he could have some time for me to talk to him. After the Liturgy I went to see him and presented him with my problems.

Son, he said, you should not be discouraged with one negative answer from the bishop. One negative answer is not yet a sign that this is the will of God for you. You made your decision for celibate priesthood not by yourself only. It was God who helped you make such a great decision. Relying on yourself and your own abilities, you would never have made such a decision. I presume that you realize that the life of a celibate priest is a life of self-sacrifice, which you freely and willingly offer to God out of love for Him and His Church for the salvation of human souls. This is a great and holy sacrifice and very much pleasing to God. This sacrifice is not a sacrifice or heroism of one moment, an hour, or a day. It is a sacrifice for every moment, and every day for the rest of your life.

What if by the negative answer of the bishop God wished to test you whether you are ready to receive from the loving hands of God all kinds of difficulties and crosses? Are you ready to conquer your own weaknesses, your own temptations, and carry your cross patiently day and night? Are you capable of taking upon yourself all kinds of difficulties, disappointments, abuses, insults, calumnies, and vicious accusations? Are you ready to take upon your shoulders all these problems and even the cross itself and follow Christ as His faithful and loyal servant for all the days of your life until your last breath?"

He then took the Bible and said, "It would be good for you to read these passages: *"My son, when you come to serve the Lord, prepare yourself for trials. Be sincere of heart and steadfast, undisturbed in time of adversity. Cling to him, forsake him not; thus will your future be great. Accept whatever befalls you, in crushing misfortune be patient. For in fire gold is tested, and worthy men in the crucible of humiliation."* (Sirach 2:1–5)

Thus, you have to be very patient and not despair when disappointments or difficulties come your way. God is a jealous lover and demands from us, especially from his priests, not only a little self-sacrifice, but all of your heart, all of your undivided love. You know the great commandment of love: *"You shall love the Lord your God with all your heart, with all your soul, with all your mind, and with all your strength."* (Mark 12:30) You must have also heard these words of the Lord: *"Whoever loves father or mother, son or daughter, more than me is not worthy of me."* (Matthew 10:37)

God has a need of priests who are ready to give themselves wholeheartedly to the ministry of the Church. He does not need weaklings who seek only their own benefits, profits, carefree life, and riches. He needs candidates who would give their heart entirely to Him, who would be ready for any sacrifice as His knights to defend the Church from snares of the evil one, build up His Kingdom on earth so that all people may gain their eternal salvation. Such priests God needs very badly in our Ukrainian Catholic Church here in our new home, and God willing, some day in our motherland. Therefore, my advice to you is, write once more to the bishop, explain the matter of the document he required of you. Should he refuse to accept you, write to the Basilian Fathers. They will, I hope, accept you.

The Earthen Vessels

I have another question for you, Father," I said. "I am very much afraid that I am too weak, that I do not have enough strength, firmness, and courage to be able to endure the celibate state of life without sinning. I panic with fear that I will fall, offend my loving God, and will cause scandal to our good and devoted faithful and will cause shame to holy mother Church."

Father Markiw replied: I am glad that you did not forget to ask me this particular question, because it is very important. Yes, son! All of us humans, especially the priests, are very much conscious that we carry a very precious treasure of divine grace in our *"earthen vessels,"* (2 Corinthians 4:7) in our frail human bodies. Relying exclusively upon our human strength, upon our courage or firmness, you will most surely fall and sin, because it is over and above our human capabilities. Even St. Peter, the chief of the apostles, the rock chosen by God himself, fell in the face of danger, and denied Christ: *"At that (Peter) began cursing, and swore, 'I do not even know the man!"* (Matthew 26:74)

Even the great Apostle of the nations, Paul, admitted, *"Even though I want to do what is right, a law that leads to wrongdoing is always ready at hand. My inner self agrees with the law of God, but I see in my body's members another law at war with the law of my mind; this makes me the prisoner of the law of sin in my members. What a wretched man I am! Who can free me from this body under the power of death? All praise to God, through Jesus Christ our Lord."* (Romans 7:21–25)

Yes, yes, without the special aid of God, no one of us could live in the state of grace. No one could withstand the invasion of temptations. We all would sin, because Jesus Christ said to His apostles and to us as well, *"Apart from me you can do nothing."* (John. 15:5) In order to receive the needed help from God, one must pray daily, must beg God the Father in the name of Jesus Christ, our Savior. We must be in constant prayer union with Christ. He so often assured us, *"Ask, and you will receive. Seek, and you will find. Knock, and it will be opened to you."* (Matthew 7:7) These very important words of our Lord may be explained thus: "If you will not ask, you will not receive. If you will not seek, you will not find. If you will not knock, it will not be opened to you." But when we do receive God's help to carry the heavenly treasury in our earthly vessels, it then *"is clear that its surpassing power comes from God and not from us."* (2 Corinthians 4:7)

You must love prayer as your best friend, your constant helper. Even as fish cannot live without the water, as humans cannot live without the life-giving oxygen in order to be able to breath. Even much more is prayer needed for your soul to live the life of grace.

There is a proverb among our people that in rough translation goes something like this, you should beg God, but you should also use your hands well. One, therefore, should pray, but he should also do everything possible to avoid sin and every occasion to sin. One should avoid persons who could tempt us to

126

sin. One should be determined to oppose such temptations, even as Our Lord said, *"If your hand is your difficulty, cut it off! Better for you to enter life maimed than to keep both hands and enter Gahanna with its unquenchable fire."* (Mark 9:43) We should, therefore, use determined means in order to oppose temptations. We should break away even from our dearest persons, if they are an occasion of sin for us.

In order to be more successful in your efforts to avoid sin and an occasion of sin, ask the Most Holy Mother of God to be your personal advocate and intercessor so that she may bring your prayers to her Son and implore him to help you. Jesus will never say "no" to his Mother. The Mother of God loves the holy rosary. Try to say the rosary daily. And always be aware of this prayer, *"Remember, most loving Virgin Mary, never was it heard that anyone who turned to you for help was left unaided . . ."*

My Meeting the Bishop

One spring Sunday there was a canonical visitation of St. John's parish in Detroit. As usual I was in church. Bishop Bohachevsky himself had the Liturgy and the homily. The concelebrants with the bishop were Father Pobutsky and Father Prokopowych. Bishop Bohachevsky was known for his regularity in canonical visitations. After the Liturgy, Father Pobutsky met me on the sidewalk and asked me to come to the rectory because the bishop wished to talk with me. I was glad to meet him.

"So you wanted to be a priest, and now what happened that you do not wish to be one?" was the greeting addressed to me. I replied, "I wanted to be a priest and still want to be one, but Your Excellency placed an impossible demand on me which I was not able to meet. This is why I came to the conclusion that you do not want me in your seminary. Here is the reply I received from Father Malynowsky, the rector of our seminary in Culemborg," and I handed to him the letter.

The bishop read the letter carefully, and gave it back to me, saying, "I did not know that! Yes, indeed, I did not know that! You write to me again, and I will accept you." Then he asked me many questions about our seminary in Hirschberg, about the teachers and the subjects that were taught there. Then followed questions from Church history, dogmatic theology, patrology, etc. He ended by saying, please write. I will be waiting for your letter.

On my way home, I stopped at Father Prokopowych's house. Both of us belong to the same branch of the senior scouts, "The Spirits of the Woods." He was curious to know what the bishop wanted from me. After I told him everything in detail, he smiled brightly and said, "You must be the first one in the world who forced Bishop Constantine to admit that he was mistaken." I said that this does not look good for me. Yet I think that an admission of one's mistake is not a sign of weakness, nor is it lowering of one's dignity, but a simple admission to being human.

The next day Father Pobutsky called me and said that he received a phone call from the Chancery in Philadelphia, reminding me to send a letter to the bishop. The same day I sat down, wrote a request for admission into the seminary, enclosed the documents as before, and mailed them. An answer came within a week, and I was accepted to St. Josaphat Seminary in Washington, D.C.

Seminary in Washington, D.C.

I arrived in Washington, D.C. just before the academic year 1949–50 had commenced. Our seminarians received their theological studies at the Catholic University of America, just about two blocks away from St. Josaphat Seminary, located at 714 Monroe Street. On the basis of my documents from our seminary in Hirschberg, Germany, I was admitted to the second year of theology.

The Rev. Stephen Hrynuck, STL, PhD was the rector. He was a very kind, peaceful and a gentle person, possessing a very good theological and philosophical education from Rome. He was known for his deep piety and great devotion to the Most Holy Mother of God. He was indeed a man of God. His character reminded me of my former rector, Father Vasyl Laba, the academic rector in Hirschberg.

The seminarians in the senior year of theology were already deacons, Joseph Shary, Paul Harchison, and George Pazdrey. All three have already passed into eternity. The junior year seminarian Joseph Nesevich, is now also with the Lord. The second year seminarians were Joseph Chacho, Paul Wasylus, and myself. Both Joseph and Paul are not among the living anymore. The freshmen year had Joseph Fedorek, Theodore Boholnick, Andrew Sagan, and

Matthew Berko. Only Boholnick and Berko are now still among the living. Wasylus and I were roommates. I was the first seminarian who came from Europe, and my English was not very good at that time. Yet they all received me in a friendly and cordial manner.

Deacon George Pazdrey was the seminary prefect at that time. It was his duty to ring the bell at 6:00 A.M. His clock must have not worked right because he was late almost every morning with the wake-up signal. After a month or so the rector appointed me to be the prefect. I remained a prefect for all the years of my stay in the seminary.

Father Alfred Rush, CSsR, a professor of Church history at the University, was our spiritual director and confessor. He would come to our seminary once a week, give us a spiritual conference, and then hear our confessions.

At the University

The education at the Catholic University of America in Washington, D.C. was very different from that at the Hirschberg seminary. First of all, the number of seminarians at the university was much larger. Each class had at least fifty seminarians. Some years had two or three separate classrooms. Each seminarian was obliged to come to the classes dressed in a black cassock, and so were the priest teachers. This university belonged to all the Latin dioceses of the United States of America. Even though many dioceses had their own seminary, selected students were sent to this university for theological degrees or to the School of canon law. In the neighborhood of the university were houses of studies of various religious orders. Some of them had their own faculty and their own school of philosophy and theology. All together there were at that time fifty male houses of study near the Catholic University.

The first few weeks of my study at the university were very difficult for me due to the lack of knowledge of the English language on the academic level. My English was on a low conversational level, which proved to be rather inadequate. I did not know enough of the scholarly terminology in English, and this made my study very difficult. At times I thought I would have to give up school, for I would not be able to pass the exams. I asked deacon Joseph Shary whether he could help me. He gave me the lecture notes for each subject in my second year. Some students in previous years were able to record the lectures by stenography or short hand, and then someone retyped and mimeographed them. They were being passed from one class of students to the other. Those notes were the solution to my difficulties. I was able every evening to carefully study the lessons for the following day. When I came across an unknown word, I used a dictionary and thus was able to understand the lesson.

Father Louis Arant, professor of dogmatic theology, liked to begin his lectures by presenting a question to the students. The questions were not easy. If someone did not prepare himself ahead of time, most probably he would not be able to give a right answer. He was teaching Mariology that semester. His question that day was, "It is the truth of our faith that Christ died for all human beings without exception. Now, a famous theologian claims that Christ did not die for the Blessed Virgin Mary, since she was immaculately conceived and never committed a sin, so there was nothing in her life that needed redemption. Was he correct?"

He started with the first seminarian in the front row, and there were fifteen in each row. I sat next to Paul Wasylus in the second row. None of the seminarians was able to give him the correct answer. When it came to me, I stood up and with my broken English I said, "Christ died for all human beings and especially for the Blessed Virgin Mary because the grace of redemption was applied to her at the moment of her conception, so that she was not cleansed from Original Sin but prevented from inheriting it. She was the only one that was pre-redeemed." Father Arant was apparently very impressed and said to the class, "This is the point." From then on I could not make a mistake in his class. I received the best grade that semester from him. It was because I was reading the class notes every evening and was prepared for his lessons.

At the end of each semester there were usually written exams. I was not yet very proficient in my English spelling. Therefore on top of the first page of my exam book I wrote a note, "Please excuse my spelling mistakes." The professors did accept my excuse and tested me on the knowledge of the subject and not on the English spelling. Thus I was able to pass all the exams the first semester.

At the school of theology there were at that time two parallel theology sequences, major and minor. The major course was much more difficult. It had more classes per week and required a knowledge of Latin, Greek, and Hebrew languages. I had these subjects already in our Hirschberg seminary, and at this university I was given credit for them. The major sequence was to prepare the student for graduate work. At the end of the fourth year of the major course the student was able to take an academic degree, a Licentiate in Sacred Theology (STL). An additional year of studies was required for students of the minor course if they wished to receive a STL degree. At the end of my second year of theology, I decided to switch to the major course.

Summer Vacations of 1950

At the end of this academic year three or four seminarians graduated, were ordained to the holy priesthood, and appointed to parochial assignments. They were Deacons Joseph Shary, Paul Harchison, and George Pazdrey. The ordination took place at our Cathedral Church in Philadelphia, and the ordaining bishop was Constantine Bohachevsky. All other seminarians were present at the ordination ceremonies and served as acolytes.

Father Joseph Shary invited me to his first solemn Liturgy of Thanksgiving at his home parish church of St. Vladimir in Elizabeth, N.J. Seminarian Matthew Berko offered to take me with him in his car. He was a member of Assumption Church of Perth Amboy, N.J., and his parents lived in a nearby town called Rahway, N.J. The next day was a Sunday, and both of us went to Elizabeth to participate in Father Shary's First Liturgy of Thanksgiving.

After the Liturgy and the reception, Matthew Berko drove me to nearby Newark Airport where I bought my first airline ticket and took the first flight from Newark to Detroit. This flight will always stay in my memory. It flew from Newark, N.J. to Philadelphia, Harrisburg, Pittsburgh, Cleveland, Ohio and only then to Detroit, Michigan. The cabin pressure was very poor, and at each landing I experienced ear pain. This was a new experience for me, and a sort of preparation for my future life when I would have to fly often.

My uncle picked me up at the airport and took me home with him. I was able to get a decent night job that was not too taxing. After a few hours of sleep, I decided to retype Father Dolnycky's Typicon, a 603-page Church Slavonic work. This unique book was old and out of print for many years already. It was not available at any of our stores. Yet it was a very important book for every priest to have. So I typed about ten pages per day and by the end of my summer vacation I completed the entire book.

While in Philadelphia at the end of my summer vacation, I stopped at the Basilian Sisters' Orphanage bookstore, located near our Cathedral church. The Sister in charge of the bookstore knew me and told me a story. She said that not long ago there was a fire in this store. They were able to get the fire out but there was some damage. When cleaning the storeroom, they had to move this big bookcase, and behind it they found this book, Father Dolnycky's Typicon. Would you like to buy it? And so, now I had two of Dolnycky's books, one original and one typed by me.

Some Changes at the Seminary

The following year at the seminary I found some changes. Seminarian Joseph Chacho, native of St. Clair, Pa., chose not to return, and my roommate Paul Wasylus transferred to Ss. Cyril and Methodius Seminary in Pittsburgh, Pa. We received three new freshmen from the minor seminary in Stamford, CT.—Michael Poloway, Theodore Danusiar, and Ray Kostiuk. There were also two new seminarians from our Seminary in Culemborg, Holland—Jaroslav Swyschuk and Lubomyr Mudry, my upper classmates from the Hirschberg seminary. Both of them completed their theological studies in Europe but Bishop Bohachevsky sent them to our seminary mainly for English language studies.

A much more important change in the seminary was the appointment of a full time spiritual director in the person of Rev. Peter Chaws, a native of Ukraine and a former pastor near the city of Sambir. With his appointment, we had the benefit of spiritual conferences every evening, and this influenced our spiritual life in a positive way. His conferences were delivered in unpretentious, simple language, always based on Sacred Scripture and the teachings of the Fathers of the Church. The American-born seminarians would have benefited much more from these conferences had Father Chaws been able to speak to them in English.

By far the greatest change during this academic year was a big surprise for the seminarians. Bishop Bohachevsky decided to erect a new seminary building. He purchased a plot of ground on a hilly location overlooking the Catholic University of America with a beautiful view over the city of Washington. Walking distance to the university was only five to ten minutes. The construction work began in September of 1950. All of us rejoiced with this great news and daily stopped at the construction site to see the progress.

On the Patronal Feast Day—St. Josaphat, Nov. 12th, there was a solemn Divine Liturgy and a special reception for the seminarians, the staff and the invited guests. The Monroe Street seminary building had very little space for guests, so only a limited number of guests were invited, the priests living in Washington, Rev. Dionisius Holowecky, OSBM, professor of Eastern Canon Law at the University, Rev. Vladimir Pylypec, the local pastor, and Rev. Dmytro Shul, an emeritus. These were invited annually.

Christmas Holydays 1950

Christmas vacation at the University lasted from Dec. 20th to Jan. 10th, and all the seminarians went home to their parents. Michael Poloway from Detroit, MI., traveled with me on a train trip home. It was good to see my relatives again. My Aunt Sophie would tell me of her correspondence with her brother, my father Michael. She told them in her letters that I was studying for the priesthood, and that made them happy. I asked her to always tell them in her letters that I was keeping all of them in my daily prayers. I was given an attic room, which was quite comfortable for my needs.

After dinner and some conversation with my relatives, I took a shower and went upstairs to rest. I could not fall asleep, so I lay there and in my memory crossed the ocean again and went back to my parents' home and my Christmas vacation with them. I knew very well that the home where I grew up was no more. Everything had been burned to the ground. Not a trace of the village or of our people was there. Even the church building was demolished. Only some parts of the thick stonewalls of the vestibule remained. The bell tower was a separate stone structure. There were three bells there before the war. The biggest one was called St. Michael, and it was purchased in 1934 from donations collected in the United States from our former parishioners. But during the war German authorities demanded that all the bells be confiscated for the war effort. Our young men brought the small bell from the chapel at the lower end of the village and added the two smaller ones from the church bell tower and delivered them to the Germans. The big St. Michael's bell was lowered down at night and buried somewhere on the church property.

But my dreams refused to acknowledge reality. They always took me back to the home and the environment in which I was growing up, going to school, coming home from the school in Sambir. In my dreams I relived the Christmases of the past. Everything was in place as though nothing had happened. There was white frozen snow outside, and frost covered the windows with artistic designs of flowers, stars, and other fantastic patterns. My mother, with my sister, Anna, were busy in the kitchen preparing for the Holy Christmas Eve Supper. In my dream I was there again and enjoyed every minute of it. Nowhere in the world would I rather be for Christmas than back home with my parents, brothers, and sister. Nowhere in the world could I experience so much mutual love, warmth, and kindness than back home.

But dreams come and go, and reality came back and faced me sternly in the eyes. I then ask myself, where are my parents, brothers, and the sister now? Do they have a home, a place to live and to celebrate Christmas in that cruel atheistic country where God is denied, religion is called "the opium of the people," our Church brutally liquidated by Stalin's murderous forces, and the bishops and most of the priests mercilessly jailed, tortured, killed or sent to the gulags of Siberia? Do my parents still have the Christmas Eve Holy Supper as they used to do at home? Did they leave a place setting for me at the supper table? Can they go to church on Christmas day? Oh, how much I would like to be with them today! And the pain of loss, a deep homesickness and nostalgia pierced my heart. I became very emotional. I felt very lonely, abandoned as an orphan. Tears filled my eyes, and streaked down my face to wet my pillow. Yes, I cried as never before.

Mary's Engagement

The day before Christmas my Aunt Sophie confided to me that her daughter Mary had found a boyfriend and invited him to come and join us for the Christmas Eve Holy Supper. She told her mother that her boyfriend Peter Boyduy was planning to become engaged to her tonight by giving her a ring. Somehow she was afraid to tell her father about Peter's plans and her mother, too, did not say a thing. This resulted in an embarrassing situation. After the supper was over, Peter got up and declared that he loved Mary and wished to marry her. He asked her parents for their consent and blessing. My Uncle Dmytro got up from the table, visibly upset, and declared, "How come everybody in the house knows about it, while I was kept in the dark?"

He walked away from the dining room into his bedroom. I went after him, sat next to him and said, "Uncle, please be calm. Control your feelings. You know that Mary loves you very much. Yet she is afraid of you and this is why she did not confide in you. She was simply afraid that you would not approve of her choice for her husband. She is in love with Peter and wishes to marry him. Should you not approve of her choice, she will obey you and refuse to marry him. What will you achieve then? If she never finds another man and remains unmarried, you will be to blame, and you will not forgive yourself. You cannot tell her whom she should love or whom she should marry."

My uncle then said, "but I always envisioned my future son-in-law to be tall and fair, and Peter is small and dark." "So what," I replied, "it is Mary who made her choice and she is the one who will have to live with him, not you. Look at them, how sad they both are, like it was a funeral, not an engagement. Go to them, embrace both of them and give them your blessing. Go, uncle."

He went to the kitchen where Mary and Peter were sitting. He apologized for leaving the room, and explained that he was surprised by the turn of events; he was not prepared for this. "But if you two love each other and really want to marry, I give you my consent and my blessing to both of you." Mary, with tears in her eyes, came to him. He embraced and kissed her. Peter then also came to him and extended his hand to him. Dmytro shook his hand, placed his right arm over his shoulders and embraced him. Sophie meanwhile went to do the dishes, quietly wiping tears of happiness from her eyes. Peter took the ring and placed it on Mary's finger. They kissed and embraced. Now they were betrothed. Dmytro gained not only a good son-in-law, but also his best friend, confidant, and helper. This was an unforgettable Christmas Eve supper not only for Mary and Peter, but also for the entire family.

Back in the Seminary

ife in the seminary during the second semester was quite normal. The seminarians worked hard to keep up with the strict academic demands of the University to be able to pass the final exams. I noticed that the spiritual life in the seminary was increasing and growing. The seminarians were seriously taking part in all the spiritual exercises as demanded by the daily schedule, but one could notice that some of them were in the chapel before the Blessed Sacrament privately in the morning before the bell for chapel rang, in the evening after the night prayers, and almost any time during the day. It was very encouraging that they would give a good example to each other in this manner.

Toward the end of the academic year on Wednesday, May 30, 1951, Bishop Constantine Bohachevsky in the small seminary chapel during a Divine Liturgy bestowed minor orders on Jaroslav Swyschuk, Lubomyr Mudry, Stephen Sulyk, Joseph Fedorek, Theodore Boholnick and Andrew Sagan.

The following week a six-day-long spiritual retreat was held especially for those who were to receive sacred orders of the diaconate and priesthood. The retreat master was Father Gregory Shyshkowych, CSsR, a renowned missionary from Canada. The priests of our archdiocese liked his style of parish mission and invited him frequently to their parishes, especially during Holy Lent. Our faithful loved his sermons and regularly attended his mission.

During our retreat Father Shyshkowych one day gave a special talk directed to those seminarians who would soon be ordained priests. I liked the talk very much and made notes of it:

The day of your ordination will soon come. You will be led by the archdeacon to the holy altar to stand before your bishop so that he may ordain you to the holy priesthood. Oh, how great, how holy, sacred, and awesome will this moment be! Stop and think, meditate deeply and seriously on the rich spiritual symbolism of the Rite of Ordination to the Priesthood so that you may fully understand and realize what you are doing there and what are the consequences for you for all of eternity.

Ordination to the sub-deaconate at the St. Josaphat Seminary, Washington, DC, Wednesday, May 30, 1951. (l. to r.): Henry Sagan, Michael Poloway, Theodore Boholnick, Ray Kostiuk, Rev. Stephen Hrynuck - Rector, Joseph Fedorek, Bishop Constantine Bohachevsky, Rev. Gregory Shyshkowych, CSsR,—Retreat Master, Stephen Sulyk, Rev. Peter Chaws—Spiritual Director, Joseph Nasevitch, Lubomyr Mudry, Matthew Berko, Jaroslav Swyschuk, and Theodore Danusiar.

"I will come into your house; I will bow in worship toward your holy temple, in fear of you." (Psalms 5:8) Yes, the archdeacon will lead you through the royal doors from the nave of the church to the sanctuary, the holy of holies. In the Old Testament *"only the high priest went into the inner one, and that but once a year."* (Hebrews 9:7) In the holy of holies *"were the golden altar of incense and the ark of the covenant entirely covered with gold. In the ark were the golden jar containing the manna, the rod of Aaron which*

had blossomed, and the tablets of the covenant." (ibid 4) In the New Testament in the holy of holies in the tabernacle on the altar lives the Lord of Heaven and earth, Jesus Christ himself, hidden in the most Holy Eucharist. Realize what a great honor is given to you, to be able to enter the holy of holies and to stand before the infinite divine majesty. Here the angels, archangels, thrones, dominions, principalities, powers, and the many-eyed cherubim invisibly worship him. *(Here) he is attended by the seraphim, each with six wings; two wings cover their faces, two their feet, and with two they fly, and they call one to the other with unceasing and incessant hymns of praise . . .* (Liturgy of St. Basil)

When Moses approached the burning bush that was not consumed by fire, he heard God speak to him: *"Come no nearer! Remove the sandals from your feet, for the place where you stand is holy ground."* (Exodus 3:5) Yet you are made worthy to enter the holy of holies with your shoes on and to stand before the face of God without being consumed by the eternal fire of the infinite holiness of God! Oh, how awesome, how holy and unforgettable is that moment in your life!

"I wash my hands in innocence, and I go around your altar, O Lord." (Psalms 26:6) You are standing in the holy of holies. Upon the request of the archdeacon, the bishop blesses you and prays, *"The Holy Spirit shall come upon him and the power of the Most High shall overshadow him."* The archdeacon will then lead you around the holy altar three times. The holy altar symbolically represents the heavenly throne of God and also Christ the Lord himself, who is mystically present upon this altar. By this triple circumambulation around the Lord's holy altar, and around the Lord himself, you are witnessing and testifying that always and everywhere and all the days of your life you will *"Love you, O Lord, my strength; the Lord is my stronghold and my refuge."* (com. Psalms 18:2–3)

"O Lord, I love the house in which your dwell, and the tenting-place of your glory." (Psalms 26:8) At each of the triple circumventions of the holy altar, you will kiss the four corners of the altar. The altar represents Christ himself. You will, therefore, kiss Christ himself. Each one of your kisses is your reply to the question of Our Lord, *"Do you love me more than these?"* (John 21:15) St. Peter replied to this question, *"Yes, Lord, you know that I love you."* At this Jesus said, *"Feed my lambs."* With your hand upon your heart could you repeat after St. Peter, *"Yes, Lord, you know that I love you."* Or maybe, God forbid, your kiss will be on the outside very nice, warm and holy, but in your heart will be hypocritical, like the kiss of Judas. (Luke 14:45)

There are three divine persons in the Holy Trinity. Therefore the number three symbolizes completeness, wholeness, permanency, and the rest of your life. By your triple circumambulation of the holy altar, you are thereby witnessing before the angels and saints in heaven, and before the whole world as well, that from now on you will dedicate all your powers of mind and soul as well as all of your talents to the faithful service to this holy altar and to the Lord God who dwells on it. This holy altar and this holy of holies from the moment of your ordination will become the center of your concerns, your daily efforts and cares. Here you will daily spend the most beautiful and the most rewarding hours in the offering of the unbloody Sacrifice of the New Testament, the Divine Liturgy; here you will celebrate the other liturgical services; here in the presence of God Himself you will dwell in heartfelt prayer, meditation and conversation with Him. Here you will preach and teach Christ crucified, the Savior of the world. By the power given to you by God Himself, here you will forgive and absolve the sins and reconcile the sinners to God. In the moments of failure and temptation, of stumbling, despair and disappointments it is here that you will find consolation, comfort, and solution to your problems. Here you will hear down deep in your heart, *"Cast your care upon the Lord, and he will*

support you; never will he permit the just man to be disturbed."
(Psalms 55:23)

Your bishop will be seated in front of the holy altar. At each of
your triple circumambulation of the holy altar, you will stop
before the bishop, kiss his hand, the epigonation, and his right
shoulder. The bishop will say to you, *"Christ is among us!"* and
you will reply, *"He is and always will be!"* By these actions you
are actually taking an oath before God and the people that you
will always love, obey, and respect your bishop, because it is by
the power given to him by God that he will be your spiritual
father, your teacher, superior, and sincere friend. In his Episcopal ministry to the Church as the Good Shepherd, he will need
your sincere but not hypocritical help, support, and cooperation. You should pray already now that your kisses of the bishop
would not be like those of Judas, but coming from your heart
filled with love, because God sees you and knows your heart.

*"If a man wishes to come after me, he must deny his very self, take
up his cross, and follow in my steps."* (Mark 8:34) During your
triple circumambulation of the holy altar, the choir will sing the
following tropar: *"O holy martyrs, you have suffered courageously
and received your reward; pray to the Lord, our God, to have mercy
on our souls."* This is to remind you that as a priest, you will be
even more than a disciple of Christ; you will represent Christ to
the faithful, and you will act in His name and stand in front of
the altar as another Christ. Therefore His words are applied to
you more than to anyone else, *"If a man wishes to come after me,
he must deny his very self, take up his cross, and follow in my steps."*
Yes, you must be ready to carry your cross, to be ready to practice self-denial, mortification, and do penance, and be faithful
to Christ even unto death.

Diaconal ordinations of Stephen Sulyk, June 7, 1951 at
St. Josaphat Seminary Chapel, Washington, DC.

You must strive to imitate Christ in all things. Like Christ you must be merciful, gracious, longsuffering and humble. Just like Christ, you must be ready always to sincerely forgive any offence done against you, always do good, love your enemies, and be always ready to suffer humiliations, calumny, and defamation, because Christ said, *"No slave is greater than his master. If they have persecuted me, they will persecute you also; if they have kept my word, they will keep yours also. But all these things they will do to you for mine name's sake."* (John 15:20)

"Do this as a remembrance of me." (Luke 22:19) Now comes the most sacred moment. You approach the holy altar, kneel on both knees, place your crossed hands upon the edge of the altar, and rest your forehead on the altar between your crossed hands. The altar represents Christ himself. You are here, therefore, like St. John the Beloved, who during the last Supper *"leaned back against Jesus' chest."* (John 15:25) From there he received the knowledge of inexpressible mysteries, and then announced with heavenly voice that," *In the beginning was the Word, and the Word was with God, and the Word was God."* (John 1:1)

The bishop places the end of his omophorion upon your head, makes the sign of the cross over your head three times, then lays his right hand on your head, and solemnly recites this formula of ordination, *"Divine grace, which always heals the infirm and supplies what is wanting, elevates the devout deacon, N., to the priesthood; therefore, let us pray for him, that the grace of the Holy Spirit may come upon him, and let us all say:* Then those in the sanctuary sing three times, *"Lord, have mercy."* Afterward the choir does the same, and all the faithful do likewise. This very moment the Holy Spirit invisibly comes down upon you, and the power of the Most High overshadows you, making you a priest of Christ forever, and impresses upon your soul an indelible sign of eternal priesthood.

The bishop will then bless your head again three times and pray over you, saying "... *grant that your servant, whom you have been pleased to ordain through me, may receive this great grace of your Holy Spirit in innocence of life and with an unwavering faith. Grant him the grace to lead a perfect and worthy life, doing all that is pleasing to you ... Fill your servant ... with the gifts of the Holy Spirit, so that he may stand worthily and blamelessly before your holy altar; preach the Gospel of your Kingdom; sanctify the word of your truth; offer gifts and spiritual sacrifices; and renew your people in the bath of regeneration ...*"

Then follows the investiture with the priestly liturgical vestments. The bishop will raise each vestment high and ask the people of God whether the candidate is worthy, saying in Greek "axios?" Those present in the sanctuary sing three times "axios!"—he is worthy! The choir does the same thing three times, and lastly the congregation in the church also sings three times "axios!" Then you shall kiss the hand of your bishop and exchange a kiss of peace with all the priests in the sanctuary.

So that you will always remember this most sacred moment in your life, the Church prescribes the following, "At the ordination Liturgy after the consecration the ordaining bishop breaks away a part of the main host, called the Lamb, and places it on the palm of your right hand, saying, *"Receive this pledge and preserve it pure and unspotted unto your last breath for you shall render an account for it at the second and awesome coming of the great God and Savior Jesus Christ."* You shall then kiss the hand of the bishop and walk to the back of the altar, place your right hand with the Body of Christ on the edge of the altar and adore the Lord. You shall hold the Lord of heaven and earth in your hand, the same Lord that was held by his Most Holy Mother Mary in her arms. Just before the celebrant is to announce, *"The holy things for the holy,"* you will go back to the bishop and return to him the part of the Holy Bread.

Diaconal Ordination

It was Thursday, June 7, 1951, that Bishop Constantine Bohachevsky came to our seminary, and during a Divine Liturgy ordained to the order of diaconate Joseph Nesevich, Jaroslav Swyschuk, Lubomyr Mudry, and Stephen Sulyk. For me it was spiritually a very emotional moment. I felt close to my namesake, St. Stephen, the first deacon and first martyr. So I prayed to him, asking him to be my special protector before the throne of God and to help me to be a good deacon.

Monday, June 18, 1951, priestly ordination took place in the Cathedral Church in Philadelphia for Joseph Nesevich, Jaroslav Swyschuk and Lubomyr Mudry. I could not attend this happy event due to my cousin Mary and Peter Boyduy's wedding in Detroit. The wedding took place at St. John's Church with Rev. John Pidzarko officiating, and I was asked to be a deacon for the wedding service.

Stephen Sulyk receives Holy Communion at his diaconal ordination, June 7, 1951, at the St. Josaphat Seminary Chapel, Washington, DC.

Academic Year 1951–1952

During my summer vacation I was able to find good employment at the General Motor Co. factory where chrome strips were manufactured for their automobiles. It was mostly women who worked at various presses where the strips were bent and shaped to fit the body of a car, and placed on a pushcart. It was my duty to take the pushcart to another press or to the finished product center.

Sometime in August I received a letter from an unknown priest, Rev. Roman Lobodych. He wrote to me, "Bishop C. Bohachevsky named me to be the new rector of St. Josaphat Seminary in Washington. The new seminary building is completed and furnished. Thus we will begin our new academic year with a new rector in the new building. You are the prefect, so come about a week before school begins so that you may have time to prepare the daily schedule and to assign a separate room for each seminarian."

I asked myself, why a whole week was necessary. I could do this task in an hour or so. But the new rector wanted me there a week earlier, so I took a train and went to Washington. On the way, I reminisced about the past in the seminary. I got used to Msgr. Stephen Hrynuck as our rector and we got along splendidly. I liked his personality. He was a very spiritual and deeply pious person, truly a priest of Christ the seminarians could emulate.

In the new seminary Father Lobodych told me about himself. He came to the United States with the recent emigration from Europe. He served recently as a pastor somewhere in California. He was ordained to the priesthood by Metropolitan Andrew Sheptytsky in 1917 together with the former rector of the Lviv Theological Academy, Joseph Slipyj, now the successor of Sheptytsky and a prisoner of the Bolsheviks somewhere in the Siberian Gulags. He told me also that he served for some years as the rector of the cathedral church of St. George in Lviv, was transferred to the diocese of Stanyslaviv, and then also elected a senator to the Polish parliament. He likewise stated to me that he never was a rector of a seminary, and that this was not a job for him. He accepted this assignment only out of obedience to the bishop. He did not hide his dislike for his present position and told the seminarians openly that he hated this kind of regimented life. Father Chaws, the spiritual director, had a positive influence on him and in his frequent conversations with him, gave him emotional support. The new rector told me, "You are the prefect of this seminary, so you run the show, and leave me alone."

The new seminarians for this academic year were Peter Ohirko, Michael Fedorowich, and Paul Hardysh from St. Basil's Minor Seminary in Stamford, CT; from the seminary in Holland came Jaroslav Fedyk.

Licentiate in Sacred Theology

During my senior year at the University I had to work much harder than before. I had to keep up with studies of the fourth year of theology. Besides studying, I tried to memorize all the material of the four years of theology summed up in the one hundred theses required for the Licentiate of Sacred Theology (STL). Some days were just too short for me to do everything that had to be done, so I worked late and drank black coffee to stay awake. This did not always help. Prior to me only Joseph Shary took the major course of theology, yet he chose not to take the test for the STL degree. I was the first one in our seminary to do so.

The second week of the month of May was designated for written exams for the candidates for the STL degree. These exams lasted two hours. Each candidate received a sealed envelope with four questions and a special notebook in which the answers were to be written. Father Francis Connell, CSsR presided over the exams. After two hours he collected all the notebooks and gave us his farewell talk with fatherly advice for the young candidates to the priesthood.

The next week, the oral exams took place. On the School of Theology bulletin board a schedule of the exams for each candidate was published with the name of the candidate and the time appointed for his exam. Some candidates used the last minutes before the exam reading over the dates that were hard to memorize, the quotes of the Fathers of the Church, or the quotes from Sacred Scripture. The exams took place in four classrooms. In each were four members of the faculty, specialists of the four sections of theology, Fundamental Theology, Christology, Mariology, and Sacramental Theology. At the appointed time the candidate would enter the first classroom and be examined by four examiners for the duration of fifteen minutes. Afterward, he would proceed to the second, third, and fourth classrooms.

Since I was the first from our Ukrainian Catholic Seminary to take this exam, most of the questions I received pertained to Eastern theology, the Orthodox Church, and how it differed from the Catholic Church in various theological fields. So in some cases they kept me longer than fifteen minutes. I had no difficulty in answering any of the questions given to me. I spoke freely on the topics so familiar to me. The next day on the bulletin board the candidates who passed the exam successfully were listed. My name was among them

The Farewell Talk of Father Connell, CSsR

After the written exams Father Connell gave the STL candidates this farewell talk:

In the town in which I was born and grew up was a parish that was served by the Jesuit Fathers. After my high school graduation, I felt a vocation to the priesthood. The Jesuit Fathers in most cases were working as teachers, and I wanted to be a preaching priest or a missionary. This is why I did not enter the Jesuit Fathers, but rather the Redemptorist Fathers. Redemptorists normally preach parish missions. After my novitiate and all the years of formation and ordination to the priesthood, my superiors assigned me to a teaching position. Now, as you see, I am already a gray- haired senior and I am still teaching, doing what I was planning to avoid in my life. Yet, I am happy and satisfied for I know that I am doing the will of God.

This is why I tell you, if you want to be sure that you are doing God's will, never ask for this or that parish or job. Never tell your bishop, I would like to do this or that or I would like to be transferred from here to there. You will then run the risk of being disappointed and dissatisfied. Just go anywhere your bishop tells you to go. It might seem to you that the position or some specific task your bishop wishes you to do might be a degradation for you, that you deserve something better. Or it might be just a temptation of the evil one who whispers to your ear thoughts of pride and rebellion against your bishop. Be strong and always remember you will never make a mistake if you do what your bishop asks you to do, for then you will be doing the will of God. This then is the point and the goal of your priestly life—to do the will of God. This is my advice for you!

To be your teacher for the years you spent at this university was a great pleasure and joy for me, because in you I see the future our Church. When in my heart I look into the future, I see before me not only future priests, but also monsignors and, God willing, also future bishops. Your growth in the holiness of life and your success in your priestly ministry will be my reward in heaven. Go, then, with my prayers and my blessings and be good, holy, and dedicated priests, for the people of God are waiting for you. They are waiting for you to bring them the Good News of salvation. They are hungry for the living Word of God, for your forgiveness and absolution, for your consolation and encouragement. They want to see in you courage and enthusiasm, happiness and joy. In you they want to see another Christ. Let us then *"pray for one another."* (James 5:16)

Dedication of the New Seminary Building

A t the end of the academic year, a festive celebration of the dedication of the new seminary building took place. An elevated platform was erected on the seminary grounds with a tent over it on which an altar was placed and other things needed for the celebration of a Divine Liturgy. Another tent was erected for the choir, and a very large one for the faithful. Early in the morning of Saturday, May 31, 1952, a large number of chairs were delivered and set up in rows.

As early as 8:00 A.M. our faithful, as delegates from our parishes, began to arrive for the celebration. Some came by buses, others by cars, trains, or even by taxis. The first thing they wanted to see was the inside of the seminary: the chapel, the kitchen, the dining room, and especially the individual student's rooms. One could notice their satisfaction and pride of having our own new seminary building. On each door of the students' rooms was a plaque with the name of the donor or donors who gave large sums sponsoring the room. Our faithful were very generous in donating money for the new seminary building.

Local police closed the streets around the seminary for city traffic, and about 10:00 A.M. a procession was formed on Harewood Road. Behind a processional cross walked the seminarians from St.

163

Basil's Minor Seminary in Stamford, CT, then our seminarians, delegates from our parishes, nuns of differed religious communities, representatives of church and civic organizations, followed by many priests in their cassocks and stoles. The bishops and the concelebrating priests were vesting in the seminary. They walked out of the building and joined the procession. The estimated number of the faithful was several thousand.

Bishop Bohachevsky initiated the celebration by performing the Rite of the Blessing of the seminary building. One or two prayers were read in English by the Apostolic Delegate. Bishops Senyshyn, Savaryn and Roborecky read other prayers. The Delegate himself blessed the first floor of the building with holy water, while Bishops Senyshyn and Savaryn anointed the walls with holy oil. Bishop Roborecky blessed the second floor with holy water.

The concelebrating clergy at the Divine Liturgy were Joseph Schmondiuk, Dmytro Gresko, Joseph Batza, and Nicholas Babak. Rev. Myroslav Charyna and Rev. Stephen Chomko served as deacons for the Liturgy. After the reading of the Gospel, Bishop Senyshyn welcomed the guests and the faithful, and the Apostolic Delegate gave a homily. The combined church choirs from the Cathedral in Philadelphia and from St. John's Church in Newark, New Jersey, sang the responses to the Liturgy under the direction of Michael Dobush.

After the Liturgy the invited guests, the clergy, and the parish representatives attended a banquet that was held in the university gymnasium hall. A total of 920 people were in attendance. Our seminarians were not invited. They just walked outside the gymnasium hall in order to satisfy their curiosity during this historic event.

Preparations for the Priestly Ordination

The historic celebrations of the dedication of the new seminary building were behind us. The bishop, the priests, and the thousands of the faithful left the seminary and went home. The workers removed the chairs, took down the three tents, disassembled and removed the platform, and cleared the seminary grounds. In the seminary were left only the rector, the spiritual director, the seminarians, and the three Italian nuns. Preparing for priestly ordination were Jaroslav Fedyk and Stephen Sulyk; to the diaconal ordination, Joseph Fedorek, Theodore Boholnick, and Andrew Sagan; to the subdiaconate, Theodore Danusiar, Michael Poloway, and Roman Kostiuk. All the ordinations were to take place in the cathedral church in Philadelphia on Saturday, June 14, 1952. In the meantime all of us had to prepare ourselves for the exams from our house courses, liturgics, church music, Church Slavonic language, and the church Typicon. Bishop Bohachevsky came back to the seminary and listened to the responses of the seminarians as the teachers were conducting the exams.

From Saturday, June 6, to Friday June 13, 1952 a Spiritual Retreat was held in the Seminary Chapel. The retreat master was again Father Gregory Shyshkowych, CSsR. I tried very hard to prepare myself for the greatest moment in my life, reflecting, meditating, and contemplating the great mystery of our faith—the Holy Priest-hood of Christ. Again and again I had to overcome doubts and fear that I would not be able to be a good priest, that I might fall, offend God, and bring shame to the Church I love. I spent hours before Christ in the Holy Eucharist on the altar. There I found consolation and assurance that He would be with me, would assist and help me.

Priestly Ordination

Friday, June 13, 1952, all our seminarians, together with our rector, Father Lobodych, and our spiritual director, Father Chaws, went to Philadelphia. After dinner in the cathedral parish hall, there was a rehearsal of the ordination ceremonies and of the Hierarchical Liturgy. Father Peter Lypyn took me into his car and drove me to his home at the church of the Protection of the Most Holy Mother of God in the Southwestern Philadelphia for the overnight stay.

Father Lypyn was a former pastor of our church in the neighboring village of Vola Myhova in Ukraine, and he knew my father and other members of my family well. Since I could not have my parents attend this most sacred moment in my life, he understood my situation and shared with me my concern. In our conversation he tried hard to keep my spirits up, knowing my thoughts would be across the ocean with my parents and the rest of the family, hoping without hope to have them come and be with me, share my joy, and receive my first priestly blessing.

Stephen Sulyk receives priestly ordination at the Cathedral of the Immaculate Conception, Philadelphia, Pa., June 14, 1952. (l. to r.): Rev. Peter Lypyn, seated is Bishop Constantine Bohachevsky, kneeling are deacon Jaroslav Fedyk and Stephen Sulyk, Rev. Basil Makuch holding the crosier.

The next morning, Father Lypyn and I drove back to the cathedral church. There gathered many family members, relatives, and friends of all the candidates to be ordained. The church was filled with the faithful, and also many priests and religious sisters as well. As Bishop Bohachevsky entered the church, Father Vasyl Seredowych, rector of the cathedral, welcomed him in the vestibule. Then there was the ceremonial vesting of the hierarch in his liturgical vestments. The ordination into the subdiaconate followed. Then the Divine Liturgy began.

After the Gospel reading, Father Lobodych gave a brilliant homily on the importance of the priesthood in our lives. After the Great Entrance, the priestly ordination commenced. Father Rector, performing the duties of an archdeacon, led both candidates into the front of the royal doors that lead to the sanctuary. First, both of us knelt down and made our profession of faith and our declaration of obedience to the Holy Father and to our bishop and his successors, while we placed our right hand on the book of the Holy Gospels. Then, having received the blessing of the bishop, we were led by the archdeacon three times around the holy altar, kissing the corners of the altar, bishop's hand, shoulder, and his epigonation. Afterward, I was the first one to kneel before the altar. I placed my crossed hands upon the edge of the altar, and between the crossed hands I rested my forehead on the altar. Bishop Constantine placed his omophorion upon my head, blessed it three times, then pronounced the words of ordination. Then my friend, Jaroslav Fedyk, followed me for his ordination.

With peaceful concentration and prayerful attention I followed the rest of the ceremonies of ordination, asking deep down in my heart the Lord and his Most Holy Mother to help me be a good priest. At the end of the rite of ordination followed the vesting into the priestly liturgical vestments. At the handing of each vestment, the bishop intoned the Greek word, "axios"—is he worthy? The priests in the sanctuary, the choir and all the faithful replied—"axios!—Yes, he is worthy.

Newly ordained priest–Stephen Sulyk, imparting his first priestly blessing, June 14, 1952 at the Cathedral of the Immaculate Conception, Philadelphia, Pa.

Now I am a priest of Christ and stand at the holy altar to the right of my bishop. As a priest I will, together with the bishop and the concelebrating priests, offer to God my first sacrifice of the New Testament—the Divine Liturgy. At that moment I felt in my soul a very deep peace, contentment, and indescribable joy. I felt as though I was at home, as though I belonged there in the sanctuary at this sacred altar. The only time I remember having a similar feeling in my whole life was back home when I was a little boy and was embraced and held in the arms of my mother. Ever since, and through the long years of my priesthood, whenever I prepare for the celebration of the Divine Liturgy and approach the altar, I get this same feeling that I belong here. The words of the Lord, calling Prophet Jeremiah, come to my mind: *"Before I formed you in the womb I knew you, before you were born I dedicated you"* (Jeremiah 1:5).

My First Divine Liturgy of Thanksgiving

In the afternoon of the day of my ordination, subdeacon Michael Poloway and I took a train to go back home. My first Divine Liturgy of Thanksgiving was planned for the following Sunday, June 22, 1952, at St. John's Church in Detroit. My old friend Father Pobutsky was not there any more. He had been transferred to our church in Shamokin, PA, and there he soon died on September 14, 1952. The new pastor at St. John's now was Rev. Emil Sharanewych. On Sunday June 15, 1952, I wanted to offer a Divine Liturgy privately. So I called the convent of Sister Servants of Mary Immaculate, asking them if I might use their chapel. They were happy to have me there. A young sister, Sister Thomas Hrynewich, attended my Liturgy and gave the liturgical responses. When Communion time arrived, she knelt down to receive Holy Communion. I looked all over for a communion spoon, but they had none. So I had no other choice but to give her communion by taking the Holy Host by my fingers which is unusual in our church. This incident remained with me, and Sister Thomas and I remain friends to this day. Moreover when I became an archbishop, I invited her to work in my chancery. Later on, I appointed her the chancellor of the archeparchy.

The First Holy Communion children of St. John's Church escorted me in a procession from the school building to the church for my First Divine Liturgy of Thanksgiving on Sunday, June 22, 1952, just before 10:00 A.M. Msgr. Joseph Schmondiuk, at that time pastor of Immaculate Conception Church in Hamtramck, MI., was my concelebrant on my right, and Rev. Peter Chaws, our seminary spiritual director on my left. Rev. Lubomyr Mudry, then the parochial vicar at St. John's, performed the duties of a deacon, while subdeacon Michael Poloway assisted him. Father Sharanewych gave a very inspiring homily. The church was filled with the faithful, and among them was my Aunt Sophie with her husband Dmytro Stec, their daughter Mary with her husband Peter Boyduy, and twenty senior members of the scout troop "Plast," to which I, too, belong. At the end of the Liturgy, all the faithful came forward and I laid my hands on the head of each and gave them my first priestly blessing.

Thanks to the efforts of Rev. John Prokopowych and the mother of Michael Poloway, the ladies of the parish prepared a banquet in my honor in the school auditorium. The hall was filled with the parishioners. At the head table with me were Father Emil Sharanewych, the pastor, Father John Prokopowych, Father John Pidzarko, Father Lubomyr Mudry, and subdeacon Michael Poloway. The main speaker was Father Prokopowych, and then the pastor spoke likewise. At the end I said a few words, expressing my gratitude to the pastor and the clergy, as well as to all who worked in the preparations and who served the tables. I asked all for prayers for my intentions so that God would help me to be a good priest.

My First Pastoral Assignment

The Chancery office in Philadelphia contacted Rev. Emil Sharanewych a day or two after my first Liturgy, asking him to inform me that I was to report to the local dean, the Very Rev. Dmytro Gresko in Cleveland, Ohio, who would inform me of my first pastoral assignment. Father Sharanewych advised me not to go to Cleveland, but just to telephone Father Gresko. I did so and found out that my first pastoral assignment was to be a parochial vicar to Rev. Dmytro Blazejowsky, pastor of St. Joseph's Church, St. Joseph, Missouri. He told me to go to St. Joseph and he would mail my assignment papers there. My papers were dated June 25, 1952, prot. #1380-52-Cb.

I packed my belongings, as well as my books, and took a train to St. Joseph. Father Blazejowsky welcomed me warmly and explained to me the situation there, of which I was not aware. He was the pastor of our parish in St. Joseph, but at the same time he was organizing two other parishes and one mission, one in Omaha, the second one in Lincoln, Nebraska, and the third one, a mission in Denver, Colorado. Rev. Jaroslav Swyschuk was his parochial vicar at St. Joseph's parish, and I would be parochial vicar at the new Assumption Church in Omaha, as well as St. George's Mission in Lincoln. He would stay in Denver and occasionally visit the other parishes. He organized these three parishes by sponsoring our people from refugee camps in Germany and by finding them housing and employment. He sponsored 125 families to Omaha, 110 to Denver and only 14 to Lincoln, because the immigration quota was then filled, and he could not get any more people to Lincoln. In Denver at first he got permission to serve the Liturgy for our faithful in a Polish Catholic church, and lived temporarily in their rectory. Then he was able to buy a small church from a Protestant congregation, had an iconostas erected in it, and lived in a sacristy. Not many priests could make such a tremendous sacrifice of themselves for the sake of the people of God, as did Father Blazejowsky.

Father Dmytro Blazejowsky

Father Blazejowsky was born August 21, 1910, a son of a poor farmer in a village called Vyslik, county Sianik, Western Ukraine. He received his high school education in the city of Peremyshl. He helped himself financially by working as an instructor to other students who had difficulties in learning. He loved to read and read every book in the school library. He graduated from high school with honors.

At first he wanted to study electrical engineering at the University of Gdansk since it was the best school in the country. Before he could be admitted to that school, he had to fulfill a requirement to have at least one-half-year apprenticeship in a factory. He did that and was admitted to the university. After one semester of studies there, he found out that due to high tuition and living costs, he was unable to meet the financial requirements. Therefore in the summer of 1931 he began an effort to obtain a passport in order to go to Prague, Czechoslovakia, and to continue his studies there. Before the beginning of the academic year in the fall of 1931, he still did not get this passport . He, therefore, crossed the border illegally, went to Prague and continued his studies there in electrical engineering.

During summer vacation of 1933 he decided to make a pilgrimage to Rome, Italy, going on foot all the way, since that year was a Holy Year. It took him six weeks to make this pilgrimage to Rome. On the way he slept mostly under open skies or in some shepherd's hut.

In Rome he first went to St. Peter's Basilica to pray. It seemed that he pleased God with his pilgrimage, because the turn of events in his life put him in the right place.

From there he went to St. Josaphat Ukrainian Catholic Pontifical College on Gianicolo hill. There he met a seminarian, George Milanyk, a student of his from his high school days in Peremyshl. Afterward he walked to Naples, Pompeii, and Ancio, where he met with our seminarians who were spending summer vacation there. He stayed with them, and then with them he returned to the seminary in Rome. There Rev. Titus Haluschynsky, OSBM, spiritual director of the seminary, asked him, "Did you ever think of becoming a seminarian, study theology, and become a priest in order to work for the good of our people? Why don't you remain in Rome and I will write to your bishop, Josaphat Kocylowsky in Peremyshl, and get him to accept you as his seminarian." Dmytro replied that he never thought of becoming a priest, but on his advice he would think about it and pray.

So he was temporarily placed in residence at the Basilian Monastery, located in Rome, Madonna dei Monti 3. In two weeks a reply came from Bishop Kocylowsky, accepting him as his seminarian. Thus his pilgrimage to Rome gained for him the grace of a vocation to the holy priesthood.

He studied diligently and successfully completed his philosophical and theological studies. He received his priestly ordination in Rome April 2, 1939, from the hands of the saintly Bishop Niaradi. Since the Second World War started in September of 1939, his return to his homeland was practically impossible at that time. He stayed on in Rome and continued his graduate studies at the Urbanianum University achieving a doctoral degree in theology in 1942. Afterward he continued his studies at the Gregorianum University where in 1946 he achieved a doctoral degree in Church history. The same year he was received by Bishop Constantine Bohachevsky as a priest of the Philadelphia Ukrainian Catholic Exarchate of the United States of America.

Yes, Rev. D. Blazejowsky, S.T.D., Ph.D. was a person of very strong will and had a completely self-sacrificing attitude for the good of the Church and the faithful. He was gifted with seemingly unlimited energy and endurance in pursuing his objective or in fulfilling his perceived duties. In addition he was very hardworking, tireless, persistent and obstinate, not paying attention to his own needs or comfort. Personally he was satisfied with the minimum for his existence, capable of living in a sacristy of his church, or in another case in the choir loft. On one occasion, when he came by train from Denver to Omaha at 2:00 A.M., he didn't want to wake me up, so he rested on a bench in the city park.

Regrettably, the Church authorities at that time did not recognize or know of his talents and capabilities and did not use them properly. His next assignment was St. Pius X Church in Houston, Texas, where he built our first church there and organized the parish. Being misunderstood, he decided to dedicate the rest of his life to scholarly rather than pastoral work. He departed in the early 1970s from the United States to Italy, and took residence in Rome where he would have at his disposition the best church libraries in the world.

Omaha, Nebraska

Now back to St. Joseph, Missouri. The day of my arrival in St. Joseph, Father Blazejowsky had one of his parishioners drive both of us to Omaha, Nebraska. The trip lasted several hours and we arrived toward evening. We took my suitcases into my temporary residence. Father Blazejowsky insisted that we visit a few parishioners. I was tired from the long overnight trip from Detroit to St. Joseph and from there to Omaha, but I went along. He could not walk slowly. His walk was very brisk and energetic, just as his speech; he was a fast talker. Everything he did, was done with speed and energy. And so we visited one home after another until about 10:00 P.M. when people were already getting ready to go to bed.

The newly organized parish in Omaha at that time had no church or rectory of its own. A religious order of nuns of German origin staffed a large Catholic hospital. On the first floor of the hospital was a large chapel with a capacity of about two hundred. Mother Superior permitted Father Blazejowsky to have his Sunday Liturgies for our faithful in that chapel. Since he had no rectory and was constantly on the go, she permitted him to stay overnight in a small room in the basement of the hospital, just a few doors from the mortuary. There was a small bed in that room, a table, and a chair. The only window was way up high under the ceiling, and under the ceiling were all kinds of pipes. This room became my first rectory!

The sisters of the hospital invited me to have my meals together with their chaplain. He was an elderly priest and a real gentleman. He used to tell me that when he took his summer vacations, he would take a train and ride all over the country. This was his joy and relaxation. This arrangement for my meals was really a great treat for me. I did not have to worry about shopping for food or cooking my meals. Besides, in that room where I stayed, there were no cooking facilities. My monthly salary as a parochial vicar at that time was only $50.00. From this amount I had to send $15.00 monthly back to the chancery to pay my school bill. The young parish had no funerals, and during my stay there I had only one baptism. The chaplain used to give me $1.00 Liturgy stipends. There was no other income.

On Sundays I had a 9:00 A.M. Divine Liturgy with a homily for the faithful. The people sang the responses themselves. Almost every Sunday there were some patients and some nuns who would attend our Liturgy out of curiosity, and to hear our people take an active part in the worship. Afterward I had to pack my vestments and everything else needed for the Liturgy into a suitcase and hurry to catch the 10:30 bus to Lincoln, Nebraska, 75 miles away from Omaha. The trip lasted two full hours. Some parishioners waited for me at the bus stop and conducted me to a Latin rite church, where the pastor permitted them to have their Sunday Liturgy. The church law at that time did not permit Liturgy after 1:00 P.M., so I had to hurry to be able to start the Liturgy even one minute before 1:00 P.M. The church law at that time required the priest who wished to celebrate a Divine Liturgy to abstain from food and water from the midnight before. I had a very weak stomach since my bout with seasickness on the boat to United States in 1948. Each Sunday my trip to Lincoln, and the late Liturgy without a drop of water were very difficult for me. I could take some nourishment only about 3:00 P.M.

After a two-month stay in the basement room, Mother Superior noticed one morning at breakfast that I was congested. I thought that it was just a simple cold. But she knew better, and immediately after breakfast she took me for a thorough medical examination. The examination showed that I had an inflammation of my sinuses. I was then assigned a hospital room and the doctors began treatment. They placed a steam blower over my head, which I had to inhale. There was no penicillin then, so they used some other kind of 10 cc. injection which I had to take hourly for 24 hours. Two weeks of such a treatment cured me completely. The doctors, however, forbade me to stay in the basement room. The parishioners found me a one-room apartment on Catherine Street to which I moved immediately; yet I enjoyed it for only two weeks.

Since Father Blazejowsky could not get any more immigrants from Germany to build up the Lincoln mission parish, he wrote to the bishop for permission to close the mission and to transfer the people either to Omaha or Denver parishes. Now Bishop Bohachevsky would never close a parish, for this would, in his mind, show that our numbers were decreasing. He, therefore, did not give Father Blazejowsky the permission he desired, and transferred me to another parish, Holy Spirit Church in Brooklyn, N.Y.

Brooklyn, New York

The chancellor, Father Platon Kornylyak, called and told me to report to Rev. Vladimir Lotowych in Jersey City, the local dean. I was sad to leave my first pastoral assignment. I got to know and love my faithful, and did not know who was to replace me. But I had no choice. I bought a train ticket, packed my suitcases and took a 1:00 P.M. train from Omaha, through Chicago to New York City. At about 6:00 A.M. I arrived in New York City. There I asked some people how to get to Jersey City by subway. People were very polite and kind to a young priest. I followed their instructions and arrived there quite early. I carried two large suitcases, and with some difficulty found the street and the house of Father Lotowych. Since it was early, I sat down on the front steps, took my book, "Office of the Hours," recited my morning prayers, and then I took out my rosary and prayed. At about 8:45 I rang the doorbell. The doors opened and a tall lady stood there. She yelled at me, "Why do you come so early in the morning, and wake the dean up? Could you not come later on?" I apologized, asked forgiveness, and explained that I came from far away, from Omaha, Nebraska, and was told by the Chancery to report to the dean. Father Lotowych heard me and asked me to come in. He handed me my documents and said good-bye. I looked at my appointment papers and noticed that they were dated September 13, 1952 prot. # 2146-52-Cb.

I then asked the dean if I could use his church to offer my daily Divine Liturgy, since I fasted from midnight, and had a weak stomach. He replied, "You are assigned to Brooklyn. Go there and say your Liturgy there. Here we have our schedule which must be followed."

I thanked the dean, picked up my heavy suitcases and went out. Slowly I made my way back to the subway station, and took a subway back to Manhattan. There again I inquired as to how to get to North 5th street in Brooklyn. The good people gave me the right directions, and by 11:00 A.M. I arrived at Holy Spirit Church in Brooklyn. Father Vladimir Andrushkiw was seated behind his desk and welcomed me warmly. The first thing I asked of him was to be able to offer my daily Divine Liturgy in his church. He gave me the keys to the church and said, go ahead!

I went to the church, looked in the sacristy for the light switches, then for the wine and the altar bread. Happily the janitor came around and helped me find the needed things. Only God himself knows if my Liturgy was pleasing to Him, for I was so weak and dog-tired, holding on to the edge of the altar while reciting the prayers and the replies of the Liturgy. I just could not concentrate on the words of the Liturgy.

My First Deanery Meeting

ishop Bohachevsky had his regular annual deanery meetings with the clergy. A week or so after my arrival in Brooklyn there was a meeting for the local deanery clergy at St. Nicholas church rectory in Passaic, New Jersey. Father Andrushkiw drove both of us to Passaic for the meeting. There were about fifty priests there already when we arrived. I greeted each one and presented myself to them, for very few of them knew who I was. It was a joy for me to be in the company of so many older and experienced priests. Even more interesting to me was to hear their conversations, mimicking their bishop, making fun of him, and passing critical remarks about him.

However, when the bishop arrived, all conversations stopped. Father Vladimir Bilynsky, local pastor, escorted the bishop to the second floor. In a short while the pastor came down the steps and asked for me, saying, "The bishop wants to talk to you." All eyes turned to me. I went up, greeted the bishop, who asked me to sit down. Immediately he started with the questions, "When did you come from Omaha? How many parishioners do we have there? Where did you reside? Where did you hold Divine Liturgies for the people? How many people attend Sunday Liturgies? How did you commute to Lincoln? How many people are there in Lincoln?

Who prepared your food? How did you like being in Omaha? What was your monthly salary in Omaha?

The bishop never was in Omaha or Lincoln. He, therefore, wanted to know everything about these two parishes. I answered each of his questions as thoroughly as I could, without any complaints or criticism. At the end I added, "I was very much surprised that you transferred me from there. There definitely is a need of a priest there. We just cannot leave so many people without pastoral ministry." The bishop then asked, "Can Father Blazejowsky minister to both parishes, Denver and Omaha?" "No, Your Excellency," I answered. "It is impossible because of the great distance between Denver and Omaha of nearly 800 miles. It takes most of the day or all of the night to travel this distance. When then could the priest celebrate the Liturgy for the faithful? He thanked me and gave me permission to leave.

During the Deanery Meeting two extensive talks were given on the explanation of the proper rubrics of the new liturgical books, published for us by the Holy See of Rome in the 1940s. A lively discussion followed in which most of the priests took part. I decided that on my first deanery meeting I would just listen and not take part in the discussion.

At the end of the meeting the bishop himself stood up and gave an extemporaneous talk. At first he thanked the host for gracious hospitality, the two who prepared the talks, and all the priests for their attendance at this annual deanery meeting and an active participation in the discussions.

Dear Fathers, in your lively discussion on the liturgical themes, and the side remarks, I could detect complaints and dissatisfaction. I understand you, since life is not always easy; it has its ups and downs. Life brings with it all kinds of difficulties and crosses. Yet a priest of Christ should imitate his Master and be able to overcome his weaknesses and bear with patience and forbearance all his difficulties and discomforts. Your parishioners watch you and learn not only from your Sunday sermons, but even more from your life and behavior; you are another Christ to them.

Here among you today is your youngest brother, newly ordained this last June, Father Stephen Sulyk. I sent him to Omaha and Lincoln, Nebraska, to help Father Blazejowsky in the organization of these new parishes. He received only $50.00 monthly salary and had no other income. He lived in a Catholic hospital basement and did not complain. Moreover, he told me, "I was very much surprised that you transferred me from there. There definitely is a need of a priest there. We just cannot leave so many people without pastoral ministry." Yet you, my dear brother priests, have old and well-to-do parishes, and yet you complain. Why? You should be happy and satisfied and give good example to your faithful."

I just laid my head into my hands and leaned it on the table from shame and embarrassment. I would have rather hid somewhere and not been there. On our way back to Brooklyn, Father Andrushkiw never mentioned a word about what the bishop said about me. This meant that he did not like such public praise of the youngest priest.

My Work in the Parish

As the school year commenced, I had to teach Saturday School of Catechism and the Ukrainian language. It was not an easy task. The boys and girls of a large city public school system were thoroughly spoiled. They got used to talking in the class, rebelling, being mischievous, and not paying attention at all to what the teacher had to say. As soon as I was able to calm down one of them, the others started up so as to bring me to lose my temper. Yet, I refused to be distracted, was calm and steady in my approach, showing them my care and love at all times. At the end of my first class, I had them all paying attention to me. I smiled at them, sang a song with them, and gave them an easy home assignment. After the closing prayer they all surrounded me and asked all kinds of questions. The next Saturday the class almost doubled in attendance. The boys and girls were happy to come to the Saturday parish school, and their parents would ask me, what kind of teaching methods did I use to interest and captivate the children?

Holy Spirit parish in Brooklyn was quite large, well organized, and well to do. There were active youth organizations, men and women sodalities and societies. There was a well-organized church choir under the leadership of Ostap Ulitsky, high school pal of the pastor, Father Andrushkiw.

One of my important duties in the parish was to visit the sick whenever they asked for a priest. Once a month, usually the first Friday of the month, I visited all the sick and the homebound. I was ready to administer to each the sacraments of Penance, Eucharist and, if need, be also the Anointing of the Sick. One Saturday evening, after the celebration of Vespers in the church, the pastor told me he just received a phone call that a certain old woman was near death. When he told me her name, I said I had visited her yesterday and administered to her the holy sacraments. Then he told me that I did not have to go again. May God receive her soul. But I said, I had better go anyway since they called and at least say the prayers for the dying. So I took with me what was needed and went by foot to Greenpoint in Brooklyn, about half an hour's walk, since at that time parochial vicars were forbidden to own or drive a car.

When I entered the house where she lived, her daughter told me her mother died almost half an hour earlier. She called the rectory to inform me not to come, but I had already left the house. The mother lay on a sofa motionless, apparently dead. I approached her and tried to talk into her ear, greeting her and telling her whom I was. I said to her, "Be sorry for your sins and I will give you absolution." Then I said loud enough the words of the act of contrition used in our Church, *"God, be merciful to me, a sinner. God, cleanse me of my sins and have mercy on me. I have sinned without number, forgive me, O Lord."* On the words, *"God, be merciful . . ."* she raised her right arm and stroked her breast. She then breathed heavily for the last time. I then gave her conditional absolution and read the prayers for the dying.

On the way home I had enough time to pray and meditate on what I just witnessed. I thanked God for his presence at the deathbed of this saintly lady, and for his help in my priestly ministry. I then asked God, "Please God, be with me at the moment of my death as you were today at the deathbed of this, your saintly soul."

There was another unusual case during my pastoral ministry in that parish. It was a case that will remain with me as long as I live. One day the pastor told me, "I just received a phone call from the wife of a very sick man in a hospital. I called the funeral director to drive you to the hospital." Immediately I went to the church, took with me the Holy Eucharist and the oils. The car was already waiting for me. I found the sick man lying in his bed in a one-bed hospital room. I greeted him and asked him whether he wished to make a good confession. He said, yes, I do! So I heard his confession, gave him absolution, administered Holy Eucharist to him, and gave him the sacrament of the sick, the anointing with holy oils. I laid my hands on his head and gave him my blessing.

He than asked me to take a seat. I pulled a chair closer to his bed and sat down. He said, "Father, what is your name? How long are you in our parish? I thank you for coming to see me, and to minister to me. You did it all so piously and even gave me your blessing. But all these your efforts are for nothing." I was shocked, and asked, "What do you mean by saying, "for nothing." "Well, Father," he replied, "I sinned my whole life, and you said a few prayers, and fixed it all up in about ten or fifteen minutes. I do not believe that it is possible to do so in such a short time."

I was dumbfounded, and thought that if the man does not believe that his sins are forgiven, then they are not. So I asked him, "Please tell me the honest truth. Did you confess all the sins you could remember, were you truly sorry for your sins?" "Yes, he said, I did confess all the sins I could remember, and was truly sorry for my sins."

I then told him the story of how Christ on the day of his resurrection appeared to his apostles, and told them, *"As the Father has sent me, so I send you." Then he breathed on them and said: "Receive the holy Spirit. If you forgive men's sins, they are forgiven them; if you hold them bound, they are held bound"* (John 20:21). This power, given by Christ Himself to the apostles, was transmitted from them to the bishops and the priests to this day. Using this power, I absolved you and forgave you all your sins. Your sins are now forgiven. But the sick man just stared at me and did not accept my explanation. I continued to tell him first the story of the prodigal son, about Mary Magdalene, and finally about the good thief on the cross. All the thief did was to acknowledge His divinity and prayed, *"Jesus, remember me when you enter upon you reign."* For this acknowledgement, Jesus forgave him all his sins, and told him, *"I assure you: this day you will be with me in paradise"* (Luke 23:42–43). It took Jesus even less time to forgive the thief all his many sins than it took me to confess and absolve you. But even this did not move the sick man. He just lay there and stared at me with unbelieving eyes.

I understood then that no matter how hard I tried to explain the teaching of Christ with my unworthy and sinful lips, it did not automatically bring conversion. Something was missing. In my heart I understood that what was missing was the holiness of life. A priest to be successful in preaching Christ must be Christ-like himself, he must be holy, so that the sick man could see Christ before him. I then placed my left hand into my pocket and touched the rosary there, asking the Most Holy Mother of God to help me. She did come to my aid and gave me an idea, a ready plan of action.

I then took the sick man's hands into my hands and told him this, "Are you ready to do me a great favor?" "What kind of favor? What can I, a sick man, do for you, Father?" he answered. Then I said, "I so firmly believe that your sins are forgiven and that when you die, you will go to heaven. But when you are there would you, please, ask God to help me be a good priest. Please, promise me that you will do that." He answered, "I do promise. I will ask God for you," and he started to cry and kissed my hands.

He did die that same day and a few days later I served funeral services for the repose of his soul.

Minersville, Pennsylvania

I t was in April of 1953 that a call came from the Chancery informing the pastor that I would be transferred to another parish, but must first present myself personally in the Chancery. As I was about to leave the rectory, and one of the parishioners was to drive me to the Chancery in Philadelphia, there were about twenty parents of the Saturday school children on the street, protesting my transfer. I went to them and told them it was not their pastor's fault that I was being transferred. The reason is that I am a young priest in the first year of my priesthood and the bishop wants me to get more experience, serving as parochial vicar to different experienced pastors. I loved being here in Brooklyn and loved teaching the children, but when the bishop commands, it is the will of God and I must obey it. I blessed them all and asked them to pray for me and to go home. But they did not, and remained on the street as my car drove away. I had made a mistake to talk to the parents. Some misinterpreted my action thinking I was agitating them. But even this mistake of mine turned out to be a blessing for me, for I did not agitate, but tried to be helpful.

When I arrived in the Chancery, Father Myroslav Charyna, who worked in the front office of the Chancery, welcomed me, and confidentially told me that the bishop wanted to name me a pastor, organizing a new parish in Miami, Florida. But something happened; someone called the bishop, and changed his mind. The bishop named Father Paul Smal, parochial vicar in Minersville, PA, to go to Florida, and I was to replace him in Minersville. I was happy at the turn of events, because in my heart I felt I was not ready, did not have enough experience to be able to organize a new parish.

A few minutes later the chancellor, Father Platon Kornylyak, entered the room and told me the Chancery would mail my transfer papers to the dean, Father Gregory Kanda, who in turn would give them to me. He told me also to go to Minersville and be a parochial vicar to Father Basil Stebelsky at St. Nicholas Church in Minersville.

I took a train and went to Minersville, my third pastoral assignment. A few days later, Father Kanda, the dean, came to see me and welcome me into his deanery. He was an elderly, tall, gray-haired man, very kind, polite, and gentlemanly. My assignment papers were dated April 22, 1953, prot. N. 946-53-Cb.

Father Basil Stebelsky, the pastor, was a young priest, only 39 years old at that time. He came to the United States after the Second World War from Ukraine. He studied at the Minor Seminary in the city of Lviv, and then at Holy Spirit Theological Academy, Lviv, Ukraine. He married Arkadia, and at the time of my arrival they had two daughters and a son, while Arkadia was pregnant with their third daughter. He was ordained in Ukraine in 1942, and was a very hardworking priest. One of his admirable qualities was his earnest desire to catechize his faithful. All his sermons, classes in the school, instructions, or talks at various meetings were based on the catechism. In his twenty-nine years in Minersville, he achieved great spiritual success; he literally educated one whole generation of his parishioners in the Catholic Faith, in our Eastern traditions, and in the love, dedication, and faithfulness to God and our Church. His successors in the parish are now reaping the harvest of his labors.

I stayed in a small room on the second floor in the rectory for only one week. With the family in that small house, there was no room for me, a celibate priest. I moved to an apartment one block away on the second floor, while on the first floor was a school classroom, since the school building could not contain all of the students. During the day it was quite noisy, but after school, I had the whole house to myself. Sister Anatole Andrews, SSMI, was the teacher in that classroom, and while I was going in or out of the house, she would invite me to talk to her class. I enjoyed communicating with the children very much and was able to make friends with them quickly. During a school break, I would invite some children to watch a baseball game on my television and they really loved this. While in Minersville, I was able to get to know all our priests, religious sisters, and many of our faithful in our parishes in that coal region. Annually, the last Sunday of July, they held a seminary day, or as they called it at that time, "the Ukrainian Day" at Lakewood Park. The bishop would come and serve Divine Liturgy in a large hall on the stage. Afterward the people remained picnicking, dancing, socializing, and getting to know each other. All our priests would come also and be with their people. The proceeds from this day would always be donated to support our St. Josaphat Seminary in Washington, D.C. When Lakewood Park was closed in the 1980s, the Seminary Day was moved to St. Nicholas Primrose Hall, near Minersville, and is still held there annually.

Youngstown, Ohio

Bishop Constantine Bohachevsky by a letter dated November 29, 1953, prot. #2457-53-Cb., named me a parochial vicar to Holy Trinity Parish, Youngstown, Ohio, where Father Leo Adamiak was the pastor. This was my fourth parochial assignment. Father. Adamiak, a young, energetic, and very talented priest, was very popular and beloved by his parishioners, especially by the young and middle aged ones. I arrived in Youngstown by train December 8, 1953.

One thing I remember well from my first night in Youngstown. Next door to the old rectory was the McKey Machine Shop Factory. My upstairs room was on the side of the factory. All night long the factory machines worked, making devilish noise, boom, boom, boom, boom! I could not sleep at all. But the next night I was so tired that after I fell asleep, I slept so well I did not hear a thing. When on the weekend the factory was closed, I missed the boom, boom, boom, boom!

This large parish under the energetic leadership of Father Adamiak was alive. There were all kinds of parish organizations, societies, sisterhoods, junior and senior sodalities, church choir under the leadership of Mr. Kohut, and many others. There were also all kinds of activities, fund raising undertakings, picnics on their own picnic grounds in a different part of the town, festivals, lotteries, etc. Saturdays, I taught children in various grades the catechism, our liturgical rites and customs, and the Ukrainian language. The altar servers were under my charge. I always attended the meetings of the Jr. Sodality. It was my duty to prepare the young couples for matrimony. So I had to write the Pre-Marital Protocols and give some instructions to the couples. When the pastor decided to make a thorough census of the parish, I visited individual homes and got to know the parishioners.

Father Leo Adamiak, later on a Monsignor and a Mitred Archpriest, treated me as his brother, and we became good friends. Later on in life we became vacation partners. He loved the game of golf, and on one occasion he took me with him to the golf course. It was the first time I ever saw a golf game. He took his driver out of the bag and hit the ball a mile. Then he gave me a five iron and a ball, and said, try to hit it. I thought this is easy. Just hit the ball and it will go. So I swung the club really hard, and missed the ball altogether. But he did not give up on me. He showed me some of the basic principles of the golf swing, and I slowly made progress. On our second golf outing, I bought an old leather golf bag with used golf clubs and we became competitors. However he used to beat me all the time!

Later on, my pastor asked me to take some driving lessons. There was an undertaker by the name of Shultz who was very friendly with us. One day one of his helpers took an old car and patiently began to teach me how to drive. Then he let me drive by myself while he was sitting next to me. I was doing very well until I had to shift gears. The car would stall, the cars behind me would blow their horns, and people were irritated and yelling at me— "get out of the way!" This was quite an experience for me. But slowly I learned to shift gears, applied for a driver's license, passed the exam and I had my first driver's license dated March 31, 1954.

Young parishioners were again and again demanding from the pastor that he change from the old Julian to the new Gregorian church calendar. They wanted to celebrate Christmas on December 25th, together with the whole country and not two weeks later.

To make such a change the bishop demanded that a vote be taken and he would give permission only if a large majority was asking for the change, and there was no danger that the opponents would leave the church.

The ballots were mailed to each home in the parish, and the parishioners were requested to fill them out and return them in sealed envelopes, placing them on Sunday into the collection basket. The results were good. Most of the parishioners voted for the change to the new Gregorian calendar. But there were a good number of elderly parishioners who either did not vote or voted against the change.

There was a need for personal visits to the homes of those who opposed the change. In the minds of our simple people, who, although they were very religious and loved their church, mistakenly identified the church calendar with the faith. They would say, it is our sacred tradition. Our fathers and forefathers celebrated Christmas on January 7th, so should we. They remembered the past in Ukraine, where our neighbors of the Latin rite would look down on us as though we were some second-class church members, and not quite Catholic. Yet, they simply did not distinguish the truth of faith and the equality of rites from the political nationalism and chauvinism.

On those visits I tried as calmly as I could to explain why the change of the calendar was preferred. We were trying to keep our young generations within our church. They were born in this country. This is their home and they have the right to observe Christmas with the rest of the American people. In many cases the opponents gave in and said for the sake of our young people we will go along and vote for the change. But there were some who made me listen to some very bitter words. They would say something like this: "Our young people do not know our traditions. They have abandoned our Ukrainian language. They became Americanized and wish to Americanize and Latinize our Church as well. Sooner or later they will leave our church. As soon as they get married to a Latin rite person, they do leave our Church. The two of you young priests are helping them to Latinize our Church and abandon her. You both are traitors to our Church."

Thanks be to God, there were not many such people as the one quoted. The children and grandchildren pleaded with their elderly relatives not to oppose the change. Thus the change of the calendar took place without much disturbance or major problems. Not one person left the parish because of the change.

It was in Youngstown that I applied for U.S. citizenship. I receive my naturalization papers and became a citizen of the United States of America in the court in Cleveland, Ohio, January 14, 1955.

Phoenixville, Pennsylvania

By a document dated January 21, 1955, prot. # 122-55-Cb., Bishop Bohachevsky appointed me an administrator of Ss. Peter and Paul Church, Phoenixville, PA, 24 miles northwest of Philadelphia. This was my fifth pastoral assignment. As I entered the rectory, there were about five men of the church advisory committee waiting. They welcomed me warmly; each one presented himself to me and wished me all the best. If I needed anything, they said, just give any one of them a call. Of the five men of the church advisory committee four were named Stephen.

One of the men present was tall, handsome, and well dressed. He lived just across the street from the front door of the rectory. His name was Peter Winnick. The next morning after I offered my first Divine Liturgy in that parish and was ready to make my breakfast, someone rang the doorbell. I opened the door and there stood a gray-haired lady, with uncombed hair wrapped over with a babushka. I asked her to come in. She presented herself to me as Mary Winnick. Then I said to her something as stupid as I ever said in my life, "Are you the mother of Peter Winnick, who was here last night?" She replied, "No, I am his wife!" I apologized for such a stupid remark, but she remembers it even now. She brought me some food for my breakfast and we remain friends to this day.

The cantor in this parish was Stephen Zguta. I remembered him from Europe. When I was in high school, he was a young cantor in our church in Sambir. Of course he did not know me at that time, but I remembered him. He and his family became my good friends. His wife would cook at home and bring a meal for me to the rectory once a day. He graduated from a professional cantors' and choir directors' school in the city of Peremyshl, now in Poland.

One of the men from the church committee, Stephen Ochrymowych, drove me to a neighboring town to a car dealer he knew, and there I bought my first car, a low-mileage used car, four door, black sedan, a 1952 Buick with an automatic transmission.

One of the persistent problems in this parish was a question of the change of church calendar from the Julian to the Gregorian. In past years, Rev. Basil Sheremeta, pastor of the neighboring parish in Bridgeport, PA, was also serving Phoenixville, and tried to please the people by conducting balloting for the change of calendar three times. All the ballots were preserved in the rectory, each one bound into a separate bundle. My good men from the church advisory committee explained to me the difficulty with the calendar. The core of the difficulty existed in a feud between two large families in the parish. Twenty-five or so years ago, two men were courting one girl. They told me her name, but I've forgotten it. After some time, she selected one and married him. Since then these two large families could not agree to anything. During the triple balloting for the change of calendar, the pastor published in the church bulletin the names of all who took part in the balloting. So, when one of these two families voted for the change, the other one would certainly vote against the change.

So, I had no choice but to conduct another ballot for the change of calendar. The results were the same as before. I then privately visited each of the families who voted against the change. I brought blank ballots with me and explained,—should you change your mind, I promise you that no one will know about it except myself, you, and the bishop. I will not publish the results of the balloting in the church bulletin. They believed me and readily signed a ballot for the change. I had only five families from among the new immigrants who remained in opposition to the change.

Generally speaking, I could honestly say that I had a very good reception from my parishioners. They were satisfied and happy with my pastoral work and were very friendly toward me. If I needed something, all I had to do was to ask, and it was done.

I had one marriage case in this parish that deserves to be noted: One of our boys came to me with his fiancé and declared that they wished to be married. They chose a date that was free on my calendar. I took the pre-marital protocol, assigned the dates of the publication of banns in the parish bulletin, and gave them right then their first pre-marital instruction. Five more instructions were to be given. They attended each of them faithfully. I was very happy that the girl, who was of the Latin Catholic and belonged to the local Slovak church, agreed to marry in our church. There are very few of those cases. Usually the Latin Catholic demands that the marriage be in their church, even though the law reads that the interritual marriage should take place in the church of the groom. After the marriage, the Latin partner usually refuses to attend our church, and so our church loses her young members. Just before I was to publish their first pre-marital banns, I receive a call from the groom to be. The man said, "Please do not publish the banns. The marriage is off. She refuses to marry in my church, and if my church is no good for her, I am no good for her." This man had a backbone, and this is the only such case in my whole priestly life.

My Work in the Bishop's Chancery

I received a letter from the Bishop's Chancery dated November 3, 1955, prot. #2416-55-Cb., in which I was ordered to commute daily to the Chancery and work there as a secretary, besides my pastoral work in the parish. A week later I began my daily Monday through Friday routine of driving from my rectory in Phoenixville, through the famous Valley Forge Park, the Schuylkill Expressway, to Philadelphia and the Chancery, at 815 North Franklin Street. The work in the Chancery could be described as a good school of discipline, punctuality, and orderliness.

Bishop Constantine Bohachevsky, as a priest during the First World War, was a chaplain in the Austrian army. His military habits of discipline, punctuality, and orderliness in his daily routine remained with him for the rest of his life. He had his set daily schedule of prayer, meditation, spiritual reading, and work. Very unobtrusively, he practiced poverty. He dressed very simply. There were no luxuries in his life or his home. He lived almost ascetically. Yet, he never talked about his private life, and very few priests knew about this side of his life. With all this, he was a man of great faith, and led a life of prayer. As a bishop he never took his monthly salary from the diocese. The only money he had on him were the stipends he received in cash from the priests for the various marital dispensations, permissions or liturgical stipends. The diocese paid his travel expenses and the utilities for his house. The fact that he never took a monthly salary was not public knowledge. Outwardly he was of calm character with a great sense of responsibility. This is why he placed the greatest demands upon himself, and from his priests he demanded honest daily work.

He had a very strict schedule of pastoral visitations of his parishes. At that time, there was only one diocese, called an exarchate, which covered the whole country. Every weekend of the year, with the exception of major holy days, he was on a visitation. In most cases he used trains for reaching the parish. Seldom did he use airplanes. Coming back home very late Sunday night, he had very little or no night rest. On one occasion when visiting the parish in Maizeville, PA, the pastor, Father Kanda, invited me to dine with the Bishop. Before he came, he wrote me a note to pick him up at the Pottsville railroad station. He asked the time of the last train to Philadelphia, which was at 7:30 P.M. He liked the Kanda family and enjoyed their company. When I reminded him that it was time to leave so as to catch the last train. He ignored me. Thus we sat there and talked until nearly 10:00 P.M. Then he asked me, "How will I now get to Philadelphia?" I answered, "I will drive you home!"

We arrived at his home in north Philadelphia well after midnight. I took his suitcase for him into the house, waited to say goodnight, and readied myself for the drive back home. He stopped me, and told me to go upstairs, showed me to a room, and said, go to sleep. You will go home tomorrow. After an hour or so, when I was going to the restroom, I saw light in his apartment. He did not go to bed that night at all. He opened the mail, and at his usual time, 4:00 A.M., he was in the chapel starting his daily routine.

Yet, by most of our priests, he was perceived incorrectly as a very strict man, unbending, merciless, money hungry, and almost a tyrant. True, when he first came into the United States in 1924, there was chaos in the exarchate. The first bishop, Soter Ortynsky died young in 1916, and for eight long years there was no bishop. The priest, administrator, Father Poniatyshyn, was not able to keep any semblance of order and clerical discipline. Priests cooperated with the all powerful parish church trustees, did what they wanted to do, set up their own salaries, and changed parishes on their own by instigating the committees to demand this or that priest. Father Poniatyshyn as the Administrator of the Exarchate was help-less, because if the priest did not get what he wanted, the parish left the Exarchate and joined the Orthodox Church.

Bishop Bohachevsky had to be a strict disciplinarian in many cases in order to save the Church. He introduced strict observance of the church law, and demanded that priests abide by it. To sup-port the diocese and later on the seminary as well, he introduced an assessment in the form of monthly cathedraticum and aluminatium, and a monthly collection for the diocese. He de-manded strict observance and regular monthly payments of these assessments. He incorporated the diocese as a non-profitable State of Pennsylvania corporation, and every parish had to incorporate their parish property into the diocesan corporation to prevent the loss of parishes. Yes, he was strict, but he had to be in order to bring order out of chaos. Every bishop who succeeded him in what are now the four dioceses will admit he is building upon the foun-dation laid down by Archbishop Bohachevsky.

I worked in the Chancery until July 1, 1957. I learned a lot in the formative years of my priesthood from Bishop Bohachevsky, and the experience served me well throughout the long years of my priestly and Episcopal ministry. I have to admit that it was not easy. My job at first consisted mostly of typing letters or other ma-terials. One mistake in typing, and the letter was returned to be retyped without any errors. Later on, I was given the task of trans-lating things from English to Ukrainian. At that time we in the Chancery did not know that the chancellor, Rev. Platon Kornylyak, was being prepared to become the first bishop of our Church in Germany. This is why bishop Bohachevsky told him to teach me the things that belonged strictly to the duties of the chancellor only. Kornylyak, not knowing what awaited him, despised these orders, but he obeyed them and showed me how do this or that. He loved his job and was afraid of losing it.

I did not mind the work in the Chancery as much as I missed being in a parish with the people. I was removed from my parish in Phoenixville early in 1956, and was a full-time Chancery worker. There was an opening in a small parish in Clifton Heights near Philadelphia. I took the opportunity to ask for it with a promise that I would commute to the Chancery daily and do everything I was doing now. This displeased the bishop very much. He never forgot it. He considered Chancery work the height of advancement.

Houston, Texas

The bishop received many letters asking for a priest for our community in Houston, Texas. In order to verify that there were enough of our faithful to form a parish, to support the church and a priest, I was told to go there and to stay for a month. I took a train November 15, 1955, from Philadelphia to Houston. The trip was long and boring. At the train station in Houston a man by the name of Victor Balaban was waiting for me. He drove me to a motel on the outskirts of the town on Airline Avenue, gave me a room, and took care of me.

Victor, who came to the United States of America after the War, was middle-aged, a very able and crafty businessman. At first he worked for a large firm that washed windows of very tall buildings in the city. Having learned the trade, he opened his own window washing firm, was able to find good workers, became a stiff competitor, and with time he became quite well to do. Then he purchased a motel on the outskirts of the city, and was now in the process of building an additional motel. With all this he was very thrifty.

One of the local Ukrainian men volunteered to be my driver. The following morning he drove me to the nearby Roman Catholic Church. I went to the rectory, told the pastor who I was, and asked his permission to say daily Liturgy, as well as Sunday Liturgy for our faithful in his church. I presented my *celebrate* (i.e., a document, stating that the holder is a priest of good standing) from Bishop Bohachevsky. He read it carefully and gave his permission. I thanked him, went to the car, got my suitcase out, went to the church and said Divine Liturgy of St. John Chrysostom in the church-Slavonic language. Apparently the pastor came to the church to see my Liturgy, and did not like what he saw! After the Liturgy he approached me and said, "If you wish to say Liturgies in this church, you must get permission from our bishop who has his offices in the city of Galveston.

The following day my driver drove to the city of Galveston to see Bishop Wendelin J. Nold. As I entered the chancery and told them who I was, the Chancellor entered the room, and joyfully greeted me, "I know you from Catholic University," he said. He asked me to come to his office, and there I explained to him that the pastor, having seen my Liturgy, demanded the bishop's written permission for me to be able to use his church. The Chancellor apologized profusely for the ignorance of the pastor. He assured me that the bishop would give me the needed permission. After a phone call from him, I went to see Bishop Nold, and showed him my *"celebrate."* He gave me the needed permission, but at the same time tried hard to persuade me that there was no need for a separate Eastern Rite parish in Houston. His priests could give the best pastoral care to all of our people. I politely assured him that I would convey his observation to my bishop.

During my month-long stay in Houston I celebrated Sunday Liturgies for the faithful, preached to them, and on weekdays I visited their homes. I took a census in which I asked such questions as, "Do you wish to have a church here in Houston? Would you attend Divine Liturgy on Sundays? How much would you be able to contribute toward this church on Sundays? It was interesting for me to learn how our people, mostly new immigrants, had accommodated themselves without our church. It was very evident that they soon would be lost to us without our Church. Very few of them went to the Latin Church. Some did not attend any church at all. Some were recruited to join a Protestant church. In one case when I asked how much would you be able to contribute to our church on Sundays, the answer was, "I would give what I give now. Every Friday a block collector comes to our house and takes one-tenth of my weekly check."

I took a plane for my return trip home. On the way home I stopped in Denver to visit Father D. Blazejowsky. As I entered the plane and took my seat, Bishop Nold entered, too, and sat next to me. All the way to Denver he tried to convince me of the absurdity of an Eastern Rite parish in his diocese. "I have enough trouble with those Mexicans. They want to sing their own hymns and to have fiestas with processions. This is not Mexico; this is the United States of America." I still remember his words.

Father Blazejowsky was very happy to see me. He was eager to tell me of his troubles and successes. He showed me his church with our icons, and the iconostas, as well as his residence. I, in turn, told him all about Houston and my month-long visit there. The next day I took a plane to Philadelphia. It was a pre-Christmas period and a lot of work had to be done in the parish, but I found time to write a detailed report to the bishop, enclosing the census cards. In reply to my report, Bishop Constantine wrote a letter to me dated December 20, 1955: "I thank you for your missionary efforts and for the detailed report of your work in Texas. Your report will be studied in order to come to a proper decision . . ."

Apparently my report pleased Bishop Constantine for soon he wrote me another letter, dated January 2, 1956, prot. # 2416-55-Cb, informing me that I was to leave Ss. Peter and Paul Parish in Phoenixville on January 16, 1956, in order to take over a full-time job in the Chancery. I admit that I did not like to leave the parish, but I obeyed and moved to Philadelphia and took up residence in the front room on the third floor of the Cathedral rectory on Franklin Street.

Father Henry Sagan, who was at that time the English editor of *The Way*, our diocesan newspaper, lived in the room next to mine. We became friends and got along very well. In our free time, we went together to see various shows or movies, and enjoyed each other's company. Father Joseph Fedorek, another classmate of mine, was at that time the Rector of the Cathedral Parish. So I had good company.

Lay People in the Parish Administration

Our first immigrants to this country came in the 1880s. For the most part they were simple peasant folk, seeking a better life for themselves and to help their relatives back in the economically poor Old Country. In order to make a living in this New World, they took the lowest menial jobs that were available to them, mostly in the coal mines of Pennsylvania. As their numbers increased, they would get together, organize themselves on weekends into societies, and sing some church hymns or national songs. They yearned for their homeland and pined for their own church, their church services, and ancestral traditions.

In the summer of 1884, Ukrainian miners in the town of Shenandoah in Pennsylvania wrote to Metropolitan-Archbishop Sylvester Sembratowych in Lviv, Ukraine, pleading for a priest of their own. "Dear Archbishop! We came to this country by ourselves, and now we are like blind men, because we lack something indispensable. We miss our God, a God whom we could understand, and whom we could worship in our own way. You, Dear Archbishop, are our father, because you are the father of all our Ukrainian people, even though we do not belong to your diocese. We, therefore, plead with you, give us priests from the Old Country, and give us your blessing for the building of our churches here in this foreign land, so that here too we may have what makes our Ukraine a holy land."

In December of 1884 Father John Wolansky, the first priest, arrived in Shenandoah from Ukraine. He served the first Divine Liturgy December 19, 1884, in a private house. No Roman Catholic priest would give him permission to use his church since he was a married priest. Eastern Catholics have an ancient tradition of married clergy. Father Wolansky visited our communities throughout the Eastern United States of America, organized parishes, and blessed their church buildings, which they erected on their own initiative.

Some other priests came from Ukraine to the United States after Father Wolansky, but all of them had a very hard time. We had no bishop of our own, and the Latin Rite bishops refused to give jurisdiction to any of the married priests. They could not understand Eastern Christian traditions and were afraid it would scandalize their celibate priests if a married Catholic priest would minister to his people in this country. Secondly, Latin Rite bishops could not understand why our people would not join their churches as many other ethnic groups did before them. The difference in church rites seemed not to matter to them.

Before they had a priest, the laity organized our first parishes according to the methods they learned from their Protestant friends with whom they worked. So they elected church boards or committees from among themselves—a president, secretary, treasurer and council members. These church committees administered the whole church property and the treasury. When we received our first bishop, Soter Ortynsky, the church committees continued to administer the church properties and considered their priest an employee of the parish committee.

The church committee set the amount of monthly salary to be paid to the priest, the cantor, the janitor, etc. In the administration of church property, they did not follow the prescriptions of church law, since they had no way of knowing what church law prescribed. At their annual meetings they voted in rules and regulations according to their Protestant exemplars and thus made their own rules and bylaws, frequently in contradiction to church law. When their pastor would not do what they wanted him to do, they cut his pay. Frequently, they refused to pay the monthly diocesan assessments to the diocese or take up a diocesan collection.

Such administration of church properties would frequently result in gross misunderstandings among the parishioners, mutual accusations of abuse of church money, mistrust, and feuds. Because of this there was no peace in the community and, of course, the preaching of the Gospel and the spiritual life in the parish suffered. There was stagnation in the parish.

Church committees would purchase land for the church's needs, erect buildings or picnic grounds, and not record it with the bishop or the diocese, but with the church committee, as the church trustees. When some misunderstanding happened to come along between the priest and the church committee, they would dismiss the priest, chase him out of the rectory, and join the Orthodox Church. When the priest was a married man with a family, it was a tragedy. This is why some of the priests gave in to the trustees, did what they wanted him to do just to be able to survive.

I heard of one case that happened in our parish in Perth Amboy, NJ, during the depression in the early 1930s. The church trustees were making homemade illegal whisky—moonshine. They would take the back seat out of a car, place the barrels there with the moonshine, cover them with a blanket, and ask the priest, dressed in his cassock with a stole, to sit on those barrels as though he was going on a sick call!

While I was pastor of St. Michael's Church in Frackville, PA, I learned that there was a priest there, Rev. Michael Prodan, in the 1940s. His wife lived in Ukraine, and he had a son studying medicine in Vienna, Austria. The all-powerful church committee would cut his pay sometimes for no reason. He had to support his wife and send money for his son's schooling. He did not have enough money left to support himself. He was literally starving.

The old St. Michael's church, Frackville, Pa.

One of the examples of such chaos resulting from trustee administration, and an example of the loss the Church had suffered in this country, was the community in the town of Canonsburg, near Pittsburgh, PA. Among the parishioners were some from the place of my birth. In the late 1890s they built a church building and a rectory on their own initiative and wrote to Ukraine for a priest. At that time the Russian Tsar was sending Orthodox priests as missionaries to proselytize among our people. They would tell our people: "The Pope does not want you. He does not want your married priests, and does not want to give you your own bishop. Come to us, and stay with your ancient traditions." This tactic worked very well. Many of our people were fooled and joined the Russian Orthodox Church. In 1905 the first Russian Orthodox Eparchy in New York was already erected.

One day a Russian Orthodox priest came to our community in Canonsburg and told them that he was a Greek-Catholic priest, sent to them by a bishop in Europe. He was welcomed and began his missionary work. In no time this parish became Russian Orthodox. Among the parishioners there was a family by the name of Lazoryschak. They came from the same village as I did, only the third door away from my home. They abbreviated their last name to Lazor. One of their sons became an Orthodox priest. He is now retired Metropolitan—Theodosius Lazor.

*St. Thérèse
of Lisieux*

*Society
of the
Little Flower*

THE WORDS OF ST. THÉRÈSE:

I understood that if all flowers wanted to be roses, nature would lose her springtime beauty, and the fields would no longer be decked out with little wild flowers. Each must shine and blossom.

Frackville, Pennsylvania

requent letters of complaints came to the Bishop's Chancery from St. Michael's Church in Frackville, Pa., against their pastor, Rev. Vladimir Pylypec. Father Vladimir was born February 14, 1902, in Ukraine. He was a tall, husky man, a former officer in the Ukrainian army after the First World War. He demanded respect and obedience from his parishioners who were not used to such treatment from their pastor. They were accustomed to treating their priest as their employee. They paid his salary, and in their minds he had to listen to them. Their little wooden framed church building was too small for their needs, and was leaning over to the left side. They had someone install steel rods to hold the walls together. For twenty-five years they took up a special collection every Sunday for the building fund of a new church. In all that time they collected only $20,440.00.

Bishop Bohachevsky knew his parishes well, and did not react to all the complaints from Frackville. But one day he received a letter from the Apostolic Delegate in Washington, D.C. with a copy of a letter from Frackville, signed literally by all the parishioners, demanding a change of pastor. He had great respect for the Pope and his Apostolic Delegate, and, therefore, he reacted immediately. By a letter dated June 24, 1957, prot. # 1136-57-Cb., he appointed me pastor of St. Michael's Church in Frackville.

Having received my marching orders, I went to the see Bishop Constantine in order to thank him for the appointment. He received me warmly and asked me to take a seat. Then he told me this, "You will take over your new parish July 1, 1957. It will not be an easy parish for you. I always had a lot of difficulties with the parishioners of that parish, or rather with their church committee. They have a very powerful church committee that does not permit the pastor do any of his administrative duties. The president of that committee is a certain man by the name of N.N. In order for you to have a better understanding of who this man really is, I will tell you a little story:

"When I, as a military chaplain in the World War I, was on the Italian front, there broke out a terrible epidemic disease—cholera. Soldiers were dying like flies. A simple soldier came up to the military medical doctor and asked him, 'Doctor, what kind of a cholera is it that kills so many soldiers?' The doctor replied, "It is our own, the Ukrainian cholera.' How else could the doctor explain a very complicated medical term to a simple soldier? And the president of the church committee in Frackville is such 'Our own, the Ukrainian cholera.' When you get there, you will find out that they want to build a new church. Don't do it, until they donate enough money for the project, otherwise you will be in trouble."

I thanked the Bishop for his kindness and the advice he gave me. I then called Father Pylypec, informed him of my appointment, and asked him to have the church committee and Father Gregory Kanda, the dean, in his rectory at 11:00 A.M. on July 1, 1957, to meet with me.

My New Pastoral Assignment

The day before I left for Frackville, I paid a visit to our auxiliary bishop, Joseph Schmondiuk, pastor of St. Nicholas in Philadelphia in order to say goodbye to him and ask his blessing. He was a very mature person with great pastoral experience. I told him I was somewhat afraid of this new assignment with all the problems facing me there. He thought for while and then gave this advice, "I understand your feelings of fear and anxiety. It is natural. You did not ask for this parish. It was Bishop Bohachevsky who made the decision to appoint you to this position. It is, therefore, the will of God that you are going to be a pastor in that town. Do not be afraid, for the Lord will be with you always. Be of good cheer. Think positively and with a smile on your face go there with courage and conduct yourself wisely and carefully. In order to be successful it is important not to be a proud dictator, but be always a humble, but decisive servant of God. Give your parishioners time to get to know you. They will observe you very carefully, and when they see in you a true man of God, they will come to love you and will follow your voice."

During my two hour-long drive to Frackville I prayed my rosary, asking God to be with me, to bless me, and show me the way. Having arrived, I parked my car in front of the rectory, left all my suitcases in the car, and rang the doorbell. Father Pylypec opened the door. He and Father Kanda welcomed me. I shook hands with the four members of the church committee. I then declared this, "Our Bishop Constantine Bohachevsky has taken into consideration your many requests for a change of your pastor. He sent me to you to be your pastor, but this under one condition that you will hand over to me all the financial books and all parish administration. If you refuse to abide by the bishop's orders, I left all my suitcases in my car. I will just turn around and go back to Philadelphia, and Father Pylypec will stay here."

Father Kanda at that point took me aside into the kitchen and whispered to my ear, "Don't do it! They will never give up their financial administration to a priest. If they refuse, what will you do then? You cannot go back to Philadelphia. To stay here, you will lose face." "Well, I will try anyway, and you just observe," I replied to the dean.

When both of us returned, one of the committeemen took out of his pocket a small booklet entitled, "The Statutes of St. Michael's Church, Frackville, Pa." He showed it to me and said, "We have these Statutes and have to abide by them. This is why we cannot give you our financial administration of the parish."

I explained this matter thus: If these Statutes were not approved by the Holy Father in Rome, or by Bishop Constantine Bohachevsky in Philadelphia, they have no legal force and are not binding in the Catholic Church. Besides, Pennsylvania state law states that each Church administers her property according to her own law. In our case it is by the law of the Catholic Church. So, according to Pennsylvania law, your Statutes are not valid and not binding. You have to understand that Christ founded our Church. In his Church God has established a certain order. The highest lawgiver is the Pope. In particular churches, it is the local bishop who alone has the right and the power to make laws. You know that Christ said to the apostles only, and not to all the people, *"I assure you, whatever you shall declared bound on earth shall be held bound in heaven, and whatever you declare loosed* on earth shall be held loosed in heaven." (Matthew 18:18) To bind or to loose is the same as to administer, to rule, to make decisions. Christ on another occasion said this, "He who hears you, hears me. And he, who rejects you, rejects me. And he who rejects me, rejects him who sent me." (Luke 10:16) Following these injunctions of our Lord, the Church from time immemorial has made laws, according to which she administers the benefits that the faithful have willingly and voluntarily donated to God's Church.

It was so from the very beginning of Christianity, from apostolic times. The goods that the faithful brought and laid at the feet of the Apostles at first were distributed and administered by the apostles themselves, and then they ordained deacons to do that. (Cf. Acts of the Apostles 6:1–6) When you go to church on Sunday, you bring with you the church collection envelope with your donation. You place it into the collection basket voluntarily. By this action you give away your property. The fruit of your labors you give away, donate to the Church as your act of thanksgiving to God for his many blessings, for your life, your wife, your children, your home, your family, your health. By this act of giving up the fruit of your labor, you acknowledge God to be your Lord and Master. From the moment you place your church collection envelope into the collection basket, it is the Church, not you, that has the right and the duty to administer those gifts you laid at the feet of the Lord. This is the law of the Church, and this is what our bishop has decided should be done in this, your parish.

I would like to be your pastor, the teacher of the law of God, your friend and your spiritual father. I would like to offer all my spiritual and physical powers for the good of your parish, your families, your children, and your elderly. I cannot do all this if you have no trust in me. If you do not trust me with your dollars, which you give to the Lord on Sunday, how will you trust my words in the pulpit or in the confessional? By this mistrust, you place your own soul in a danger of the loss of salvation. Will you believe me when in the confessional I will absolve you from your sins? Will you believe then that your sins are forgiven? You will come to me for Holy Communion. I will place into your mouth a piece of consecrated bread dipped in consecrated wine. Will you believe then that it is really and truly the Body and Blood of our Lord, God and Savior Jesus Christ?

I will agree to be your pastor only when you will convince me that you have trust in me, that I am not a thief, that I will not steal the church's money.

Then one of the committeeman said, "Father, we will permit you to sign checks with us." "No, my dear men, it is I who will permit you to sign checks with me so that you may have trust in me, that you will come to know that I will never take a single penny that does not belong to me, that once and for all you may come to know that I am not a thief, that I am a priest and a servant of Christ," was my reply.

There was silence. No one said a word, nor did I. They looked at each other and said, "Ok, Father, we agree to give over to you all of the administration of the parish, if you agree to be our pastor." I said, "Good, I accept your offer. Hand the books over to me, and go and help me take my suitcases from my car into the house." Father Kanda came to me, embraced me and congratulated me. So did Father Pylypec. I thanked God for his help and guidance.

My First Steps in the New Parish

The first two months in the parish I dedicated to acquainting myself with my parishioners. I frequently met with many of them on different occasions, visited their homes, and wanted to know their wishes and their plans concerning their parish. I took a complete census, and while doing so I got to know them much better. With every day I became more and more convinced that there was a critical need for a new church building. In no time I became an enthusiast of this idea.

On Sunday August 18, 1957, I began publishing a weekly Parish Bulletin. At first it was only a two-page sheet, but later on I increased its size and content. The Parish Bulletin with time became a communicator and a pulpit for the pastor. In the first edition of the bulletin I wrote this message:

In the past you tried to collect the necessary funds for the erection of a new church building of which you and your children would be proud. The years passed and you were not able to collect a sufficient amount of the necessary funds. Yet, I am convinced that this community of good and faithful Christians is capable of achieving this goal, provided that all of us will work together, have sufficient interest in it, and cooperate. Do not expect someone else to come to your aid. No one will come and give you hundreds of thousands of dollars, if we ourselves will not do it.

Here is my plan of action. I believe that if we put this plan into practice, we can achieve our goal. First, let each working member of this parish donate toward the Building Fund of our new church the amount he earns in the first hour of every week. Let this be your gift of love for the new house of God among us. One out of the forty hours of work weekly should not be too big of a burden for anyone. Secondly, let the unemployed members of this parish try to donate at least one dollar for this Building Fund. One dollar should be possible for anyone to donate weekly. In our weekly Parish Bulletin I will publish the donations of all who will give one dollar or more.

Until then, Sunday collections from both Divine Liturgies amounted to about $95.00 to $100.00 weekly. Usually parishioners donated only $0.25 weekly. This first Sunday when the Bulletin was published there were 36 single dollar bills in the collection. The next Sunday there were 72 bills in the collection. In the following Sundays the amount increased to 104, then to 112, 130 and more. Sunday collections increased from $100.00 to $300.00 and in a short time we achieved the sum of $400.00 plus every Sunday. From Sunday, August 18, 1957 to the end of the calendar year the balance of our treasury was $5,734.37. When at the end of the year I had a meeting with the members of the church committee and read this report to them, the president of the committee, Mr. N.N. took me aside and said, "Father, cross my heart, I will not tell this to anyone. Tell me, where did you get all this money? It is impossible that we could have collected it in our church."

In March of 1958, I encouraged the ladies of the parish to start their own fund-raising project for the new church by making "pirohies" every Friday, a sort of dumpling, very popular with our people, used on days when no meat should be eaten. The project became very popular in the town, and there were many buyers. Even elderly men would volunteer to help the ladies. In four years this project alone added $18,688.00 to the Building Fund.

A Pre-Christmas Bazaar was organized yearly in November. It lasted a whole week. Many volunteers were needed for this project. The enthusiasm was very high in the parish, and there were a sufficient number of women and men who came daily and worked very hard. Each year this project's net income amounted to at least $5,000.00.

The parish was alive, and fund-raising projects multiplied. I frequently met with the activists of the parish. They themselves brought up suggestions of how to raise more money: picnics, lotteries, the sale of Christmas cards, and school children selling candies from door to door. But one man who worked in a cigar factory suggested a most unique project. He would supply us with sufficient number of cigar boxes. Our volunteers would cut a small opening in the lid of the box, big enough for money to be inserted into the box. On top of each box we pasted a printed text that read, *"Penny per person per meal, to be put into the box by the seal, for our new church to treasure, should be a pleasure."*

My Pilgrimage to Lourdes

The year 1958 marked the centennial anniversary of the apparitions of the Most Holy Mother of God in Lourdes, France. Our bishops were planning a large pilgrimage to this miraculous place to celebrate this anniversary. Bishop Joseph Schmondiuk chaired this project, and Father Basil Sheremeta, pastor of Ss. Peter and Paul Church in Bridgeport, PA, was the bishop's assistant for this project. Someone called me and said that there was still one place open and would I like to join this pilgrimage? I decided to go. The time was short. I got an application for a US Passport, mailed it by overnight mail to our congressman in Washington, D.C., and in a day or two I had my passport. Then I mailed the needed check to Father Sheremeta, paying for the costs of the pilgrimage. This was to be my first vacation as a priest. Father Theodore Weneck, OFM, from the Sybertsville Franciscan Monastery, was to substitute for me in the parish.

About twenty priests and over one hundred lay people were in that pilgrimage from our Church in the United States. From our parish in Frackville, Mrs. Julia Melnic and her daughter Lorraine joined the pilgrimage. Approximately one half of the pilgrims departed a week earlier by boat. The other half left by chartered airplane from Philadelphia airport. I was in the second group. The airplane was old, decrepit, and dated from World War II with very narrow and uncomfortable seats. No food was served, not even water. It departed from Philadelphia after a great delay, and we had to stop twice to refuel. Several people became ill in flight.

In Paris our two groups met and continued the trip on three large buses. First we visited some noteworthy places in the city of Paris. The next day we were on our way to Lourdes, stopping in several places to see the sights. We arrived in Lourdes August 7, 1958. Many of our faithful, priests and bishops from other countries, were already there. As I arrived in front of the famous grotto, I was overwhelmed. At first I tried to take some pictures, and then to my embarrassment I noticed that people were praying, some of them were actually kneeling on the hard stones, and I a priest, was taking pictures. The first day we took part in the procession with the sick, in the candlelight procession, and in the Stations of the Cross.

Our bishops and many priests as concelebrants in front of the famous grotto celebrated our solemn Hierarchical Liturgy, where one hundred years ago the Mother of God appeared to St. Bernadette, and where many miraculous cures had taken place, and the faith of millions was revived, strengthened, and increased. I was one of those whose faith was strengthened and increased. As our buses were leaving this holy place early in the morning of August 7, 1958, I felt spiritually uplifted and my heart was full of indescribable joy. I thought in meditation that I would like someday to come back here, not with a pilgrimage, but alone or in a small group and spend time here just in prayer.

Our buses crossed high rocky alpine mountains and traveled along the northern shores of the Mediterranean Sea east to Italy. We traveled through the city of Nice, near Monaco, and stopped overnight in a hotel in Geneva. The organization of this tour was very poor. It took several hours to register 120 pilgrims for hotel rooms, and it was past midnight when I got my room. The travel agent who was hired to plan and organize this pilgrimage was not an honest man. He apparently stole a lot of money and did not pay the hotel bills as he should have done.

Next morning, we had a tour of the city of Geneva and then left, passing through the cities of Milan, Verona, and Padua, to Venice. Some of us hired a gondola and had a delightful trip through the canals of Venice to St. Mark's Cathedral. The square before the cathedral was full of pigeons, whole crowds of them. Inside the cathedral we enjoyed the beautiful architecture and the famous mosaics. On our way to Rome, we stopped at Assisi, the town where St. Francis lived. We had a tour of the city and the Cathedral of St. Francis.

In Rome we stayed in an old hotel near the famous Pantheon, not far from the Colliseum. The next day we had a tour of the city of Rome and the Vatican. Of great interest for me were the catacombs of St. Calista, the ruins of ancient Rome, the Vatican museum and our St. Josaphat Seminary on the Gianicolo hill. Wednesday, August 13, 1958, our buses took us to the special sight Castel Gandolfo, the summer residence of the popes. The square before the papal palace was filled with pilgrims from all over the world. At a certain moment a window was opened and Pope Pius XII appeared. He greeted the pilgrims, gave a very brief talk, then gave his blessing. I was deeply impressed with the sight of this stately, dignified, and saintly person. This was the first time I ever saw a pope. Less than two months later he died on October 9, 1958.

My Dreams Are Fulfilled

Having returned back home, the first thing I did was visit the sick. There was an old woman, Mrs. N.N. who had gangrene on the large toe of one of her feet. Before I left on the pilgrimage, she was in a hospital. Since she refused to have her toe amputated, they released her. As I entered the house, her doctor was visiting her. I gave her a medal and a little bottle of the Lourdes holy water. The doctor poured some of the water on the surgical dressing and wrapped the toe with it. In a day or two, I was told, the toe just fell off and there was no sign of gangrene.

When my films were developed, I announced that if anyone was interested in the Lourdes pilgrimage, I would show the pictures and share with them my impressions from the trip. The questions asked of me gave me an opportunity to relate to them the story of St. Bernadette, the appearances of the Most Holy Mother of God, and following events.

Life in the parish was very active and enthusiastic. My parishioners were now convinced that their dream of a new church was coming slowly to be fulfilled. By the end of the 1958 there was $55,000.00 in the church treasury. At the annual meeting, the parishioners themselves suggested that each family in the parish be assessed the sum of $250.00 for the building fund of the new church. This assessment added to the building fund in 1959 the sum $24,130.00. The success in the increase of the building fund gave the parishioners and me hope that we should begin our first steps toward the achievement of our goal.

After some inquiry, I made an appointment with an architect, Mr. Freeman, from Reading, Pa. In the past he had designed several of our churches. He came to Frackville on almost a weekly basis and listened to the building committee's and my suggestions and wishes. Every time he came back he brought new sketches or ideas incorporating our wishes. On his suggestion we agreed to a church building without a basement. He said that the basement, limited the size of the church building, would cost so much that for this same money we could build a hall as a separate building larger than the church itself.

When all of us agreed as to the shape, size, and the architecture of the design, I mailed the preliminary designs to the Chancery, asking for approval. I believe that Archbishop Bohachevsky was not too happy with my request, incredulous that such great success was possible in Frackville in such a short time. I was asked to come to an administrative board meeting in the Chancery and explain my proposal. I did as he wished and found that the Archbishop was undecided whether I should get this permission. Bishop Schmondiuk came to my aid, when he said, "He collected the money, and if by the time construction will commence he will have more than one-half of the needed funds, I would grant him the permission to proceed with the final plans. When these are ready, he should ask for approval of the contract. Then we can say yes or no." There were some minor suggestions from the board members as to the specifics of the design. I thanked them and promised to take their suggestions into consideration. The architect made the necessary changes in the preliminary plans, and I mailed them back to the Chancery. The reply came dated February 19, 1959, prot. #2800/58/Ch., with the approval of the preliminary designs and the permission to proceed with final plans and the specifications.

It was not only Archbishop Bohachevsky who had a very low opinion of St. Michael's parish in Frackville, but my brother priests in the deanery as well. We had very close fraternal and friendly relationships. Especially in the wintertime, we would be invited to a different rectory once a week to play an innocent card game, talk, and joke among ourselves. On one such occasion the conversation turned to the possible construction of a new church in Frackville. They could not believe that I would venture into such a project especially in such a poor parish, like St. Michael's in their eyes. I assured them that not only would we build a new church but also another building, a parish auditorium. At that Father Stephen Bachynsky from St. Clair burst out laughing, and asked, are you joking?

I was young and only five years in the priesthood. When considering how well everything was going with all of my pastoral work and with the dreams of all the parishioners as well as mine for a new church, I realized that all this success was not due to my talents or capabilities. Here I could see very clearly that the hand of God was guiding everything, and blessing this parish and me.

When final plans and specifications were ready, and the ten contractors presented their bids, the building committee and I, in the presence of the architect, selected the contractor, Whalen Brothers from Pottsville, PA. Construction cost for the church building and the separate hall amounted to $135,000.00. I sent the plans and specifications to the Chancery for final approval. I stated the amount of the funds that we had available for construction, and asked permission to take a loan from the Providence Association of Ukrainian Catholics in the sum of $35,000.00. Permission was received promptly.

From this moment on everything progressed well. On Sunday, June 28,1959, a blessing and breaking of the ground for the new church took place. One could read real joy and happiness on the faces of the parishioners. The dreams of many years were being fulfilled. The next day the contractors moved in with their equipment. The engineers began the survey of the plot, and marked the lines of the building with wooden stakes and lines of cord between them. Then the excavation began. The work was progressing very satisfactorily. On the sidewalk there were always some people, mainly parishioners, watching the progress with great interest.

In April of 1960 the construction of the new church building was completed. The auditorium was to be a building on the site of the old church. It was to be much larger than the old church. This is why the contractor began his work in the back and on the sides of the old church, laying foundations and raising walls. Only the front of the old church was not touched so that the faithful could use it. We were able to get pews for the new church already, some stained glass windows, and the new iconostas were in the making.

Holy Name Society members carry the tabernacle from the old to the new St. Michael's church, Frackville, Pa., April 10, 1960.

It was Palm Sunday, April 10, 1960, when Archbishop Constantine Bohachevsky had his pastoral visitation in the nearby town of Mahanoy City, and in the afternoon at 3:00 P.M. came to Frackville. He blessed the cornerstone of the new church, into which was placed a commemorative document with a short history of the parish, and a list of all living parishioners who became founders and benefactors of this new house of God. After this ceremony, all the faithful, the clergy and the Archbishop went in procession to the old church. The Archbishop presided at a Moleben Service in order to give thanks to God for all the graces and blessings of God that were bestowed upon the members of the parish in this old house of God. After the reading of the Gospel, Msgr. Constantine Berdar, local Dean, delivered a homily in which he eloquently expressed gratitude to God for the living and the deceased members of this family of God's children, for the river of graces that flowed throughout the past years upon the faithful in the daily Divine Liturgies, and all the sacraments administered here—Baptisms, Chrismation, First Holy Communions, weddings, as well as funerals and anniversaries. The faithful and even some of the priests were moved emotionally by the words of the preacher and wiped tears from their eyes.

At the conclusion of the Moleben service, a solemn procession was formed in order to transfer from the old church to the new some of the liturgical items, and especially the Most Blessed Sacrament. The most distinguished senior in the parish, Mr. Andrew Koropchak, who served as a sacristan, carried the Gospel Book, the Holy Name Society men carried the antimension, the candlesticks, the tabernacle and the altar itself. At the very end the Blessed Eucharist was to be carried by the Archbishop, but he told me that I should do it. With fear of God and with faith I carried my Lord and God. This procession was very moving and emotional for me. It marked the summit of the years of prayers, planning, and work. It was the crowning point of all the efforts, work, struggle, and generosity of most of the parishioners. As the procession was making its way out of the old church and proceeded into the new one, for some reason it reminded me of the procession of Israelites from Egypt into their Promised Land.

The procession left the old church, but some of the faithful remained behind. Many older women stayed there, saying goodbye to the old church by kissing the icons of the old iconostas, and remained there crying. As a point of interest, the deacon doors and the royal doors of this iconostas originally belonged to St. George's, the first church in Minersville, that stood way up on top of a steep hill. It was so high that a casket could not be carried into the church; it had to be pulled up by ropes. When the new St. Nicholas Church was built in 1930s these doors were donated to St. Michael's church in Frackville. Now as we moved into our new church, I donated this old iconostas to our church in Manville, N.J.

As the procession entered the new church, the Holy Name Society men placed the altar in the center of the sanctuary, covered it with altar covers, placed the tabernacle on it, the candlesticks, the antimension with the holy relics of a martyr under the top altar cover, and the Holy Gospel Book in the center. Afterward we had a service called the Supplication. The kivot with the Blessed Eucharist was placed on the altar, and then everyone knelt down and we prayed to our Eucharistic Lord to bless this parish as it entered the new house of God, bless the founders and benefactors, the donors and builders. At the end there was a solemn blessing Benediction of the faithful with the Blessed Eucharist. As I turned around to face the congregation, I was surprised to see the 300 seating capacity of the new church was almost full. There were few empty seats. Not only the faithful were moved to tears of joy, but also the Archbishop was visibly moved to see this great success which at first he could not believe possible.

To complete this project, a lot of work and planning had yet to be done. Over the main entrance into the church a beautiful mosaic was fashioned, portraying the Oranta, the Most Holy Mother of God with hands raised in prayer. A marble altar with bronze baldachin, as well as the small altars on each side of the sanctuary were built. A brass tabernacle was made especially for this church, with the Eucharistic host designed on its doors. Two large triple candlesticks, matching the tabernacle were likewise made. The famous iconographer, Sviatoslav Hordynsky, designed a new iconostas and had it made by a skilled wood craftsman in New York. He himself painted all the icons and designed the stained glass windows in the sanctuary and on the facade of the church.

When the auditorium was completed, it had to be properly furnished. First the kitchen was equipped with all modern equipment, and the stage was outfitted with a curtain and backdrops. The hall received an elegant wooden parquet floor. The auditorium received a folding partition to make two classrooms or two meeting rooms. New tables and chairs were purchased. The bar and the cloakrooms were also equipped.

Two parishioners, John Badida and Nick Shabowsky, were skilled carpenters and homebuilders. They helped me a lot whenever I needed something done. They closed in half of the porch in front of the rectory to make a small parish office. On the left side of the rectory, they constructed a spacious garage with a door into the office.

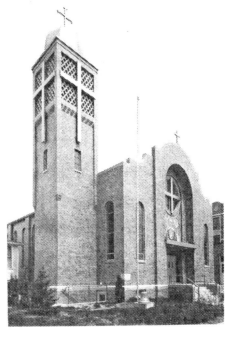

The new St. Michael's Church, Frackville, Pa.

Even with all the expenditures to equip the new church and auditorium, we still had enough money to meet the monthly payments on our mortgage to the Providence Association. In fact, in 1961 I was making large payments on the principal to save on the interest. Before I was transferred, I had enough money in the treasury to liquidate the mortgage, but did not want to leave my successor without any money in the treasury.

The Archbishop was evidently very impressed with the progress at St. Michael's in Frackville. Every time he had to visit our deanery, I received a note in the mail, "Please pick me up at the railroad station in Pottsville at such and such a time, and take me to this or that parish. After the celebration, take me back to the station." On one occasion in October of 1960 there was a fiftieth parish anniversary celebration in Hazleton, Pa. I picked the Archbishop up and started to drive him to the destination. As we were going through wooden terrain between Shenandoah and Hazleton and were about two hours early, he asked me to pull off to the side and stop for he wanted to talk to me. He said that he was looking a for a good candidate to run in the elections for the position of the President of the Providence Association of Ukrainian Catholics in the United States. Who do I think would be a good candidate, he asked? I suggested a few priests, but none of them was suitable in his judgment. Then he said, "How about you? I think you would make a good candidate. You were able to manage well the church committee and the parishioners in Frackville, so you will be able to manage the "pany" (the intelligentsia) in the Providence Association."

I had no love for a job of this kind and tried very hard to convince the Archbishop that I was not the man for this position. First of all I was too young and they would not respect me. All these top men in the Providence Association are deeply involved in Ukrainian political partisanship. I hate politics and especially the divisive partisanship among Ukrainian politicians. Providence is a fraternal insurance company. I have neither knowledge nor any experience in dealing with this kind of business. So, I pleaded with the Archbishop not to consider my candidacy for this position. After I took the Archbishop back to the railroad station from

Hazleton, and went home, I felt very guilty to have said "no" to my Archbishop. After some time, I sat down and wrote a letter to him, apologizing for my behavior and stating that, even though I am convinced that I am not a good candidate for the position he proposed to me, I will, if he still wants me, accept the candidacy. He replied that by that time he already asked another priest who had accepted the offer.

By December of 1960 my parishioners and I were ready to start preparations for a solemn consecration and dedication of our new church and the blessing of our new auditorium. We selected the 4th of July 1961 as the best day, when all are free from work and the priest is free as well. I wrote a letter to the Archbishop and asked him to come to Frackville July 4, 1961, and do us the honor of consecrating our new church. The reply was positive and he marked the date in his calendar and stated with God's help he intended to be with us. Apparently it was not the will of God for him to rejoice with us on July 4, 1961, because God called him home for his eternal reward January 6, 1961. Bishop Joseph Schmondiuk, temporary administrator of the Archeparchy, was the one who came to Frackville July 4, 1961, and celebrated with us the solemn consecration and dedication of our new church and the auditorium. Seventy priests attended this festive and beautiful day of St. Michael's in Frackville.

Back to Philadelphia

After the death of Archbishop Bohachevsky, the Holy Father appointed Bishop Ambrose Senyshyn, OSBM of Stamford, Connecticut on August 14, 1961, as the new Archbishop of Philadelphia for Ukrainians and Metropolitan of our Church in the United States. At the same time, Bishop Joseph Schmondiuk, auxiliary in Philadelphia, was appointed bishop of the Eparchy of Stamford. Even before the installation of both of the new bishops, I was transferred from St. Michael's in Frackville to St. Nicholas in Philadelphia as a parochial vicar to Bishop Schmondiuk. The day was October 4, 1961, when I had to say goodbye to my beloved parish, my dear parishioners, whom I got to know and love, and especially to the new church and the auditorium. It was a heart-breaking move for me. But, after long prayer in the sanctuary before the Holy Eucharist, I was lifted up spiritually, and thanked God for all the blessings and graces he had poured out on me and my parishioners here at St. Michael's during the last four years and three months of my stay in this parish. As I was driving away from Frackville, I stopped at the hospital in Pottsville and then at the nursing home in Schuylkill Haven to say goodbye to the sick of St. Michael's parish whom I used to visit regularly.

St. Nicholas parish in Philadelphia was at that time a thriving parish. Bishop Schmondiuk just completed the construction of a new school building and engaged the Basilian Sisters to teach in it. There were over seven hundred families in the parish. Besides me, there was also Father Julian Slonsky, as a parochial vicar. He was an elderly gentleman who did not live in the rectory, but in his private home. In the parish were a lot of the new immigrants, and among them an unusually large number of professionals. The old church was very small and could hardly contain the large congregation so we celebrated four or five Liturgies on Sundays. The rectory was a three story high row house. Bishop Schmondiuk was an energetic man, hard working and industrious. He would not tolerate a woman in the house, so we had no housekeeper. An elderly man would bring prepared food for us into the rectory. Frequently, the bishop would go out to a restaurant to eat and take me with him.

The installation of the new Metropolitan-Archbishop was held December 11, 1961. I could not attend it because someone had to stay home and attend to the needs of the parish and the school. Bishop Schmondiuk was planning to move to his new assignment in Stamford on the 19th of December 1961. Yet, when he came back from the installation of the Archbishop, he changed his plans and began packing his belongings. Msgr. Stephen Knapp, his personal friend, was with him and helped him. I helped carry the packages of books and suitcases into his car. He left the same day.

In the evening of the day after he left I received a delegation of parishioners in the rectory, about eleven persons, with a list of demands. A lady, N.N., was in charge of the delegation. When I read the list of demands, I asked them why didn't they come here with this list yesterday when the pastor, Bishop Schmondiuk, was here? Do you want me, an assistant pastor, to correct a bishop? No new pastor was assigned yet. I am only a parochial vicar and am awaiting instructions from the new Archbishop. I have no authority to deal with your demands. But they would not give up and claimed that I most certainly will get the assignment. Well, I said when I do get the assignment as your pastor, then come to me and I will deal with your demands. These people were most difficult. Their demands for the most part dealt with the school, the Sisters, and the teachers, who did not use enough of the Ukrainian language in teaching their children.

The new Archbishop might have learned of the demands that some of the parishioners presented to me and, therefore, did not assign me as administrator or pastor. I was flabbergasted and could not understand why I had to be subjected to such an uncanonical status, not having the necessary faculties to administer the parish, yet I just had to act as an administrator. I was patiently waiting for the Archbishop's decision, which came in March of 1962. I was assigned to administer Assumption Parish in Perth Amboy, New Jersey. It was March 22, 1962 when I left St. Nicholas parish in Philadelphia, and drove to Perth Amboy for the first time. This was the parish where Msgr. Jaroslav Gabro had been pastor for the last eleven years. He was named the first bishop of the St. Nicholas Eparchy in Chicago, and in the interim Msgr. Michael Fedorowich was his assistant just as I was for Bishop Schmondiuk.

Perth Amboy, New Jersey

ssumption parish in Perth Amboy, N.J. at that time had nearly 500 households. The first Ukrainian immigrants came to Perth Amboy in the 1880's. At first they attended St. Stephen's Latin Rite Polish church, and around 1892, together with their brothers from the Carpatho Ukraine, built St. John the Baptist Church. However, unity and peace among these two groups of parishioners did not last long. Outside influences, especially political intrigues from abroad caused a split among the parishioners. At their annual parish meeting in 1908, the Ukrainians were asked to leave; they were not wanted there.

The Ukrainian parishioners were able to buy a small church with a rectory on Wayne Street from the Polish National congregation. The Polish National congregation converted and rejoined St. Stephen's parish. In the 1940s the pastor was able to buy a large plot of ground on the corner of Meredith Street and Alta Vista Place. The pastor at that time, Rev. Jaroslav Gabro, was able to construct a new church and a rectory on the new parish grounds. The construction of a spacious parish school building began in 1961. On my arrival, the school building was completed on the outside, as well as the auditorium and the three classrooms on the first floor. The second floor was not yet finished.

A church committee ruled the parish with its president John Swalick, who was at the same time chief of police of the city. John was very helpful to Msgr. Gabro and kept the parishioners in line. However, one month after my arrival in Perth Amboy, John Swalick died suddenly of a heart attack. Bishop Gabro came back from Chicago for his friend's funeral.

In July of 1962 the church committee called a general parish meeting for the election of a new president. The church hall was filled with parishioners. By that time I made enough friends among the parishioners to be able to consult with them confidentially. They urged me to run for the presidency of the parish. When at the meeting I announced my candidacy, the younger parishioners supported me, while the older ones opposed me. When the discussion turned into loud and angry shouting, I got up and asked to speak.

From what I have heard here so far, I come to the conclusion that many of you do not trust me with the administration of the church money and property. If you would like to have an outside opinion of my administrative skills, why don't you call on someone in my former parish, in Frackville, Pa? And if that is not satisfactory to you then, do not elect me your parish president. But mind you, then I will know that I am not worthy of your trust and will be forced to act accordingly.

I will do my best to teach you and your children the Gospel Truths. I will with love serve your spiritual needs, visit the sick, serve all the church services regularly, hear your confessions, marry your young couples, and bury the dead. But I will absolutely refuse to have anything to do with the finances of this parish. Let the president you elect take care of all the financial matters of the parish. Do not ring my doorbell or come to me with your money. My hand will not touch your money. Ask your newly elected president to come to the rectory and take all the architectural school plans, since the construction is not completed. It will be his duty to see to it that it is completed. I will have nothing to do with the finances of this parish, because by your vote you will have given me proof that I am not to be trusted. I will pray that God would bless you and your new president. God love you.

With that I left the meeting hall and went to the rectory. It was less that a half-hour later that two men came to my door, rang the doorbell and asked me to come back to the meeting hall, since I had been elected president of the parish.

Toward the end of this same year, Archbishop Senyshyn informed the pastors that he had procured one insurance policy for all the church properties in the Archeparchy. He asked the pastors to cancel as of the 1st day of January 1963 any property insurance policy they had, since they will be covered by the diocesan insurance policy. Now the Perth Amboy parish property was not recorded in the Diocesan Corporation, but rather with the church committee. The insurance agent N.N., was vice-president of the parish committee. At that time we had 15 individual property insurance policies to cover all the properties the parish owned. As soon as I announced the decision of the Archbishop, the insurance agent called a secret meeting of the church committee without informing me about it. They hired a lawyer, our own parishioner N.N., and sent a letter to the Archbishop, informing him that he had no right to insure the parish properties since they do not legally belong to the Archdiocese. He may as well insure the Brooklyn Bridge.

The Archbishop was outraged. He called me and asked me to come to Philadelphia to see him. How dare they write such an arrogant letter to me, he told me. Then he asked: "Can you change the parish property incorporation from the church committee to the Archdiocesan Corporation?" I said that I would give it a try if he gives me his support in case trouble starts in the parish. He said he would support me all the way.

When I returned home, I called some of my trusted parishioners, explained to them the situation, and consulted with them.

They all agreed that our church properties should be legally rein-corporated under the diocesan corporation so that no one ever could alienate any part of it without the Archbishop's permission. The next thing I did was hire a lawyer and asked him to proceed with the case.

At the first meeting of the church trustees with the lawyer held in the church hall on March 17, 1963, a resolution had been taken with accordance of the New Jersey State law to reincorporate the legal holdings of the of the Ukrainian Catholic Church of the Assumption in Perth Amboy. According to the New Jersey law the Archbishop would then be the president of our church corporation, his vicar general or the chancellor would be the vice-president, the pastor—secretary-treasurer, and these three would elect two lay trustees.

This resolution of the trustees according to the demand of the State Law had to be published in the church bulletin and posted on the church doors for three consecutive Sundays. Following the three Sundays, a general church meeting had to be called, and a vote of the majority of the members of the parish had to decide on the trustees' resolution, the reincorporating of the church properties.

The meeting of the parishioners was called for Sunday, April 29, 1963 after the 11:30 A.M. Liturgy. I prayed hard, imploring the Lord to help me keep peace and harmony in the parish, to avoid divisions and dissatisfaction among the parishioners. And God was with me. In the Church Bulletin for Apr. 29, 1963, I published an article in which I explained the dangers entailed in holding the parish properties in the present incorporation:

> Our present corporation . . . means that all our church proper-ties, theoretically speaking, could be disposed without the per-mission of our Archbishop. This could prove to be very dangerous. We do not know the future, but we know the past. And the past teaches us a very important lesson. Some day some-one might come into our midst that could mislead enough pa-rishioners, create disorder or even turn this church, rectory,

school, and cemetery into something other than what you and I believe. And our Archbishop could not help us then because under the Present Corporation he has no legal right to our church property. But someone might say: 'This will never happen!' Under our present setup this is quite possible for the same has happened before to other parishes, where those good people who valued their Catholic faith more than anything else were forced to leave their church, which they helped to build, and to buy new land and build a new church.

Just recently our Archbishop placed all our churches and their properties under one insurance policy and thus negotiated a much better insurance coverage for a much smaller annual premium. In our parish alone the savings on the new diocesan insurance would amount almost to one thousand dollars annually. Yet because of our present corporation this new diocesan insurance is not valid for our parish, and we cannot take advantage of the annual saving.

Should we sign our parish properties over to the Archbishop? No! Our Archbishop said that he does not want us to do that. He wants no part of our parish properties. All that our Archbishop wants is what the Holy Father commands all Catholics to do, namely, that we give our Archbishop a voice in the administration of our parish properties . . .

The meeting was calm. There were neither harsh arguments nor much discussion. I explained to the people the benefits of the new church property insurance coverage. While insuring all of our parishes on one policy, the Archdiocese was able to secure the best possible benefits. All our church buildings have replaceable value coverage, i.e., should a building burn down, the insurance company will give us the amount of money needed to replace the building. One individual parish could never afford such coverage. It would be out of reach for a parish. After this explanation a vote was taken and an absolute majority voted for the reincorporation. There were no ill effects in the parish after the meeting. Peace and harmony prevailed.

The Parochial School

I had three classrooms ready for the opening of the school in the fall of 1962 with the first two grades. Bishop Gabro told me that the Basilian Sisters promised him to supply their sisters to staff his school. When I wrote to them, quoting Bishops Gabro, they replied that they were not able to keep their promise due to the shortage of vocations. Then I wrote to Sister Servants in Sloatsburg, N.Y. The reply was the same. The only religious community left were the Missionary Sisters of the Mother of God in Stamford, Connecticut, who just recently opened another house in Philadelphia. In both places they conducted a nursery-daycare center. In my letter to their general superior, Mother Andrea Spikula, I wrote that they should consider my offer for the good of their community. In order to be able to get some vocations, they should be visible in our parishes, work with our people and our youth. I am sure that they consulted their founder, Archbishop Ambrose Senyshyn, OSBM, and the reply was positive. I would get two sisters but only in September of 1963.

In the meantime I had to find a contractor to finish the second floor of the school, i.e., six classrooms, principal's office, two rooms for the faculty kitchenette and lounge, office of the school nurse, the library and the music room. While doing all this, I had to find enough money to meet monthly mortgage payments that Bishop Gabro took from the Providence Association for the construction of the school building in the amount of $150,000.00.

In front of the school building a huge pile of dirt remained from the excavation for the school building foundation. The original contractor just left it there. I was able to find a local contractor who agreed to haul all this dirt to our cemetery, level it there and landscape it. A total of 92 truckloads of dirt were hauled to the cemetery, and the vanishing dirt pile was leveled and a school playground built in its place.

Where there is a will, there is a way, and there is God to come to your aid. One Sunday after the Liturgies I met a very skilled carpenter and a homebuilder by the name of Walter Krus, our own parishioner. He was out of work at that time. I asked him to step into my office. We talked of the needed work to be done on the second floor of the school building. After we went to the school and actually saw the second floor, he agreed to do the job by himself while the parish agreed to pay for his labor and material. He did not have to hurry since the school would start in the following year, i.e., in September of 1963 with only two grades, and then we would add one grade a year. The second floor classrooms would be needed in September of 1966. Walter was an excellent craftsman and did the job solidly as though he was working for himself. He, wife Mary, and their four children are my friends to this very day.

Before school started in 1963, I had to make some arrangements for the Missionary Sisters' living quarters. There was no apartment for rent in the neighborhood that would fit their needs, so I decided that both I and my associate, Father Walter Wysochansky, would move into the school building temporarily, and give the rectory to the Sisters as their convent. Walter Krus divided the large library room in the school building into two rooms, one for a bedroom and the other for a living room. There was a rest room there already and he just put in a shower stall. This would be my apartment for the next three-and-a-half years. Father Wysochansky occupied the two rooms designated for the faculty's facilities. Parish offices would be located in the two large rooms right over the main entrance to the school auditorium, designated as the music rooms. In the rectory were two small office rooms. I had Walter Krus remove the partition and make a chapel for the Sisters. Later on, we had a small iconostas built for that chapel.

On the corner of our property at Alta Vista Place and Padarewski Avenue there was a fenced-in brick shed containing pressure pumps for the city gas company. We needed this corner to have a place where our new rectory could be built. Thus we would own one complete city block. I went to the nearby city of Woodridge to the main offices of the gas company and asked to see the president. I presented to him our need for that corner property and offered to pay for it. He said he had no other place to put the pressure pumps. I told him the great city of New York has their gas pressure pumps under ground. Why can you not locate your facility under the sidewalk with smaller and more efficient pumps? He agreed to it, had his lawyer prepare the necessary papers, and the church was able to get the needed property.

I then contacted Mr. Freeman, the architect from Reading, PA. He agreed to visit me. After a short discussion on the needs of a parish rectory for at least two priests, a guest room and a housekeeper's apartment, he went home. After some weeks he came back with ready preliminary sketches. I called some members of the church committee as well as some of the Holy Name Society to review the sketches and give me their opinion. Their input was helpful. One man suggested that a small elevator be installed for elderly priests and for hauling heavy things to the second floor. After these changes were incorporated into the preliminary plans, I sent them to the Chancery for approval. A positive reply came within a week. After the finished plans and the specifications were ready, they were given out to contractors for bids. Further process went without a hitch.

As the construction of the new rectory commenced, I hired two brothers, student engineers of landscaping, who were home from school for summer vacation, to design a landscaping plan for the whole block of our property. They did a magnificent job. The two brothers suggested that we install an underground water sprinkling system to keep not only the grass but also all the shrubs alive. We gave the plans to several landscaping firms for bids. Before the landscaping job began, we inquired whether it would be feasible to have our own water well drilled to be used for the sprinkling system. No one could give us an exact reply, because no one knew for sure whether there was sufficient water here at reasonable depth. The firm we asked to drill near the convent's garage, asked the State of New Jersey for their opinion and a permit. The whole project became a failure, for the drilling hit solid rock, the same one upon which Manhattan is built, and after six hundred feet of drilling very little water was found. They capped the pipes and abandoned the project. We got water from the city for our sprinkling system.

I invited Sviatoslav Hordynsky, the iconographer, to design for us a small shrine to be erected on an elevated spot between the church and the new rectory. I selected the icon of the Most Holy Mother of God Oranta. He designed the icon in a mosaic as well as the limestone shrine itself. Before the landscaping began, the shrine was up and was included in the landscaping plans.

When in early 1967 the rectory and the landscaping were completed, I invited the Archbishop to bless and dedicate the new rectory and the shrine. The rite of the solemn blessing took place on Sunday, April 16, 1967, after which there was an open house. Many parishioners took the occasion to go through the whole rectory, and they were pleased with what they saw.

The Life in the Parish

The Perth Amboy parish was active and bursting with life. With the opening of the school, interest in the life of the parish increased. Sisters Josepha Kruchinsky and Yosaphata Litvenczuk organized the school parents into a PTA. They held regular monthly meetings and ran various fund raising activities. There was an active Holy Name Society in the parish as well as the Sisterhood of St. Ann, the junior and the senior Sodalities, and the Altar Boys Association. To pay the school bills, fundraising activities had to be increased. We organized the game of Bingo, licensed by the State of New Jersey, running it twice a week. Here the men of the Holy Name Society and the school PTA gave us a helping hand on the floor of the bingo hall and in the kitchen.

While in Perth Amboy for over nineteen years, I kept my friendships alive with some of our priests. To the circle of my friends belonged first of all the two native sons of the parish, Msgr. Leon Mosko, stationed permanently at St. Basil's College in Stamford, CT, and Father Matthew Berko. They were always invited to come back home and participate in any parish festivities, and they never refused an invitation. Msgr. Leon Mosko frequently came home to visit his aging mother and his brother John, his wife Helen, and their children, who lived near the church. Father Leon's mother was the only parishioner who faithfully attended the daily Divine Liturgy. I had a great regard for her, for in her I saw a walking saint. Her presence in the church for the morning Liturgy always up-lifted me and gave me spiritual support and encouragement.

To the circle of my priestly friends belonged Msgr. Leo Adamiak from Youngstown, Ohio, Msgr. Peter Fedorchuck and Msgr. Emil Manastersky, both from St. Basil's College in Stamford. We formed a golfing foursome. In all the years in Perth Amboy, and even later on when I moved back to Philadelphia, we kept our friendship going by vacationing together a week or two in wintertime and also at least one week in the summer time. I remember well one such vacation in February of 1963. We drove in my car to Fort Lauderdale in Florida, lived in a motel and played golf daily. One morning we picked up a newspaper and a large headline read—Ukrainian Catholic Metropolitan Archbishop Josyf Slipyj was re-leased from his eighteen-year long imprisonment in the Siberian gulags, arrived in Rome, and was embraced by Pope John XXIII. His release was attributed to the efforts of the Pope through Presi-dent John F. Kennedy.

I took another memorable vacation in July of 1974 with my friend Peter Fedorchuck. He made all the arrangements with a travel agency. We flew to Scotland, rented a car, drove on the wrong side of the road all the time and golfed every day at a different golf course. We started our golf tour with the famous St. Andrew's course and played it twice.

The travel agency made all the reservations for us. With a good road map in our hands, we drove every day to a different golf course, took some clubs out of our golf bags so they would not be too heavy, carried them ourselves, played eighteen holes in the morn-ing, had our lunch, and played another eighteen in the afternoon. The last day of our vacation in Scotland, we did not golf but took a trip north to the famous Loch Ness Lake, where the fabled mon-ster was supposed to be in the water. This was the best of my golf-ing vacations.

Our foursome endured for many years. We enjoyed each other's company. Msgr. Fedorchuck and Msgr. Manastersky would come one week to Perth Amboy and we would play on the local golf course, and another week I would drive to Stamford and play there. It was in June of 1974 when Peter Fedorchuck came to Perth Amboy and we played. I had a hole-in-one on the eleventh 183-yard hole.

Msgr. Fedorchuck's brother Joseph with his wife and children, as well as his two sisters, Theresa and Anne Polit and their son Thomas, became my friends and I was frequently invited to their home or for meals after our golf game. But this was not to last. The good Lord called home first Msgr. Emil Manastersky, October 12, 1995, and just a few months later, Msgr. Peter Fedorchuck April 27, 1996. It was with a deep feeling of sorrow and with a pain of loss that I celebrated their funeral Liturgies.

My Unforgettable Visit to the Holy Land

At the suggestion of my friend and vacationing companion of many years, Msgr. Leo Adamiak of Youngstown, Ohio, I gladly agreed to go with him on a tour to the Holy Land, which took place October 10–20, 1977. The tour was organized by Rev. Clement E. Humbard of Youngstown, Ohio, a Protestant minister. The group consisted of about 37 persons. Besides the two of us in the group were also Mr. & Mrs. Joseph and Helen Zarconi, Mrs. Mildred Sawczak, Mrs. Jenet Perko, all of Holy Trinity Ukrainian Catholic Church, Youngstown, Ohio.

The Group met in Youngstown. They departed to the Pittsburgh Airport. From there they took the 6:45 P.M. flight to JFK Airport in New York. It was Monday, October 10, 1977. I joined the group at the JFK Airport. We checked in as a group and boarded the Jordanian ALIA flight for Amman, departing at 10:00 P.M. The flight was uneventful and we arrived the next day, Tuesday, October 11, 1977 at 2:30 P.M. in Amman, Jordan. A bus took us to the Grand Palace Hotel, University Avenue, Amman. The city of Amman is the ancient Philadelphia, capital of the desert kingdom of Ammon in the Old Testament times, known as the Decapolis (ten cities) with her mythical, biblical, and archeological sights. The rest of the day was without a planned program so that we were able to rest well after a long flight.

The following day, Wednesday, October 12, 1977, a bus took us on a trip to the fabulous Mount Nebo, Petra, and the famous Rose City, which amazed all of us. Our day commenced with a brief visit to Madaba, originally a Moabite town and of special interest for its mosaic of the country, including Jerusalem, as it was in the 6th century A.D. Then we visited Mount Nebo a short distance away. It is a traditional site from where Moses saw the Promised Land and where he died (*Deuteronomy 32:49; 34:1*). Our route continued over a modern highway built over "Kings Highway" of the time of Moses. Our travel guide explained that in this area Esau, the eldest son of Isaac and Rebekah and twin brother of Jacob, wandered. He said that the Moslems accept "Ain Mussa" as the place where Moses struck the rock and water came forth. Westward from there, toward the Dead Sea, he pointed out, is Machaerus, where the head of St. John the Baptist was presented to Salome. The travel guide knew all this historical information as though he was reading it from a book. Petra, he said, is partly carved out of the multi-colored sandstone cliffs and partly freestanding in the classical manner. As ruins today, they form a sight of unforgettable splendor. Here are the Street of Columns, the Triple Gate, Sela mountain-fortress of Edom, High Palace, a primitive Nabatean palace, and other ornate tombs and temples. Petra could easily be the eighth Wonder of the World.

On Thursday, October 13, 1977, we left the hotel in Amman and boarded our bus. On our way to Jerusalem the trip took us on a fascinating drive through the Jordan Valley to Qumran Caves, and the Dead Sea—1,292 feet below sea level—the lowest point on earth, explained our travel guide. Other biblical sites we were able to see included the Mount of Temptation and the city of Jericho. We stopped on a road at a sycamore tree. A legend has it, said the travel guide, that it was the tree Zacchaeus climbed to see Jesus. Here we started a practice of reading from the Bible the section pertaining to the place we were visiting. After the reading, one of the preachers would make a brief commentary. It was my turn to read the passage and to give a commentary. This practice was very good and made the trip much more memorable.

Next, our bus took us on a steadily climbing road for some twenty miles on our way to Jerusalem. All around us was the Judean Desert. We stopped for a while at the Good Samaritan Inn. Here we read from the Bible the parable of the Good Samaritan. Again we stopped in Bethany, the town associated with the two sisters Mary and Martha and their brother Lazarus, the friends of Jesus. Here we read from the Bible about Jesus raising Lazarus from the dead. I was amazed how very familiar with the New Testament was our Jewish travel guide.

On the Mount of Olives we saw a small round chapel in which was a footprint in a stone. Tradition has it, explained out travel guide, that this was the place from which Jesus ascended into heaven. In Bethlehem we saw the Church of the Nativity of Christ, inside of which is the Grotto of Christ's birth. This was the place where prayer came easily. My heart was filled with great joy to be able kneel where the shepherds knelt, where Mary and Joseph adored the Divine Infant. To enter the Grotto we had to pass an Orthodox priest who was collecting alms. Each of us gave him something. There we were able to see the Tomb of St. Jerome and the Christmas Bell. From there we motored past the Shepherd's Field and the Caves, by the Herodion to Rachel's Tomb. From there we traveled through the modern section of Jerusalem to our hotel, National Palace on Zahara Street.

Friday, October 14, 1977, we started with morning worship at the Garden Tomb and Calvary. The Protestants regard the Garden Tomb as the actual Tomb of Christ, without denying that the one in the Church of the Holy Sepulcher might be the real one. Objective archaeologists have discovered that the Garden Tomb dates back to the 5th century B.C. There is a tomb carved out of a stone wall in that Garden. There is an opening to the tomb. Inside is a flat bench to receive the body. A large round stone was on a side, which could be rolled over the entrance of the tomb. The field in front of the tomb with some rows of benches is used for their worship. Msgr. Leo Adamiak and I sat on a side, not participating in their worship service.

From there we went to the old Walled City of Jerusalem. First we visited the Pater Noster Church. Helena, the mother of the emperor Constantine, had this church built beside the cave in which is it believed Jesus spoke to his disciples and where He taught them the Lord's Prayer. The Persians destroyed this church in 614, but the Crusaders constructed an oratory on its ruins in 1106. In front of the church on the columns of a covered passageway are the attractive tiled panels on which the Lord's Prayer is inscribed in sixty languages. We found one in the Church Slavonic language.

Next we visited the Garden of Gethsemane, where our Lord went with His disciples after the Last Supper, where He prayed: *"My Father, if it is possible, let this cup pass me by. Still, let it be as you would have it, not as I" (Matthew 26:39)*. This is the place where Judas betrayed Christ with a kiss, and where Jesus was arrested. They say that the olive trees live a very long time. We were told that some of the old trees in the Garden might have been witnesses of Christ's betrayal. Later on I found out that this is not true. They are only 500 years old!

Here we read from the Bible passages pertaining to Christ's prayer, betrayal, and the arrest. The commentary was very moving. It was a happy and at the same time an awesome thought to stand where Jesus stood, where He was in agony and where *"His sweat became like drops of blood falling to the ground" (Luke 22:44)*. Inside the church in the sanctuary in front of the altar is a large boulder on which Christ leaned while praying to His Father. Msgr. Adamiak and I offered our Eucharistic Liturgy on the altar before the famous boulder. This church was built in 1924. A consortium drawn from twelve nations financed it. It is called Church of All Nations or the Basilica of the Agony. It has on its façade a glistening golden mosaic depicting Jesus carrying the suffering of the world. This church is the successor to two earlier churches, the first erected in the 4th century but destroyed by the earthquake in the 740s, the second an oratory built over the ruins by the Crusaders was abandoned in 1345 for reasons unknown.

Gethsemane lies on the lower slope of the Mount of Olives. The Valley of Kidron separates Jerusalem from the Mount of Olives. The summit of the Mount of Olives rises about 250 feet above the Dome of the Rock. From there we saw a magnificent panorama of the Old Walled City of Jerusalem. It was from this point of view that Jesus Christ, as He was entering the city of Jerusalem for the last time, cried over the future of his beloved city: *"Coming within sight of the city, he wept over it and said: 'If you only had known the path to peace this day; but you have completely lost it from view! Days will come upon you when your enemies encircle you with a rampart, hem you in, and press you from every side. They will wipe you out, you and your children within your walls, and leave not a stone on a stone within you, because you failed to recognize the time of your visitation"* (Luke 20:41–44).

Having entered the Walled City, we visited the Coenaculum or the Upper Room where Jesus had his Last Supper with the disciples. It is a part of the King David's Tomb complex. The Coenaculum was a site of Christian worship during the Byzantine period. The Franciscans acquired it in the middle Ages, but the Turks later expelled them. Under Ottoman rule the Coenaculum became a mosque and Christians were barred from entering. The southern wall still bears the *mihrab*, the prayer niche hollowed by the Muslims when they converted the chapel into a mosque. Many visitors mistake the first large room for the real thing, but one needs to walk across the hall to enter the much smaller chamber beyond which is where Jesus is believed to have shared the Last Supper with his disciples. Here we read from the Bible the account of the Last Supper, and one minister gave a very impressive commentary. For us it is the hallowed place where the Sacrifice of the New Testament of the Holy Eucharist was established, where the priesthood of Christ was first confirmed upon the apostles, and where the Risen Christ appeared to them, the doors being closed, and gave the power to forgive sins. I wish I could have stayed there alone and spent some time in prayerful meditation or by offering a Eucharistic Liturgy where the Last Supper took place.

The next visit was to a church of St. Peter in Gallicantu. It is almost hidden by the trees and the slope of the hill. The church of St. Peter 'at the Crowing of the Cock' is the traditional site of the denial of Jesus by his apostle Peter *'before the cock crows three times'* (Mark 14:66–72). Built on the foundation of previous Byzantine and Crusader churches, the modern structure is also believed to stand on the site of the house of the High Priest Caiaphas, where Jesus was taken after his arrest. A cave beneath the church is said to be where Christ was incarcerated overnight.

We walked into the Old Walled City. The sights, sounds, and smells of the bustling area transported us back in time to the Jerusalem of Ancient Palestine, for life has changed very little through the centuries. Strolling the narrow streets and lanes of the market, we made our way to the Hebrew Temple area. Today two great Moslem mosques rise from the paving stones—Golden Dome Mosque of Omar or "Dome of the Rock," and the Mosque of Al-Aqsa. Al-Aqsa is a functioning house of worship, accommodating up to 5,000 praying worshipers at a time.

The Dome of the Rock encloses the sacred rock upon which Abraham prepared to sacrifice his only son Isaac and from which, according to Islamic tradition, the Prophet Mohamed was accepted into heaven to pray with the other saints and Allah himself. The Dome was built between 688 and 691 A.D, making it one of the oldest surviving Islamic monuments in existence. In the interior in a center is a wooden fence, which rings the sacred rock. To enter the Dome of the Rock we had to take our shoes off and leave them outside.

Orthodox Jews may not enter the mosque, because they might inadvertently trespass on the site of the Holy of Holies, the innermost sanctuary of the Temple containing the Ark of the Covenant. Only the High Priest is permitted to enter, and even then only on Yom Kippur.

In stark contrast to the magnificence of the Muslim's Dome of the Rock, the Western Wall is nothing more than a bare stone wall. However, it still manages to be one of the most captivating places in all of Jerusalem. It is part of the retaining wall built by Herod the Great in 20 B.C to contain the landfill on which the Second Temple compound stood. The Temple was destroyed in 70 A.D, but since the *Shehina* (Divine Presence) is believed never to have deserted the Wall, it is regarded as the most holy of all Jewish sites. During the Ottoman period, the Wall grew as a place of pilgrimage where Jews would come to mourn and lament their ancient loss—hence the name, "Wailing Wall."

Watching the black-garbed devout Jews rocking backward and forward, bobbing their heads in prayer and occasionally breaking off to press themselves against the Wall and kiss the stones, I admired their strong faith.

Via Dolorosa, or Way of Sorrows, winding up through the Muslim and then the Christian Quarter, is the route Jesus took as He carried his cross to Calvary. By the 8th century, some stops had become customary. The route first went from Gethsemane around the outside of the city walls to Caiaphas' house on Mt. Zion, then to the Praetorium of Pilate at St. Sophia near the Temple and eventually to the Holy Sepulchre. In the Middle Ages, with Christianity divided into two, the Via Dolorosa was twinned—each of the two claimed routes primarily visiting chapels belonging to either one or the other. In the 14th century, the Franciscans devised a walk of devotion that included some of the present day Stations of the Cross, but had as its starting point the Holy Sepulchre. This route was eventually modified by the desire of European Christians to follow the order of events of the Gospels, finishing at the site of the Crucifixion rather than beginning there.

The Church of the Resurrection stands on the spot of Christ's crucifixion and His resurrection. At the start of the 1st century, this was a disused quarry outside of the city walls. According to the Gospel of St. John (*John 19:17,41–42*), Jesus' crucifixion occurred at a place outside of the city walls with graves nearby. Archaeologists have discovered tombs dating from the correct period, so the site is compatible with the biblical account.

Until at least 66 A.D, Jerusalem's early Christian community held celebrations of public worship at the tomb. Hadrian filled in the area in 135 A.D to build a temple dedicated to Venus, but the Christian tradition persisted. Some 200 years later, Constantine and his mother, Helena, chose the site to construct a church to commemorate the Resurrection. To make room for the new development, substantial buildings had to be demolished. Work on Constantine's church commenced in 326 A.D.

Saturday, October 15, 1977, we traveled southward from Jerusalem to Hebron. Hebron is a city of biblical times, located some twenty miles from Jerusalem. It lies in a depression in the mountains of Judea. The hills, which surround it, rise to an altitude of 3,300 feet. From there we motored to Masada. Herod the Great built a magnificent winter palace on a frees-tanding, sheer-sided plateau some 3,200 feet high above the Dead Sea. This massive rock formation jutting out from the edge of the Judean Desert has come to be a most widely known symbol of human dedication to freedom.

Herod built a fortified palace complex, including a synagogue. In 66 A.D, as part of the Great Revolt, refugees from Jerusalem joined a group of Jewish Zealots at Masada. After the fall of Jerusalem in 70 A.D, the Roman army, commanded by Flavius Silva, began to mop up the rebellion at Masada. During the ensuing two-year siege, the Romans built a massive ramp to bridge the chasm between the great abutment and the main plateau up to the walls of the fortress. When defeat was imminent, the 930 survivors carried out a pact of mutual homicide rather than surrender to slavery and disgrace. The view from the summit is one of the most scenic. The ruins of Masada can now be reached by a cable car. Some historians now question the truth of the death of the zealots. Masada is today the place where many young recruits take their oath of loyalty and service in the Israel Defense Forces in a ceremony that closes with the pledge: "Masada shall not fall again."

Some of us wanted to take a swim in the Dead Sea, but time did not permit it. So we returned to Jerusalem for dinner and overnight stay.

Sunday, October 17, 1977, our bus took us north from Jerusalem following the foothills of Judea, along what were once camel caravan paths. We motored into the pages of biblical history and into the sights and sounds of today. First we passed the biblical town of Anathoth about five or six miles north of Jerusalem. Now the town is knows as Anata. About three miles further we passed another biblical town of Gibeon, then Bethel and Shiloh, Arimathea and Jacob's Well. We stopped at Jacob's Well, went to see it and drink some water from it. This is the place where Christ met the Samaritan Woman (John 4:4–42). We crossed Samaria into the famous Valley of Jerzeel and then into Galilee.

From there we traveled to Nazareth, the boyhood home of Jesus. It is a tranquil town nestled in the hills of Lower Galilee and overlooking the lush green Valley of Jerzeel. With its white stone houses, curving lanes, alleyways and olive trees, it is probably little different from the town of the days when Jesus lived there with Mary and Joseph the carpenter. In 326 A.D, Emperor Constantine, at the request of his mother, Queen Helena, built the first church in Nazareth, a Byzantine basilica, over the traditional site of Mary's home. When Moslems invaded the country in 636 they destroyed the city, and it lay in ruins until its restoration by the Crusaders in the 12th century. A hundred years later, the Saracens massacred the Christian population and demolished the Crusader churches. In the 17th century a group of Franciscan monks were permitted to return to Nazareth.

The Basilica of the Annunciation, whose construction was completed in 1966, dominates the present town. Built over the ruins of the Byzantine and Crusader churches, elements of which have been restored, it marks the traditional site of the Annunciation. The basilica is noted for its art forms drawn from many nations of Christendom.

From there we traveled northeast and passed the town of Cana where Jesus at a wedding, at the request of his Mother, changed water into wine (John 2:1–11). We arrived at the Sea of Galilee for the overnight stay at the Ron Beach Hotel in Tiberias.

Monday, October 17, 1977—Before we started on our trip, we admired the Sea of Galilee, also know as Lake Tiberias and as Sea of Gennasaret. It is a serenely beautiful sweet water lake framed by the mountains. To the west rise the hills of Galilee flanked by the lush Plain of Ginnosar, and to the east the Golan Heights. The Jordan River flows through it from its sources in the North to the Dead Sea in the south. The Sea is fourteen miles long, nine miles at its widest, and 700 feet below sea level. The Sea of Galilee is Holy Land's largest freshwater lake and the country's main water reservoir. On the northern shores is Bethsaida, Capernaum, Tabgha, the Sanctuary of the Primacy, the Mensa Christi (Table of Christ), and the Mount of Beatitudes. Along the western shore is the Plain of Ginnosar, the village of Magdala, the home of Mary Magdalene from whom Jesus cast out "seven demons," and Tiberias.

From Tiberias our bus took us to Capernaum, which was the main center of Jesus' work and teaching. Many parables and miracles are recorded of his activities in or near this town. Here He made his second home, after Nazareth, *"his own city"* (Matthew 9:1). Here along the shores of the Sea of Galilee Christ called Simon Peter and his brother Andrew, James, and his brother John, the sons of Zebedee, to be his apostles. Peter's house and a neighboring synagogue have been excavated and reconstructed by the Franciscan Custody of the Holy Land. Up the hill to the west is the Mount of Beatitudes where, according to Matthew's version, Jesus preached His famous "Sermon on the Mountain." Nearby to the northwest is Kozarin.

From Capernaum the bus took us south to the lower end of the Sea of Galilee where the River Jordan continues its flow south. There we witnessed the baptism of adults by a Protestant minister and his helper. The three of them were in the water up to their chest. Two men would tilt the one to be baptized backward three times until his head was immersed in the water.

Almost in the middle of the beautiful Valley of Jerzeel the Mount of Tabor rises high. We visited Mount Tabor and the new Basilica Church standing over the spot where Christ was transfigured. From there we traveled northwest, passing the village of Nain where Jesus raised the son of a widow from the dead (Luke 7:11) to the city of Haifa and Mt. Carmel. From there we motored south through Caesarea, the Plains of Sharon, Appek, and Lydda to Tel Aviv and the Tal Hotel on Hayarkon Street.

This was the end of our tour of the Holy Land. The following day, Tuesday, October 18, 1977, we boarded TWA flight #881 and departed at 9:10 A.M. from Tel Aviv to Athens, Greece. There we spent a few hours and viewed the imposing Acropolis with the majestic Parthenon, the Temple of Zeus, Socrates' Prison, and the

Dionysus Theatre. We saw likewise the Areopagus—Mars Hill on whose rock St. Paul gave his famous speech to the Athenians. At 4:50 P.M. we departed Athens on Alitalia flight #481 for Rome and Hotel Ritz-Sporting on Piazza Euclide.

I was grateful to the Lord for giving me the grace to see the Land of Jesus Christ. For nowhere in the world is there such a rich abundance of history, of sacred places that call to mind the great deeds of our God and His sacrifice to save humanity. Ever since, when I recite the Holy Rosary and meditate on the mysteries in the life of Christ and His Mother, I place myself mentally in the place and surrounding now familiar to me, and my prayer is much more meaningful and intimate.

Language Difficulties

Toward the end of the Second Vatican Council, all the Roman churches in America abandoned the Latin language in their liturgy and used the English language exclusively. Many of my parishioners in Perth Amboy were of ritually mixed marriages going back to 1918 or even earlier. We had many such families for at least two generations. When English was introduced into the liturgy by our good neighbors of the Latin Rite, and we still used the Church-Slavonic language, many of our young couples left us and went there.

Our bishops at that time were at the Council and there was no one to consult as to what we were to do. Yet Bishop Schmondiuk of the Stamford Eparchy wrote a letter to all his priests, giving them permission to use the English language in the liturgy wherever there was a need. True, some months later he withdrew that permission. Yet many priests in his Eparchy introduced the English language, using an approved text prepared by Archbishop Senyshyn while he was still in Stamford.

I consulted some of my priest neighbors, especially Msgr. Victor J. Pospishil, pastor of our Church in Carteret, N.J., a renowned canonist and author of many books and articles. He told me that the salvation of souls is the highest law. I should, therefore, use my own pastoral judgment and, if there is a real need of the English language in my parish, then I should not hesitate to do what is needed for the salvation of souls, a real canonical counsel!

At that time I had three Liturgies on Sundays. Now, with the new law, it was possible to have a Sunday Liturgy on Saturday evening, after 4:00 P.M. So I introduced my first English Liturgy on Saturday at 5:30 P.M. But before I did so, I explained to the faithful for several Sundays my motivation for doing so. I told them how many young couples we have lost already, without blame, for they do not understand the Ukrainian or Church- Slavonic languages. The reaction in the parish was not bad. I received very few complaints.

There were available at that time small pew booklets of the Divine Liturgy with the English text parallel to the Ukrainian. I purchased enough copies of those booklets and placed them in the pews so that my faithful could follow, understand, and take an active part in the Liturgy. But there are in our rite liturgical services those who are served only once a year, e.g., Christmas Eve, Epiphany, the Holy Week, and Easter Sunday Resurrectional Matins. There was no Ukrainian or English translation of these services at that time.

In my spare time in the evenings I started the work of compiling and translating bi-lingual texts of these liturgical services. My first project was a booklet of the Resurrection Matins for Easter Sunday. At first it was not even a booklet, but just loose leaves stapled together. The reaction of my parishioners was exuberant. Some said it was the first time in their lives that they understood this service. This gave me the needed encouragement to work even harder. The next project was a 114 page booklet, containing the bi-lingual translations of the services connected with Christmas, New Years Day, and Theophany, especially the long service of the Blessing of Water on Theophany day, published in 1972. My next booklet was the Holy Thursday Service with the reading of the twelve Passion Gospels. In 1980 I published a booklet containing "Good Friday Vespers."

These booklets became very popular. They were copied and recopied by many priests throughout the country, even by the Orthodox priests. Later on, when I was in the Chancery, we had these booklets retyped on a computer and were selling them in our Byzantine Church Supplies store.

To See My Parents Again

The last time I saw my parents was in January of 1944. The cruel events of the war forced me to leave them. Yet in my heart I was always with them, frequently thought of them, prayed for them daily, and even dreamed about them. In 1946 they were forcefully resettled into Ukraine in the Soviet Union. My yearning to see them once again encouraged me to join a tour of 36 other tourists, organized by the Kobasniuk Travel Agency from New York City. Not to be conspicuous, I did not use my clerical garb, but civilian attire instead. Our flight took us first to Moscow where we were taken by a bus on a sightseeing tour of the city. The next day we flew to Kiev, the capital of Ukraine. There we spent some four days sightseeing and taking side trips. Then we flew to Lviv in Western Ukraine.

The bus took us to our hotel. In front of the Inturist Hotel was a mob of people awaiting our arrival. These were mostly relatives of the tourists from the United States of America. I was seated on the right side by the window in the back of the bus. Someone came to my window and was waiving to me. I did not react because I did not know who it was. The man then took his passport out of his pocket and, opening it, placed it on the window for me to read. I read his name, and could not believe my eyes. It was my youngest brother John. The last time I saw him he was only seven years old. Now he was a grown man. I used to send my parents my pictures, so they knew my appearance, but I never got John's picture and could not recognize his face. When I finally got out of the bus, I embraced and kissed him. He led me to another group of people. Among them I recognized my sister Anna. After we embraced, she presented to me the rest of my relatives whom I was seeing for the first time. "This is Helen, our brother Wasyl's wife; this is Slavko, their son, and the seven year old girl is their daughter Orysia; this is my son John, who just finished his military service; these two are my daughters—Maria and Olga. My husband Nicholas and our brother Wasyl will come to see you tomorrow." Next I asked my sister, "How are our parents?" They are well, she replied. They hope that you will be able to come to see them at home in Sambir.

The Catacomb Nun

All the tourists were told that they couldn't leave the city without a specific permit from the hotel manager (read, a KGB agent). So, daily I would go to see him, asking his permission to go to the city of Sambir, some 74 kilometers away. The reason I gave was that my father was a disabled war veteran, and he asked to see me. His daily reply was that today we have no available car to take you there, come tomorrow. It was the Soviet Union, and you just don't rent a car as you would in the free world.

One day an old lady with her daughter came to see me in the hotel. It was the mother of Peter Boyduy, my cousin Mary's husband. The other lady was Peter's sister. Before my departure on this trip, Peter asked me to give his mother $100.00. So I did give her an envelope with the money. Thinking that in the hotel rooms there might be secret microphones, I asked the two ladies to go out with me to a park across the street from the hotel. The day was sunny and warm.

There we found a bench and sat down. The mother, about eighty years old, sat on my left, and her daughter some fifty years old on my right. They began a conversation with me in a very low voice, almost whispering. The daughter said she was a religious sister, a nun of the order of St. Basil the Great. She told me the following:

"Before the war I was elected a bursar for the whole province. In 1946, when the Bolsheviks liquidated our Ukrainian Catholic Church, all the seminaries and the convents were likewise liquidated. Then I was arrested, sentenced to eight years of hard labor, and sent to a concentration camp in Karaganda. By God's help I was able to survive and finally came back home. There are many other Basilian nuns. They live privately, do not wear monastic habits, and some work as nurses in hospitals in order to be able to make a living. There were six nuns in one small house. In the hotel where you are staying there are Sister Servants of Mary Immaculate who work as cooks in the kitchen. But no one there knows they are religious sisters. At home they observe their normal daily schedule of common prayers, meditation, spiritual reading, and examination of conscience. Once in a great while, one of our underground Catholic priests would visit them, hear their confessions, serve a Divine Liturgy for them, and consecrate the Eucharst for them, which they keep hidden and have adoration whenever they can. One of us is always watching. When someone comes to the house and we do not know who it is, we consume the Holy Gifts, and have to wait for another visit from our priest."

The Sister continued: "On one occasion as I was on my way to visit our sisters near the city of Ivano-Frankivsk. I did not walk on the main streets, but on paths that lead across the fields and meadows so as not to meet anyone. I was passing a high school when I noticed that all the school children were being assembled on the school playground and formed a circle. I love children very much and was curious to know what they were up to. I hid myself behind some bushes, observed and listened to what was going on.

"Soon, some important man came out of the school building and gave a spirited talk on atheism, using the same old arguments that everyone knows already and doesn't believe. I noticed that the students did not pay attention to him because some of them were quietly sneering and making fun of him. The speaker might have noticed something and raised his voice, saying, 'I know that among you are some who still believe in some religious superstitions and fables, and may be secretly wearing a cross under your shirts. This you cannot do in this school. This is strictly forbidden.'"

"He then he approached a girl some twelve or thirteen years of age and said to her, 'I know that under your dress you wear a cross. Take it off and throw it to the ground so that all may know that you do not believe in such superstitions.' The girl yelled out, 'Never, never, never.' She just shook her head right and left to let him know that she would not part with her cross. The man then put his left arm over her back, and with his right hand reached underneath her dress, got her cross out and took it off from her. He then threw the cross to the ground and demanded that she step on it. She began to cry and, sobbing bitterly, said, 'I will never do this.' So he put his foot on the cross, turned his foot right and left, thus pushing the cross into the mud.

"This was the end of the school assembly. Children were dismissed and each went his way home. I sat there for over an hour, and when I was sure that no one was there anymore, I went there, dug the cross out of the mud. I brought this cross with me to give it to you, so that you may give it to our Basilian Sisters in the United States of America that they may know how much we have to suffer for our faith. I wrapped the cross in a handkerchief and I placed it on the bench next to me. Do not look at it now for two KGB agents who are following us from Ternopil are observing us. One of them is sitting on a bench over there, and reading a newspaper, and the other one on our left is looking at the flowers." I slowly lowered my right hand to the bench, took the cross, put it into my pocket and thanked the nun.

At My Parents' Home

Toward the end of the week I finally got permission to visit my parents, hire a car and also a driver. I paid the manager for the use of the car and for the driver. On the way to the city of Sambir, the driver was trying to ask me all kinds of personal questions with details about my life in the United States of America. At first I tried to answer him in generalities, then I took out of my pocket two packages of American cigarettes and pushed them over toward him, pointing with my finger—this is for you. He thanked me by nodding his head, and immediately he turned the radio on really loud. Apparently there was a hidden microphone in the car. The radio noise would have killed it.

When we were approaching the city of Sambir, I observed with real interest the changes that occurred in the city since the last time I was here. There were so many changes. More buildings had been built. The city was more than twice the size it was in the early 1940s. My parents lived in a section that before the war was considered a suburb. Now it was part of the city.

When I arrived at my parents' home, tears of joy glistened in the eyes of all in the house, especially in the eyes of my parents. My mother embraced me with trembling arms and kissed me. I kissed her hand. My father was speechless at first. Slowly we all embraced and kissed. We then sat down to a table covered with all kinds of goodies on it. I said the prayer before the meal and blessed the food. My brother Wasyl gave the driver a bottle in a paper bag, and asked him to come back at 4:00 P.M.

I was trying to get to know my brother's children—Slavko and Orysia. So I asked them some questions, as I normally do when I speak with children. But I was not prepared to speak to children in the Soviet Union. I asked, whether they received their First Holy Communion yet? Under those conditions it was a wrong question to ask. Children were forbidden to attend church, and I did not know that. Slavko's reaction was sincere. He started to tell me, "Uncle, you do not know how evil these communists are . . . ." His father interrupted him sharply, "Be quiet!" The fear of the terror of the Communist rulers was so great that these poor people were afraid to talk, even privately at home.

My father then related a story that happened that year in their church during the Lenten season. School children were forbidden to attend church. But a teenaged girl, dressed as an old woman, went to church on a Sunday with a group of old ladies. Those who observed people going to church, normally one of the teachers from the school, did not notice her. Stalin liquidated our Ukrainian Catholic Church in 1946, and now a Russian Orthodox priest was serving in our church building. The teenaged girl stood in line for confession. When her turn came, she approached the priest, and knelt down. He could not see her face but her young voice betrayed her. He refused to hear her confession, got up and started to yell at her. Then he turned to the congregation and scolded them publicly for sending children to confession. Do you want trouble for me? He asked. The girl started to cry aloud and to sob. The other ladies tried to console her, but she could not stop crying for a long time.

What an ugly example or caricature of a pastor who would not shepherd his sheep. He was, rather, the one of whom our Lord said, *"The hired man—who is no shepherd nor owner of the sheep— catches sight of the wolf coming and runs away, leaving the sheep to be snatched and scattered by the wolf."* (John 10:12) But I should not judge him. Let the Lord be the judge of him and me as well.

I had a camera with me. So I asked every one in the house to come outside where I could take better pictures. I took some group pictures as well as individual ones. To this day this is the only remembrance I have from those memorable days. I thought there would be an opportunity for me to sit down with my parents and have a quiet conversation with each of them and share some of my past experiences with them. But there was no time left. My sister Anna came and insisted that I go to her house and visit with her family. I could not say no to her. My sister lived with her family on the next street. The house there was full of their family members and their friends. I could hardly eat anything more. But I enjoyed their company, had a lively conversation, and answered their questions about life in America. My brother-in-law, Nicholas Ryszwec, stated that every Sunday he listens to the Vatican radio, which broadcasts our Divine Liturgy with a homily. He said he placed the radio on a windowsill, and opened the window so that the neighbors could hear it too. Time was passing quickly. Soon I had to go back to my brother's house, and the driver was already there to take me back to my hotel in Lviv.

It was time to say goodbye. It's a very painful goodbye when one has not seen his parents for so many long years. My father at that time was already 78 years old. The thought came to my mind that this is most probably the last time I will see both of them in this world. The goodbye was like a funeral, full of pain, grief, and tears. My mother decided to go with me to Lviv and spend some time with me in the car. When I left their house, the street was full of people, neighbors and friends. They all knew I was a Catholic priest. One lady placed something into my pocket. She whispered to me, read it later, not now. I blessed all of them and said a tearful goodbye.

On the way to Lviv, I got the note that the lady put into my pocket, and read it. "Please tell the Holy Father, the Pope of Rome, that we did not abandon our Catholic Faith. We will remain for as long as we live what we always were, loyal Catholics."

I enjoyed my mother's company so much. We were able to exchange many thoughts in a low voice so the driver could not hear us. He just listened to some Polish radio program. Before I entered the hotel, we said goodbye. She went to stay overnight at the house of one of our friends, Dmytro Rapko, from Balnycia. I did not know that this was the last time I would see my mother. Two years later, as she was on her way home from Sunday Liturgy with her daughter, she collapsed and died.

Dmytro Rapko was a son of another disabled war veteran from Balnycia. His father sent him to a high school in Peremyshl. He married a priest's daughter from Balyhorod. During the war he joined the Ukrainian Insurgent Army (UPA), and became an officer. After the war, he was arrested by the Bolsheviks and sent to the Gulags. After Stalin's death, his wife was able to have amnesty applied to his case, and he was released. He worked as a bookkeeper for some agency. One day Dmytro came to my hotel, took me into his car and drove me to his house. I spent a pleasant time with him and his family. About a month after my return to the United States of America, I received a letter from my uncle Nicholas Sulyk in Poland, saying, "I learned here that you visited with Dmytro Rapko while you were in Lviv. I hope that you did not say too much, because his wife is an active agent of the KGB."

Late in 1970, my father wrote to me, "Son, I am getting old and frail. Before I die I would like to see you once more, but come in your clerical garb and offer a Divine Liturgy here in our church in Sambir. I will talk to our priest, and I am sure he will not object." My Aunt Sophie wished to go with me on this my second trip that lasted from May 20, to June 5, 1971, again with a tour of the Kobasniuk Travel Agency. When we landed in Moscow, during the check and control, all the tourists went through without any difficulty, but I was searched thoroughly, and the prayer books I got for my relatives, all the holy pictures, rosaries, and medals were confiscated. Apparently, when I wrote to my father that Aunt Sophie and I would be there, he must have gone to the local Orthodox priest, asking permission for me to offer Divine Liturgy in his church. This same priest, who refused to hear the confession of a teenaged girl in 1957, must have reported my father's request to the KGB, and they were ready for me on my arrival in Moscow.

Most probably this was likewise the reason why I was refused permission to visit my father in Sambir.

But it turned out better for father and me that I did not travel to see him in Sambir. My brothers brought him to the hotel in Lviv. While all the relatives were visiting with my Aunt Sophie in her room, I was able to spend the day alone with my father in my room. True, I was not able to celebrate a Divine Liturgy for him, so that he could see me at least once in his lifetime at the holy altar as a priest. But he was happy to be with me alone and to share with me so many memories of the past in his and my life. Again, this was our last meeting, the last time I saw him in this world.

Father Walter Ciszek, S.J.

While preparing for my second trip to Ukraine, I asked Father Walter Ciszek from the Pope John XXIII Jesuit Center in the Bronx, N.Y. to substitute for me in the parish during my absence. There was no parochial vicar in the parish at that time. Father Walter was born of Polish parents in Shenandoah, Pennsylvania, grew up and went to school with many of our Ukrainian boys and girls.

After graduating from high school, he decided to be a priest and joined the Jesuit Order. During his seminary days, Pope Pius XI in 1929 appealed to the Jesuit seminarians to volunteer to be future missionaries in the present Soviet Union. Ciszek liked the idea and wrote a letter to the Jesuit General Superior in Rome, volunteering his candidacy as a future missionary in Russia.

In the fall of 1934 he was called to Rome to study theology at the Gregorian University and likewise the Byzantine rite and the Russian language at the Russicum College. He was ordained June 24, 1937. Since missionary work in the Soviet Union at that time was impossible, he was assigned in November of 1938 to a Jesuit parish in Albertin, the Belarusian territory of eastern Poland. He was there when the Second World War began September 1, 1939. When the Soviets occupied eastern Poland, his parish became part of the Soviet Union. Father Ciszek and his friend Father Makar

Nestorov decided to take the opportunity to go secretly into Russia.

On their way, they stopped in the city of Lviv to see Metropolitan Andrew Sheptytsky. They confided in him their secret plans to volunteer as laborers for work in the woodworking factories behind the Ural Mountains. The Metropolitan tried to convince them that such a mission was very dangerous. When they, however, insisted on their own plan, he gave them his blessing to go there for one year only, under the condition that they would only learn of the local conditions and situation, and not engage in any missionary work. Then they should come back and report to him.

They left Lviv on March 15, 1940 under assumed names and with false passports in a railroad boxcar. When in June of 1941 Hitler attacked the Soviet Union, both of them were arrested as spies of the Vatican. In August of 1941 they were transferred to the ill-famed Lubianka prison in Moscow. Ciszek spent five long years of interrogations and tortures there. He was sentenced and condemned to the concentration camps in the Norilsk district of Siberia. After twenty-three years of confinement, Ciszek was freed in October of 1963, and exchanged for two Soviet spies, who were imprisoned in the United States of America.

Father Ciszek came to Perth Amboy a few days before my departure to get acquainted with his duties in the parish. This gave me an opportunity to get to know him better and to learn of some of his experiences in his long confinement. One thing interested me more than anything else. How was he able to find in himself so much spiritual stamina and endurance not to give in or break down and to remain faithful to his priestly vows. His answer was very simple: "I always kept in mind that I am not alone, that God is always with me." When I asked him about his sufferings or tortures, he did not want to talk about that. He said, "Right now I am writing a book. When it is ready and published, I will send you a copy so that you may read all about my experiences."

One evening when we sat together and had a friendly conversation, I said, "The Soviets are forcibly Russifying all of Ukraine, resettling hundreds of thousands of Ukrainians into Russia and

Russian people into Ukraine. They forcibly liquidated our Ukrainian Catholic Church, imprisoned all our bishops, thousands of priests, and many outstanding lay people. We know that our Church exists there in modern catacombs, but for how long? If the Soviet Union exists another ten or twenty years, I doubt we will last that long. The older generations will die out, and the new ones, nurtured in atheism as "the Soviet people," may not keep the faith.

His reply was very interesting. "Looking at the conditions in the Soviet Union with human eyes, it seems that the situation is hopeless. I fully agree with your conclusions. We, however, should never forget that the atheistic chieftains in the Kremlin are not the ones who decide the fate of nations. It is God who makes the decisions. From what I have personally witnessed and experienced, everything tells me that your Ukrainian nation and your Church are indestructible. In every concentration camp or gulag in which I resided, over fifty percent of all inhabitants were Ukrainians, the greatest part from Western Ukraine. These are deeply religious people. They are not ashamed of their faith. They would pray publicly, sing church songs and hymns, and unashamedly give glory to God. All other prisoners admired them for their courageous faith. No, my dear father, such a nation as yours will never die out, because God is and always will be with them."

My Work in the Archeparchy

While at the time I was an administrator of St. Michael's in Frackville, Archbishop Constantine Bohachevsky on June 11, 1959, appointed me a promotor of justice in the diocesan marriage tribunal. This appointment demanded of me not only frequent trips to the Chancery, but also forced me to get some books in that field and study up on the matter at hand. This appointment lasted until 1974.

Archbishop Ambrose Senyshyn appointed me on July 19, 1963 an examiner of junior clergy on the Sacred Scripture. Later on in July of 1968, he appointed me a member of the Archeparchial Finance Council. This lasted until 1975.

In July of 1964, Msgr. Michael Poloway, the Chancellor, called me and informed me that the Archbishop was inviting me to have a luncheon with him at the Barkley Hotel in Philadelphia. What the occasion was or the reason, the Chancellor could not say. During a delicious luncheon, the Archbishop asked me to volunteer for a position of rector of St. Josaphat Seminary in Washington, D.C. It was a great surprise to me, for which I was not prepared. I always tried to obey my bishop and would have done so right there, but my sense of responsibility before God admonished my conscience not to rush into this thing. This is why I asked the Archbishop to kindly give me a few days to think about it and to pray for God's guidance.

I realized that the position of a rector, particularly in our situation, brings with it a very grave responsibility for the proper formation of future priests. I was not prepared to take this position in the next two or three weeks. Seriously, I needed more time to prepare myself by reading up on the law and the pertinent literature, and/or by consulting other rectors. So I wrote to the Archbishop, asking for more time to prepare myself for this very important position. He then appointed Msgr. Constantine Berdar as the new rector.

Through the efforts of Archbishop Senyshyn, I was named a Papal Chaplain with the title of a monsignor on May 31, 1968. At the same time, eight other priests of our Archeparchy were elevated to this same dignity: Stephen Hrynuck, Roman Lobodych, Michael Fedorowich, Basil Losten, Myroslav Charyna, Russell Danylchuk, John Bilanych, and Basil Makuch.

After the death of Archbishop Senyshyn, Bishop Losten, as the Apostolic Administrator of the Archeparchy, appointed me on September 27, 1977 to the college of the Archieparchial Consultors, and on September 28, 1977 as a member of the Archieparchial Corporation.

On the initiative of the parish church committee in Perth Amboy, N.J., and especially of the Missionary Sisters of the Mother of God and the school faculty, the parish prepared an observance of the 25th Anniversary of my priestly ordination on Sunday June 26, 1977. There was a solemn Divine Liturgy in the morning of which I was the main celebrant. My good friends Msgr. Leon Mosko and Father Matthew Berko were my concelebrants. Msgr. Leon gave an excellent and inspiring homily. In the afternoon there was a large banquet in our spacious school auditorium with Bishop Basil Losten in attendance. On this occasion Bishop Losten raised me to the dignity of an archpriest, by a letter dated May 5, 1977, prot. # 577-77-Cb.

There were some 37 priests present at the banquet, as well as my aunt and uncle, Sophie and Dmytro Stec, as well as my cousin

Mary Boyduy and her daughter, Lydia Boyduy, Msgr. Fedorchuck's two sisters, Mary and Peter Polit, Theresa Fedorchuck and Mrs. Joseph Fedorchuck, John and Ollie Mysak, Mr. & Mrs. Walter Lahotski from Stamford, and many others. The school children presented a delightful concert, and afterward the church choir sang a few songs. I was given a gift from the parishioners of a Ukrainian embroidered priestly vestment. In my concluding remarks, among others, I said:

"Today my heart is filled with the sentiments of gratitude and love for all of you, my parishioners, my spiritual family. The presence of so many of you here today, which I have never expected, is for me the greatest reward for all my efforts here, and a stamp of approval for my work. The last fifteen years have been the happiest years in my life. This is so because of you, who have given me your love, your respect, and your whole-hearted cooperation in every undertaking . . .

So, if I had to relive my life over again, do you know what I would choose for my vocation?—Priesthood! Yes, priesthood, because it is the most rewarding and the most satisfying life to be able to work for the best employer in the universe—for God himself and for his people and his Church. Yes, indeed, I would choose the priesthood again and again with all its problems and difficulties, if I had to start my life over again. Today is the first day of the rest of my life, and I am happy that I am a priest."

Changes in Episcopate

The Holy Father, Paul VI, named, Bishop Joseph Schmondiuk of Stamford, CT, as the new Metropolitan-Archbishop of Philadelphia for Ukrainians, October 1, 1977, succeeding the late Archbishop Ambrose Senyshyn, OSBM, who died September 11, 1976. Even after his formal installation, it was months before Archbishop Schmondiuk moved to Philadelphia and took his residence in Archbishop Bohachevsky's house on Medary Avenue in North Philadelphia. He appointed Father Andrew Baunchalk, a very capable and energetic young priest, as his private secretary.

Archbishop Schmondiuk did not enjoy his new position for long. On Christmas day, December 25, 1978, he celebrated the Hierarchical Divine Liturgy in his cathedral church, preached a spirited homily, and then was invited by Msgr. Moskal, the rector of the cathedral parish, for a breakfast in the rectory. He was in good spirits and enjoyed the priests' company. Afterward Father Baunchalk invited him to his mother's house in Wilmington, Delaware, for a Christmas dinner. He gladly accepted the invitation of his private secretary. Toward evening, the Archbishop returned home on Medary Avenue. They took the Archbishop's three Alaskan Huskies out for a walk. Then both of them went into the chapel for the recitation of the Priestly Office. Following this, the Archbishop, before he went upstairs to his apartment, extended his hand to shake Father Andrew's hand, saying, "Thank you Father Andrew for a beautiful day." Father Andrew at that moment was trying to get a cigarette out of his pocket, and before he could extend his hand to the Archbishop, the Archbishop collapsed, falling down to the floor, dead. The dogs then attacked Father Andrew, apparently blaming him for the death of their master. He barely got away. Father Andrew Baunchalk told this story to me personally.

The College of Consultors elected Msgr. Stephen Chehansky, a senior priest and a pastor of St. John's Church, Northampton, PA, as the interim administrator of the Archeparchy. He did not involve himself too much in the matters of the Archeparchy and left all the day-to-day decisions to be made by the Chancellor, Msgr. Robert M. Moskal.

Archbishop Schmondiuk's body, in accordance with his wishes, was buried at the Holy Spirit Cemetery of the Stamford Eparchy that he established at Campbell Hall, N.Y

Pope John Paul II Visits Our Cathedral

The new Pope's first visit to the United States of America was to begin October 2, 1979. His visit to the Ukrainian Catholic Cathedral in Philadelphia was planned for October 4, 1979. One week before the visit, the Apostolic Delegate in Washington, D.C. announced that the Holy Father, on September 21, 1979, had named Msgr. Myroslav Lubachivsky, the spiritual director of St. Basil's Seminary in Stamford, CT, as the next Metropolitan-Archbishop of Philadelphia for Ukrainians. Immediately he was named an Apostolic Administrator of the Philadelphia Archeparchy, even before his Episcopal ordination. Now he would be the one who would officially welcome the Holy Father in our Cathedral.

It was August 29, 1979, that our Chancery announced that the Holy Father would be in Philadelphia for two days, the 3rd and 4th of October. It was through the efforts of Cardinal John Krol, then the Archbishop of Philadelphia for the Latins, that the Pope would visit our Cathedral.

Pope John Paul II visits the Immaculate Conception Ukrainian Catholic Cathedral, Philadelphia, Pa., October 4, 1979. (l. to r.): John Cardinal Krol—Archbishop of Philadelphia, Msgr. Myroslav Ivan Lubachivsky,—newly appointed Metropolitan Archbishop of Philadelphia for Ukrainians, (To the right from the Holy Father): Augustine Cardinal Cassaroli–Secretary of State and Archbishop Paul Marcinkus from the Vatican.

The time of the Holy Father's visit was scheduled for 8:00 A.M. On that day as early as 5:00 A.M. our faithful began to arrive and take their seats inside the Cathedral. They arrived by buses, cars, or trains from all over the country. They were the representatives from all our parishes. They were given admission tickets to the Cathedral. Even before 7:00 A.M. there were more that three thousand faithful, priests, and nuns admitted inside the Cathedral. In front of the pews were some 200 school children, dressed in their Ukrainian national attire. On both sides before the entrance to the Cathedral were several hundred Ukrainian girl and boy scouts in their uniforms. North Franklin Street was packed with about five thousand people standing on the sidewalks and on empty lots.

The Holy Father's caravan arrived. Cardinal Casaroli, the Secretary of State, Cardinal John Krol, and many bishops accompanied him. Before the entrance to the Cathedral, Msgr. Robert M. Moskal, rector of the Cathedral, with our traditional bread and salt, welcomed him. Msgr. Moskal asked the Holy Father to bless the new Cathedral building. While privately saying some prayers, he blessed the Cathedral with holy water. Then two priests, Rev. James T. Melnic and Rev. Thomas Sayuk, blessed the walls of the cathedral with the holy water.

At this time of the year the sun was quite low, shining very brightly over the horizon from the cloudless skies. It was shining from east to west right through the large clear glass window over the entrance to the Cathedral and like a huge reflector it illuminated the huge mosaic of the Most Holy Mother of God, Oranta, with hands raised in prayer, on the wall behind the altar. This caught the eyes of the Holy Father. He stopped right beneath the choir loft, and just looked at the icon and prayed silently while the huge crowd of people applauded him. He seemed not to pay attention to the applause, as though the beauty and the size of the icon captivated him. The Blessed Mother seemed to be welcoming among her Ukrainian children her beloved son, the first Slavic Pope. After a long silence, the Pope began to walk forward, extending his hands and greeting the people on the right as well as on the left side.

When he reached the children in front of the pews, he went to them. They surrounded him. He patted some on them on the head, others he embraced and kissed on the forehead. All the children tried to kiss his hand. In front of the iconostas, the cardinals and the bishops stood in one row. The Pope passed them and entered the sanctuary through the open royal doors. He knelt down before the altar, placed both, his hands on the altar, rested his head on them, and prayed there for long while. Following his examples, the cardinals, the bishops, and all the people in the church knelt down as well.

Afterward, standing before the royal doors, the Holy Father began his talk, at first in Ukrainian and later in English. The television cameras followed his every move and telecast his talk throughout the world. I sat in the pews with the rest of the priests and tried to remember his talk.

"I have always highly regarded the Ukrainian nation for many years. I have known of the many persecutions and injustices you had to suffer. This was and is now a very important matter for me. I am likewise aware of the efforts of the Ukrainian Catholic Church throughout her history to always remain faithful to the Gospel and be united with the successor of St. Peter. I cannot forget the numerous Ukrainian martyrs in the past as well as in the recent times, whose names in most part are unknown, and who preferred to rather give up their lives than to abandon their faith. I am acknowledging this in order to express my deep respect for the Ukrainian Church and for her proven loyalty in her suffering . . . ."

Episcopal Ordination of Metropolitan Myroslav Lubachivsky

On October 26, 1979 our Chancery made this announcement: "The Vatican Congregation for the Eastern Churches informed us that the Holy Father John Paul II will be the ordaining bishop of the Episcopal Ordination of the newly appointed Metropolitan-Archbishop Lubachivsky. The concelebrants will be Metropolitan Maxim Hermaniuk, Bishop Losten, and Bishop Gabro. The ordination will take place November 12, 1979, on the Feast of St. Josaphat, at the Sistine Chapel in the Vatican at 5:00 P.M."

This unusual and unexpected decision of the Pope was a great surprise to all and became the subject of many articles and commentaries in the press. I joined the pilgrims to Rome for this unusual Episcopal Ordination. The bishops and the priests resided at St. Josaphat Ukrainian Seminary in Rome. The day before the ordination, there was a rehearsal in the Sistine Chapel headed by Bishop Myroslav Marusyn. I and other priests were asked to concelebrate. The next day His Beatitude Cardinal Slipyj joined the Holy Father. For me it was a great honor and privilege to be able to serve the Liturgy with the Holy Father at the altar in the Sistine Chapel right at the world famous painting on the back wall of the chapel of the Last Judgment by Michelangelo. The deep impressions of this Liturgy will remain with me always. After the Liturgy, all the celebrants processed out of the chapel, through a sacristy, and assembled in a spacious hall. There the Holy Father greeted each one of us personally.[3]

After the Liturgy we were invited to the Columbus Hotel for a reception. The next day, all our bishops and priests served a Divine Liturgy in the Basilica of St. Peter at the altar of St. Basil the Great under which is preserved in a glass casket the body of St. Josaphat, the Ukrainian martyr for the unity of the Church.

---

[3] The other concelebrants were: Archbishop Hermaniuk of Winnipeg; Bishop Jaroslav Gabro of Chicago; Bishop Platon Kornylyak of Munich; Bishop Basil

My Return to Lourdes

On the suggestion of my good friend, Rev. Theodore Weneck, OSM, I made my return visit to the world-famous shrine in Lourdes, France, in June of 1980. There were six persons in our small group. There were a husband and wife from Cleveland, Ohio, friends of Father Theodore Weneck, Sister Thomas Hrynewich, SSMI, from St. Josaphat Seminary, Washington, D.C., Rev. Basil Lar, pastor of Sts. Peter and Paul Church, Ansonia, CT, Rev. Theodore Weneck, OFM from the Franciscan Monastery, Sybertsville, PA, and I, pastor of the Assumption Church, Perth Amboy. N.J.

Our only goal was to be in Lourdes and not to visit any other sites. So we had no cameras, and no pictures were taken. We made out of this visit to this sacred shrine a kind of weeklong spiritual retreat. Each day we started with a Divine Liturgy in the Ukrainian Chapel, which was located on the left-hand side of the vestibule of the shrine. There is a Ukrainian Catholic mission not too far from Lourdes. The pastor of that mission is Rev. Vasyl Pryjma who was with me in the Seminary in Hirschberg, Germany. He was building at that time a small Ukrainian church in Lourdes, across the river from the shrine. He is the one who takes spiritual care of our pilgrims at the Lourdes' shrine and was able to get our chapel ar-

303

ranged with our altar and a large icon of the Blessed Mother behind the altar. Near Lourdes there was at that time a convent of Ukrainian Sisters Servants of Mary Immaculate from Yugoslavia. One day we visited the sisters in their convent.

Following the daily Liturgy, we went back to the hotel for a breakfast. After a brief rest, all of us went to the shrine and spent about an hour in private prayer, adoration, and meditation. Afterward we took a walk on the grounds of the shrine. In the afternoon we joined the procession of the sick with singing of Marian songs. In the evening followed the candle light procession and the recitation of the holy rosary.

One day all of us went to the chapel where confessions are heard daily in various languages. I remember making a confession of my whole life there. The Most Holy Mother of God of the Lourdes shrine helped me make this spiritual retreat be one of the most memorable in my life.

Other Changes in Episcopate

The new Pope, John Paul II, unexpectedly called all our bishops from the free world to the Vatican for a special Synod March 24, 1980. The Pope personally presided at this Synod and asked our bishops to elect a terna, i.e., three candidates, from among whom he would appoint one as the coadjutor to the aging Major Archbishop of Lviv. By this action the Holy Father wished to emphasize that the so-called Synod of Lviv of 1946 was invalid. This so-called Synod was called by Stalin's henchmen, although not one single Ukrainian Catholic bishop could attend for they all were imprisoned by then. There were two Orthodox bishops present at that Synod but legally they could not make decisions for our Catholic bishops, and thus the Synod's decision for our Church to liquidate herself and join the Russian Orthodox Church, was just a legal camouflage. This is what Pope John Paul II wished the Communist leaders of the Soviet Union to know, that our Catholic Church in Ukraine is not liquidated, that legally she exists and has a successor to the throne of the Lviv Metropolitan.

Our bishops did elect a terna. The following day the Holy Father appointed from among the elected terna, the new Archbishop of Philadelphia, Myroslav Lubachivsky as the coadjutor, an auxiliary bishop with the right of succession to the Major Archbishop of Lviv, Cardinal Josyf Slipyj. Thus in a matter of just a few months the Philadelphia Archeparchy became vacant again. Archbishop Lubachivsky was appointed once more an Apostolic Administrator of the Archeparchy until a new Metropolitan Archbishop is appointed.

Bishop Jaroslav Gabro of Chicago became ill and in a few short weeks died March 28, 1980. Thus we had two Episcopal sees vacant in the United States. I attended the funeral services for Bishop Gabro, my predecessor in Perth Amboy. It was indeed a very sad occasion. Realizing the needs of our Church in the United States of America, I included in my daily intention a prayer that God would bless our Church with good, holy, and capable leaders.

Who Will Be Our Next Metropolitan?

With the election of Archbishop Lubachivsky as the coadjutor to Cardinal Slipyj and with the death of Bishop Gabro, the question as to who will be the next metropolitan and the next bishop of Chicago were predominant, especially among the clergy and, as well among the lay people. Some steadfastly insisted that, following past history, it was always the bishop of Stamford who ascended to the metropolitan's throne after the passing of the Metropolitan. It was so after the death of Archbishop Bohachevsky that the Bishop of Stamford, Ambrose Senyshyn, became his successor. Likewise after Senyshyn's death, again the Bishop of Stamford, Joseph Schmondiuk succeeded him as the metropolitan in Philadelphia. So, they said, now it's Bishop Basil Losten's turn to become an archbishop. Others did not agree with the historical precedence, and prophesied that someone else would be elected to this prestigious position. Both sides, however, agreed on one thing, namely that Bishop Losten would not refuse the appointment.

John Paul II was the first Pope to give our bishops the right to hold synods outside of the territory of Ukraine. The Synod of Bishops would elect the terna for each vacant Episcopal see. The Congregation for the Eastern Churches, with the services of the

Apostolic Nuncio in Washington, would then conduct a very strict check of the suitability of the three candidates, and make its recommendation to the Holy Father.

Those who were very interested in the question as to who would be our next metropolitan were some of our outstanding lay people, especially those who had a close relationship with Major Archbishop Cardinal Slipyj in Rome. It is possible that Cardinal Slipyj himself asked them who in their opinion would be good candidates for both vacant sees.

Some of my priestly friends, some lay people, and even some of my parishioners began to include my name among the possible candidates. I would get regular telephone calls in the evening from those interested in this question, speculating on any possibility of this or that candidate, specially from one in our Chancery. I did not know anything and no one confided in me. I had to tell the truth to all who asked me about my candidacy, "I am not a candidate! No one ever asked me if I would accept if I were ever asked. Personally, I can assure you that I do not desire this great burden upon my shoulders. I am very happy as a priest and this I wish to remain for the rest of my life."

One day I received a phone call from Leo Rudnycky, professor at LaSalle University in Philadelphia. He is married to Christine Luznycky, a daughter of Gregory and Nina Luznycky. Gregory is a renowned journalist, a historian, and my good friend. He said, annually in the fall we have a set of weekly talks and discussions at the Filial Branch of the Ukrainian Catholic University here in Philadelphia. Would I be so kind, he insisted, to give a 30 to 45 minute talk on the subject, "The important needs of the Ukrainian Catholic Church in the United States of America at the present time." I agreed, prepared a talk, and on the appointed day drove to Philadelphia.

There were about sixty elderly ladies and gentlemen, all from the intellectual elite. They all listened very attentively to my presentation. When the discussion period began, they asked very informed questions concerning the life of our Church. I gave extensive answers and explanations, especially concerning pastoral difficulties, problems with religious and priestly vocations, and the mobility of our faithful. Rudnycky told me privately at the end that my question and answer period was the best part of my presentation.

As I was driving home, one thought began to bother me, "Why was I invited to give this talk? Apparently they, too, think of me as a possible candidate for a Metropolitan and wished to appraise my abilities and then report to Cardinal Slipyj in Rome."

Synod of Ukrainian Catholic Bishops

ajor Archbishop Cardinal Slipyj, with the blessing of the Pope, called a Synod of Bishops to convene in the Vatican, November 24 to December 2, 1980. During that Synod I received a phone call at about 3:00 A.M. The phone ring woke me up. Thinking that someone was dying in the parish, I turned the lights on and grabbed the phone receiver. To my great surprise I heard the familiar voice of Father Dmytro Blazejowsky calling me from Rome.

"Father Stephen," he said, "I just received very joyful news. Yesterday at the Synod of Bishops, you were elected as one of the three candidates for the Metropolitan of Philadelphia. So I wanted to share this joyful news with you." I was speechless and could not answer him. Only after he insisted over and over again, "Do you hear me, are you there?" was I able to come to myself and talk to him. I said, "Do you know what you did to me? You poured a bucket of cold water over my head. I would rather not know this news. But how is it possible that a very high church secret, a pontifical secret, was divulged so early? Could it be that one of the bishops was making fun and told this story so that people would have something to talk about?" He told me that he couldn't tell me how he knew this, but assured me it is the truth. I thanked him for the call, turned the light off and tried to go back to sleep. This was impossible. So I took the rosary into my hand, knelt down at my bedside, and started to pray. I placed my life into God's hands and prayed, "*My Father, if it possible, let this cup pass me by. Still, let it be as you would have it, not as I*" (Matthew 26:39).

This prayer was on my lips daily. I kept the news from the Synod to myself and did not share it with anyone. Apparently I was not the only one who learned of the news from the Synod in Rome. I was amazed that there were no more daily speculations and guessing games. From that day on, the daily phone calls ceased. I thought to myself, if the news from the Synod were true, it would take many months for the screening of the candidates, before the nominations could take place. In my pre—and post-Christmas parish work, I even forgot about the whole thing.

The Nomination

I was in the process of visiting homes in the parish with the Theophany blessing, as were other priests in the Archeparchy. Now even my parishioners stopped asking me questions about my possible candidacy for a bishop. All the noise somehow stopped and everything was quiet. But it was only the stillness before a storm.

Monday, January 19, 1981, was a normal day for me. I celebrated my daily Divine Liturgy with the Missionary Sisters of the Mother of God singing the liturgical responses. During my breakfast I read the daily newspaper. Afterward I went to my office, took the money from the Sunday collection from the safe, and took it to the bank. On my way home I stopped at the local hospital to visit my sick parishioners. By the time I returned home, the mailman had already delivered my daily mail. I opened and read my mail, typed some of the responses, and answered some phone calls. Right after my luncheon, I took the Ukrainian newspapers that arrived in the mail with me upstairs to my sitting room and lay on the sofa for a little siesta.

My siesta was interrupted by a phone call. The call was from the office of the Apostolic Nuncio in Washington, D.C., Archbishop Pio Laghi. His secretary called to inform me that the newly arrived

Nuncio wished to see me and that I should go to Washington for a talk with him. When I asked what is it all was about, he replied, when you come here the Nuncio will tell you. I asked then, whether it should be tomorrow; he said no, not tomorrow. Tomorrow was the inauguration of President Reagan, and the Nuncio is invited to attend the affair. Come Wednesday, and keep this conversation confidential.

This is how it all started. I was quite upset with the phone call from the Nuncio. I knew what it was all about, and it disturbed me no end. But I had to take hold of myself to keep my peace and do what seemed to be God's will for me. I made the necessary phone call to book a reservation on an airplane to Washington and back the same day. I could not get over the fact that there could have been a screening of the candidates in such a short time. The Synod was over December 2, 1980, and it was only January 19, 1981. Perhaps the screening was done much earlier, like after the death of Archbishop Senyshyn, or after the death of Archbishop Schmondiuk. If it were done earlier, then not one priest who received the questionnaire betrayed the secret. I knew then why the priest from the Chancery called me almost daily just to speculate about possible candidates. He must have known my name was among the candidates long ago.

Wednesday morning, January 21, 1981, without saying a thing to anyone, I drove my car to the Newark airport, parked it, and took my flight to Washington, D.C. The pilot informed us that we might arrive a bit late because of the heavy air traffic at Washington airport due to many passengers leaving the city after the presidential inauguration. I took a cab from the airport and arrived at the Nunciature just before noontime.

A nun opened the door for me, greeting me with grace and kindness. After I told her who I was, she asked me to sit down while she contacted the Nuncio. Soon she came back and asked me to go upstairs to the second floor. There Archbishop Pio Laghi was waiting for me and invited me in to his living room, asking me to take a seat. He was somewhat older than I, a friendly person with a pleasant smile. "I arrived in Washington only two days ago, he said, and brought with me your appointment papers. The Holy Father appointed you the new Metropolitan-Archbishop for Ukrainians in Philadelphia. Will you accept the appointment? I hope that you will not say no to the Holy Father?"

I replied, "Do I have to give you a definitive answer right now? I need some time to pray about what I should do. I do not want to make a mistake in my life about such an important matter. I do not wish to say no to the Holy Father, but on the Judgment Day before God, it will be I who will have to give an answer for my actions. I need some time to reflect if I am capable to take such a big burden on my shoulders."

The Archbishop replied, "You do not have to give me the answer today, here and now. On your way home you can pray and reflect and then, when you get home, call me and give me your answer. But you must be aware that it was the Holy Father himself who selected your name from among the candidates presented by your Synod of Bishops. He would be very disappointed if you would refuse this high dignity and honor. Should you decide to accept it, call me and at the same time write a letter addressed to the Holy Father, stating your acceptance of this nomination. Send the letter to me, and I will forward it to the Holy Father."

Archbishop Laghi got up. He thanked me for visiting him, and as I was about to leave, he said, "About fifteen minutes ago Father Innocent Lotocky was here. He was appointed by the Holy Father the new Bishop of your Chicago Eparchy."

My Decision

When I arrived back home it was already dinnertime. After the meal, I went to church to pray. No one was there, except of course our Lord in the Holy Eucharist in the tabernacle. I knelt down before the holy altar and prayed with all my heart and soul.

"My Heavenly Father, I come to you today with a heavy heart. I need your help to make maybe the most important decision in my life: should I accept the appointment offered to me by the Holy Father or not? Without your help I am not able to make this all-important decision.

I am afraid that I am not strong enough to carry this big burden on my weak shoulders. I fear that in my weakness I might falter, fall, and bring shame to your Church. You know me better that I know myself. You know that I love you, and wish to serve you faithfully for the rest of my life. But you also know all my intimate thoughts and desires, my weaknesses, my many sins, my feebleness, and deficiencies.

My dear Jesus, give me today the needed courage and stamina to say no to this appointment. Let not the shining miter be a temptation for my pride and me. Bring me to my senses and do not let me make this big mistake by accepting this appointment for it is over my head and my capabilities"

I then got up from kneeling, kissed the altar, and sat down on one of the chairs behind the altar. I said no words of prayer anymore, just looked at the tabernacle in the silence of my heart. I firmly believe that Jesus Christ, the Son of God, is really and truly present in the Holy Eucharist in the tabernacle. For some years already I would come daily at this time of the day to the church and spend an hour in adoration of our Eucharistic Lord.

So I just looked at the tabernacle and united my heart and soul with the Lord. After a while I heard in my heart very clear and unmistakable words of the Lord.

"O you of little faith, why did you doubt? Why do you have such a little trust in me? Why don't you recall my words recorded by the Prophet Isaiah, *"For my thoughts are not your thoughts, nor your ways my ways, says the Lord."* It would be good for you to also recall the words of my chosen Apostle Paul and apply them to yourself, *"God chose those whom the world considers absurd to shame the wise; he singled out the weak of this world to shame the strong. He chose the world's lowborn and despised, those who count for nothing, to reduce to nothing those who were something; so that mankind can do no boasting before God. . . . Let him who would boast, boast in the Lord."*

I do know all your weaknesses. You do not have to remind me of them, for long ago I said, *"Before I formed you in the womb I knew you."* You should rather recall my words recorded by St. Paul, *"My grace is enough for you, for in weakness power reaches perfection."* I know also all of your sins, but I did forgive them long ago. In spite of all your weaknesses, I have chosen and appointed you that you may go courageously and bear fruit in patience. Do not oppose my will! *"Do not let your heart be troubled, or be afraid."* I will be with you always."

There was no way for me now to oppose any further the will of God. I could not find a single excuse that would justify me before the tribunal of God on Judgment Day for not accepting the nomination. So, I got up, laid myself down on the floor in a cross form before the altar, and said, "I am yours, O Lord, do with me what you wish. I dedicate all my episcopal life and work to the powerful Protection of my Heavenly Mother, the Most Blessed Mother of God, Mary.

With peace in my heart I went back home. In the morning of the next day, I called the Apostolic Nuncio and informed him of my positive decision. Afterward I wrote a short letter to the Holy Father.

"Most Holy Father, Your Apostolic Nuncio in Washington, D.C., the Most Reverend Archbishop Pio Laghi, informed me that Your Holiness has appointed me Metropolitan-Archbishop of Philadelphia for Ukrainians. By this letter I wish to express my sincere gratitude to Your Holiness for placing trust in me and for this high distinction given to my unworthy person.

It was only out of obedience to Your Holiness, as the successor to St. Peter, that I gave my consent to this appointment, even though my conscience forces me to admit to Your Holiness that I am not worthy of this high office.

Offering my priesthood, my future episcopacy and myself to the Protection of the Most Holy Mother of God, I humbly ask your Apostolic Blessing. (Signed) Stephen Sulyk."

The Events that Followed

Tuesday, January 29, 1981, public announcement of my and Bishop Lotocky's nomination by the Holy Father was made by the Vatican and simultaneously by the Apostolic Nuncio in Washington, D.C. From that moment on, my telephone rang frequently. Congratulations and best wishes came from some bishops, priests, and lay people. Newspapers asked for my statement, biography, and a photo. Sisters Servants from Sloatsburg, NY, called with congratulations and informed me that Sister Jacquelyn would make a set of episcopal vestments as their gift for me.

I invited a few of my priestly friends to my rectory for a short meeting to ask their advice. It was their suggestion that I should immediately inform His Beatitude Cardinal Slipyj of my nomination and ask him to ordain me a bishop in his church of St. Sophia in Rome. Bishop Lotocky agreed to my suggestion and sent his letter to Cardinal Slipyj. The same day I wrote to Cardinal Slipyj:

"Your Beatitude, I was informed today that the Holy Father, John Paul II, appointed me Metropolitan-Archbishop of Philadelphia for Ukrainians. I feel obliged to express my deep gratitude to Your Beatitude for presenting my candidacy and to the Synod of Bishops of the Ukrainian Catholic Church for electing me.

The good of our Church to which you dedicated your entire life, to strengthen our Church and to achieve for her the Patriarchal dignity, will be the goals of my Episcopal ministry as well.

Kindly accept the assurance of my filial respect for you and my episcopal cooperation. I humbly request your blessing for my episcopal ministry.

Following the prescriptions of canon 321,1, #2, of *"Cleri sanctitati"* I ask you to bestow upon me the grace of Episcopal Ordination. I propose the date as Sunday, March 1, 1981, at the Church of St. Sophia in Rome."

I called the office of the Cardinal in Rome and read my letter to his secretary before I mailed it. The next day, February 2, 1981, Rev. Ivan Dacko, the Cardinal's secretary, called me, and stated, "You do not realize what a great joy you have caused His Beatitude and all of us here in Rome by requesting that he give you the Episcopal Ordination. His Beatitude wrote you a letter and I am going to read it to you now:

"Thank you for your letter dated January 29, 1981, transmitted to me by way of a phone call. I accepted your letter with joy for in a great and important moment of your life, you turned to me in the words of the Psalmist, *"Direct my steps according to your word; let not any wickedness rule over me"* (Psalms 119:133).

I welcome you into the sacred college of our Ukrainian Bishops and pray that God will bless you in your important episcopal ministry for the development and increase of the Philadelphia Archeparchy and for the good of our entire Church so that you may *"live in peace, safety, honor and health for many years, and rightly impart the word of your truth."*

In reply to your request, I will impart on you the Episcopal Ordination in Rome, March 1, 1981, in the Church of St. Sophia so
that our joy may be full and that we may *fulfill all justice.*

My Episcopal Ordination

On Tuesday, February 24, 1981, I departed from New York City's JFK Airport to Rome. I went early as to have some time to prepare myself spiritually for this most important moment in my life. I had spent several hours daily, making my private spiritual retreat in my church in Perth Amboy. I planned to spend at least three more days in St. Josaphat Seminary chapel in Rome.

My first day in Rome I paid a visit to Cardinal Vladylslav Rubin, the Prefect of the Congregation for Eastern Churches. I met him for the first time November 12, 1979, during the Episcopal Ordination of Archbishop Lubachivsky. I spoke to him in English, and he replied in good Ukrainian. He told me he was born in Ukraine of a Ukrainian mother and a Polish father. Thus he spoke both languages fluently. My next visit was to Bishop Myroslav Marusyn who lived at that time at St. Josaphat's Seminary. I got to know him first at Holy Spirit Seminary in Hirschberg, Germany. Very little time was left for me to go to the chapel for meditation.

His Beatitude Josyf Cardinal Slipyj bestows an episcopal mitre to
Archbishop Stephen Sulyk

The following day, Sister Servants from their Generalate in Rome
invited me for a luncheon. This again took some hours from my
free time. I used this opportunity to order a set of episcopal vestments and a folding miter for traveling purposes. The next day
Sister Lydia Korotkova, SSMI, from the Ukrainian program of the

Vatican Radio asked me to prepare a short greeting to be broadcast to Ukraine on the day of my Episcopal Ordination. She would come to the Seminary and record it on a tape recorder. I could not say no to her. Thinking that one of my relatives might be listening to the Vatican Radio, I agreed to prepare something. Among other things I said this:

> ". . . My Brothers and Sisters in Ukraine. On the occasion of my Episcopal Ordination today, I wish all of you to be strong and firm in your faith that Christ and his Church are invincible. Our Church was built on the rock of St. Peter. This is why all the powers of hell, of human denials, persecutions and malice will not overcome her. Christ and his Church have lived in Ukraine for one thousand years already. You, therefore, may be assured that our Church will continue to live as long as Ukrainian people are alive . . ."

The following day in the church of St. Sophia in Rome there was a rehearsal of the ceremonies connected with the Hierarchical Liturgy and of the ordination itself. There, to my great surprise, I met some of my dear friends from the United States of America who came especially to Rome to attend my ordination. Among them were: Msgrs. Emil Manastersky, Peter Fedorchuck, Leo Adamiak, Leon Mosko, Peter Skrincosky, Robert Moskal, Stephen Chomko, Revs. Peter Lypyn, Michael Pyrih, and Thomas Barylak. A great joy for me was the presence in Rome for my ordination Archbishop Gabriel Bukatko from Yugoslavia, Bishop Platon Kornylyak from Germany, Bishop Neil Savaryn from Canada, and Bishop Basil Losten from Stamford, CT, USA. Yet the most pleasant surprise was for me to see in Rome my Aunt Sophia, her daughter Mary, and my first cousin Theodore Sulyk from Poland.

Sunday, March 1, 1981, the two candidates, the concelebrating clergy, and the bishops all gathered at the nearby building of St. Clement's Ukrainian Catholic University. At the appointed time a procession was formed and all processed to St. Sophia Church. The celebrant and the chief consecrator was His Beatitude Cardinal Slipyj; Bishops Neil Savaryn, Basil Losten were the co-consecrators.[4]

The other concelebrants were bishops: Myroslav Marusyn, Gabriel Bukatko, and Platon Kornylyak. The duties of the archdeacons were performed by: Rt. Rev. Isidore Patrylo, OSBM, for Bishop Lotocky, and Archimandrite Lubomyr Husar for me. Rev. Ivan Dacko served as a deacon. Rev. Petro Steciuk served as the master of ceremonies.

Cardinal Slipyj at that time was eighty-nine years old and was weak in his legs. During the act of my episcopal consecration, Bishop Marusyn approached me as I was kneeling before the altar with an opened Gospel book over my head, and laid his right hand upon my head, joining the other two co-consecrators, reciting with them the form of ordination.

In preparation for the Episcopal Ordination Liturgy at the St. Sophia Basilica, Rome, Italy, March 1, 1981. (l. to r.): Rev. Ivan Dacko, Rt. Rev. Isidore Patrylo, OSBM—Archimandrite of the Basilian Fathers, Msgr. Stephen Sulyk, Rev. Innocent Lotocky, OSBM, and Rev. Lubomyr Husar.

---

[4] The other concelebrants were bishops: Myroslav Marusyn, Gabriel Bukatko, and Platon Kornylyak. The duties of the archdeacons were performed by: Rt. Rev. Isidore Patrylo, OSBM, for Bishop Lotocky, and Archimandrite Lubomyr Husar for me. Rev. Ivan Dacko served as a deacon. Rev. Petro Steciuk served as the master of ceremonies.

At the conclusion of the Episcopal Ordination Liturgy, March 1, 1981 (l. to r.): During the Episcopal Ordination at the St. Sophia Basilica, Rome, Italy, March 1, 1981. Archbishop Stephen Sulyk with his main consecrator–His Beatitude Josyf Cardinal Slipyj. Archbishop Myroslav Marusyn–Secretary of the Congregation for the Eastern Churches; Bishop Basil Losten–Eparch of Stamford; newly ordained Bishop Innocent Lotocky, OSBM–Eparch of Chicago; His Beatitude Josyf Cardinal Slipyj; (behind him) Rev. Peter Steciuk; Archbishop Stephen Sulyk; Bishop N. Savaryn, OSBM–Eparch of Edmonton; Archbishop Gabriel Bukatko–Eparch of Krizevci, Croatia and Bishop Platon Kornyljak–Exarch of Germany

After the reading of the Gospel, Cardinal Slipyj, while sitting in the royal doors, read his homily. Here are some segments of it:

"Our soul rejoices in the Lord because today by the power of the Holy Spirit and by the laying of our hands we have transmitted Christ's sacred authority to two teachers of faith, hierarchs and pastors of our holy Ukrainian Catholic Church. We all rejoice today because our suffering Church in Ukraine, as well as the one in the free world, by this event gives testimony that she is alive, strives, and perpetuates Christ's work by fearless confession, suffering and by these new apostles in the persons of the hierarchs—Stephen and Innocent.

By these my tired hands I transmit to you a holy touch that of the Servant of God Metropolitan Andrew (Sheptytsky), my great predecessor of the Kiev-Galician See. Thus through the apostolic succession you have embarked on the one-thousand-year-old course of bishops-successors of this venerable see upon which sat and ruled giants of the spirit who were all for all among their people, especially at times of disasters and enslavement . . . .

Here in this basilica of St. Sophia, as though a sister of the Kievan Sophia, are present the spirits of our great and holy predecessors, Vladimir, Olga, Josaphat, and Andrew. We stand before them . . . with our obligations to guard their great heritage, their apostolic faith, our native devoted piety, the sacred rites of our Church and nation and to be on fire with love of the Lord and his eternal truths . . ."

After his homily the Cardinal remained seated and motioned to me to take his place at the altar. I was honored to have to take the place of the Major Archbishop at this holy altar, even if it were only for this part of the Liturgy. At the end of the Liturgy he wanted to vest me in the Eastern rite hat with a white veil, but I asked him to postpone it till the next day and then give it to me privately.

Since he was the only prelate in our Church to wear such a head-piece, someone might misinterpret this as though he is marking me his successor. I did not want this to be done as a part of the ordination ceremony.

During the Episcopal Ordination at the St. Sophia Basilica, Rome, Italy March 1, 1981. Archbishop Stephen Sulyk with his main consecrator - His Beatitude Josyf Cardinal Slipyj.

A Festive Reception

In the evening of the same day there was a festive reception at St. Josaphat's Seminary on Gianicolo Hill, marking the occasion of the two episcopal ordinations. Cardinal Rubin, Bishop Marusyn, Father Sophronius Mudry, OSBM, and the rector of the seminary gave special talks. All of them greeted the newly ordained bishops, congratulating them and wishing them a lot of success. At the end I got up and gave my talk. In it I expressed my deep spiritual feelings at the episcopal ordination. I had mixed emotions rooted deep in my soul, the feelings of joy and of the fear of God, as well as of sincere heartfelt gratitude. I expressed my gratitude to God, to the Most Holy Mother of God, to His Holiness Pope John Paul II, to my parents who did not live to see this day, and to all there present. Then I continued:

> "What a deep gratitude fills the heart of a priest toward his consecrator through whose hands he receives the apostolic succession of the apostolic powers, the grace of the fullness of the holy priesthood, which no one has ever earned.
>
> Deep down in my heart I do experience today such emotions. These are strengthened by the consciousness that the Providence

of God granted me the grace that His Beatitude, Cardinal Josyf Slipyj, laid his hands upon my head, unworthy as I am. These are the hands of a confessor of faith, the hands that were privileged to be tortured by the enemies of God, that were suffering for the faith of our fathers, for the unity of the Holy Church, for the faithfulness and loyalty to the successor of St. Peter. It was through these hands that I received today the grace of God, which binds my episcopacy by an unbreakable chain with our silent and suffering Church in the catacombs of Ukraine, the Church of the new martyrs and confessors.

I think that no one could say that he has earned the episcopal dignity. This is true especially in my case . . . Yet by the judgment of Cardinal Slipyj and of the Synod of our Bishops, as approved and appointed by His Holiness Pope John Paul II, I was called to be the Metropolitan- Archbishop of Philadelphia for Ukrainians. This was done not to reward me for the past, but in order to expect from me sincere efforts in the future. I wish, therefore, to assure His Beatitude and all of you my brother bishops, that I will, with the help of the grace of God, with all my strength imitate your brilliant example . . ."

The following day at 7:30 A.M. all of our Bishops present in Rome with His Beatitude Cardinal Slipyj concelebrated a Divine Liturgy in St. Peter's Basilica at the altar of St. Basil the Great, under which rests the body of our great priest-martyr, St. Josaphat.

The same day the Congregation for Eastern Churches arranged for a reception at the Hotel Columbus, honoring the two newly ordained bishops. Present were Cardinal Rubin, Archbishop Silvestrini, and Bishop Marusyn, all our Bishops present in Rome, as well as our priests residing in Rome. There were no speeches. At the end I thanked Cardinal Rubin for the honor extended to the newly ordained two bishops.

Tuesday, March 3, 1981, Bishop Lotocky and I went to see Cardinal Slipyj to extend to him our personal thanks for ordaining us.

He received us graciously and was very happy to see both of us. On this occasion he asked his secretary to read his letter dated March 3, 1981, prot. # 9378/81. In this letter he insisted that we keep our ancient traditions, which had been abandoned and forgotten, i.e., that we wear the Eastern episcopal hat covered with a veil, white for the metropolitans and black for bishops. He then asked me to come closer to him. He placed on my head the hat covered with a white veil. I thanked him, embraced him, and kissed him.

Visiting the Holy Father

Wednesday, March 4, 1981, the Holy Father had a public audience at the Pope Paul VI auditorium in the Vatican. The two newly ordained bishops were escorted to the stage, joining six Latin Bishops. After the Holy Father's talk, he asked the bishops on the stage to join him in bestowing the Apostolic Blessing to the attending visitors. Afterward we were escorted to separate rooms where I met my Aunt Sophia, her daughter Mary, my cousin Theodore Sulyk from Poland, Father Peter Lypyn, and others.

In a short while the Holy Father came into the room, greeted me warmly, and asked in Polish, where was I born? I replied—in a small village in the Carpathian Mountains.—What was the name of your village? He asked again. I said, Balnycia. Then he said, "I was there, while walking through these mountains in a summer, but all the houses there were burned down. Nothing was left." Having said that, his cheeks got somewhat red. Apparently he felt the pain in my heart for the loss of my homeland. He then changed the subject and recalled our Cathedral church in Philadelphia and the imposing mosaic behind the altar. He greeted each present there with me, and took a group photograph. Then he left to the next room where Bishop Lotocky and his friends were awaiting for him.

Return to My Parish

hen my airplane landed at the JFK Airport in New York, and the passengers were disembarking, going through the passport control, some official came up to me and asked my name. When I told him who I was, he took my passport, escorted me through the control, bypassing the long line into a room full of our people. There were representatives from our New York City parishes, Father Anthony Borsa, local dean, Sister Stephanie—superior general of Sister Servants of Mary Immaculate, some twenty boy and girl scouts, representatives of other youth organizations, and a group of my parishioners from Perth Amboy. I was greeted with speeches and flowers. The Plast members were especially happy, for I was the first of their members to achieve this high church position.

I thanked one and all for this most pleasant surprise, greeted each one personally and gave them my blessing. The Perth Amboy group told me that they had a busload of parishioners ready to welcome me at the airport, but an unexpected snowfall made it impossible.

As soon as I arrived in Perth Amboy, I noticed that the church was full of people. They all were waiting for me. First I went into the rectory, put my cassock, mantle, and miter on, and to went to church. The choir began to sing the hymn welcoming a bishop. I knelt before the royal doors and prayed with deep emotions. I got so emotional that I could not speak a word! I just stood in front and asked each one to come to me, imparting to each my episcopal blessing.

The following Sunday, March 8, 1981, I offered my first Pontifical Divine Liturgy in my parish church with the concelebration of two priests and a deacon. The activists in the parish organized a farewell banquet for me in the afternoon of that Sunday in the school auditorium. Msgr. Leon Mosko was the master of ceremonies; Msgr. Emil Manastersky was the main speaker, while Msgr. Victor J. Pospishil, a renowned canonist and author of many books, gave remarks of his observations of our close cooperation while we were neighboring priests. Present were also two Latin rite priests, Msgr. Michael Churak, pastor of the Holy Trinity Church, and Rev. Stephen Horwath, pastor of Our Lady of Hungary Church, Perth Amboy.

The Missionary Sisters with the school faculty prepared a concert of songs and national dances, while Mr. Roman Lewycky, church choir director, likewise gave a presentation of several selections of church hymns. Representatives of the parish organizations stepped forward and each gave a short farewell talk and a gift to me. At the end of the program, I gave a short farewell talk, thanking God, the Blessed Mother, the Patroness of this parish, for their graces and help given to me during my pastoral ministry of nineteen years in this parish. I thanked the clergy present for their friendship and for being with me on this memorable occasion. Above all I thanked all the parishioners for putting up with me for so many years, for their good will and splendid cooperation. I concluded thus:

"Among you I always felt at home as among my own brothers and sisters, and such you always were for me. I would be very happy to be able to stay with you as your pastor for the rest of my days, but the Lord God has ordained other things for me, another place of work and other duties. I am a servant of God

340

and have humbly accepted His will. This is why I have to leave you. But I am not abandoning you. I am taking all of you with me and will carry you in my heart for the rest of my life. You will always be in my prayers. I hope that you, too, will remember me and sometimes with a good word will mention my name to God in your prayers. God love you one and all!"

Visit to the Orthodox Metropolitan

The Archieparchial Committee selected the date for my installation as Tuesday, March 31, 1981. I had about three weeks to pack my belongings, especially my many books, and to move them to my residence in Philadelphia. I selected as my successor in the parish Rev. Roman Dubitsky. I knew him since he was in high school. In March of 1981, Father Roman was pastor of St. Nicholas Church, Wilmington, Delaware. When I called him and proposed to him to be my successor at the Assumption Church in Perth Amboy, he tried very hard to convince me that he should stay in Wilmington. But on my insistence, he finally agreed, and within a week he came to Perth Amboy.

I decided that before I move permanently to Philadelphia I should take the opportunity to make an official visit to the Ukrainian Orthodox Metropolitan Mstyslav Skrypnyk in nearby South Bound Brook, N.J. I called his office, but he was not home at that time. His secretary took my name and my telephone number and promised to call me back. He returned my call and I was given Thursday, March 23, 1981, at 10:00 A.M. for my visit to him.

Dressed in my eastern cassock, the monastic hat with the white veil, and accompanied by Father Roman Dubitsky, I came to South Bound Brook at the appointed time. I was met by two orthodox priests and escorted to the Metropolitan's residence. He was exuberantly happy with my visit and showed his happiness in many ways. First we exchanged a kiss of peace in the Eastern style. Then we continued with a very friendly conversation, inquiring of my election by the Synod of Bishops, my appointment, my episcopal ordination by Cardinal Slipyj in Rome, and of the date for my installation. He offered as gifts to me several liturgical books newly published by his Church.

"I would like to show you our memorial church and the museum, but I am awaiting a photographer from the Ukrainian daily newspaper *Svoboda*, he said. At that time one of his priests came in and announced that the photographer had arrived. The two of us, accompanied by Father Roman Dubitsky and the two orthodox priests, went to the St. Andrew Memorial Church, commemorating the horrible forced famine of 1932–33 in Ukraine, organized by Stalin, which caused the death of some seven to ten million Ukrainians. He explained to me the specific architectural qualities of the church structure. Then I was led to the museum in the lower level of the church. With certain pride, the Metropolitan showed me some very beautiful, priceless, and rare liturgical books, items belonging to worship from past centuries, and some insignia from the period of the Kozaks and Hetmans. From there we went to the nearby cemetery where rest the mortal remains of many outstanding Church and lay personages.

As I was saying goodbye to him, he thanked me profusely for my visit and promised to send me some of the pictures taken by the photographer. Not one picture was developed, because, as the photographer apologized, being in a hurry he did not load the film into the camera correctly.

My Installation as Metropolitan-Archbishop

The Installation Divine Liturgy Tuesday, March 31, 1981, was attended by all our Ukrainian Catholic Bishops from the United States of America.[5] The long procession of many religious sisters, several hundred of our priests from all over the country, the seminarians from our minor St. Basil's Seminary in Stamford and from St. Josaphat's Seminary in Washington, D.C., and many bishops all processed into the Cathedral church. The rite of the installation took place before

---

[5] In attendace were: Archbishop Myroslav Ivan Lubachivsky of Philadelphia; Basil Losten of Stamford and Innocent Lotocky, OSBM of Chicago; all of our Bishops from Canada—Metropolitan Maxim Hermaniuk, CSsR of Winnipeg; Isidore Borecky of Toronto; Andrew Roborecky of Saskatoon; Neil Savaryn, OSBM from Edmonton; and Jerome Chimy, OSBM from New Westminster. Present also were—Efraim Krevey, OSBM, from Curitiba, Brazil; Platon Kornylyak from Munich, Germany; Augustine Horniak, OSBM from London, Great Britain; and Andrew Sapelak from Argentina. Present likewise were Metropolitan-Archbishop Stephen Kocisko from the Pittsburgh Byzantine Archeparchy; his auxiliary John Bilock; and Bishop Michael Dudick from Passaic. From among the Latin rite Bishops were—Cardinal John Krol; his four auxiliary bishops, Apostolic Nuncio Archbishop Pio Laghi from Washington D.C. Ukrainian Orthodox Metropolitan Mstyslav Skrypnyk and his auxiliary Archbishop Constantine, were accompanied by three of their Orthodox priests. All together there were thirty-three Catholic and two Orthodox bishops.

the Divine Liturgy. I was sitting in the royal doors. The Apostolic Nuncio, Archbishop Pio Laghi, opened the rite with a short word of welcome. Then Msgr. Michael Poloway read in English the so-called Papal Bull, appointing me to this position, and in Ukrainian by Msgr. Stephen Hrynuck. Then the Apostolic Nuncio read a short Prayer of Installation, escorted me from the royal doors to my throne on the right side in front of the iconostas. I sat down and he handed me the crosier, the symbol of my episcopal authority. We then exchanged a kiss of peace. Afterward the deans, as representatives of all the clergy, came to me, kissing my epigonation, my right shoulder and my hand, thus pledging love and obedience to me. As I looked into the congregation my heart was filled with joy to have seen there all my relatives present: my Aunt Sophia, my Uncle Dmytro Stec, their two children, Mary and Frank, and Mary's children, Steven, Lydia, Theresa, and Donna.

Archbishop Pio Laghi, Apostolic Nuncio, installing Archbishop Stephen Sulyk, March 31, 1981.

In my homily I said:

"Approach with the fear of God and with faith! With these words a deacon invites the faithful to receive Holy Communion during Divine Liturgy. Likewise I stand on this holy place before the face of Almighty God and before you, my most honored and beloved brothers and sisters in the Lord, *"with the fear of God and with faith!"* I stand with the fear of God because fright has entered my heart, asking do I have sufficient strength to fulfill the great task the Lord God has placed upon my shoulders? I stand with the faith of God because, following the example of St. Paul, I must address his words to myself, *"Strength is made perfect in weakness."* (2 Corinthians 12:9) So, *"the Lord is my strength!"* And *"I can do all things in him who strengthens me."* (Philippians 4:13) Your kind and so numerous presence here today for these celebrations diminishes my fright, because of your expressed desire to aid me in my difficult episcopal ministry . . .

Archbishop Stephen Sulyk as homilist at his Installation Liturgy, March 31, 1981.

I come to you with a sincere heart and with the intention to serve you with all the powers of my soul and mind. I come so that with your help and cooperation we may not only preserve our Church and rite, our native traditions and heritage, as well as our ethnic identity. I come that we may further develop, increase, and strengthen these our treasures and then hand them over to our posterity.

I make the words of the Servant of God, Metropolitan Andrew Sheptytsky, my own, "I would like very much to wipe the tears from the eyes of those who are crying, to console those who are saddened, to strengthen those who are weak or ill, to cure everyone who is sick, elucidate everyone who is in darkness. I would like to become all for all of you so that all of you might be saved. May I die today and not know the joy eternal, may I be separated from Christ so that you, my brothers and sisters, who are my kinsmen according to the flesh, be saved!" These are the only wishes and desires of my heart.

So, my dear altar brothers and religious sisters, and you, the People of God, accept me as your spiritual father and pastor of your souls. Help me with your prayers and your sincere cooperation. For in unity there is strength. When we come to *"Love one another so that we may be of one mind,"* as it befits the members of the one family of God's children, then God will be with us, as well as his grace, peace, and blessings will be upon our Church and our nation."

Installation Liturgy group picture. (l. to r.): Michael Dudick—Eparch of
Passaic, Andrew Roborecky—Eparch of Edmonton, Innocent Lotocky,
OSBM–Eparch of Chicago, Stephen Kocisko–Metropolitan of Pittsburgh,
Msgr Raymond Revak, Metropolitan-Archbishop Stephen Sulyk, Rev. Roman
Dubitsky, Maxim Hermaniuk, CSsR–Metropolitan of Winnipeg, Basil Losten–
Eparch of Stamford, Isidore Boretsky–Eparch of Toronto, Rev. Walter
Bilynsky, Andrew Sapelak–Eparch of Buenos Aires, Michael Hrynchyshyn,
CSsR–Exarch of France, Emil J. Mihalik–Eparch of Parma.

In the afternoon of the same day there was a great banquet in
my honor in the Hotel Sheraton in Philadelphia. All our bishops
who concelebrated at the Installation Divine Liturgy were present
as well as most of our priests, religious sisters, and over one thousand faithful. Msgr. Leo Adamiak spoke in the name of the priests
and Gregory Luznycky in the name of the laity; Bishop Losten on
behalf of our bishops, and Metropolitan Hemaniuk, CSsR, in the
name of the Synod of Bishops.

The words of Gregory Luznycky were valuable and are worth
repeating:

On this, the first day of occupying the Metropolitan's see by Archbishop Stephen, we the lay people welcome you and, handing over to you our hearts, we ask you to inspire us with love for our Church just as your parents have inspired you. Our Church is the only one capable of diminishing the day's mutual acrimony, and teaches us to give our life with love for our friends. Teach us to love our Church, for she is the only one capable of teaching us the virtues of self-sacrifice, obedience, and discipline and with it the unity of mind of soul, because without these there never will be a victory.

Our dear Metropolitan Stephen, we the lay people sincerely welcome you and ask you to share with us your faith and the consciousness of the historical mission which God himself gave our Church and nation to fulfill.

In my talk at the banquet I tried to sketch out a program of my episcopal ministry as I envisioned it in my heart.

"The festive character of the august assembly here this afternoon is not only personally gratifying, but also spiritually satisfying. I see your presence here as a tangible expression of your willingness to support and assist me in bearing the formidable burdens that have been placed on my shoulders with the office of metropolitan and archbishop. Your encouraging words and gracious assurances are comforting and strengthening as I prepare to face the multitude and many-faced challenges and problems that await me. I would like to review some of the more important areas of my concern with you at this time.

I would like to find ways and means to assist our underground Church in the catacombs of Ukraine. The dedication, zeal and spirit of sacrifice of these bishops, priests, and faithful are, I believe, the reasons God continues to shower us in the free world with blessings and all sorts of good things. It is our duty—born of a debt of gratitude on our part for the splendid example of devotion to the true Church they give the world—that we seek ways to support, strengthen, and encourage our suffering Church. From the messages they are able to get to us, it is clear that nothing so elates and invigorates them as does news of how well we in the free world support and promote our Ukrainian churches; how zealously we preserve and spread our Ukrainian religious, cultural and national heritage; and with that spirit of unity we Ukrainians work together, striving to reach our sacred goals. No, we cannot and will not forget them ever . . .

To our Orthodox and Protestant brothers, I extend the hand of friendship and embrace you with the kiss of brotherly love. Times and circumstances are long gone when we were in opposition or even in competition with one another. For past failures in Christian charity, please accept our humble and contrite plea: in the name of Christ, forgive us! Henceforth let us assist each other in strengthening our respective churches and cooperate in fostering Christian love among all Ukrainians. And if we are to compete with one another, let it be in our love for Christ and our fellow man . . .

A magnificent building was erected here in Philadelphia fifteen years ago, our Ukrainian Catholic Cathedral. It is the pride of our Church, being the largest Ukrainian Catholic church anywhere, including Ukraine, and it is one of the largest in Eastern Christendom. My predecessor began the completion of the interior decoration of the Cathedral, and I will continue it.

In addition, a modest Archdiocesan Office, a residence for the Archbishop and a new rectory for the Cathedral Parish will be built. The Archdiocesan Chancery Office and the Archbishop's living quarters are now located in three unconnected row houses, some 150 years old; leaky firetraps, ready to be demolished and expensive to maintain. While the expenditures connected with

these projects are considerable in view of present inflated building costs, I know that our Ukrainian people, in their generosity,
will gladly support them . . .

There are a number of other tasks and challenges that face us:
Raising the funds necessary to maintain our seminary; Develop-
ing a viable eparchial youth organization; Establishing continuing religious education centers for adults; The preparation for
Ukrainian and English liturgical translations for our return to
our genuine Eastern liturgical traditions; The strengthening of
our weekly newspaper, *The Way*; The organization of pastoral
centers for our retired faithful in Florida; The preparation of a
dignified commemoration of the Millennium of Christianity in
Ukraine in 1988; And others, which I shall not even mention
here today.

That which faces us is a formidable agenda, but it can be carried
out with the help and blessing of God and with the full cooperation of you, my dear priests and faithful."

Two days later, Thursday, April 2, 1981, the Installation of
Bishop Innocent Lotocky, OSBM, took place at the St. Nicholas
Cathedral in Chicago. I took an active part in these festivities and
as a metropolitan I personally conducted the Rite of the Installation. In my homily I said:

"It has pleased Divine Providence that the Most Rev. Bishop Innocent Lotocky be placed upon the cathedra of the Ukrainian
Eparchy of St. Nicholas in the Blessed-by-God City of Chicago.
I as Metropolitan of the Ukrainian Church in the United States
have the privilege to bring to completion the decision of His
Holiness, Pope John Paul II, who appointed Your Excellency to
this holy office, fulfilling the wish of the Holy Synod of Bishops
under the leadership of His Beatitude Joseph Slipyj, the Father
and Head of our Ukrainian Church.

Our Church places her trust and hope in Bishop Lotocky, expecting from him that he would not only be a zealous and alert shepherd to you, dear priests, religious and people of this Eparchy, but that he will also be a valuable member of the Episcopal College of the Ukrainian Church, and with his wise counsel and proven devotion to God's Church promote the welfare of our Ukrainian Church in this country as well as in the whole world.

You, dear people of the Eparchy of Chicago, are entitled to receive as your second bishop a man of the ability, zeal, and dedication of Bishop Lotocky. It is so because you have shown your first bishop, Jaroslav Gabro of blessed memory, affection and love as an expression of your spiritual joy at being led by such a loving and kind bishop as he was. I was deeply moved in observing the signs of affection you bestowed upon his body at the time of the Funeral Liturgy. I have not yet seen any priest or bishop receiving from his faithful as many kisses, accompanied by tears, as you in your kindness and grief expressed sincerely at his burial. God, knowing your filial devotion to your bishop, has graciously willed to send you another zealous successor and shepherd in the person of Bishop Innocent.

It is not necessary for me that I introduce Bishop Innocent to you since the remembrance of the apostolic zeal with which he worked among you as the pastor of this church, which will be his cathedral, is still alive. Show yourself grateful for the action of the Holy Spirit who was present in the intentions of His Beatitude Major Archbishop Joseph, in the election of the Holy Synod of our Church, and in the ratification by His Holiness John Paul II, by gladly, willingly, and readily giving him your complete and dedicated obedience, trust, and cooperation as your spiritual father and shepherd . . ."

The Beginnings of my Episcopal Ministry

There is a saying that all beginnings are difficult. I found that to be true. After almost twenty-nine years of pastoral work, all of the daily rhythm of my life had been broken. Up until now there was not a day that I would not have some pastoral relationships or dealings with my parishioners, with the teachers in the school or the students. Having become a bishop, all of this ceased. Now my daily work consisted of simple office work, answering phone calls, listening to complaints, writing, or reading. The chancery was located at that time in a row house at 815 North Franklin Street. Most of the daily work of a bishop is office work and endless meetings. In my first days and weeks as a bishop I longed for the warmth and friendship of my parishioners in Perth Amboy. In addition to the feeling of having lost something, my coworkers in the chancery did not receive me warmly. They seemed to be indifferent or maybe even envious. When I introduced some minor changes in the daily office routine, they pulled back and became remote.

Now I found out that my experience in the two years I worked in Archbishop Bohachevsky's office became very valuable. I already knew the ins and outs of chancery work. Yet, I needed reliable and trustworthy help. When one day the Provincial of the Sister Servants from Sloatsburg, N.Y., paid me a courtesy visit, I asked her whether she could spare someone to come work in this office and help me. She was not prepared to give me an answer right there. So I suggested, could you give me St. Thomas Hrynewich since she had some canon law courses at the Catholic University in Washington, D.C., while working in our seminary as a cook? My question cheered her up, and she replied, "Oh yes, I will be happy to have Sister Thomas come here and work in the chancery for you." She became my right hand for the twenty years of my episcopal ministry. Later on, I made her vice-chancellor, and later, I made her a chancellor, since I had no available priest to take this position.

I lived then in a very narrow three-story row house building at 818 North Franklin Street, next to the cathedral parish rectory. My bedroom and sitting room were on the second floor, while on the third floor I had my chapel. At first I ate with the cathedral fathers. But this was not the best arrangement. The fathers needed their privacy, and so did I. So I asked the Sister Servants for a sister to be my cook and a housekeeper, while living in the convent. They could not spare a sister for this purpose. So I asked the Missionary Sisters of the Mother of God who have a house just one block away and conduct a nursery for the pre-school children. Their answer was inspiring for me. "This is why we are here, to serve you, our Metropolitan."

A special event happened during my first weeks as a bishop in Philadelphia. One day I was low and somewhat depressed. I do not recall the reasons why I felt so. While in this state of mind, I was kneeling and praying in my chapel, adoring our Lord in the Holy Eucharist in the tabernacle. My heart was heavy and I must have complained to the Lord. Suddenly I heard loudly and clearly in my heart, *"Did I ever abandon you?"* This inaudible voice was so powerful that it changed my thinking and my attitude. I realized how true this voice was. Indeed, God never abandoned me. He was with me since my birth and protected me always. It is I who seem to forget this fact sometimes and behave as though I was all alone and abandoned. As long as I live, I will never forget this voice. Every time I recall this voice, it lifts me up and gives me courage and strength to go on and face whatever problems or difficulties are in my way.

It was during my first month in office that the Basilian Sisters invited me to visit their Mother House in Fox Chase, a suburb of Philadelphia, on Tuesday, April 28, 1981. I was welcomed with bread and salt by Sister Theodosia, the Provincial Superior, offered a Divine Liturgy in their chapel, gave a homily and then was treated to a delicious meal. After dinner a few of the younger sisters escorted me to see their beautiful buildings: Manor College, the Academy, the dormitories, and their library. As we were about to enter the library building one of the sisters asked me, "Archbishop, what do you think of women priests?" Without much reflection I replied, "The same as did Jesus Christ, our Lord!" Later on as I was driving back home, I realized that God was with me and it was He who gave me the words of my reply to the sister infected by feminist ideas.

Orthodox Metropolitan Mstyslav's Official Revisit

June 17, 1981, the Ukrainian Orthodox Metropolitan Mstyslav paid me an official visit. He arrived in Philadelphia with two of his priests. I knew of the time of his arrival and was waiting for him. We exchanged a kiss of peace, as it is traditional in the Eastern churches, and escorted him to our new and beautiful cathedral. I was accompanied by three of our priests from the Chancery. The royal doors were opened, we entered the sanctuary and kissed the altar and again exchanged a kiss of peace. I asked him to take a seat while I said a few words of greeting:

"The 45th chapter of the book of Genesis describes a very moving scene, how after many years of separation Joseph made himself known to his brothers in Egypt. *"No one else was about when he (Joseph) made himself known to his brothers . . . I am Joseph, he said to his brothers. Is my father still in good health? Thereupon he flung himself on the neck of his brother Benjamin and wept, and Benjamin wept in his arms. Joseph then kissed all his brothers, crying over each of them; and only then were his brothers able to talk with him."*

Your Beatitude! Our meeting today is a mirror of the biblical story just quoted. The two of us are brothers, two sons of the same mother, Mother Ukraine. We have met here today in this holy place, and have recognized each other and rejoice. Our meeting in this church of the most holy, most pure and Immaculate Mother of God has likewise a very significant meaning. Our Heavenly Mother embraces both of us as her sons. She is the same Queen Mother to whose powerful protection Jaroslav the Wise dedicated our nation. Please accept my most sincere thanks and gratitude for the honor of your kind and brotherly visit. I hope and pray that all our bishops and priests as well as the faithful could always live and practice brotherly relationships with your bishops, priests, and your faithful. This is the will and the command of our Savior and God, Jesus Christ. You and I *"must do this if we would fulfill all of God's demands"* (Matthew 3:15).

Mstyslav Skrypnyk–Metropolitan of the Ukrainian Orthodox Church in the United States visits Archbishop Stephen Sulyk June 17, 1981.

He thanked me and said a few words of greetings to me but was not prepared for something more elaborate. We then walked out of the church. He was in a hurry to get somewhere for an appointment and declined my invitation to stop in my house or office.

My First Auxiliary Bishop

As the result of the persistent efforts of Coadjutor-Archbishop Lubachivsky in Rome, the Holy Father on Friday, August 14, 1981, appointed Msgr. Robert M. Moskal as my auxiliary bishop. At that time he was the rector of the Cathedral parish and the chancellor of the Archeparchy. His episcopal ordination took place on Tuesday, October 13, 1981, in our Cathedral Church. I was the main consecrator while Bishops Basil Losten and Innocent Lotocky were the co-consecrators. Coadjutor-Archbishop Lubachivsky came from Rome for this festive occasion to rejoice with his very close friend. With him came also Msgr. George Milanyk, the undersecretary of the Eastern Congregation.

It happened that the Stamford Eparchy was observing its 25th Anniversary on Sunday October 11, 1981. Cardinal Rubin, the Prefect of the Eastern Congregation, was invited to this celebration. So he also came to Philadelphia and took part in the festivities of the episcopal ordination of Msgr. Robert Moskal. Our Major Archbishop, Cardinal Josyf Slipyj, was not able to come. In his private letter to me he expressed his indignation because I accepted an auxiliary while I was at that time still young, and there was no real need of an auxiliary bishop. Apparently his Coadjutor-Archbishop did not inform the Major Archbishop of his efforts on behalf of Bishop Moskal.

Episcopal Ordination of Bishop Slavomir Miklos

During the Synod of our Bishops, which was held in Rome from January 31 to February 12, 1983, Rev. Slavomir Miklos, spiritual director of our Seminary in Zagreb, Yugoslavia, was nominated by the Holy Father to succeed the late Archbishop Gabriel Bukatko as the bishop of the Krizevi Eparchy. He informed us that his episcopal ordination would take place March 25, 1983. He invited me personally and pleaded for me to come and attend his great day.

In order to maintain friendly relationships with all our bishops, I decided to make the long and tiring trip to Yugoslavia. Bishop Basil Losten decided likewise to make the trip. We traveled together and arrived at the airport in Zagreb Tuesday, March 22, 1983. The Coadjutor-Archbishop Lubachivsky, who arrived from Rome with Father George Dzudzar, a native of Yugoslavia and a doctoral candidate at the Pontifical Oriental Institute in Rome, welcomed us.

In the bishop's residence in Zagreb we were welcomed by Bishop Joachim Segedy, the administrator of the Eparchy, Bishop-nominee Slavomir Miklos and Sister Servants who were employed there. After a meal we were escorted by Father Dzudzar to visit the Latin Rite Cathedral of Zagreb, the largest one in the Balkans. There rest the earthly remains of Cardinal Aloysius Stepinac and Cardinal Franio Seper. One could always see fresh flowers and lighted vigil lights on both of these graves. There are always some faithful kneeling and praying there for favors through the intercession of these two great churchmen. On the wall beside each grave there hung tablets with expressions of gratitude for favors received.

From there we went to see the huge Seminary building, some 300 years old. Next to it was a parish church. Bishop Slavomir used to live in this seminary and was the spiritual director. Entering the old church building, one's eyes rest immediately on the beautiful and majestic iconostas. The tabernacle was made in a shape of the Old Testament Tabernacle. In the sacristy one could see in a glass-covered case a shroud (Plaschanytzia) over two hundred years old, woven with gold and silver threads, made in Ukraine.

On Wednesday, March 23, 1983, Father George Dzudzar drove Bishop Losten, Coadjutor Archbishop Lubachivsky and me to the center of their Eparchy, the town of Krizevci, situated Northwest of Zagreb. When this Eparchy was first erected in the year 1777, the Empress of Austria, Maria Theresa, donated 300 acres of land, a church, and a school with a dormitory building. The communist government of Yugoslavia confiscated almost all the land. It was a great loss for the eparchy and the bishop. We were able to visit the old buildings, old church books, and the archives. The church at that time was under repair. Electrical lights were being installed there for the first time. Basilian Sisters were taking care of the church and the grounds while conducting a home for the aged.

The following day, Thursday, March 24, 1983, we went to a town called Rus'key Kerestur, a place where the episcopal ordination was to take place the next day. On our way we stopped and visited several of our parishes. In the city of Banialuka we visited the pastor, Father Zenon Sagadin. His sister was a teacher in the Perth Amboy, N.J. parish school while I was pastor there. Bombs destroyed his beautiful church building during the last war. During our long trip to the destination we visited parishes in Khorvachany, Lishnia, Perniavor, and Vukovar.

Rus'key Kerestur is a town of over six thousand inhabitants, consisting entirely of immigrants from Carpatho Ukraine and their descendants who preserved their language and church traditions to this day. In their beautiful church in front of the iconostas were two tablets, marking the burial places of their former bishops— Dionisius Niaradi and Gabriel Bukatko. I was told that when Archbishop Bukatko was being buried in 1981, they were able to see through a glass cover on the casket, the face of Bishop Niaradi as though he were alive, not corrupted at all. Those of our priests and bishops who knew Bishop Niaradi have always claimed that he was a very saintly person.

Friday, March 25, 1983, the Feast of the Annunciation, a procession was formed at 9:45 A.M. consisting of over seventy priests of the Byzantine and Latin Rite, various religious and the Bishops of both Rites. The main celebrant and the main consecrator was Archbishop Myroslav Marusyn the Secretary of the Eastern Congregation in the Vatican.

Saturday, March 26, 1983 was a cold and rainy day. Bishop Losten and I visited the Latin Cathedral in the city of Diakovo. The local bishop, Cyril Kos, gave us a tour of the cathedral and explained its architecture and the artistic decorations in it. The bishop invited us for lunch. The next day was Sunday. We visited our parish in the town named Novy Sad where Father Roman Myz was pastor. We celebrated a hierarchical Divine Liturgy, and I was a homilist. After a delicious luncheon we departed to visit our parish in the town called Sremski Mitrovychi. Father Stephen Pitka welcomed us and explained that this town is famous because Roman emperors had their summer residence here. This town is likewise famous because in it lived St. Demetrius who died a martyr's death in the 3rd century.

Monday, March 28, 1983, Bishop Losten and I departed from Yugoslavia to return home full of many impressions and good memories.

50th Anniversary of the Forced Famine in Ukraine

1983 marked the 50th anniversary of the horrible forced famine in Ukraine, organized by Stalin's criminal terrorists to break the back of Ukrainian resistance to his plan to take away the land from the farmers for the collective farms. His military forces and police confiscated all the grain from the farmers the previous year, so that the farmers had nothing to sow and cultivate on their farmland. Consequently, there was no harvest in 1932 and worse yet in 1933. The farmers were forbidden to go into the cities for help. So they starved. Historians estimate that between seven and ten million Ukrainians died as a result of the forced famine in 1932 and 1933 in central and eastern Ukraine.

Sunday, May 15, 1983 was set-aside in the United States of America for prayer and fasting in memory of the victims of the forced famine. Each parish had a Divine Liturgy offered for the repose of the souls of the famine victims. The main celebration was held in South Bound Brook, N.J., at the Ukrainian Orthodox Center. I was invited to concelebrate a requiem service with the Orthodox bishops and to preach a homily. I accepted the invitation, for it was my heartfelt desire to come closer to our Orthodox brothers, always praying that the Lord would grant us the grace of unity in his Church.

It was an outdoor celebration before their memorial church with thousands of Catholic and Orthodox people present. I concelebrated with Metropolitan Mstyslav and bishops Mark and Izjaslav. Present was also a Ukrainian Protestant Evangelical pastor, Vladimir Borovsky. Here are some excerpts from my homily:

We pray today and commemorate the millions of our brothers and sisters, sons and daughters of our Ukrainian nation, who died fifty years ago from the horrible forced famine, organized by the criminal occupation powers. Our spacious steppes and flowering villages were then covered with the corpses of the sons and daughters of Ukraine . . . Ukraine was crying then, but the free world was deaf and silent, looking the other way. The Western press and mass media of communication were silent and could not see or hear the cries, the moaning and wailing of the starving millions of our brothers and sisters. There was no one to sympathize with our people or to give us a helping hand. Where was the Red Cross or the many other world beneficial organizations?

With the sight of this horrible horror and tragedy of our nation in the years of 1932–33 we, becoming numb from pain, ask ourselves: Why did the merciful Lord permit this tragedy to befall our people? Why did the right hand of God not slay the criminal blood-red Babylon? Why did our innocent farmers have to suffer death while the evil and malicious were triumphant? Why were the truth and love defamed at the banquets prepared by the iniquity and injustice? Why?

Our Christian faith has answers to these questions. Christ himself taught us that suffering is not always a punishment for sins. He said that suffering frequently is a proof of God's epochal Providence, special mission. On one occasion the disciples asked Christ about the man born blind, *"Was it his sin or that of his parents that caused him to be born blind? Neither, answered Jesus:*

370

*It was no sin, either of this man or of his parents. Rather, it was to let God's works show forth in him." (*John 9:2–3)

If God's works are to be shown forth in our nation, then the following Christ's words are referred to us as well, *"If you find that the world hates you, know that it hated me before you."* (John 15:18)

St. Paul states that, *"Whom the Lord loves, he disciplines"* (Hebrews 12:6). *"For my thoughts are not your thoughts, nor are your ways my ways, says the Lord. As high as the heavens are above the earth, so high are my ways above your ways and my thoughts above your thoughts."* (Isaiah 55:8–9)

Indeed, the Lord God does not delight in the moaning and tears of his beloved children. To gain for us the eternal joy of heaven Christ took upon himself horrible sufferings. He suffered the most horrific pains, mockery, scorn, and the betrayal of his friends and his people, the contempt and the insults and the death on the cross. Our suffering is only a drop into the ocean of pain and suffering our Lord bore on the cross. *"Rejoice instead, in the measure that you share in Christ's sufferings. When his glory is revealed, you will rejoice exultantly."* (1 Peter 4:13) In the plans of Divine Providence the way of the cross of our people there is a secret mission, a mission not known to us now, but it will be revealed. *"God makes all things work together for the good of those who have been called according to his decree."* (Romans 8:28)

371

New Buildings for the Archieparchial Administration

Our first bishop, Soter Ortynsky, OSBM, resided in a row house, at 818 North Franklin Street in Philadelphia. His Chancery Office was located in the building next to his residence at 816 North Franklin Street. One year before the second bishop Constantine Bohachevsky, arrived in the United States of America in 1924, Father Maxim Kinash, pastor of the cathedral parish, purchased a three-story row house at 815 North Franklin Street on October 30, 1923. It must have been used as a bank in the past for in the front office behind a simple plywood door was a huge walk-in vault with a large round steel door. Bishop Bohachevsky established his residence in this building on the third floor, while the lower two floors were used for chancery purposes.

This building could not adequately serve the administrative needs of the diocese. The rooms, with the exception of the library room on the second floor, were small. Archbishop Senyshyn in the 1960's purchased a building next door to it, at 813 North Franklin Street. On the second and third floors, doors were made through the walls to connect the two buildings. . But the floor level in the next building was much lower and it became cumbersome and awkward to use the connections. Both buildings were about 150 years old, leaky, and their maintenance was very expensive.

Archbishop Bohachevsky saw the need for a new and more modern cathedral, chancery, and residence buildings. His departure into eternity January 6, 1961 did not give him the opportunity to fulfill his plans. His successor, Archbishop Ambrose Senyshyn, OSBM, concentrated all his attention on erecting a new and representative cathedral building. Afterward with Council Vatican II, and his frequent trips to Rome, then some other difficulties, as well as a long illness, prevented him from completing his building plans. The very short duration of episcopal ministries of Archbishops Schmondiuk and Lubachivsky did not offer them a chance to do that either.

Residence of the Metropolitan Archbishop, Philadelphia, Pa.,
build in 1983

Actually Archbishop Lubachivsky did engage an architect, Joseph Novicky, and had preliminary sketches made of a new chancery across the street from the Cathedral. It was to be a five story high building, a square tower-like structure, with parking garage in the basement, a chapel on one side and the Byzantine Church Supplies Store on the other side of the first floor. The cathedral rectory and the living quarters were to occupy the second floor. The chancery would occupy the third and the fourth floors, while the fifth floor was to be the Archbishop's residence.

I called a meeting of the Archdiocesan Consultors and showed them the preliminary designs of the proposed new chancery building. Most of them did not like the concentration in one building under one roof of the chapel and the store, of the cathedral parish and the diocesan chancery, which are different in nature and might cause complications in daily life. The question of privacy was likewise raised. The cathedral fathers might not be happy to have the diocesan business interfere with the parish business. I agreed with their opinions and added that I personally would like to go to work and then go back home after working hours. Living just one floor above my working place might create a cramped situation.

After long discussion we decided to consult with the architect for his opinion should we wish to have separate buildings erected to locate the various needs. The architect's opinion was that the cost of separate buildings might be somewhat higher, but not too much. Since we have an adequate amount of land, there would be no problem. It was Archbishop Senyshyn who was able to receive from the city's Redevelopment Authority several parcels of land situated across the street from the cathedral building. We all agreed to this proposition and asked Mr. Novicki to prepare new preliminary sketches for the chancery, the rectory, and the archbishop's residence. We likewise asked him to take into consideration the architecture of the cathedral building and come out with some ties between them so the whole complex would have architectural unity.

The architect, our building committee and myself met on a weekly basis and discussed his designs and sketches. He proposed a chancery building of three stories with a full basement and foundation strong enough so that a fourth floor could be added when-ever needed. We suggested some modifications of the office spaces, and a reception room.

The rectory, according to his design, was to be erected to the left of the chancery, connecting with the chancery building at the dining room and consisting of two stories. It was to have a full basement. The first floor was to have offices, a dining room, living room, kitchen, pantry, laundry room, and two guest rooms. The second floor was to have three two-room apartments with another two-room apartment over the chancery dining room as the housekeeper's living quarters. It was to have a three-car garage.

The design of the archbishop's residence was the most compli-cated one. The architect changed his mind several times as to the arrangement of rooms and the other spaces. Finally we agreed to his last design. It was to have a half basement, two-car garage. On the first floor would be a kitchen and dining room, a laundry room and a pantry, a large living room and a small reception room with a small office. Then there was to be a two-room apartment for the archbishop's priest secretary, and a chapel. The size of the chapel was dictated by the size of a beautiful highly artistic iconostas, which we inherited from the late Archbishop Bohachevsky's chapel in his residence, located on 705 Medary Avenue in North Philadel-phia. Archbishop Lubachivsky at the suggestion of one of our bish-ops, sold that residence, but the cathedral priests were able to save the iconostas from it.

When the architect had all of the final construction plans and the specifications ready, and our administrative board with the building committee approved them, he gave them out to ten con-tractors for bids. On the appointed day when the bids were to be delivered, we had the architect, the consultors and the building committee present for the ceremony of the opening of the bids. Some of the bidders were parked outside waiting for the news as to which one of them would be selected. We accepted the bid of the P. Agnes Construction Company. The signing of the contract took place July 14, 1982. The construction cost was about $3,500,000.00. Soon afterward the contractor moved in with his equipment and the work was begun. Each parish was assessed according to its size and capability and, thanks to our good priests, the money was coming in on a regular basis so that we had no difficulty in meeting the huge monthly construction bills.

As the walls of the chancery were going up, I decided that it was a mistake to have a connecting door from the chancery's dining room to the rectory. The cathedral priests need their privacy and so does the chancery staff. So I ordered that doorway closed in by bricks and another door from the dining room was cut out of the existing wall to the outside. The construction of the three buildings was coming to a conclusion in the early fall of 1983. I had to travel to Rome, Italy, to take part in the World Synod of Bishops that would last the whole month of October. So I called a meeting of the deans in order to plan and make proper preparations for the official dedication of the new buildings. At the same time we had to plan for some kind of observance of the 25th Anniversary of the establishment of our Philadelphia Metropolitan Province by Pope Pius XII August 6, 1958. Also we were to commemorate the one hundred years since our first priest arrived from Ukraine to our parish in Shenandoah, PA, to mark a one hundred anniversary of our Church in the United States of America. I appointed Bishop Robert M. Moskal to chair this committee and assigned to them the task of preparation.

The Committee worked well and prepared everything for the celebration that took place Saturday, November 12, and Sunday, November 13, 1983. Saturday at 4:00 P.M. a festive concert was held at the Northeast Public High School auditorium, Cottman and Algon Avenues, Philadelphia. I opened the concert with a word of welcome to our distinguished guests and the faithful. The main speaker was Archbishop Pio Laghi, the Apostolic Nuncio from Washington, D.C. The artistic program of the concert consisted of such performers as Martha Kokolska, soloist; Roman Rudnycky, world famous pianist; our local Metropolitan Choir with Osyp Lupan as its director; the Ensemble of Bandurist Singers with Julian Kytasty as its director; and the Prometheus Choir with Michael Dlaboha as its director.

Cathedral Rectory, built in 1983

Chancery Office of the Metropolitan Archbishop, Philadelphia, Pa.
built in 1983.

Sunday, November 13, 1983 from 9:00 to 11:00 A.M., there was an open house in the new chancery building. The clergy and the faithful came in large numbers to view the new structure and its spacious layout. Afternoon at 1:00 P.M. a Solemn Blessing and Dedication of the three new buildings took place. Afterward a procession was formed from the chancery to the cathedral and a hierarchical Divine Liturgy was celebrated at 2:00 P.M. I was the main celebrant. After the Liturgy, a festive banquet was held at the Philadelphia Center Hotel, 1724 JFK Boulevard. There were over nine hundred guests present. His Archbishop-Coadjutor Lubachivsky read a letter of congratulations from the Major Archbishop Cardinal Slipyj from Rome. The main speaker was Msgr. Myroslav Charyna in Ukrainian, and Msgr. Leon Mosko in English. I had the concluding remarks.

The following day all the Ukrainian Bishops present at the dedication ceremonies remained in Philadelphia for a fraternal get-together, an exchange of ideas concerning the good of our Church. After a group photo and luncheon, all departed for their respective homes.

The Death and Funeral of Patriarch Josyf Slipyj

I t was Friday, September 7, 1984, when the sad news went out from Rome throughout the world that at 10:45 A.M. local time, there fell asleep in the Lord in his 93rd year of life the Father and the Head of the Ukrainian Catholic Church, Major Archbishop and Cardinal, Josyf Slipyj. He was a man of God's Providence, a worthy successor to the great Servant of God Metropolitan Andrew Sheptytsky, and a promotor of his ecumenical ideas, an outstanding scholar, fearless confessor of faith, and a dedicated advocate of the idea of a Kievan Patriarchate for the Ukrainian Catholic Church.

Having received the sad news, I immediately wrote a letter to all our priests ordering a period of a forty-day mourning, and to have a Divine Liturgy offered in all of our churches on the day of the funeral, September 13, 1984, for the repose of the soul of the late Cardinal. Likewise I ordered that from the date of this letter his successor, Archbishop Lubachivsky, as the new Major Archbishop, is to be commemorated in all liturgical services.

I learned that the body of Cardinal Slipyj was transferred to the church of St. Sophia in Rome on Saturday, September 8, 1984. Liturgies for the repose of his soul were being offered frequently by visiting priests. The Holy Father, John Paul II, came Saturday to pay his respects to the late Cardinal, prayed for his soul, and then

381

bending over, he kissed the forehead of the deceased and said, "He fought for a just cause."

I departed for Rome to attend the funeral on Monday, September 11, 1984, and stayed at St. Josaphat Seminary on Gianicolo Hill. There I met other bishops and more of them were coming daily. The funeral services commenced on Wednesday, September 12, 1984, at 4:30 P.M. Major Archbishop Lubachivsky was the main celebrant, and the rest of the bishops as well as many priests concelebrated.

The following day, Thursday, September 13, 1984, a Funeral Liturgy was held outdoors. The altar was erected on a platform before the entrance to the church, and many chairs were placed in rows on the grounds before the church to accommodate the church dignitaries. All others had to stand. Numerous groups of lay people came from the United States of America, Canada, England, Austria, Germany, France, Belgium, Poland, and Yugoslavia. Among them were many outstanding community and political leaders. The first two rows of chairs were occupied by 14 cardinals, members of the diplomatic corps at the Vatican, the King of the Netherlands, Father Wilfred Van Straaten, a great friend of the late Cardinal, US ambassador to the Vatican Peter Murphy, and many others. A wooden casket with the body of the late cardinal was placed on a stand in the center of the grounds.

All our bishops with Major Archbishop Lubachivsky at the head, and many priests, processed from the University building to the altar. In his eulogy His Beatitude Lubachivsky gave a short biography of the deceased. He ended his talk thus:

> The late Cardinal Slipyj became a symbol of the Ukrainian Catholic Church, her standard-bearer and a role model of patriotism and of love for the fatherland, as well as a confessor of Christ and Ukraine. He was the rock, as it were, upon which a heroic Church is being built. He became a symbol of fidelity, generosity, steadfastness, and courage. He was the true pastor and a prophet sent by God Himself to show us the true way to the spirit of the Ukrainian Church. Ages will pass and he will

continue to shine as an exemplar of unity of divine with the human, of religious with the national, of the transient with the eternal . . ."

Here is an excerpt from the Italian eulogy given by Archbishop Marusyn:

We render our deep reverence full of reverential respect and gratitude to the great hierarch of our century . . . His name is famous from the rising to the setting of the sun, because for eighteen long years he bore the shackles for the sake of the name of Christ. Together with the other bishops of the then flowering Galician Metropolia, he was imprisoned for Christ's sake, for the Holy Church, for his fidelity to Peter's chair, and led to an inequitable tribunal. The unjust trial on the innocent pastor of the flock of Christ in Western Ukraine took place in Kiev, the mother of Ukrainian cities, where one thousand years ago the light of Christian faith shone forth. Metropolitan Josyf then took upon his shoulders a cross, similar to the one of the Son of God, and carried it to a Golgotha of jails and exiles, concentration camps and forced labor, of cruelty, hunger, and cold in the midst of sickness and pain . . .

This Church is shedding tears now over the grave of her hierarch and pastor, because she knows well whom she is losing. The whole Catholic world is crying together with our Church, because the Mystical Body of Christ is one, and if one member is ill, the whole organism feels indisposition. Yet, at such times as this, divine power and wisdom come to our aid, bringing consolation and hope for better days . . ."

At the end of the Funeral Liturgy, Father Ivan Choma read excerpts from "The Last Will and Testament of Patriarch Josyf." After the concluding requiem service several bishops and priests carried the casket around the church to the sorrowful melody of "Holy

God, Holy Mighty, Holy Immortal, have mercy on us." Afterward the body was taken into the crypt of the church, His Beatitude Lubachivsky sealed the grave, and everyone sang the mournful hymn of "Everlasting Memory."

After the funeral services, all the bishops were invited to the dining room of the University building for a luncheon. During the luncheon Father Ivan Choma read to all present the decision of the Chapter of the Canons (Krylos) of the Lviv Archeparchy. His Beatitude Myroslav Ivan Lubachivsky is now the successor to Patriarch Josyf, i.e., the Major Archbishop of Lviv and the inheritor of the title Patriarch. Some bishops remarked that the "Krylos" was actually usurping the apostolic powers of the successor of St. Peter.

A commemorative dinner "tryzna" was held the same day in the evening at the "Domus Mariae." It was opened by a member of the "Krylos," Father Lubomyr Husar, and in his remarks he repeated the decision of the 'Krylos" that His Beatitude Myroslav Ivan Lubachivsky is the heir of the title Patriarch. Those present gave evidence of their approval of this decision by prolonged applause. Afterward Father Husar asked me to speak in the name of the Synodal Fathers. Here are some excerpts from my talk:

> It seems not too long ago that his tortured hands rested upon my head so that Divine Grace in the form of the fullness of priesthood came upon me. I recall this with sadness in my heart, and begging farewell to you, my consecrator, I pray 'O Lord God, as you adorned him with spiritual honor among men, so also receive his soul in to the glory of your angels and saints, and number his soul with all those who pleased you from the beginning of time . . .'

> Before us is the majestic person of our hierarch. He is our great Church and national leader, the spiritual father of Ukrainian people, who occupied the metropolitan's throne for forty years. Yet, almost half of these forty years he spent in prisons and concentration camps. Forgive us, our Spiritual Father, that the thou-

sands of your faithful in your own city of Lviv could not escort you to your eternal rest. There now your cathedral of St. George is closed to us, and her bells are silenced. Their glorious sounds are not ringing out your farewell into eternity, because your and our land is in captivity of the atheistic enemy of God. Forgive us that the Ukrainian Army is not giving you a 21-gun salute, the leader of millions of Ukrainian souls. O, unforgettable our Vladyko, instead of these, now are rising up to the throne of God in heaven heartfelt prayers of the millions of your silent and catacomb Church from cold Siberia, and prison cells of your faithful priests for the repose your soul. In all of our churches in the free world Divine Liturgies are being offered today for your saintly soul's eternal rest with the angels and saints in heaven . . ."

Monumental painting depicting the Baptism of Ukraine.

Artistic Decorations of the New Cathedral Building

The new Cathedral, a version of Hagia Sophia in Constantinople (Istanbul), building was erected by the efforts of the late Metropolitan-Archbishop Ambrose Senyshyn, OSBM, (+ September 11, 1976) between 1963 and 1966. The structure is in the form of an octagon with the extensions to the West for the sanctuary and the sacristies, and to the East for the vestibule and the choir loft. A Venetian gold mosaic covers the dome. Below the dome there is a drum band, consisting of 32 windows with an arch form. The entire structure is 144 feet (52.43 meters) long. To the top of the cross over the dome it is 119 feet (43.28 meters) high. Inside, the diameter of the dome is 88 feet (32.31 meters) long. The height of the church to the center of the dome is likewise 88 feet (32.31 meters) high. The sanctuary's floor is 42 x 42 feet (12.80 x 12.80 meters), and its height is 58 feet (or 15.85 meters).

The Immaculate Conception Ukrainian Catholic Cathedral,
Philadelphia, Pa., built in 1964.

The 32 windows below the dome were made of thick chunks
of colored glass. They were installed during the actual construction. Each of these windows represents a coat of arms, which has
some connection to the history of the Ukrainian Catholic Church
in the United States of America. There are coats of arms of the
Popes—St. Pius X, Pus XI, Pius XII, John XXIII and Paul VI. There
are the coats of arms of our bishops: Metropolitan Andrew
Sheptytsky, Soter Ortynsky, OSBM, Constantine Bohachevsky,
Ambrose Senyshyn, OSBM, and of the following religious commu-
nities: Basilian Fathers, Redemptorist Fathers, Franciscan Fathers,
Basilian Sisters, Sister Servants of Mary Immaculate, Missionary
Sisters of the Mother of God. There are likewise coats of arms of
the Philadelphia Archeparchy, the Stamford Eparchy and the St.
Nicholas in Chicago Eparchy. Then there are coats of arms of the
United States of America, Ukraine, Pennsylvania, Volynia, Podilla,
Bukovina, Carpatho Ukraine, Kholm, Lemkos, Halich, Lviv,
Peremyshl, Ivano Frankivsk, and others. Yet this heraldic panorama,

full of interesting symbols and details is so high that one cannot see them from the floor of the cathedral.

In the very center of the dome is the circular icon in mosaic of our Lord the Ruler—Pantocrator. The icon is 18 feet in diameter. Peter Andrusiw, a very famous artist, composed this icon. This mosaic representing pure Byzantine iconography, is the most beautiful one in the whole cathedral, and was installed at the end of the construction in 1966. Christ is represented on this icon as a teacher, advocate, and judge. With the background of the icon sky blue, it is located in the very center of the dome from which thirty-two golden rays radiate. These symbolically represent Christ, *"The real light that enlightens every man who comes into the world"* (John 1:9).

The interior of the Immaculate Conception Cathedral
in Philadelphia, Pa.

The builder of this cathedral, Metropolitan Ambrose Senyshyn, OSBM, requested the iconographer, Christine Dochwat, to design several sketches of an icon of the Most Holy Mother of God, the patroness of this church, to be located on a large flat wall behind the altar. One of her designs was selected, enlarged and sent to Italy to be set in a mosaic. This icon is to remind us of the one in the Hagia Sophia Church in Kiev on the indestructible wall. The Most Holy Mother on this icon has on her chest in a large circle a great panagia-medalion that represents her Son, the Son of God, radiating heavenly purity, her virginity, and at the same time her maternity. This grand and monumental icon was installed in the cathedral in 1967 before there was an iconostas.

Archbishop Joseph Schmondiuk (+ *December 25, 1978)* was planning to install an Italian marble iconostas in the cathedral, while the icons on this iconostas would be made of mosaics. However, the engineers, having inspected the structure, advised against such a move, fearing that the floor would not be able to support so great a load. His successor, Metropolitan Myroslav Lubachivsky, placed an order with Christine Dochwat, to design a wooden iconostas. He signed the contract, but before it was completed, he was appointed a Coadjutor to Cardinal Slipyj and moved to Rome.

Graphic representation of the Cathedral of the Immaculate Conception, Philadelphia, Pa.

Archbishop Volodymyr Sterniuk from Lviv, Ukraine visits Archbishop Stephen Sulyk May 17, 1991.

Creation of a New Eparchy—St. Josaphat in Parma

The Philadelphia Archeparchy at the time I inherited it was very extensive as far as territory was concerned. I had to take an airplane in order to visit our parishes in Western Pennsylvania, Ohio, or Florida. To drive those distances was impractical and time consuming. I made regular pastoral visitations in order to get to know better my priests and faithful and for them to know me better. I wanted to know the conditions in each parish, their spiritual life, the catechetical instructions of the youth and the adults, the economic conditions, parish devotions and activities. Normally I celebrated Sunday Liturgy, was the homilist, and after the Liturgy I would go to the church hall where the faithful had assembled and spend some time with them. I would socialize with them, inquire about their health, their family life, employment, economic conditions, their parish life and activities. They would ask me all kinds of questions, and I tried to give each a satisfactory answer.

Such pastoral visitations were mutually very beneficial. The faithful were very happy to see their bishop and welcomed me warmly. I used each of the pastoral visitations to share with the faithful my concerns about the welfare of their own parish, the growth of their spiritual life, especially the great need of priestly and religious vocations so as to preserve our Church for future generations.

To be able to maintain a good relationship with the parishes, I thought that such pastoral visitations, to do some good, should take place at least every two to three years. When I was installed, I inherited 112 parishes, 134 priests (96 diocesan, 12 religious, and 26 retired), 210 religious sisters, two deacons, and 15 parochial schools. The most practical seasons for visitations were winter and springtime. The fall was very busy with all kinds of episcopal meetings, synods, and parochial celebrations of parish or priest's anniversaries. With all the parishes and the great distances between them, I could not implement my vision of parish visitations as frequently as they should be made.

Already in 1956, Bishop Bohachevsky saw the need for dividing his territory and erecting another exarchate. He made the necessary arrangements with the Apostolic See of Rome and separated from his exarchate all the parishes in the State of New York and in the New England States, thus establishing the Stamford Eparchy. It was Pope Pius XII who made the official formation of the Stamford Eparchy on July 20, 1956, and named the auxiliary bishop of Philadelphia, Ambrose Senyshyn, to be the first Exarch of Stamford. At that time the Apostolic See of Rome was in favor of such a division, for it had plans for permanent ecclesiastical structures for our Church in the free world. Thus the Holy See raised the Winnipeg exarchate to the status of an Archeparchy Nov. 3, 1956, thereby erecting a Metropolitan Province of Canada. The Philadelphia exarchate was raised to the status of an Archeparchy July 12, 1958 and thus the Metropolitan Province of Philadelphia was established. The Stamford exarchate was raised to the status of an Eparchy.

Bishop Bohachevsky made further necessary arrangements to form the St. Nicholas Eparchy in Chicago. He, however, did not live to see it established. He died Jan. 6, 1961, and Pope John XIII erected the Eparchy July 14, 1961, naming Bishop Jaroslav Gabro as the founding bishop of that Eparchy. It was at that time that there were plans for another ecclesiastical unit somewhere between

Chicago and Philadelphia. Due to various circumstances this last plan was not put into practice.

After I learned about this plan, I called a meeting of our bishops and presented them my ideas as to how we should realize it. I proposed to divide the Philadelphia Archeparchy by separating from it about one-third of all the parishes. The line of division would give the new eparchy all the parishes in Western Pennsylvania, in Ohio and in all the states east of St. Nicholas in Chicago Eparchy, down to and including the State of Florida. The Philadelphia Archeparchy would retain the State of Virginia. The State of Florida, having a warm climate, attracts many of our elderly people from the Northern United States of America and Canada to settle permanently there. It would be a good addition to the new eparchy where it could experience growth.

The bishops were in agreement with my plan. The only remaining question to be solved was to find the episcopal see, i.e. a parish with a representative church to serve as the cathedral. The discussions narrowed to St. Josaphat parish in Parma, Ohio, where a new church was being built. There was a large unused circular building, planned for a possible high school, that could be utilized for a chancery and other diocesan needs. I recalled then the example of Bishop Bohachevsky. When in 1956 he planned to erect the Stamford exarchate, he proposed his auxiliary, Bishop Senyshyn to be the first Exarch of Stamford. Following this example, I proposed my auxiliary Bishop, Robert M. Moskal, to be the first and the founding eparch of the new eparchy. The bishops applauded my proposition. Next came the name of the new eparchy. Since in the city of Parma there is already a Ruthenian Eparchy by the name of that city, I proposed that the name should be "St. Josaphat Eparchy in Parma." Having received the consent of the bishops, I prepared the necessary papers and sent the whole case to the Apostolic See of Rome for approval and promulgation.

It was in December of 1983 that the Apostolic Nuncio in Washington, Archbishop Laghi, informed me that Pope John Paul II, on December 5, 1983, had established the St. Josaphat Eparchy in Parma and appointed Bishop Robert M. Moskal as its first Eparch.

On Sunday, January 15, 1984 there was a farewell banquet in honor of Bishop Moskal held at the Cathedral auditorium in Philadelphia. People were present from the cathedral parish, from St. Ann's parish in Warrington, and from Annunciation parish in Melrose Park, all parishes in which he had served. All together about 500 persons attended this banquet, including about ten priests along with Archbishop Coadjutor Lubachivsky from Rome.

The formal creation of the new eparchy and the installation was set to take place Wednesday, February 29, 1984. An episcopal ordination of Bishop Basil Filewych was held on February 27, 1984, at St. Josaphat church in Toronto, Canada. I was invited to be one of the co consecrators. The mass media had broadcast warnings from the early morning that a great snowstorm was to come late in the day. The Ordination Liturgy was held at 2:00 P.M. Bishop Moskal and I left the church after Holy Communion and took a taxi to the airport just as snow started to fall. It was probably the last flight from Toronto to Cleveland, Ohio, that day. The next day the airport was closed.

In spite of the great snowstorm the festivities of the creation of St. Josaphat Eparchy in Parma took place as scheduled. True, some bishops and priests who planned to attend this celebration could not come. Archbishop Pio Laghi called in the morning of February 29, 1984, stating that he would not be able to come and delegated me to perform the rite of the creation of the eparchy and of the installation of its first bishop.

About 1,300 faithful participated in the Liturgy. Although thirty-eight bishops were planning to participate, only fifteen were able to come. Bishop Moskal was the main celebrant.[7]

---

[7] The concelebrants were Metropolitan Stephen Kocisko from Pittsburgh; Bishops Michael Hrynchyshyn from Paris, France; John Bilock from Pittsburgh; and Andrew Pataky, from Passaic. Present were the Latin Rite Bishops Archbishop Edmund Szoka from Detroit; Anthony Pilla from Cleveland; James Hoffman from Toledo; Edward Pevek, auxiliary from Cleveland; and the auxiliary bishops from Philadelphia, Francis Schulte, John Graham, Martin Lohmuller, Edward Hughes and Louis DeSimone.

The concelebrants were Metropolitan Stephen Kocisko from Pittsburgh; Bishops Michael Hrynchyshyn from Paris, France; John Bilock from Pittsburgh; and Andrew Pataky, from Passaic. Present were the Latin Rite, Bishops Archbishop Edmund Szoka from Detroit; Anthony Pilla from Cleveland; James Hoffman from Toledo; Edward Pevek, auxiliary from Cleveland; and the auxiliary bishops from Philadelphia, Francis Schulte, John Graham, Martin Lohmuller, Edward Hughes, and Louis DeSimone.

I presided, and before the Liturgy began, I read the Papal Bull of the erection of the St. Josaphat Eparchy in Parma; Msgr. Leo Adamiak read the Nomination Bull of Bishop Moskal in English, and Father Ivan Tylawsky read the same in Ukrainian. I then performed the ritual of the installation of Bishop Moskal and the Divine Liturgy began.

At the banquet that followed the Liturgy in my remarks among other things, I said: "Dear Bishop Robert, you were welcomed as the founding Bishop of your Eparchy by a huge snow storm. My wish for you is that this would be the last storm in your life . . ."

Michael Kuchmiak, CSsR— My Second Auxiliary Bishop

t took almost four years before I was able to get another auxiliary bishop. It was on March 8, 1988, that the Apostolic Nuncio, Archbishop Pio Laghi, informed me that the Holy Father appointed Father Michael Kuchmiak, CSsR, as my auxiliary bishop. Father Kuchmiak at that time was pastor of Holy Family parish in Washington, D.C. He was one of three candidates elected by our Synod of Bishops.

Learning of this news, I made the following announcement, "I am grateful to our Synod of Bishops and especially to the Holy Father John Paul II, for appointing Bishop Kuchmiak as my auxiliary Bishop. I welcome him with open arms for I know him to be a good and serious person, straightforward and pleasant, always smiling. He has a long pastoral experience both in Canada and in United States and will be of great help to me in this Archeparchy."

The episcopal ordination of Bishop Michael Kuchmiak took place in our cathedral on April 27, 1988. I was the main consecrator, while Metropolitan Maxim Hermaniuk CSsR, of Winnipeg and Bishop Innocent Lotocky, OSBM, of Chicago see co-consecrators. Thirty-six bishops of the Byzantine and Latin Rites, some 130 priests, and over fifty religious sisters were present at the ordination Liturgy. Bishop Robert M. Moskal was the homilist. After the

Liturgy, all were invited to attend a banquet held in our cathedral auditorium.

Bishop Michael remained pastor of Holy Family parish in Washington, D.C., frequently coming to Philadelphia to help me in any way he could. He gladly would take a pastoral visitation for me or any other substitution. There was between us good, harmonious, and friendly cooperation, for he is a holy and dedicated man of God. I was truly sad when on July 11, 1989, the Holy Father appointed him an Exarch of Great Britain.

Efforts to Obtain from the Holy Father a Ukrainian Catholic Patriarchate

ishop Augustine Horniak, OSBM was the first Exarch of our Church in Great Britain since 1961. He is a very capable and talented person, wholeheartedly dedicated to God, his Church, and his Ukrainian people. His faithful were mostly Second World War veterans of the Ukrainian Army organized in 1943 by the German occupation forces. Later in the 1970s, this exarchate would become the worst battlefield for the Ukrainian Catholic Patriarchate.

Our Major Archbishop, Cardinal Josyf Slipyj, residing in Rome, was making every possible effort to have the Holy Father create a Ukrainian Catholic Kievan Patriarchate. Yet his efforts were not successful due to the fact that the territory of our Church at that time was occupied by the Soviet Union, which in 1946 had officially liquidated our Catholic Church and forcefully joined it to the Russian Orthodox Church. To erect our Patriarchate outside of the Soviet Union from our eparchies in the free world was irregular in the mind of the Apostolic See. Actually the greatest difficulty was and still is the Vatican's policy of trying to gain Russia's favor in order to achieve possible unity of the Orthodox and the Catholic Churches. Many years have passed, the Soviet Union has ceased to exist, and the Vatican policy of trying not to offend Russia in the slightest way has miserably failed. It seems that even our present Holy Father John Paul II has been finally convinced of this failure and made an official visit to Ukraine in June of 2001, amid the fierce protests of the Russian Orthodox Church and its Patriarch Alexius II.

The second reason of the failure to convince the Holy Father to erect a Ukrainian Catholic Patriarchate at the time of Cardinal Slipyj's efforts was the fact that the latter was unable to convince all his bishops to work with him for this cause. Some of our bishops were not convinced that this was the best idea at that time and refused to cooperate and support Cardinal Slipyj's efforts in this regard. The reason for this disunity among our bishops is hard to say. Some said the reason for the lack of unity might have been in the way the individual bishops were treated by the Cardinal. Others claimed that the reason was the failure of not clearly presenting the very idea of a Patriarchate.

In order to force the bishops to cooperate with the Cardinal, a lay patriarchal movement was formed in all our dioceses in the free world. They organized local chapters, diocesan chapters, and national organizations. In Philadelphia a World Patriarchal Organization, uniting all the local and national organizations was organized. They began to publish a monthly journal, *Patriarchate*. In it were well-written articles supporting the idea of a Patriarchate and condemning the bishops who were not active supporters of this idea.

During the Holy Year of 1975, the Patriarchal Organization organized a huge pilgrimage to Rome. Some four or five thousand pilgrims were present at St. Peter's Basilica in the Vatican for the Divine Liturgy on July 12, 1975. The main celebrant was His Beatitude Cardinal Slipyj. During the main entrance of that Liturgy, a concelebrating priest, Rt. Rev. Ivan Hrynioch, while carrying the chalice, commemorated His Beatitude Slipyj as the Kievan and Galician Patriarch. The Patriarchal Organization accepted this as the official proclamation or erection of the Ukrainian Catholic Patriarchate. They said all we need now is the Holy Father's blessing or approval, which may come later, but our Patriarchate exists already. From that day on His Beatitude signed his letters as "Patriarch," sometimes adding "and Major Archbishop." From that day on, three of our bishops began to commemorate our Major Archbishop as Patriarch in all liturgical services and demanded that their priests follow their example. They were: Isidore Boretsky of Toronto, Ivan Prasko from Australia, and Neil Savaryn of Edmonton. Other bishops refused to do so and, therefore, became targets of attacks by the patriarchal organization.

The worst religious war began in Great Britain. Bishop Horniak proclaimed that he would be the first one to commemorate our Patriarch in the Liturgy as soon as the Holy Father promulgates our Patriarchate. Otherwise it would be a falsehood and a sin of rebellion to call someone a Patriarch when in reality he is not. He forbade his priests to commemorate the "Patriarch" in the Liturgy. This started a rattle in his Exarchate. A great majority of his faithful demanded that he retract his decision and start to commemorate the Patriarch or else they would not donate any funds for the support of the church. Two or three priests came to Great Britain from Rome and in opposition to Bishop Horniak began serving Divine Liturgies in private homes and in some rented facilities, commemorating the Patriarch. This action actually started another church within the church in England. The church was split in two. This however, did not convince Bishop Horniak to give in to their demands. He remained steadfast in his decision, and most of his priests supported him.

Years after the death of Cardinal Slipyj, when Cardinal Lourdusamy was the Prefect of the Congregation for the Eastern Churches, Bishop Horniak was retired by the Holy See on September 29, 1987, due to the efforts of the Patriarchal Organization and the Major Archbishop Lubachivsky. This was the thanks and gratitude for his loyalty and support of the policies of the Apostolic See of Rome! A great wrong was done to this good and dedicated bishop. The rebels were rewarded, and the defender of the policies of the Vatican was punished. Not once since was he invited to attend one of the Synods of our Bishops. Yet his retirement did not resolve the problem of the rebellion in our Church in Great Britain. Those people who rebelled against Bishop Horniak never returned to their churches. Probably through the sin of rebellion they lost the grace.

The opposition to Archbishop Ambrose Senyshyn, OSBM from the Patriarchal Society reached its crest in 1971 when the Apostolic Delegate in Washington announced that the Holy Father appointed an auxiliary bishop Msgr. John Stock. The Patriarchal Society had no objection to the person of John Stock, but objected to the method of his nomination. They protested the fact that the nomination was done outside of our Synod and without the knowledge of Major Archbishop Cardinal Slipyj. When some weeks later it was announced that the Holy Father appointed a second auxiliary bishop in the person of Msgr. Basil Losten, the protests increased.

Both candidates traveled to Rome to visit His Beatitude Cardinal Slipyj and to ask him to be their main consecrator. He categorically denied their request. Then the date for the ordination of both candidates was set as May 25, 1971, at the cathedral church in Philadelphia. Invitations went out to all of our bishops and Latin bishops, as well as to the representatives of each parish. Admission tickets to the cathedral were printed so as to maintain order and have seating available for the invited. The preparatory committee for this celebration expected some protests, so they informed the city police and asked for help to keep order and proper decorum. Security police were present likewise inside the cathedral church. Someone had counterfeit invitation tickets printed, exactly like the official ones, so that many of the protesters walked into the cathedral.

On the street the city police placed barricades along the sidewalks so as to keep the street open for the procession. The demonstrators were well organized. They came by cars and buses from as far as Cleveland, Ohio. They brought with them some of the organized youth, like the Scouts "Plast." They carried large portraits of Cardinal Slipyj and posters with offensive slogans.

During the procession to the cathedral the demonstrators greeted the priests and the bishops with emotional and offensive screams of "traitors"; they spat on them and waived their fists.

Inside the cathedral, as soon as the ceremony began of introducing the candidates and of the reading of the nomination documents, the demonstrators began to chant their own hymns, e.g. "anaxios"—"he is not worthy," or the funeral hymn "Everlasting Memory." Later on they stopped singing and began to recite aloud prayers one after another. Archbishop Senyshyn then ordered the whole ceremony and the Divine Liturgy not to be sung, as it is normally done, but simply recited. The reporters and the TV cameras recorded it all and the world learned about our problems.

Luckily, I was not present at this celebration. At that time my Aunt Sophia and I were in Ukraine visiting my father. But Cardinal John Krol was present and was presiding at the ordination ceremony and the Liturgy. Years later when I became a bishop, Cardinal Krol told me this about the demonstration: "Do not blame your people for this demonstration!"

Preparation for the Jubilee

Our bishops visited the Holy Father John Paul II on November 20, 1978, and presented to him a draft of their plan for the preparations for the Millennium Jubilee of the Baptism of Ukraine, which was to be observed in 1988. They asked the Pope to bless their plans. He responded with a lengthy letter, addressed to His Beatitude Cardinal Slipyj, and dated March 19, 1978. It was an historical document of great value. In it, among many other things, he said:

> While fulfilling the office of the Servant of this community, I address all the churches and Christian communities with whom we are not in full unity, but all of us are united by Christ. We, who follow Christ, Who sent his apostles *"to the ends of the earth"* with our thoughts and reflections now fly to that blessed land of Rus' (Ukraine), which one thousand years ago accepted the Gospel and Baptism. With our spirit let us penetrate again the history of this Christian community. Let us admire and delight in it; let us enter into her spirit; the spirit of faith we emphasize, the spirit of prayer, and of constant submission to Divine Providence. Let us dwell in the places where Christ is being glorified and His Mother is being venerated. Finally through the media-

tion of His Mother, we entrust to our Savior all of the descendants of this Baptism, which the blessed Rus' before one thousand years received from Him who is *"The Father of the World to come."* (Isaiah 9:6)

Inspired by the words of Pope John Paul II: *"I address all the churches and Christian communities with whom we are not in full unity, but all of us are united by Christ,"* I got the idea of a common preparation for the Millennium Jubilee together with our Orthodox brothers. I prayed for this intention and then sat down and drafted a project of *a Common Appeal* to be signed by the Orthodox Metropolitan Mstyslav and myself.

"In the Year of the Lord One Thousand Nine Hundred Eighty Eight, we shall observe the Millennium of Baptism of Rus'-Ukraine, attained by the Equal to the Apostles—Vladimir the Great.

Our people in their native land, languishing in a cruel captivity, are not able to freely and properly render thanks to God for the grace of Baptism of our ancestors as well as for the grace of God we all received. The atheistic state authorities have destroyed our church buildings while our Churches have been liquidated and made illegal. Our people now pray in the modern-day catacombs. The church bells, which called our people to church and worship, have been silenced. Our people are persecuted for their faith in God and their love of their homeland. The enemies deny our people the right for independence. They ruin our culture and Russify the people.

We, who by the grace of God live in a free world, have a sacred obligation to properly prepare and in 1988, united as one people, render thanks and glory to God for the grace of Baptism and for the one thousand years of the light of the Word of God . . .

We, your hierarchs and pastors, appeal to all of you in the United States of America: The leaders of church and national organizations, the cultural, educational and community organizations, the professional associations and youth organizations to send your representatives to a meeting in order to elect One Representative Committee of Preparations and Celebrations of the Millennium of Baptism of Ukraine in 1988.

The meeting will be held Saturday, March 23, 1985 at 1::00 A.M. at the Ukrainian Cultural and Educational Center, 700 Cedar Road, Philadelphia, PA.

Given at South Bound Brook and Philadelphia, the 17th day of February 1985 A.D.

(Signed)

+ Mstyslav—Metropolitan of the Ukrainian Orthodox Church in United States of America

+ Stephen—Metropolitan of the Ukrainian Catholic Church in the United States of America.

I sent my project to Metropolitan Mstyslav by a trusted person. He accepted my project, at first with great misgivings and mistrust. Having read it carefully, he liked the idea and, having made some minor corrections in the text, he signed it and send it back to me for publication.

The reaction of the Ukrainian press was very positive. The Ukrainian daily, *Svoboda*, having published the text of the Appeal, made this editorial comment: "This is a consecutive historical document, which is a clear proof that there exists now a spirit of unity among our churches, a spirit which commands all Ukrainians to unite for the sake of a common observance. . . . A very sincere thanks to our Hierarchs for their Appeal."

The Observance of the
Millennium

E very parish in our Archeparchy was asked to organize a
Millennium Parish Committee and start planning local
celebrations in 1988. In Philadelphia we started our preparations by organizing a Millennium Choir with seventy members
under the leadership of Michael Dlaboha. This choir initiated our
celebrations of the Millennium on Sunday, June 1, 1986, with a
Grand Concert held in our Cathedral church at 4:00 P.M. It was a
mighty song of gratitude to God for giving us the grace of being
the followers of Christ and able to glorify his Most Holy Name.

I accepted an invitation from Bishop Efraim Krevey, OSBM and
traveled to Brazil in order to partake in the official celebration June
27–30, 1985, of the Millennium in his Eparchy in Curitiba. In August of 1987 I took a weeklong trip to Australia in order to participate in the celebration of the Millennium with Bishop Ivan Prasko
in the capital city Canberra.

The official celebration of the Millennium of the Philadelphia
Archeparchy was held on Pentecost Sunday, May 22, 1988, with a
hierarchical Divine Liturgy at 2:00 P.M. Delegates from all our parishes
and most of our priests were present. Invited were likewise all the
Ukrainian and Ruthenian Bishops from the United States of America,
as well as the Latin Bishops from Pennsylvania. Bishop Innocent

Lotocky, OSBM, gave a spirited and eloquent homily. Before the Creed, I led the faithful in the renewal of their Baptismal Promises.

The main celebration took place in the Vatican with the Holy Father John Paul II. The celebration began with a Divine Liturgy on Friday, July 8, 1988, at 9:00 A.M. in the Basilica of Santa Maria Majore. The main celebrant was His Beatitude Myroslav Cardinal Lubachivsky. With him were all our bishops from throughout the free world. Concelebrating were about 250 priests. Some 6,000 pilgrims came from all our settlements in Western Europe, the Americas, and Australia. No one was able to come from Ukraine.

Saturday, July 9, 1988, there was a concelebrated Moleben to the Most Holy Mother of God at 9:00 A.M. in front of St. Sophia Church. In attendance were about 23 cardinals, a number of the Latin bishops. The Holy Father arrived by helicopter and presided at the Moleben. Here are some excerpts from Cardinal Lubachivsky and the Pope's homilies:

> This our church was erected on the Roman soil. She gathers us together who are dispersed throughout the free world. With her name and the structure this church reminds us of Kiev and the beginnings of our Christianity, and unites us with our native land. This house of God is for us a small particle of our native land of Ukraine . . .

> Your Holiness, the sons and daughters of Ukraine greet you on the occasion of this Holy Jubilee of the Baptism of Ukraine. We greet you in front of this Church of the Divine Wisdom, which for us is the symbol of our independence, our struggles, representing our faith in Christ's victory with the words: *"The Lord is my stronghold, and my God the rock of my refuge."* (Psalms 94:22)

> Holy Father, bless our Ukrainian people and our suffering Church. May this our Jubilee with your apostolic blessing be a pledge of our freedom . . .

After the reading of the Gospel, the Holy Father gave his homily in Ukrainian and in Italian:

This Millennium reminds us that ten centuries ago on the banks of the Dnipro River the Gospel was announced to the people who, thanks to the bath of regeneration, became part of the Church, the Mystical Body of Christ.

In our thoughts, full of gratitude, let us go back to the Baptism of Vladimir and Olga, as well as to each baptism conferred throughout the centuries upon the lands of the Kievan Rus' as to the messengers of the word of salvation. In each baptism the mercy of the Blessed Trinity is realized and confirmed is that which is dearest to each human being: his great value, his high dignity, and the freedom of God's children . . . .

Meeting the Holy Father, John Paul II, at St. Sophia Basilica, Rome Italy, during the Millenium celebration, July 9, 1988.

After the Moleben, the Pope went inside the church where the bishops and the representatives of various communities were able to meet him personally and exchange a few words. The same day at 9:00 P.M. a great mass of the pilgrims assembled at St. Peter's Square in the Vatican. The bishops served a Moleben to St. Vladimir. Bishop Innocent Lotocky, OSBM, preached a homily. After the Moleben, at a sign given by the master of ceremonies, Mr. Vladimir Luciw, all the members of the youth organizations lit their torches, and the people lit their candles. In the darkness of the night a huge flaming cross was formed the length and the width of the large square.

It was at that moment that a window on the top floor of the Apostolic Palace was opened and the Holy Father appeared in it.

Through the loud speakers he greeted the assembled masses in Ukrainian, and then in Italian explained the reason of this celebration.

Sunday, July 10, 1988, marked the crowning of all celebrations. At St. Peter's Basilica in the Vatican, a hierarchical Divine Liturgy was celebrated in Ukrainian at the main altar, standing over the tomb of St. Peter the Apostle. At 9:30 A.M. a majestic procession took place going from the vestibule through the center of the church to the main altar. The Holy Father, John Paul II himself, headed the procession of about 250 priests and all our bishops. He was the main celebrant. His throne was erected in the center of the Basilica in front of the main altar. To his right and his left were seats for the concelebrating bishops. His Beatitude Cardinal Lubachivsky began the celebration by blessing the four sides of the world with the triple and double candelabra and singing: *"Lord, Lord, look down from heaven and see; visit this vineyard, and protect what your right hand has planted . . ."* The combined church choirs composed of six hundred singers sang the responses to this Liturgy beautifully. Their harmonious voices rose high and filled the huge spaces of the largest church in Christendom.

While the Ukrainian Catholic Church in Ukraine was forcefully liquidated and exists only in the modern-day catacombs, here in the free world this Church is celebrating its Millennium together with the successor to St. Peter in a most festive and majestic way. Polish Cardinal Henryk Gulbinowicz of Wroclaw, present at our Liturgy, told me: "In 1966 when we observed our Millennium in Poland we did not have such a majestic celebration as you have here today."

Vatican radio broadcast this Liturgy into Ukraine while Italian TV was transmitting it for three hours to its viewers. The commentators in Italian were Rev. Vasyl Sapelak and Rev. Alexander Dzerowytch.

The Holy Father in his homily among other things said:

The Apostolic See has always felt a strict obligation to support the Ukrainian Catholic faithful in their right to remain in the Catholic unity and to retain their own liturgical rite and traditions. For this reason Metropolia, eparchies and exarchates were erected with their own hierarchy for the Ukrainian Catholic faithful who live in the Diaspora.

My dear brothers in the Episcopate! My most beloved brothers and sisters in the Lord! Here, near the grave of St. Peter; closer to it rest the earthly remains of your beloved martyr, St. Josaphat. Here we together render thanks and gratitude to the Most Blessed Trinity for the invaluable gift of Baptism, for the numerous spiritual fruits shared in the Divine Mysteries in the community of faith and in the bonds of love . . .

From my sincere heart I embrace you as your brother and as the first in all the history of the Church, Pope from the Slavic people. Together with you I start a pilgrimage to the hill of Kiev where on the banks of the wide River Dnipro stands a monument of St. Vladimir. I fall on my knees before the icon of the Mother of God Oranta in the St. Sophia Church in Kiev and entrust to her the entire destiny of the Ukrainian Catholic Church. O, Mother of God, cover us with your sacred Protection and shelter us from all evil.

Saint Peter and Paul, saintly princes Vladimir and Olga, holy fathers Anthony and Theodosius of the Monastery of the Caves, saints Boris and Hlib, the holy martyr Josaphat always intercede for us, your faithful children. O, Jesus Christ, have mercy on us and save us for you are good and love mankind . . .

The same day, July 10, 1988, at 6:00 P.M. a Grand Concert took place in the Paul VI Aula. The huge auditorium was filled to capacity. The Holy Father entered and greeted all with the Ukrainian, "Slava Isusu Christu!"—Glory be to Jesus Christ! It took him almost twenty minutes to pass from the rear to the front of the hall. He was shaking hands and greeting people on both sides of the aisle.

His Beatitude Myroslav Cardinal Lubachivsky welcomed the Pope with a short speech and opened the concert. The same combined choir, which sang the Liturgy in the Basilica gave this concert. The performance of each composition was done at a highly professional level. Mr. Vladimir Luciw from Great Britain performed the duties of a master of ceremonies and announced each performance in Italian and Ukrainian. During the concert, a life-size statue of St. Vladimir was unveiled on the stage. It was a gift of our bishops to the Holy Father.

At the end of the Concert program, the Holy Father stepped forward, greeted and congratulated the choir members and their director, took a group photo with them, then sat down and gave a brief talk:

> To you I address my sincere greetings, wishing to express my great joy as well as my admiration for all you were able to achieve today, using the talents of the Ukrainians who live in the Diaspora only. Together with my coworkers from the Vatican Curia and my guests I had the opportunity to admire the language of your art, your singing, your music, and all of this was indeed a spiritual delight.

> Look at the rock from which you were hewn." (Isaiah 51:1) Thus speaks Prophet Isaiah to his people. Today's evening is filled with episodes, which call forth the memory of a nation's piety and are a reminder to "look at the rock from which you were hewn." Christ with his Gospel is that rock. Your acceptance of which into your culture permitted such a blossoming of beauty.

> Christianity made possible in the Kievan Rus', homogeneous at that time, the creation of its own culture upon the national and religious background. The language of Sts. Cyril and Methodius became the language of authors and scholars, of the Sacred Scripture, especially of the Gospel and the Psalter, and became the exemplar of the art of the word. Even the folk art, which grew out of a pagan background, with time went thorough a process of sanctification, and was expressed in special works of religious poetry and literary genre.

> The culture of the Ukrainian nation grew out of the heritage of St. Vladimir's Baptism, and this is why it is rooted in the ground of Christian Europe . . .

416

Millennium Celebrations in Czestochowa

I am convinced that it was John Paul II himself who persuaded the Polish Bishops to invite the Ukrainian Catholic Bishops to their famous Marian Shrine in Czestochowa so we might celebrate the Millennium of the Baptism of Ukraine. This is the place closest to our native land, presently under the Soviet Union, where our Church is illegal and persecuted. These celebrations took place Saturday and Sunday, September 10th and 11th 1988.

Bishop Kuchmiak and I arrived in Warsaw the morning of September 8, 1988. Basilian Fathers, Sister Servants, and Father Theodore Majkowycz were waiting for us. Someone had made special arrangements so that the airport authorities took both of us into a VIP room where the police checked our passports so we did not have to stand in line with the rest of the passengers. The Sister Servants invited both of us to their convent for a luncheon. There we met Sister Philomena who came from Ukraine and the catacomb Church, dressed as a peasant woman, to attend this celebration. Father Majkowycz was very friendly with me, because some years ago he wrote and asked for financial help to be able to buy a car so that he would be able to reach his distant parishes on Sundays. With the help of some of my friends I was able to help him. Now he felt obliged to help me while I was in Poland. His brother Theodore became my driver for the duration of my stay in Poland.

Following the luncheon, we were taken to the Basilian Monastery, located on 8 Miodowa Street. There we met with the other bishops who had arrived before us. In the evening the Basilian Fathers prepared a festive dinner to which Cardinal Joseph Glemp, the Primate of Poland, was invited.[8]

Cardinal Glemp welcomed us with a short speech, and Metropolitan Hermaniuk thanked him on behalf of all of us for being with us and inviting us to Poland. Afterward cars took all our Bishops to the residence of the Polish episcopate for an overnight stay. This residence was built especially to house Bishops' Conference of Poland and has conference rooms as well as a number of comfortable sleeping rooms for the bishops.

The next day, September 9, 1988, Cardinal Glemp invited all our bishops as well as some priests to his house for a luncheon. His house, or rather a palace, is located directly across the street from the Basilian Monastery. After the luncheon with speeches, the Cardinal took us on a tour of his palace, showing us especially the huge artistic paintings and other artifacts.

In the afternoon, the Basilian Fathers drove us in two cars to Jasna Gora in Czestochowa. We got our rooms in the old monastery building, next to the famous Basilica. In the evening of that day all our Bishops with Father Isidore Patrylo, the Protoarchimandrite of the Basilian Fathers and Father Sophronius Mudry, OSBM, Rector of the St. Josaphat Seminary in Rome, concelebrated a Prayer Service to the Most Holy Mother of God before her miraculous icon. The large Basilica was filled with our faithful from all over Poland. During the Prayer Service, Father Rubin Abramek, the Superior of the monastery, welcomed all of us with our Millennium pilgrims in this famous place of pilgrimages.

---

[8] Present were His Beatitude Cardinal Lubachivsky, our Major Archbishop; Archbishop Myroslav Marusyn—Secretary of the Congregation for the Eastern Churches; Metropolitan Maxim Hermaniuk, CSsR, of Winnipeg; Bishop Basil Losten of Stamford; Bishop Michael Hrynchyshyn, CSsR from Paris, France; Slavomir Miklos from Yugoslavia; and Bishop Michael Kuchmiak, CSsR from Philadelphia. There were likewise some of our priests from Rome, United States of America, and Canada.

Saturday morning Myroslav Ivan Cardinal Lubachivsky with the two Metropolitans celebrated Divine Liturgy before the miraculous icon of the Most Holy Mother of God. The official opening of our celebrations was at 10:00 A.M. Saturday with a hierarchical Divine Liturgy at the Basilica with Archbishop Marusyn as the main celebrant and Fathers Theodore Majkowycz and Julian Gbur as concelebrants. Other bishops presided with the Senate of the Catholic University, as well as many other dignitaries.

In his well-prepared homily Archbishop Marusyn stated that the miraculous icon of the Most Holy Mother of God of Czestochowa was a witness of the Baptism of Ukraine one thousand years ago. This icon was brought from Byzantium to Kiev as a dowry of Anna, the wife of Vladimir the Great. He then sketched a short history of this icon and how it was brought to Czestochowa some 600 years ago. At first this icon was kept in Kiev, afterward in the city of Polock at the Convent of St. Euphrosina. From there Prince George, the son of King Leo of Halych, took the icon to his capital city of Belz. Prince Wladyslaw Opolski, vice regent of the Hungarian King Ludwig, conquered the city of Belz in 1377. He then just heisted the icon and transferred it to the West, giving it to the Pauline Fathers in Czestochowa in the year 1382.

Our church choir from Peremyshl sang the responses to the Liturgy. After the Liturgy I was a witness to how Father Abramek congratulated Archbishop Marusyn for his excellent homily and asked for a copy of his homily because he never heard this story of the icon.

In the afternoon the programs of the celebration followed one after another. The faithful had an opportunity to view the exposition portraying highlights from the history of our Church. A concert was presented by four hundred school children from the various places of their settlements in Poland. In poetic and musical form they portrayed scenes from the Baptism of Ukraine and scenes from the tragic history of the Ukrainian Catholic Church.

Because the number of our faithful present there was so large that they could not assemble in one place, the program was arranged in such a way that two or more different activities were taking place at one time. Thus at 4:00 P.M. Bishop Hrynchyshyn,

CSsR, with ten priests celebrated a Divine Liturgy for about one thousand school children and some three thousand faithful. At the same time in the "Papal Hall" a concert of Ukrainian religious hymns took place. Before the opening of the concert, Cardinal Joseph Glemp had a talk, stressing the point that here in Czestochowa it is appropriate for the Ukrainian Catholic Church to celebrate their Millennium of Baptism because here we all are united in one faith and one love of the Most Holy Mother of God.

At 7:30 P.M. a well-organized procession of young people took place on the very large ground of the monastery, called "The Way of Faith of Our Ancestors." With a cross bearer in front, there followed the banner bearers, the faithful, and the clergy all carrying lighted candles. The procession proceeded from one station to another. Each station was dedicated to a separate scene from the history of our Church. The first one was to honor Sts. Cyril and Methodius, then came St. Vladimir and Olga, St. Josaphat, and the last was dedicated to the martyrs of our Church of the present time, marked by three high crosses.

The procession in the darkness of the night with a sea of lighted candles and torches was very inspirational and prayerful. During the two-hour long procession there were readings of the Gospel, church hymns, and meditations at each of the stations. It was a kind of public profession of faith and a demonstration of the love for our Church and her traditions. On a high platform of the monastery were seated Cardinals Lubachivsky, Glemp, and Macharski, and all our Bishops observing the progress of the procession.

The high point of the celebration in Czestochowa was the hierarchical Divine Liturgy with Cardinal Lubachivsky as the main celebrant, with all our bishops and about seventy priests concelebrating. From the Polish Catholic Church Cardinals Joseph Glemp, Franciszek Macharski, Henryk Gulbinowicz, and fifteen other bishops were present. The Liturgy was celebrated on the outside on the high platform of the monastery, while thirty thousand faithful were gathered on the huge grounds where the procession had been held the night before.

Before the Liturgy commenced, the Superior of the monastery Father Rubin Abramek said some welcoming words: "The Mother of God of Czestochowa waited six hundred years for her children from Ukraine to come to her and be with her." From the Ukrainian Church in Poland spoke Father Ivan Martyniak, Vicar General. He read a telegram from the Holy Father with very warm greetings and blessings for all present here.

These two days of our celebrations in Czestochowa, filled with liturgical celebrations, concerts, and prayerful programs with great masses of our people, many priests and bishops, became a huge manifestation and profession of our Catholic faith, as well as an eloquent expression of our gratitude to God for the grace of baptism.

Throughout Poland by Car

After a luncheon on Sunday, September 11, 1988, Archbishop Marusyn, Father Majkowycz and I left Czestochowa by car and traveled through the cities of Krakow, Tarnow, Rzeszow, and Sianok to the village of Komancza, located in the eastern Lemkivschyna. Father Majkowycz was the pastor of Komancza parish. We lodged at the Latin Nazarene Sisters' Convent. The late Cardinal Stefan Wyszynski was interned in this convent for two years by the Polish Communist authorities. We were welcomed warmly and hosted with a delicious supper.

The following day, Monday September 12, 1988, Archbishop Marusyn and I traveled by car to visit the village Balnycia, my birthplace. The roads were very good, newly built by the Polish Army. We passed villages Radozhyci, Oslavycia, Lupkiv, Smilnyk, Vola Myhova, and just before the village Maniw we turned right on a dirt road to go to Balnycia. Hardly anyone has lived in those villages since the people were forcefully resettled in 1946–47. There were one or two homes in Vola Myhova.

My first impressions when we arrived in the lower part of Balnycia were very painful. I was away from this village since 1944. It was very strange to see a very familiar landscape and no one there, not even an animal. Not a single house, only a chapel across the ravine behind a creek still stood there surrounded by weeds and shrubs. Once a year on Pentecost Sunday there was a procession from the church to this chapel, Divine Liturgy would be celebrated, and then water would be blessed in a small spring just before the chapel. People believed that the water from this spring had some miraculous curative powers.

Once this place was alive. Where the tillage fields were before, now they were overgrown with pine trees especially planted for use by the paper mills. We went to the place where our church once stood. Only the lower part of the stone vestibule was still standing. The large iron cross from the top of the church tower was leaning against the stone fence. There was a cemetery around the church. I found the grave of my oldest brother. His tombstone was overturned. I could not find the graves of my two other brothers who died during the last war and my grandfather's grave. Archbishop Marusyn and I sang the requiem prayer service for the repose of the souls of my dear ones.

From the church site we traveled further to find the place where my home once stood. The house was built in 1929. All I could see was one huge emptiness. There was no point of reference. Finally I noticed a cluster of fruit trees. That was our orchard. By these trees I determined the place where our home once stood. Theodore Majkowycz, our driver, went there and plucked a small apple from a tree. I took that apple and gave it to my sister later on when I met her in our Uncle Nicholas' house in northwestern Poland.

From there we went back to the paved road and turned right to the village of Maniv. Again we stopped to see the place where the church once stood. Not far from that place stood a single house, but no one could be seen in it. We kept going on through former villages of Scherbanivka, Zhubriache, and the town of Tisna. From there we traveled the road that led to the town of Balyhorod through the former villages of Habkovychi, Jablinka, Lubne, and Bystre. We stopped in Balyhorod to see the brick church that stood, doors and windows broken, the roof full of holes, and the interior ravaged. Years ago my father would take me with him when he traveled by horse and buggy to this town for shopping.

We continued our trip to the city of Lisko and from there through the former villages of Hlynne, Wilshanycia, Stefkowa, Ustianova Dolishnia and Horishnia to the town of Ustriky Dolishni. All along the road all we could see were empty fields and abandoned villages. Father Theodore Majkowycz served three parishes: Komancza, Ustriky Dolishni and Peremyshl. After a short rest, our driver turned around and we started on our trip back to Komancza through Lisko, Chashyn, Kulashne, Schavne, and Repid.

The following day, Tuesday, September 13, 1988, was a festive day for the parish in Komancza—the dedication and consecration of a newly-built church. Archbishop Marusyn was the main celebrant. Concelebrating were Bishop Losten and myself, as well as fifty priests who came from Czestochowa for this occasion.

Wednesday, September 14, 1988, Archbishop Marusyn left for Warsaw to take a plane back home to Rome. My driver and I left Komancza and stopped in the city of Horlyci at the Basilian Sisters' convent. They welcomed me cordially and treated both of us to a meal. Soon afterward we started on a long trip to the city of Wroclaw (Breslau), located in western Poland, formerly in Germany. I had an invitation from Henryk Cardinal Gulbinowicz to visit him and to offer our Divine Liturgy in his cathedral. Another invitation I received was from our priest in that city, Father Petro Kryk. Some time ago he wrote to me, asking for help to buy a tabernacle for his church. I did order a bronze tabernacle for him from a firm in Chicago and shipped it to him.

It was evening when we arrived in Wroclaw. The Cardinal received me warmly, treated me to a dinner, and, after some small talk, he showed me to my bedroom for a night's rest. The next morning I went to our church where Father Kryk with his parishioners welcomed me. I served a Moleben and had a homily. The tabernacle looked very nice on the altar. Afterward the Cardinal invited me to see his Archdiocesan Museum. Showing me some old documents, he tried to convince me that Wroclaw was always Polish. In the evening of the same day I had a hierarchical Divine Liturgy in his cathedral. The choir from our parish church sang the responses. I prepared a homily and Father Kryk translated it into Polish, so I preached in Polish for the first time in my life.

Friday, September 16, 1988 Theodore Majkowycz and I departed from Wroclaw, driving north through former German lands to a town named Trzebiatow, near the Baltic Sea shores where my Uncle Nicholas Sulyk and his sons lived. I stayed at the house of his son Ivan, and the next day he took me to see his father. My Uncle Nicholas was waiting for me in the doorway of his house with a welcome that is traditional for bishops. He held in his hands a loaf of bread and some salt on a tray and gave a beautiful speech, saying how happy he is to have lived to see the day when I would enter his house, the first from our family to have become a Metropolitan. I gave him and his wife, Marka, a hug and a kiss. He insisted on kissing my hand. My sister Anna was there from Ukraine.

Saturday, September 17, 1988, the local pastor, Father Pavlo Malynowsky organized a parish Millennium Celebration. Since the church was not large enough to contain the many people, he had a platform built on the church grounds with a canopy overhead. Before the Liturgy I was welcomed by the school children from the parish with songs, poems, and flowers. Afterward there was a wedding of my uncle's granddaughter Hrazyna with Ivan Podubinsky. All these arrangements were made by the pastor, not only to honor me, but also my uncle who had served there as a cantor for many years.

The next morning I traveled to Warsaw and served a Divine Liturgy in the Basilian Monastery chapel. Monday morning I was taken to the airport for a flight home to the United States of America.

Visiting My Birthplace

When I returned home from the trip to Czestochowa, I sat down in the evening and started to write a letter to my brothers and sister in Ukraine of my impressions from visiting my birthplace after forty-four years of absence. When I started writing, the ideas smoothly flowed into my mind and I put them on paper via a computer.

My visit to the place where our native village stood made a profound and unforgettable impression on me. For many years I dreamt to see once more in my lifetime the place where I was born, where I grew up, started school, and spent the carefree years of my young days.

For me this is the only such place. In the whole world there is no other. From my early days when I was not quite eleven years old, from the 5th grade on, I was already away from home. At first it was in the school in Sambir. Later on I was forced to share the destiny of a refugee in a foreign land, among strange people and an unknown language. I sorely missed the love of my parents and you, my dear brothers and sister, the warmth and the security of our home. Many a time I wished I could have shared with our parents and you my joys and sorrows, but that was not to be. There was no one to give me advice or encouragement. Loneliness in a foreign land is a bitter pill to swallow. This is why very often I had dreams that took me back home to our native village, our home, and our church on a hill, the green meadows and dense forests. I had these dreams although I knew that our village and our home are no more.

Finally in this, the Jubilee Year of the Millennium of our Baptism of Ukraine, God permitted my dreams to be fulfilled. On the occasion of our Millennium celebration in Czestochowa, I had the occasion to see once more the land of my birth. I traveled by automobile from Komancza through the former villages of Radozhyci, Oslavycia, Lupkiv, Smilnyk and Vola Myhova. Just before Maniw we turned right. The road led us through thick forest, as though it was an admission gate, into the scenery where once our village Balnycia stood.

Although I knew well that no one lived there any longer, subconsciously I hoped against hope to meet somebody to share the joy of my homecoming. In my school days when I was returning home for Christmas or Easter and walked from the railroad station up the road, our faithful dog would always come running to welcome me. With his joyous barking he seemed to announce to all: "Our Steve has come back home!" Today I couldn't hear even a dog's bark. No one came to meet me. No one welcomed me home, only the dark autumn skies covered with gray clouds silently looked down on me, while the ground, wet from the rain, seemed to say: "My son came back to me!

I looked at the landscape of our village and did not recognize it. There is not a single home left in it, no church, no sawmill at the lower end of the village, nothing. My heart ached from seeing this great and total ruin. This is the place where our people lived for many centuries, where they prayed to God and raised their families. From dawn to dark they toiled on their fields to earn their daily bread. Now these fields are overgrown with weeds and bushes.

"This is a picture portraying the ruin caused by the people of this the twentieth century. The century of colossal progress and fantastic inventions, of technology and civilization, and at the same time the century of most cruel wars and brutal wild animal-like barbarism no less than the ancient Mongolian hordes. We are observing our Millennium of Baptism this year. The Gospel of truth, love, mercy and forgiveness of even the worst enemies was preached for a millennium. Yet, is this ruin a witness of Christian morality and human kindness? Is it possible that Christians are capable of such barbarism and cruelty on innocent women and children, the elderly and the infirm? Yes, they are capable of such crimes only because they permitted the darkness of modern paganism to enter their hearts.

Looking at this our hallowed land in total and horrible ruin, I prayed in my soul: 'Almighty and merciful God, what kind of a horrible sin did these poor farmers, my people, commit that You permitted this horrible ruin to fall on them? To love this land, this Church, the native language and freedom is a good and praiseworthy thing, a virtue for all but the Ukrainian people. For Ukrainians this somehow is a crime that deserves this rude and barbaric punishment.'

I then in my heart I heard this answer: 'Recall that my dearest Son, who was the most holy and innocent one, suffered also unjust cruelties and horrible death on a cross. Then He suffered alone. Now He is not alone anymore. Since the Baptism of Vladimir, all who are baptized in Christ have put on Christ and become His Mystical Body. Christ now continues to save people, continues to make up for the horrible crimes of humanity. In his glorified body He cannot suffer anymore. This is why He chose your people, part of His Mystical Body, so that like Simon the Cyrenean of old, they would help Him carry his cross today. As it was then, so it will be now, that the way of the cross will end. It will be followed by the Easter Sunday morning and the glorious Resurrection; victory and freedom will inevitably follow for all who remain faithful to me."

World Synods of Bishops

As a result of Vatican Council II, a World Synod of Bishops was established in order to introduce a collegial method of decision-making in important matters. Normally such synods were held every three years. In the preparatory phase of such a Synod, once the main topic was selected, a booklet called *Lineamenta* was prepared and mailed to each Bishops Conference and each Eastern Catholic Church. The *Lineamenta* contained an outline of the topic subject matter with questions after each chapter. All the bishops were asked to answer these questions. They in turn should have asked their priests likewise to give their answers. In this way the collegial method of decision-making is extensively widened.

The answers to the questions of the *Lineamenta* were mailed to the Secretariat of the Synod in the Vatican. The preparatory Committee would study the answers and from them compose a final working document called *Instumentum laboris*. This, in turn, was mailed to all the elected delegates from the Bishops' Conferences, to the Eastern Catholic Patriarchies, the Metropolias outside the Patriarchates, and to the invited delegates.

On the basis of the *Instumentum laboris,* the Synodal fathers would prepare their input into the Synod or the so-called "intervention." As a Metropolitan outside of the Patriarchate, I was called *ex officio* to six consecutive World Synods of Bishops. The first such Synod I attended began September 29, and ended October 29, 1983. The topic of the Synod was *"Penance and Reconciliation."* In my intervention I wanted to present one important concept in the theology of the Eastern Church. There were only about fifteen hierarchs of the Eastern churches. All others were of the Latins, and this point of view of the Eastern Church should have been interesting to them.

In my intervention I spoke of reconciliation as seen by the Eastern theology. Eastern theology speaks of *deification,* or, from the Greek, *theosis."* The biblical theme that gave rise to this concept is found in the Second Letter of Peter (1:4), which speaks of *". . . becoming sharers of the divine nature. . . ."* *Deification* is also the way in which the Gospel of John and the letters of Paul seek to express the greatness of the gift of divine grace. Closely connected with *deification* is Paul's teaching about the Mystical Body of Christ: *"You, then, are the body of Christ. Every one of you is a member of it"* (1 Corinthians 12:27).

For the Eastern Fathers and church writers, *deification* was never a mere metaphor. For instance, St. Maxim the Confessor writes: "God has created us in order that we may become partakers of the divine nature, in order that we may enter into eternity and that we may appear like unto him, which brings into existence everything that had no existence before" (Ep. 43rd ad Joannem cubicularium, PG 91,640).

In the doctrine of *deification,* grace is not something created, coming like creatures *ex nihilo* (out of nothing). It is rather the living God in His act of coming to the faithful. This understanding of grace as God's own energy is much more theocentric than the scholastic concept of created grace.

When deified, the human being possesses within limits, by grace what the Holy Trinity has by nature. Possessing the divine energy-grace means having God not in the divine essence but in the divine energies, which are inseparable (though distinct) from the divine essence.

Such imagery and such concepts are employed to stress that God really comes to human beings wholly and entirely, through His grace-energy. Though a mystery itself, the Eucharist helps shed some light on the mystery of deification. The Eucharistic Christ is present wholly and entirely in each fragment after the Eucharistic Bread is broken. Hear as well the way in which St. Cyril of Alexandria speaks: "Our return to God is understood to have come about not otherwise than through Christ our Savior, through participation of the Spirit and through sanctification. For the Spirit joins us, so to speak, unites us with God so that having accepted the Spirit we become sharers of the divine nature" (Cf. Johannem XI, 10; PG 74,544 D-545A).

In 1985 the Holy Father called an Extraordinary Session of the World Synod of Bishops for two-week-long deliberations, from November 24 to December 8. This Synod had one main theme, the 20th Anniversary of the close of Vatican Council II.

I used this opportunity to call the attention of the Holy Father and of the bishops of the world to the plight of our Church in Ukraine.

"In a few days we shall mark the twentieth anniversary of the declaration of the Vatican Synod II concerning religious freedom, *Dignitatis humanae*, promulgated December 7, 1965. The introduction to this document states:

"This Vatican Synod states that the human person has the right of religious freedom." It further states: "This freedom consists in this that all people should be free from compulsion, be it from single individuals or a community and from all human authorities, so that in religious matters . . . no one is to be forced to act contrary to his own conscience . . . privately, publicly, personally, or in conjunction with others." Further on we read in this document: "It follows from this that public authorities are forbidden by force or fear or by other methods to impose on their citizens the acceptance or renouncement of any kind of religion or to interfere in that one chooses for himself or leaves a religious community."

I have cited this document because history has never known such a concentration of religious persecution, especially of Christians, as it is being done today. These millions of people who live under communist rule, which actually destroys every religion, comprise half of all humanity. As a bishop of the Ukrainian Catholic Church, I feel pain because my Mother Church in the Soviet Union legally does not exist. Her bishops, priests, and the faithful make up a catacomb church in this our enlightened century. If they are not actually imprisoned, then they live in constant danger of being jailed or be deported into one of the numerous concentration camps.

What can we do, free members of the Catholic Church, in order to aid our brothers and sisters in these modern catacombs?

The only help in the face of this brutal tyranny is moral pressure and protests from among the Catholic community. In the past, insistent protests were made only when the Apostolic See informed us that it is our duty to condemn such cruelty.

I wish to recall that the communist authorities did not treat such protests seriously because they felt that these protests were not spontaneous nor were they expressions of real dissatisfaction. Yet we know that communist governments are very sensitive to public actions and opinions, because such an opinion reflects on the relationships with other nations.

These governments evaluate the protest of Catholics against a religious persecution as a manifestation by Rome itself. They do not consider these protests to be true expressions of feelings. They understand the protests of aliens as such that have no influence on any one.

This is why it is important that the whole Catholic Church in the Free World be united in one serious and continuous protest against the communistic suppression of religious freedom. The Jewish communities could serve us as an example. They do not have a central leadership, yet personal protests continue, and rightly so, whenever a communist government commits an anti-Semitic action. And they attain concrete answers.

Even when our protests and demonstrations may have small or no influence on the atheistic government, our brothers and sisters in Ukraine, Lithuania, and Latvia and in other parts of the Soviet Union, China, Vietnam, Cambodia and in many other countries will receive moral aid. This will sustain them in their endurance. There is no doubt that our Catholic brothers and sisters as well as other believers will be grateful to us.

May I propose to Your Holiness, and to the entire assembly to teach all members of the Catholic Church:

1. To openly and publicly protest against the persecution of all Christians by the communist governments;

2. That the protest be spontaneous and that they may begin in all the countries by their own hierarchs;

3. That local churches ask their own government to demand from the Soviet Union and other communist countries to give all believers, especially Catholics, the full use of the religious freedom and the freedom of church life. Thank you!

An ordinary session of the Word Synod of Bishops was held in the Vatican during the month of October 1987. Its theme was: "The role of laymen in the Church." In my intervention I spoke again on the persecution of our Church in Ukraine. The summary follows:

Most Holy Father, My brother Bishops, I speak as the representative and the Metropolitan of the Ukrainian Catholic Church in the United States of America. Because of our close ties with our brethren behind the Iron Curtain in Ukraine, I speak so that their voices might be heard by this distinguished Synod and that the

Church share in witness of our heroic Underground Church and its faith in Jesus Christ and its loyalty to the See of Peter in Rome.

While I shall omit the tortuous history of my Church, I shall concentrate on the role of the laity whose cooperation has made possible the celebration of the Millennium of the Christianization of Ukraine next year. In particular, I wish to give testimony of the active role the laity played in the development of the Ukrainian Catholic Church in the United States of America during this century.

The Ukrainian Catholic Church in the Soviet Union, where five million people faithful to the See of Peter were forcefully suppressed and annexed to the Russian Orthodox Church in 1946. In spite of this, bishops and priests continue, over the years, to be secretly ordained and religious communities continue to organize and function. But their work is severely curtailed by the Soviet police. Often, the courageous laity of the Underground Church have paid for their fidelity to the Church with prison, exile, and even death. But they have kept their faith alive.

In a real sense, the persecution of the Church in the first centuries of Christianity is being repeated today in the Soviet Union. The cruelty of the Roman emperors and other enemies of Christ has been replaced with more "refined," if we may use the term, methods of torture and mistreatment. The vast majority of modern confessors and martyrs today are lay people. With this heroic example in mind, I submit to the Synod the following proposals:

The Synod should publicly give recognition to the suffering laity in all countries suffering persecution both in Soviet Union and in all communist countries throughout the world.

Meeting the Holy Father, John Paul II, during the World Synod of Bishops in October of 1983.

Pleasant Surprise

During the World Synod of Bishops in October 1987, the Primate of the Polish Catholic Church, Joseph Cardinal Glemp, extended an invitation to all Ukrainian Synodal Fathers and to some Ukrainian Catholic priests residing in Rome, to an all-Ukrainian dinner at the Pontifical Polish College, October 8, 1987. During the dinner Cardinal Glemp gave the Ukrainians a pleasant surprise. All of us were convinced that the ideal came directly from the Holy Father, John Paul II. In his talk Cardinal Glemp in summary said:

We invited to this Polish College our Ukrainian brother bishops and priests of the Ukrainian Catholic Church. The Ukrainian Catholic Church is now preparing for its Great Jubilee, a Millennium of Christianity. This Church is present here today by its most distinguished representatives. We understand the feelings and difficulties of our Ukrainian brothers, because we ourselves observed our Millennium 22 years ago in Poland. From this Eternal City our thoughts fly to our native lands and to all the places in the world where our people have settled.

We now stand on the eve of the Millennium of Christianity in Rus'. This concerns not only our churches but whole Christianity as well, and likewise the culture that was developed from Christianity there . . .

I hope that next year God will permit you and us to stand together on the Jasna Gora in Czestochowa to join our "We praise you, O God."

On our way from the Polish Seminary to St. Josaphat's Seminary I stated that it would be proper and expected that we invite the Polish Hierarchy to our seminary for a dinner. The date selected was October 17, 1987. Father Sophronius Mudryj, OSBM, the Rector, agreed to take care of all preparations and invitations. Cardinal Lubachivsky was one of the three presiding cardinals at the Synod. He agreed to give an appropriate speech.

On the day of our dinner for the Polish hierarchy the following guests came: Joseph Cardinal Glemp, the Primate of Poland; Francziszek Cardinal Macharski, Metropolitan of Krakow; Henryk Cardinal Gulbinowicz, Metropolitan of Wroclaw; Archbishop George Stroba, Metropolitan of Poznan; Archbishop Bronislaw Dombrowski, Secretary of Polish Bishops Conference; Bishop George Dobrowski, undersecretary of Polish Bishops Conference; Ignatius Tokarczyk, Bishop of Peremyshl; Zenon Grocholewski, Bishop of Kelcy; Bishop Wladyslaw Jendrusiak, Secretary of the Apostolic Signatura; Ryszard Karpicki, Bishop of Lublyn; and Msgr. Stanislaw Dziwisz, private Secretary of Pope John Paul II.

In his talk Myroslav Ivan Cardinal Lubachivsky in summary said:

Our encounter today is a manifestation of great meaning and joy, because today we can pray together and have a fraternal meeting on the eve of the Great Jubilee of the Millennium of Baptism of our people. First of all, I wish to thank Your Eminence, the Primate, for your kind hospitality by which you received us, the representatives of the hierarchy of the Ukrainian Church, last week, Thursday October 8, 1987.

Right now I recall a document of historical value, which was promulgated in 1965 by the Primate Stefan Wyszynski. In it, in the name of all the bishops of Poland, he addressed the Bishops and the people of Germany on the eve of the Millennium of the Baptism of Poland, as a gesture of forgiveness, unity, and love. This took place during the Vatican Council II. The one who inspired this action, in a great measure, was the Metropolitan of Krakow, Karol Cardinal Wojtyla, our present John Paul II.

Standing here today on the eve of the Great Jubilee, the Millennium of Baptism of Rus'—Ukraine we, the hierarchs of the Ukrainian Catholic Church, extend our fraternal hands to our Polish brothers in a gesture of unity, mutual forgiveness, and love.

World Synods of Bishops in 1990, 1994 and 1997

The Eighth World Synod of Bishops, held in October 1990 at the Vatican, was on the theme of priestly formation. Below is a summary of my intervention:

My remarks are related to #41 of the *Instrumentum laboris*, where it is said that, "candidates of both the Latin and Oriental rites ought to be introduced to the doctrinal traditions of each other," as well as the statement in #25, which reads, "the cooperative efforts of all persons entrusted with formation work is to take into account the necessities of the Particular Church.

I would like to make an appeal for this cooperation and exchange. My plea is for the recently liberated churches of Eastern Europe and their great needs. They are in need of many things—primarily the establishment of their own seminaries and formation programs.

The liberated churches of the East are in the process of reorganizing their seminaries and formation programs. There is a great need for qualified teachers of ecclesiastical disciplines. Seminaries that are being reopened in the East are in need of textbooks and manuals. Libraries have to rebuild. Books and theological literature are indispensable tools in the work of educating priests. In this area, too, the West can assist the liberated churches of the East.

The Ninth World Synod of Bishops took place in the month of October in 1994. The theme was "The consecrated life and its role in the Church and in the world." My intervention in summary was:

To restore institutes of consecrated life to their cherished and necessary role in the Church, there must be a genuine reform of the consecrated life, a reform on returning to the roots and spiritual patrimony according to the evangelical counsels and the spirit of the founder. This reform means that the religious would reject the pressure of the secularistic fashion of our times and return to the life of Christ. The evangelical counsels must be taken seriously and earnestly without watering them down. The religious life must be lived out with all its necessities and demands in a spirit of obedience, poverty and chastity, comparable to that, which was practiced by our Lord and his Most Holy Mother. Reforming institutes of consecrated life in the West in this way would renew and restore them to the apostolic heritage of the Early Church, which to this day still remains a main source of holiness and strength of all the Eastern Churches, both Orthodox and Catholic, and would faithfully adhere to the teachings of the Fathers of Vatican II which stated, "In the East are to be found the riches of those spiritual traditions which are given expression in monastic life especially."

At the Opening Papal Liturgy of the World Synod of Bishops, September 29, 1990 at the Basilica of St. Peter, Vatican City. Vested in the Eastern Episcopal vestment. (L. to R.) Bishop Sophronius Dmyterko - Eparch of Ivano-Frankivsk, Ukraine; Archbishop Stephen Sulyk and Archbishop Maxim Hermaniuk - Winnipeg, Canada.

In Diplomatic Service

Since the visit of Michael Gorbachev, the President of the Soviet Union, to the Holy Father, John Paul II, in the Vatican on December 1, 1989, the situation of the Ukrainian Catholic Church in the Soviet Union has drastically changed. Gorbachev gave a promise to the Holy Father to give freedom to our Church. The Apostolic See of Rome sent a delegation to the Patriarch of Moscow, headed by Cardinal Willebrands. This delegation deliberated with the Russian Orthodox representatives January 12 to 17, 1990. As a result of these deliberations a document was agreed upon, called *"The recommendations concerning a normalization of relationships between the Orthodox and the Catholics of the Eastern rite in Western Ukraine."* Number 8, of the Recommendations read:

> In order to make decisions pertaining to the practical questions, which will arise before the Catholics of the Eastern rite, both sides have agreed to request that a mutual Commission be established, composed, besides the representatives of the Holy See and the Moscow Patriarchate, of the representatives of the Catholics of Western Ukraine. Each side of the Commission should have an equal number of representatives, one or no more than

two. The purpose of this Commission is to ascertain that mutual agreements be made in the spirit of Christian charity and fraternal cooperation. There is a need of immediate decisions pertaining to the church buildings, which were taken over by the Catholics of the Eastern rite without consent of the parishes. This should take place in accordance with the law pertaining to the registration of Catholic parishes.

To represent the Holy See, the Holy Father appointed Archbishop Marusyn, the secretary of the Eastern Congregation, and myself to this Commission. The representatives of our Church in Ukraine were Archbishop Vladimir Sterniuk and Bishop Sophronius Dmyterko. Archbishop Pio Laghi, the Apostolic Nuncio, informed me of this appointment on about February 22, 1990. He asked me to immediately send my two passport size photos to the Eastern Congregation so that the Secretary of State may prepare a Vatican diplomatic passport for me and get an entry visa to the USSR as well. I contacted Archbishop Marusyn by phone and learned that I had to be in Rome no later than March 3, 1990. The work of the Commission was planned for March 5 to 15, 1990.

I packed my suitcase and departed on Friday, March 2, 1990, arriving in Rome the next morning. A young priest from St. Josaphat Seminary met me at the airport and said that he was told to take me directly to the Eastern Congregation. I disagreed and told him to take me first to the Seminary, and in ten minutes I will be ready to go to the Congregation. I needed to wash my face, shave, and brush my teeth, as I had spent the whole night I on the plane.

In the Congregation Archbishop Marusyn greeted me and said that both of us should go immediately to see Archbishop Edward Cassidy, President of the Pontifical Council for Promoting Christian Unity. Archbishops Cassidy gave me a copy of the *"Recommendations"* and asked me to read them and get acquainted with them. As soon as I started to read, I asked: "Why does this document not call our Church in Ukraine a Church but just "Catholics of Eastern Rite." The reply was, "This was the wish of the Orthodox side during the meeting in Moscow in January of this year."

After I completed the reading of the document, I asked Archbishop Cassidy, "Are you going to take part in the meeting of the Commission together with us?" He replied that only Archbishop Marusyn and I will take part in the work of the Commission." To that I stated, "If so, then our trip to the USSR will be a waste of time, energy and money. Our deliberations will not be successful if you permit the Ukrainians alone to negotiate with the Russians." "Why do you think so?—asked Archbishop Cassidy. I retorted, "First of all, Russians have ruled the Ukrainians for centuries. They are used to ignoring our opinions and doing what they want to do. Secondly, if you were with us, the Orthodox would know that the Vatican is serious about the matter and sends its best diplomats to help solve the problem. Neither Archbishop Marusyn nor I are diplomats, while the Orthodox will most certainly select the best bishops for this purpose." Cassidy then said, "I agree with you but it is too late to make changes in our plans. Let it be so. The two of you go alone and do your best."

The following day, Sunday March 4, 1990, I paid a visit to Myroslav Ivan Cardinal Lubachivsky in order to find out whether he had some wishes or instructions for me. Actually he was expecting me and was ready. In an envelope addressed to the Catholic members of the Commission, he had a list of ten demands of our Church to the Commission. I promised to personally deliver each envelope to the addressee.

The Quadripartite Commission consisted of the delegates from the Vatican, the Moscow Patriarchate, the Ukrainian Orthodox Exarchate of Kiev, and the Ukrainian Catholic Church in Ukraine.

The two Vatican delegates attired in their cassocks departed from Rome on Monday, March 5, 1990, at 9:00 A.M. by plane to Milan. There we transferred to a Soviet airplane and arrived in Moscow at 4:30 P.M. local time. A young and pleasant Russian Orthodox monk, named Nestor, met us at the airport. He was a member of the Foreign Department of the Moscow Patriarchate. He drove both of us to "Hotel Ukraine." After we had a short rest and a dinner, he drove us to the "Kievan" Railroad Station in Moscow. On our way there he stopped to visit his mother and invited us to come with him. He himself lived in this luxurious apartment with his mother. I knew then that he belonged to the chosen elite of the Soviet society. We boarded a direct non-stop train to Kiev, which left Moscow at 10:00 P.M. and arrived in Kiev the next morning at 11:00 A.M.

The sleeper car was quite comfortable, but the interminable noise made by the train wheels as they hit the rail joints made sleeping very difficult. At daybreak I got up, shaved, washed, and dressed. I got out of my suitcase my breviary and prayed for the success of this mission. Afterward I stood at a window and observed the landscape. The train passed towns and villages, but nowhere could I see a church building. All the churches had been destroyed or turned into some other use by the atheistic authorities. I saw the first church building in Ukraine when we arrived in Kiev.

Father Nestor was on the train with us and we met him at the train station in Kiev. He soon found a driver who took us to the hotel "Ukraine." We left our suitcases in our hotel rooms and were escorted by Father Nestor to the home of the Ukrainian Orthodox Exarchate, the residence of Metropolitan Filaret (Denysenko), located on 36 Pushkin Street.

The Vatican delegates were greeted by Metropolitan Filaret, Metropolitan Methodius (Nimtzov) of Voronizh and Lypetz, Archbishop Theodosius (Dykun) of Kamenetz Podilsky, Archbishop Irynej (Serednij) of Lviv and Drohobytch, Bishop Jonathan, auxiliary of Kiev, and Father Alexander Shvetz. The two delegates from the Ukrainian Catholic Church, Archbishop Vladimir Sterniuk and Bishop Sophronius Dmyterko, were absent. It was decided to send them a telegram over the signature of Archbishop Marusyn, inviting them to come to Kiev. The language used was exclusively Russian.

The absence of the two Catholic delegates showed that they had not been informed. Whose duty was it to inform them ahead of time so they could be prepared, and, if necessary, consult with their priests? Naturally, it was the one who made the agreement with the Moscow Patriarchate in January of 1990, the Vatican. Had they known of their participation in this Commission, they would have been prepared and consulted with their priests as to the disputed church buildings. The Vatican delegates had no way of knowing which churches were involved. This information came exclusively from the Orthodox delegates, which made the Commission biased and inequitable from the start. Now I understood why Archbishop Cassidy refused to participate in this Commission.

After a luncheon and a discussion as to how the Commission was to proceed, all the members left to visit Mykola Kolesnyk, a person who was authorized in matters of religion by the Council of Ministers of the Ukrainian Soviet Government. He explained to the members of the Commission the position of the Ukrainian Government concerning the process of the legalization of the Ukrainian Catholic Church. In his presentation he stressed the importance of this Commission, which must make a decision on each controversial church building and prepare a signed report for each case. This report will be transmitted to Kiev and then to Moscow for approval. Only then can a parish be registered and exist legally.

In this cumbersome process of the legalization of the Ukrainian Catholic Church I immediately saw a cleverly deceitful scheme of obstacles and delay for many years to come. The Commission was scheduled ahead of time to work for only a few days in which to decide on many disputed church buildings. In the meantime, the whole process of legalization would stop working. This scheme was concocted so as to help the few Orthodox in a parish hold on to the church building, while the Catholic majority whose fathers or forefathers actually built the structure, would remain without a church building. Our Catholic faithful, who suffered severe persecution since 1946 and remained faithful and loyal Catholics, would not easily agree to such an unjust and perverted process. At that time I was sorry I got myself entangled in the work of this Commission.

Mykola Kolesnyk led the delegates to a building of the Council of Ministers. He walked along with me and kept peppering me with all kinds of questions. I used this occasion to ask him one question: "I was told that your government is concerned about religious unrest in Western Ukraine. If you really want peace, I suggest that you simplify the process of the legalization of the Ukrainian Catholic Church by first giving the Catholics their St. George's Cathedral in Lviv. By doing so you will demonstrate good will, and your understanding and compassion toward your citizens. If you refuse to do so, you will lose, because these people who suffered liquidation of their Church, persecution, and imprisonment, will not easily give up, and eventually will achieve their goal." He did not react to my proposal.

At the Council of Ministers, Maria Andrijivna Orlyk, the substitute Prime minister, received us. In her welcome she assured us that the Ukrainian Government would do everything possible to speed up the process of the legalization of the Ukrainian Catholic Church. She wished the best to our Commission and promised that the Government will approve all our decisions. Apparently Mykola Kolesnyk told her of my concerns.

We had a few free hours left of the day, so Archbishop Marusyn and I asked Father Nestor to take us to the Caves Monastery (Pecherska Lavra). They assigned a monk to be our guide. He took us on a tour of the upper and lower caves, explaining to us every detail. They are long, tunnel-like corridors dug out of dark granite. There are many bodies of the saints, absolutely incorrupt, entombed in wall cavities. This is the miraculous marvel of these caves. Some scholars try to explain this by the special atmospheric condition inside the caves. But what causes this condition and why only there? The relics of the most famous saints we saw there were the founders of this monastery, Saints Anthonius and Theodosius.

The following day, March 7, 1990, the two absent Catholic members of the Commission arrived by an overnight train. Both acknowledged that they had not been informed about their membership in this Commission. The meeting began with a welcome by Metropolitan Filaret:

"I welcome the members of the Commission of the Moscow Patriarchate, of the Holy See, as well as representatives of the Catholics of Eastern Rite from Western Ukraine. I welcome you in the city, from which Christianity spread all over our vast country . . . This Commission faces not an easy problem, which we should solve. We should do everything, so that on our Galician land there would be peace between the Orthodox and the Catholics . . . As the Metropolitan of Kiev I wish all the success to this our Commission in its work.

This Commission should be guided be the *Recommendations,* agreed upon by the delegates of the Catholic Church and the Moscow Patriarchate at their meeting in Moscow, January 12–17, 1990. These *Recommendations,* as all us of know, were approved by the Hierarchical Sobor of the Moscow Patriarchate as well as by the Holy See and Pope John Paul II. This is why they form the basis of our work."

At that time Archbishop Sterniuk asked, "Where are those *Recommendations?*

Archbishop Marusyn replied, "I have them and will give you a copy."

Then Filaret continued, "In the *Recommendations* the main idea is derived from the fact that in Galicia there are Orthodox as well as the Catholics of the Eastern Rite. We should start from those realities and order the motions in such a way so that between them there will be peace, although it will not be an easy task. We should reject some ideas, which state that there is no room for the Orthodox in Galicia. I think that these are not serious ideas and they should not guide us . . . It is necessary that the faithful should believe that this Commission is able to resolve their problems in a peaceful way. Should the faithful not believe that this Commission is able to resolve their problems in a peaceful way, they will employ different methods. They will seize the church buildings. Today the Catholics are seizing them; tomorrow the Orthodox will do the same. In such a case our Commission will have no reason to exist and we will not fulfill the duties laid upon us by Pope John Paul II and the Hierarchical Sobor . . ."

Archbishop Marusyn, as the head of the Catholic delegates, thanked the host for his greetings. He expressed his joy to be in Kiev for the first time, where there are so many more sacred things that unite us, rather than those that divide. We pray to the Lord that we be able without unnecessary quarrels to do the work entrusted to us by our Church authorities.

Archpriest Alexander Shvetz then made this proposition: "At the start this Commission should make a decision that Catholics must give back to the Orthodox all the churches they have seized illegally. Should we refuse to do so, we will then only add fuel to the fire. I was informed yesterday that the Orthodox are already organizing fighting groups, which will forcefully impound their churches. This is why we should inform our people that we reject all kinds of violence."

All members of the Commission agreed that all violence, if such exists, should be absolutely rejected so that peace may rule among the people of Western Ukraine.

Archbishop Sterniuk stood up and said, "You are condemning violence, but you do nothing to avoid it. Christian charity demands justice. If there is no justice, there can be no charity. If e.g., a thief has stolen something, you say that he may keep it, that it belongs to him, and that he does not have to give it back to the right owner. A stolen item belongs to the one from whom it was stolen. So justice demands that stolen goods be returned to the right owners."

There was no comment on Sterniuk's statement. It just passed by their ears as though they did not know or understand what he was taking about. Could it be that the Orthodox moral theology differs from other Christian morality? No, but their hearts were hardened by the Stalinist immorality with no justice, no charity, but brutal force and violence. Thus ignoring Sterniuk's brave and demanding statement, they turned their attention to other things, to drafting a common statement for the press. In it they pushed and pushed such appeals as—there should be no demonstrations or other methods of pressure so the Commission may be able to work in a normal way. I objected to the words by which demonstrations be forbidden. "It goes against what Mr. Gorbachev is now proclaiming—"glasnost"—openness, candor and "perestroika"—restructuring of society. Ukrainian Catholics in the Soviet Union, brutally liquidated, forcefully joined to the Russian Orthodox Church, are now demonstrating by hundreds of thousands, demanding their freedom. And the government does not stop them. Why should we do so?" Sterniuk's statement was ignored, so was mine. They just did what they wanted, ignoring our objections.

At the first break in our meeting, I handed over to the Catholic delegates the sealed envelopes I brought from Rome from Cardinal Lubachivsky. I had a small tape recorder with me and recorded all the sessions of the Quadripartite Commission.

Six Days in Lviv

Thursday, March 8, 1990, all the members of the Commission left Kiev and flew to Lviv. The Vatican members of the Commission were welcomed at the Lviv airport by about two hundred people, carrying Ukrainian flags and a portrait of Metropolitan Sheptytsky. Many priests and religious sisters led them with two Bishops—Philimone Kurchaba, CSsR, and Julian Voronowsky. Two young girls presented bouquets of flowers to the two archbishops, and speeches of welcome were given. A young Sister Servant recited an emotion-laden poem of welcome. The two bishops advised us to go with them to the Church of Transfiguration of our Lord, where many people were waiting for us.

When we arrived by car, the church was filled with people, and the overflow crowd was standing outside. Archbishop Marusyn and I came to the altar, made a deep bow, kissed the altar and prayed for a while. Then Marusyn spoke to the people, thanking God for giving our people a living faith that persevered in the most trying tests throughout decades of atheistic persecution. He gave to all present an apostolic blessing from the Holy Father. I spoke after him and expressed my great joy for the grace of being able to be with them, my brothers and sisters in the Lord, to see their undaunted faith and their firm loyalty to the successor of St. Peter.

I greeted them in the name of all our bishops, priests, religious, and the faithful in the United States of America and assured them of our continuing prayers for our Ukrainian Catholic Church in the catacombs of Ukraine.

To give due thanks to the Lord for this our encounter with the faithful of our heroic Church in Ukraine, Archbishop Marusyn intoned a popular hymn to the Mother of God, *"Za vsich molyshysya, Blahaya . . ."* (You pray for all, O Good one . . .) All the faithful fell to their knees and continued wholeheartedly the mighty hymn. For fifty years they had not heard this hymn, and yet they did not forget it. Before the War this hymn used to be sung during the May devotions to the Mother of God. The Orthodox did not practice this devotion, so the people could hear it only in the underground Church. The spontaneity of the singing brought tears to my eyes. It was their faith, made strong and firm throughout the decades of persecution, that now publicly and unashamedly sang the glory of God. Now I recalled the testimony of Father Walter Ciszek concerning the strong faith of the Ukrainian Catholic prisoners in the Gulags of Siberia.

We resided and conducted our meetings in the Hotel "Dnister." We met for the first time after a luncheon on Thursday. The first topic of discussion was the methods we should use in achieving our decisions. The Orthodox delegates were very well prepared. Each bishop had his assistants in another room, and a pack of documentation on each disputed church building. Bishop Irynej Serednij began by presenting one case of one disputed church after another, reading alleged proofs, insisting that there are very few Catholics and the majority of residents are Orthodox. There was no way of disputing his figures or questioning their veracity.

The Catholic members of the Commission were taken by surprise. The two bishops from Ukraine were not organized. They still lived in an underground Church. Archbishop Sterniuk lived in one small room on the fourth floor, where there was hardly enough space for a small bed and a little table loaded with books and papers. Bishop Dmyterko did not have any better accommodations in the city of Ivano-Frankivsk. Both of them were completely unprepared for the work of this Commission. They did not present one single case of a disputed church. Thus the Catholic members of the Commission delayed any decision-making.

During our first break I approached Archbishop Sterniuk and whispered to him to demand the return of our cathedral in Lviv, St. George's church and the residence, as our condition of any further work in this Commission. As soon as we returned to our seats, he did that. But the head of the Orthodox delegation, Metropolitan Methodius was visibly frustrated. He tried to explain away this demand, postpone it to the last, and then he apparently came across an idea. "The case of St. George's Cathedral and the residence is not in the competence of their delegates. This case will be decided probably by a wider Commission, composed of members of both sides." I then objected saying: "*The Recommendations*" are the only basis agreed upon in Moscow in January of this year upon which this Commission is to work. There you do not find a single exception. All disputed churches are subject to this Commission. Archbishop Sterniuk just disputed the ownership of the Orthodox Church of St. George's in Lviv. You, therefore, cannot state that this Commission is not competent to decide on it." He was cornered and he knew it. So he changed the subject and said that the entire Commission has to make plans to take a trip and visit some of the disputed churches. I expected Archbishop Sterniuk or the other Catholic members to come to my support, but no one did and the Orthodox just dropped the subject.

The following day, Friday, March 9, 1990, the whole Commission took a trip to the city of Zolochiv so that we could see both disputed churches. Archbishop Marusyn was especially happy with this trip because this is where he attended his high school, and on his way to the school daily he would stop in the church of the Resurrection to serve as an acolyte for the Divine Liturgy.

On our return trip Archbishop Marusyn and I stopped in the village of Kniazhe, some seven kilometers from Zolochiv. This was Marusyn's birthplace. At first we stopped at the local cemetery and visited the graves of his parents. The two of us served a Memorial Service for the repose of the souls of his parents. As he was kneeling in private prayer, I took several pictures of him and the two graves and later on I sent them to him for a remembrance. From there we went to the local church and there met a lot of people who somehow observed our visit to the cemetery and knew we would stop to see the church. As we entered the church and were passing the cantor's seat, Marusyn recalled, "This is where my grandfather, my father, and I sat, singing responses to the liturgical services." People soon filled the whole church to see one of their sons who became a high Church dignitary. Marusyn spoke to them, telling them who he was and how happy he was to see his native village once more in his life. There were some who remembered him as a young student, but most did not, for fifty years is a long time. He gave them his blessing, said good-bye, and we departed. On our way we stopped and walked to a side street to visit his parents' house. In it lived two women, his relatives. We entered the house, were treated to a snack, and bid them goodbye.

Saturday, March 10, 1990, the Commission had planned to travel to the city of Ivano-Frankivsk. A large gathering of the Catholics in Ivano-Frankivsk who were just waiting for the Commission to arrive foiled the plan. The Orthodox members of the Commission refused to go there. This same thing happened to the plans to go to the city of Mykolayiw. So the Commission planned to go to the city of Stryj without notifying anyone.

Before we started on our trip, a discussion began as to where the Catholic members of the Commission should serve their Sunday Liturgy. They were invited to Transfiguration Church. The Orthodox Bishops were against this, because, as they said, the Catholics forcefully and illegally seized this church. The presence there of the Vatican delegates would be a sign of approval of their action. They proposed the Church of St. Onuphrius, but Bishop Dmyterko protested, saying this is a small church and our people would like to see our guests. Then I proposed this, "Two or three of you could be our guests at the Transfiguration Church, sit there and watch our Liturgy and hear what we have to say to our people." They looked at each other and gladly accepted my proposition.

Sunday, March 11, 1990

This was the Second Sunday of the Great Fast (Lent). Archbishop Marusyn was the main celebrant of St. Basil's Liturgy in the Church-Slavonic language. Concelebrating were myself, Archbishop Sterniuk, Bishops, Sophronius Dmyterko, OSBM; Philimone Kurchaba, CSsR; Michael Sabryha, CSsR; Julian Voronowsky (Studite); local pastor Father Jaroslav Chukhniy and a guest from Canada, Father Andrew Chirowsky. From among the Orthodox delegates came Metropolitan Methodius, Archbishop Theodosius and Father Alexander Shvetz. Before the Liturgy, as the Orthodox entered the sacristy, we shook hands. As Methodius shook hands with Bishop Voronowsky, he demanded: "Kiss my hand!" Voronowsky replied, "I am also a bishop." "Then why do you not wear a panaghia, only a cross?" retorted Methodius. Voronowsky said, "Because I have none as yet. Besides a panaghia does not make a bishop!" The Orthodox took their seats in the right "Krylos." The local church choir sang the responses except for the Creed and "Our Father," which were sung by the whole congregation. Archbishop Marusyn gave a homily toward the end of the Liturgy. The church was filled with the faithful and three thousand stood outside. This was some demonstration of their Catholic faith for the Orthodox to see!

After the Liturgy the Vatican delegates were escorted to the right sacristy. Twenty delegates of the Committee for the Defense of the Ukrainian Catholic Church were there waiting for them. They asked us to take our seats and began to welcome us with speeches. The first one to speak was Irene Kalynec, then Ivan Hel, and others. All of them demanded that we immediately cease our deliberations with the Russian Orthodox Church, because all these Orthodox bishops are hardened Stalinists, staunch communists, and fierce enemies of the Catholic Church. Archbishop Marusyn gave his reply to the delegation. He thanked them for their warm welcome and promised to take their request into consideration. As we were leaving the sacristy, Father Chirowsky handed me a sealed envelope, asking me to please read it and give it to Marusyn to read.

We had our luncheon as soon as we returned to the hotel. Afterward numerous members of my family, who live in the city of Sambir some 75 kilometers away, were waiting for me. I have two brothers and one sister with their families, children and grandchildren. I had no time to read the letter I received from Father Chirowsky until that evening:

"To the Vatican Delegates, Archbishops Marusyn and Sulyk . . . . You had no occasion to get acquainted with a number of documents pertaining to the situation in the region of Western Ukraine, where there exist efforts of some destructive forces, to provoke cunningly a conflict between the Orthodox and the Catholics . . . What is necessary is to raise the question of the violation of human rights, to acknowledge as non-existent the nonhuman and illegal so-called "Sobor of Lviv of 1946," which devoured thousands of innocent people, which to this day gives the right to denigrate the human dignity of the Ukrainian Catholic Church, as well as a full and complete legalization of this Church to positively solve all the problems of this our region. Without the above, any kind of negotiations as equal partners between the Russian Orthodox Church and the Ukrainian Catholic Church—all of this is one big counterfeit. Your press release to avoid violence is actually a clever camouflage to violence on the side of the totalitarian regime against the Ukrainian Catholics who continue to bear the burden of defamation as "the fascist," "criminals," and "enemies of the people," etc.

The refusal of rehabilitation and legalization of the Ukrainian Catholic Church, the refusal of acknowledging it as a fully legal historical Church of the Ukrainian people, and the efforts to force Ukrainian Catholics parishes to register as "newly erected" are the last relics of the Stalinist policies, directed toward physical and spiritual genocide. Today all the progressive forces of society recognize this for what it is . . .

We have no reason to speak about criminality in the field of relationships between churches. There are criminal actions on the side of our opponents, such as endeavors to provoke us by criminal elements, by alcoholic intoxication, by lies or fights . . . All this reveals evidence of interest of the antidemocratic forces, including the Russian Orthodox Church . . .

We know that you are not politicians . . . Involuntarily you have entered the field of clever political play with opponents who were perfectly schooled in evil and cunningness. If you are coming with Christ's words, with a Christian mission, then arm yourselves with the truth. For "Blessed is the man who has not walked in the council of the wicked . . ."

The Ukrainian Catholics await from the Apostolic See not the secret conversations at the table of the Stalinists, but an open and honest truth, a word of truth concerning our RIGHT TO BELIEVE AND TO LOVE GOD. Realize that you have entered deliberations not with spiritual pastors, but with those to whom "most dear is the memory of Stalin, the uncrowned emperor." Not only Ukraine but also all of Orthodox Russia, which is ill

459

from the evident errors of the patriarchs, awaits your honest and sincere word . . ."

The letter was dated March 10, 1990, and signed by: Irena Kalynec, parliamentarian, Ivan Hrechko, chairman of the Commission for the Freedom of Conscience, Theodosius Starak, editor of *Veera Bat'kiv*, and Stepan Chmara, parliamentarian. As I finished reading this letter, I took it to Archbishop Marusyn. Having read it, he said, "Stephen, you and I cannot oppose the will of our people."

On the request of Bishop Dmyterko, I went to the Basilian Fathers Monastery and Church of St. Onuphrius in Lviv. The church was filled to capacity with the faithful. The overflow crowd filled the street before the church. Bouquets of flowers welcomed me; children were strewing flowers on the floor before me. Two strong men were pushing the crowd aside to make room for me to enter the church and reach the altar. I knelt down before the altar and prayed, thanking God for the grace of faith of these good people. Then I said a few words to the assembled people:

"I am grateful to God for giving me the grace of being able to be with you in this holy church. You are my brothers and sisters in the Lord. You have come here today not only to welcome a Ukrainian Catholic Metropolitan from the United States of America, but mostly because your hearts are thirsty for God and His true Church. Your hearts are thirsty for freedom to be able to pray and glorify God with your whole heart and soul. For the last half of the century of the liquidation of our Ukrainian Catholic Church, persecutions, imprisonment, and atheistic propaganda, you did not lose your faith in God. You remained faithful to your ancestral Catholic faith and Church. And God has rewarded you for your faithfulness to Him. He gave you a gift of unshaken faith, strong as granite, and a burning love for God and your neighbor.

I, therefore, implore you, as your father and brother, keep God's gift in very high esteem. Keep it as your most precious treasure. Nurture and increase it with all your might. Diligently and patiently hand it over to your children and grandchildren from one generation to the other. Thus our holy Catholic faith will always be that indestructible bulwark, our strongest defense, and our mighty armament against all the enemies. As long as there is such a firm and unshakable faith in God in the hearts of our Ukrainian people, no one can conquer or defeat us, because God will always be on our side and with us. He Himself will protect and defend our people and our country.

I pray the Almighty and merciful God, Father, Son, and Holy Spirit, to bless all of you, your families and relatives, that His abundant graces, love, and might be always with you, protect, defend, and preserve you for many years. Amen."

There was no one to help me pass through the thick mass of people as I was leaving the church. Everyone tried to kiss my hand or just to touch my cassock. Patiently I made my way slowly through the church where everyone was standing, for there were no pews; only a bench or two along the sidewalls for the elderly.

Meeting the Bishops of the Catacomb Church

onday, March 12, 1990, the work of the Quadripartite Commission was interrupted for the Vatican delegates to be able to meet with their brother bishops of the Ukrainian Catholic Underground Church. The meeting took place in the same room where our Commission met. This was an unforgettable moment since it was for the first time that brother bishops met and got to know each other. This applied not only to the two Vatican delegates, but likewise, to some of the bishops from the Catacomb Church who also met each other for the first time.

Archbishop Marusyn in his introductory words "expressed his great appreciation, gratitude, and admiration for their heroic faith, their faithfulness and loyalty to Christ and his Church. He thanked them for their courage to take upon their shoulders the burden of episcopacy, the heavy load of Christ's yoke, and that in these unspeakably difficult circumstances."

The Holy See needs certain information from each one of you, the underground bishops, so that you may be officially acknowledged and recorded in the Vatican directory, the *Annuario Pontificio.* He then distributed printed questionnaires and asked each one to reply to every question.

Present were: Vladimir Sterniuk, CSsR, Philimone Kurchaba, CSsR, Sophronius Dmyterko, OSBM, Michael Sabryha, CSsR, Julian

Voronowsky, a studite monk, Irynej Bilyk, OSBM, Pavlo Vasylyk, Ivan Semedij, and Josyf Holovach.

Archbishop Marusyn gave a short explanation of their canonical status and of the status of our Church as a Major Archbishopric, equal to a Patriarchate. He stated:

> "When, with the help of God, the time will come when it will be possible for the Apostolic See to establish normal Church structures in Ukraine, then at your own Synod under the leadership of our own Head and Father, our Bishops will be able to commonly decide the problems which now might not be settled and might disturb some. Thus with patience and with fraternal love wait for the day when the Holy Father will be able to normalize our Church structure."

The Bishops from Ukraine had some questions to which Marusyn and I tried to give satisfactory answers or explanations. After a group photo we all went to a luncheon in the hotel.

The Conclusion of the Commission's Work

The Vatican delegates received Vatican diplomatic passports from the Secretary of State and airline tickets with reservations for a return flight from Moscow to Rome on March 15, 1990. We had a reserved flight from Lviv to Moscow March 13, 1990, in the evening. Thus the Commission could work only Monday afternoon and Tuesday morning, March 12 & 13 1990.

Archbishop Makarius, the Orthodox bishop of Ivano-Frankivsk, arrived Monday afternoon and joined the Commission. He gave a fiery speech, pleading with the Commission to assign him the Armenian church and two other churches in the city of Ivano-Frankivsk, since all other churches were handed over by the city authorities to the Ukrainian Catholics. He had no church at all and nowhere to serve the Liturgy.

All eyes turned to Bishop Dmyterko. He had to defend his position, and he did it very skillfully. "I am not a dictator, but a servant of God and of my people. I cannot force my priests or my people. Before I can give you my consent, I first have to present the case to my priests and the faithful." For over three hours the Orthodox side pleaded with Bishop Dmyterko to release some churches, but he did not give in. Finally he agreed to release the former Armenian church to them, but this was not enough for them, and they had to postpone the case for a later time.

Tuesday we had a morning session, since the afternoon was the time for preparation for travel. The Orthodox demanded that we prepare a common declaration to be published in the press. I was fiercely opposed to such a declaration, knowing from the past that it would be used as their propaganda tool. Archpriest Alexander Shvetz rudely interrupted my presentation. He would not let me finish a sentence. This irritated me to no end. I raised my voice and said, "Father, in the cultural world, a priest would never dare to interrupt when a bishop is speaking. I don't know what your custom is in the Soviet Union. I think that it is not different from the rest of the cultured world. If you dare to interrupt me once more, you will have to leave this room or else I will leave." Metropolitan Methodius looked at him and pointed to a corner to sit there and be quiet. I did not know at that time that he was a pastor in the city of Sambir where my relatives live.

The discussion on the wording of a declaration lasted for two hours until Archbishop Marusyn finally agreed to sign it. But before the discussion was over Archbishop Sterniuk got up and made the following statement:

"Dear Bishops, all of us in this Commission tried to do the work that may satisfy someone. However, we did not do what would satisfy our Church. Our Church awaits from this our gathering, from the delegates of the Apostolic See, from the Orthodox and from ourselves as well, that we would do much more than merely assign church buildings. I think that we should start such work that would satisfy our Church. Yesterday I gave the Orthodox my project of such a work, which contains fifteen demands. (These were the letters I brought from Rome from Cardinal Lubachivsky). Today I gave these demands to the Vatican delegates. These demands are so indispensable for our Church that without their fulfillment our existence is impossible, that is, with full legalization of our Church, without returning to us our Cathedral of St. George, etc. These are necessary questions for us, which hurt us very much.

You have your staff with you. You have your offices and your workers. You have your living and working facilities and the necessary help to do your work. We do not have all that. I do not have someone to help me edit a document. Yet people keep on coming and asking for this or that. This is why I consider the work of this Commission unsatisfactory and I wish to terminate my work here. I ask to be excused by the Vatican delegates and by the Orthodox bishops as well. I just cannot continue this, and I terminate my work in this Commission. I greet all of you. I will pray for you. Please forgive me. I say goodbye to all, wishing you a pleasant trip, and that you may live happily in the grace of God."

Archbishop Marusyn then asked of him, "Would you please permit me to say a word, or would you prefer to just leave?"
Sterniuk, "I will just leave!"
Marusyn, "I would like to say only one word."
Sterniuk, "I would not wish anything else."
Marusyn, "If you do not wish it, I will not say a word."
Dmyterko, "Please, Vladyko, what if the Orthodox side would agree to your demands."
Sterniuk, "Maybe, I don't know if they would agree. At present it all is now enough. I just cannot!" With these words Archbishop Sterniuk left.

I turned to Marusyn and whispered to him, "If he had informed us of his plans, we all could have all walked out of here, thus demonstrating our unity."

As we were leaving the meeting room, a priest approached me and said, "His Beatitude, Patriarch Lubachivsky sent his secretary to Lviv. Father Ivan Dacko is here in Lviv." I knew that Cardinal Lubachivsky inquired at the Holy See if he could send Father Dacko as one of the delegates to the Commission. He received a negative reply since members of the Commission had to be bishops.

On the Way Back to Rome

Both Vatican delegates were on their way back to Rome on Tuesday, March 13, 1990, taking a flight from Lviv to Moscow. At that time one could take a direct flight to Rome only from Moscow. We used our free day in Moscow visiting some outstanding churches. Our driver and guide was Father Nestor. While passing the famous Tretiakivsky Art Gallery, Father Nestor went to the guard at the gate and received permission for us to enter the gallery. The gallery was closed to all visitors. All we wanted to see was the famous icon of the Mother of God known as "Vyshorodska." Vyshorod is a town near Kiev, where the icon was originally located. This miraculous icon is one of the most famous in the world of iconography, especially in the Eastern Slavic world of Byzantine origin. It was ordered painted by Kievan prince Yaropolk and delivered to Kiev in 1134 and placed in a church in Vyshorod near Kiev. In 1165 a prince from Suzdal, named Andrew Boholubsk stole it and took it with him to Moscovia, to the city of Vladimir. This is why this icon is also called "Vladymirska." During the reign of Dmytro Donsky in 1394 this icon was transferred to Moscow and placed in the Dormition Cathedral in the Kremlin. After the Bolshevik revolution in 1917 the icon was transferred to the Tretiakivsky Art Gallery in Moscow. This icon is also called

"Mother of God of Tenderness," because its basic element is compassion. The Infant Jesus is depicted as sitting on the right arm of the Holy Mother, and with his arm He hugs her neck. This icon in the Art Gallery was displayed behind a glass case.

In the afternoon of that day Father Nestor drove us out of town to the Monastery of Zagorsk. He introduced us to the Superior and asked his permission to visit the sights of the huge monastery and for someone to be our guide. The Superior asked an elderly monk (he might have been a priest) to be our guide. He showed us some beautiful church art, churches, chapels, the seminary, etc. This monk stopped for a moment on a sidewalk looked at us and asked, "Are the two of you uniates?" I replied, "Yes!" He then turned his head towards us and spit on us, turned around and started to walk away. Father Nestor yelled at him, saying, "What are you doing, you crazy man. Don't you know that these two are Vatican diplomats?" He did not pay any attention to him, and just walked away. It is an age-old custom among the Orthodox to spit upon the devil. During the Rite of Baptism there is a prayer of exorcism. At that moment the sponsors with the child, or the one to be baptized if he is an adult, turn about and face the West, that is they turn their backs to the priest. The priest then asks them, "Do you renounce Satan, together with all his works, all his angels, and all service to him, and all his arrogance? The sponsors, or the one to be baptized if he is an adult, respond: "I do renounce him!" The priest then says, "Then spit on him!" The sponsors, or the one to be baptized if he is an adult, spit toward the West. Thus this monk considered us Eastern Rite Catholic bishops as devils. How far from Christ's true spirit of love of neighbor or even of an enemy was the behavior of this Orthodox monk? And how deep is the rift between the Catholic and the Orthodox churches?

We arrived in Rome Thursday, March 15, 1990, at 7:00 P.M. The following day, March 16, 1990, both of us visited Archbishop Cassidy and reported to him on the work and failures of the Commission. In the afternoon I visited Cardinal Lubachivsky. He tape-recorded my extensive report to him on the events and failures of the Commission. Saturday, March 17, 1990, both of us were invited by the Holy Father to dine with him. He was very interested in even the smallest details, not only about the Commission, but also especially on the present situation and life of our Church in Ukraine. He asked very many questions that revealed that he was very well informed. At the end he thanked both of us and gave us his blessing.

On Monday, March 19, 1990, I took a flight home. I thanked God for His help and His Mother for her maternal protection during my diplomatic mission.

A Monument to Metropolitan Sheptytsky

The Philadelphia Archeparchy as well as the whole Province owes a great debt of gratitude to the Servant of God Andrew Sheptytsky. Our first immigrants came to the United States of America in the 1870s when our national designation was "Ruthenian." From the very beginning they started to organize their religious life by building churches. They wrote desperate letters to our bishops in the Old Country begging for priests. The first priest, Father Ivan Wolansky, came to the United States of America in December of 1884. He was a married priest, as are diocesan priests in Ukraine. Metropolitan-Archbishop of Lviv, Sylvester Cardinal Sembratowych, sent him to the United States of America. Latin bishops of the United States of America would not accept our married priests, and our faithful refused to attend the Latin church services and were yearning for their own Particular Church, and traditions.

The servant of God Andrew Sheptytsky statue, Philadelphia, Pa.

The first one to care for the spiritual needs of our immigrants was Metropolitan Andrew Sheptytsky. He sent many more celibate priests, mostly religious, Basilians and Redemptorists, and later on the Basilian Sisters and the Sister Servants of Mary Immaculate. At the same time, he made insistent efforts at the Vatican and with the Holy Father St. Pius X, to appoint a bishop for our faithful in the United States of America and Canada. There was rigid opposition to this idea on both sides of the ocean on the part of the Latins.

The dedication of the Sheptytsky statue, Sept. 27, 1992.

In 1902 the Holy See appointed Canon Andrew Hodobay, a priest from the Priashiw Eparchy, as an Apostolic Visitator. According to his own admission he was at the same time "an official agent of the Hungarian state authorities." Their state policy was that there be no unity between our people who migrated from the territories occupied by Hungary and those who came from the Galician territory. This is why Hodobay completely ignored the parishes and the priests from Galicia, and tried to take under his control the fraternal organization "Soyedynenie." By this action he created great disunity among the priests and instigated fierce fights between the priests from the Mukachevo Eparchy and those from the Priashiw Eparchy. As a result of this, many faithful, trying to rid themselves of Hungarian interference, looked for a safe harbor by joining the Russian Orthodox Church. This forced the Holy See to recall Canon Hodobay in 1906.

The Latin bishops of the United States of America were opposed to a nomination of a Byzantine bishop in the United States of America. They had their hands full with their ethnically different faithful, parishes, and priests: Irish, Italian, French, German, Polish, Slovak, Lithuanian, Slovenian, and Hungarian. Each of these ethnic groups tried to safeguard its own traditions, language, and customs. The bishops at that time were in the main Irish, and they guided the Church with an iron hand.

In order to preserve unity in the Latin Church, great efforts were needed. They were not always successful, for a large group of Polish Catholics, opposed to the iron dictatorship of the Irish, organized an independent Polish National Church in the United States with a married clergy.

James Cardinal Gibbons, Archbishop of Baltimore, Maryland, from 1877 to 1921, proposed to the Holy See a very simple solution concerning the Greek-Catholic Ruthenians: "Let the Ruthenians in the United States of America become Roman-Catholics. In three or four generations they will become the same as all other Americans anyway." Fortunately the Holy See did not follow this proposition.

The Russian Orthodox Church was very interested in the difficulties of the Eastern Catholics in the United States of America. After the division of Poland, the Russian Orthodox Church forcefully liquidated the Ukrainian Catholic Church on the territories occupied by Russian armies. They wanted very much to liquidate her also in the United States, for they were afraid of the influence of the Ukrainian Catholics upon the Ukrainian Orthodox from the Russian occupation. The Russian government generously funded the Russian Orthodox Mission in the United States of America, and this Mission had great success. The Mission was able to prey on the difficulties our priests and parishes had with the Latin Bishops. They exploited those difficulties by saying to our people: "The Pope does not want you. Why don't you come back to us?" And many did leave the Catholic Church and joined the Russian Orthodox Church, so that in 1905 the Russian Orthodox Church was able to establish its first Eparchy in New York City.

Metropolitan Andrew Sheptytsky, realizing what the plan of the Hungarian government was, and exploiting the failure of Hobobay's mission, commenced very lively diplomatic activity. He frequently went to Rome, Vienna, and Budapest, demanding an appointment of a Ukrainian bishop in the United States of America. As a candidate for this position he proposed Father Soter Ortynsky, OSBM, a tireless missionary, a brilliant orator, and his classmate from their theological studies. The Hungarian government, disturbed by the Russian proselytism and the danger coming from the Russian missionaries now working on the Ukrainian territories under Hungary, finally gave consent to Ortynsky's appointment, under the condition that Ortynsky's successor would have to be one of their priests.

The Servant of God Andrew Sheptytsky statue erected on the place where the old cathedral church was

The appointment of Ortynsky was made by Pope Pius X March 4, 1907. Stephen Soter Ortynsky was born January 29, 1866. He joined the Basilian Order in 1885, studied at the Jesuit College in Krakow, and was ordained July 18, 1891. He spoke six European languages well. His nomination was to be an auxiliary bishop to each Latin Rite bishop in the United States where our faithful lived. Metropolitan Sheptytsky ordained him a bishop at St. George's Cathedral in Lviv May 12, 1907. The co-consecrators were: Constantine Chekhowych, Eparch of Peremyshl, and Gregory Khomyshyn, Eparch of Stanyslaviv. The homilist was Rev. Ivan Wolansky, our first priest in the United States of America. Ortynsky arrived in the United States of America August 27, 1907.

Bishop Ortynsky made Philadelphia his episcopal see, and thus it became the center of Ukrainian Church and cultural life in the United States of America. In the fall of 1908 he purchased a church building on North Franklin Street from the Methodists. He likewise purchased a house next to the church at 816 N. Franklin Street where he made his residence and his office.

Metropolitan Sheptytsky, on his way to the International Eucharistic Congress in Montreal, Canada, stopped in Philadelphia in July 1910, and visited several of our larger parishes. On his return trip from Montreal he stopped again in Philadelphia, and on October 2, 1910, consecrated the Cathedral Church with 38 priests as concelebrants. Present were the Papal Legate to the Eucharistic Congress, Cardinal Vanutelli, the Latin Archbishop of Philadelphia, and many other dignitaries.

Thus Metropolitan Andrew Sheptytsky has to be considered as the founder and father of the Ukrainian Catholic Church in the United States of America. The year 1992 marked the centennial anniversary of his priestly ordination September 2, 1892, by Bishop Julian Pelesh of Peremyshl. I considered that it would be right and proper to mark this anniversary in some special way. After some consultation, it was decided that a statue of Sheptytsky would be the right thing to do, and it would become a lasting memorial in his honor for future generations to remember him and his deeds.

In 1988 I contacted Leo Mol (Molodozhanyn), a renowned sculptor from Winnipeg, Canada. He agreed to do the project, and for this purpose came to Philadelphia to further discuss the project and to see the site where the statue would be located. I proposed the site where the old Cathedral Church had existed, especially where the sanctuary was. He agreed with my proposition. I asked him to make Sheptytsky look as he did, when he last visited Philadelphia in 1920.

Leo Mol sent me a black and white photo of a model statue of Sheptytsky January 17, 1989. My first impression of the model was that it was majestic. On it Sheptytsky looked as though he was full of energy, authority, and majesty, as Moses might have looked. In his letter to me of January 27, 1989, he wrote: "I am happy that my project of the statue found your approval. To realize the project I have to proceed with the enlargement of the model and then with casting it in a mold in bronze. In Canada there are no facilities for this kind of work. I have to go to Germany with this project. If everything goes well, I can commence the project towards the end of April, and hope to have it cast in bronze towards the end of October or the beginning of November. Besides, I have yet to work on the pedestal for the statue . . ."

Meanwhile, we had to prepare the grounds for the stature. There were three empty buildings standing there which had to be demolished at 816, 818 and 820 N. Franklin Street; 816 was the former rectory; 818, Auxiliary Bishop's residence; and 820, the Byzantine Church Supplies Store. We contracted the work of demolition of the buildings, and it was done expediently. Then we had to hire a landscaping contractor, have him design a plan for our approval, build concrete walks, pour a solid foundation for the statue, and plant some trees and shrubs.

The statue arrived crated in a casket-like box on May 4, 1990, and it was stored in the rectory garage until the time of its installation.

The committee for the celebration of the one hundredth anniversary of Metropolitan Andrew Sheptytsky's ordination planned the affair for Saturday and Sunday, September 26 and 27, 1992.

The larger-than-life statue was raised to the granite pedestal one week before the scheduled celebration, then covered with a thin linen cloth.

The schedule for the celebrations included a symposium on Saturday at 10:30 A.M. in the school auditorium where Bohdan Procko presented a very interesting display of colored slides on the theme, "Metropolitan Andrew Sheptytsky and the Ukrainian Catholic Church in the United States of America." After lunch, Wasyl Lencyk from Stamford, CT, read a paper, entitled, "Archbishop Sheptytsky and the Culture of Ukraine." At 2:00 P.M. Father Athanasius Pekar, OSBM gave a talk on, "Andrew Sheptytsky as a Basilian." There were more than one hundred participants in the symposium.

On this occasion, I published a pastoral letter in which I tried to present the great efforts and merits of Metropolitan Sheptytsky on behalf of the Ukrainian Catholic Church in the United States of America. On Sunday I celebrated a Hierarchical Divine Liturgy at 10:00 A.M. in the Cathedral with all the Bishops of our Province as concelebrants, as well as Metropolitan Hermaniuk of Winnipeg and Bishop Hrynchyshyn from Paris, France, together with many priests. Many religious sisters and the faithful filled the spacious Cathedral. Metropolitan Hermaniuk was the homilist.

The official unveiling of the statue took place at 3:00 P.M. All the bishops and the priests present there concelebrated a Moleben Service to the Most Holy Mother of God with myself as the homilist. After the Moleben, all the clergy went out in a procession to officially unveil the statue and bless it.

At 4:30 P.M. a concert was held in the school auditorium. It was opened by Bishop Paska's brief remarks. The Church Choir "Boyan" from Perth Amboy, N.J., and the Ecumenical Choir from Olyphant, Pa. gave a series of well-prepared and well-executed presentations. Then Bishop Michael Hrynchyshyn gave a talk on the Beatification Process of the Servant of God Metropolitan Andrew Sheptytsky. The Philadelphia Choir "Prometheus" gave a number of presentations to conclude the concert.

This is how the Philadelphia Archeparchy marked the 100th Anniversary of Metropolitan Andrew Sheptytsky's priestly ordination. We raised his statue, the first one anywhere, to acknowledge that he is the Father and the heavenly Protector of the Ukrainian Catholic Church in the United States of America. On a separate pedestal we placed the bell from the old Cathedral Church, which Sheptytsky had blessed October 2, 1910.

My Participation in the Ukrainian Synods of Bishops

Our present Pope, John Paul II, soon after his election to Peter's throne, gave our Church the right to call regular Synods of Bishops outside of the territory of our Church, i.e. Ukraine. Previously we were not permitted to do this. The first Synod I attended after my appointment as a Metropolitan Archbishop was called by the Major Archbishop Josyf Cardinal Slipyj to take place in the Vatican January 30 to February 12, 1983. The bishops of the Catacomb Church in Ukraine were not able to participate in these Synods. Only bishops from the free world participated.

The first Synod I attended was a great event in my life, an honor and distinction. I prepared myself carefully so as not to burden the Synod with my inexperience, but to add something constructive. At that time there was a Presidium of the Synod composed of the Major Archbishop or his Coadjutor and the two Metropolitans— Maxim Hermaniuk, CSsR of Winnipeg, Canada, and myself. The sessions of the Synod were guided by a moderator from among the members of the Presidium, alternating at each session. Major Archbishop Josyf Cardinal Slipyj did not attend the sessions of the Synod due to his advanced age and deteriorating health. He came to the last session however, read his talk, and stayed for the group picture.

During the first session on liturgical questions, I presented the following proposition: "In our preparations for the Millennium of the Baptism of Ukraine, the Synodal Committee on Liturgical Matters will study the possibility of establishing in the Church calendar one Sunday in a year for the honor and glorification of *"All Saints of Ukraine."* Then I gave the following reason for the proposition:

"During the one thousand years of Christianity in Ukraine there were frequent cases where our faithful sacrificed their lives in defense of the faith in Christ or for the unity of Christ's Church. This happened yet in times of internal strife among the princes, and during the invasions of the Mongolian hordes. It happened even more frequently in later centuries when there were attempts to destroy the Union of our Church with Rome. I will cite an historical example. When Russian Tsar Peter I was passing with his army the city of Polotsk on July 11, 1705, he entered the Cathedral Greek Catholic Church while the Service of Vespers was being conducted. There he personally killed two priests with his sword. He then entered the sanctuary, took the ciborium out of the tabernacle, and threw the Blessed Sacrament on the floor. When Father Zaykowsky, OSBM, got on his knees and tried to pick up the consecrated hosts, the tsar cut off his ears and commanded his soldiers to take him out and to hang him. When the Tsar came back into the church after the hanging, he killed five more priests and commanded that the bodies be burned so that 'the Uniates would have no relics to venerate as martyrs.' To this day the Church did not canonize these seven priests.

Especially in the not-so-distant past, during the Second World War, our Church had a great number of martyrs and confessors who are known only to God. In the 1940s when Stalin and his henchmen tried to liquidate our Church, then how many thousands of nameless martyrs and confessors were there? They died for their Catholic faith in the tortures of prison basements, in

My first Synod of the Ukrainian Bishops.

A group photo of the Synodal Fathers, February 1, 1992. (L. to R.): Ephrem Krevey, OSBM - Eparch of Brazil; Bishop Dmytro Greschuk - auxiliary of Edmonton, Bishop Myron Daciuk, OSBM - auxiliary of Winnipeg; Bishop Jerome Chimy, OSBM - Eparc of Westminster, Bishop Platon Kornyljak - Exarch of Germany; Bishop Innocent Lotocky, OSBM - Eparch of Chicago; Bishop Michael Hrynchyshyn, CSsR - Eparch of France; Bishop Ivan Prasko - Eparch of Austrailia; Archbishop Stephen Sulyk- Philadelphia; Archbishop Maxim Hermaniuk, CSsR Winnipeg; Rev. Ivan Choma; Patriarch Josyf Slipyj; Rev. Ivan Dacko; Coadjutor Myroslav Lubachivsky; Bishop Neil Savaryn, OSBM - Eparch of Edmonton; Bishop Isidore Boretsky - Eparch of Toronto; Bishop Andrew Sapelak - Eparch of Argentina; Augustine Horniak, OSBM - Exarch of Stamford; Bishop Robert Moskal - Eparch of Parma; Rev. Ihor Monchak (secretary).

the gulags of Siberia, and in prison camps of Kazakhstan. How many more died during Hitler's occupation of our country? Most of them were killed at night so that there were no witnesses, and no records were kept. My former pastor in Maniw (1930–1934), Rev. Zenon Krupsky, was also killed in the Sambir prison when in June of 1941 the German army attacked the Soviet Union.

This is why I consider it proper for our Synod to select one Sunday in the Church calendar so that our faithful may have an opportunity to venerate those nameless heroes of our faith."

The Synod unanimously voted on my proposition and assigned the fourth Sunday after Pentecost as the Sunday of all Saints of Ukraine. The Basilian Fathers were asked by the Synod to compose the propers for that Sunday. One of their priests, Father Sebastian Sabol, OSBM, an outstanding writer and a poet, composed a very rich and poetic service, and it is included in their "Molytvoslov" (Breviary), published by the Basilian Press, Rome—Toronto 1990, pp. 778–784.

Archaic Words in the Liturgical Texts

The 1983 Synod of Bishops voted in the following decision: "This Synod charges the Liturgical Committee to translate from the Church-Slavonic to the Ukrainian language the "Archierarticon," published in 1973 by the Congregation of the Eastern Churches." There existed a Synodal Intereparchial Liturgical Committee under the leadership of Josyf Cardinal Slipyj, which made the first translation of the Divine Liturgy from the Church Slavonic to the Ukrainian language in 1968. But this Committee was no longer in existence. This is why this Synod elected a new Synodal Liturgical Committee to make the necessary translations of the liturgical texts. The chairman of the Liturgical Committee will always be the Major Archbishop. I was elected as the executive chairman for the translation of the Ukrainian Liturgical texts. Another Subcommittee was chosen for the translation of English texts, and Metropolitan Hermaniuk and I chaired this one. It would be my duty to find expert linguistic scholars who would make the actual translations in both the English and Ukrainian liturgical texts.

At that time I had no way of knowing what awaited me in this particular section of my work for the Synod, how great would be the unpleasantness, how sharp the disagreements would become, how ungrateful my job would be. Had I known all this, I would never have agreed to do it. But, who knows the future? Only God; the future is not ours to know.

I accepted my election to this Committee with humility and I declared to the Synodal Fathers, "I am not a philologist or a linguistic scholar. I personally cannot do this kind of work. But I will try to find someone who is capable of doing such a work. I, therefore, cannot be held responsible for the mistakes of the scholars." We all agreed that the translated texts should be sent to the Major Archbishop, and he, in turn, to all the bishops for their input. The bishops, in turn, would send their remarks and observations back to the Major Archbishop. When all the observations were implemented or properly explained, the corrected text was to be sent back to the Major Archbishop who would then send it to all the bishops for their approval.

There was a discussion at this Synod concerning the archaic words used in the Ukrainian Intereparchial Committee's translation of the Divine Liturgy of 1968. They demanded that the new translation eliminate archaic words and replace them with words of literary Ukrainian language. Coadjutor Archbishop Lubachivsky was an enthusiast for the cause of eliminating archaic words. But there was no decision taken on this matter at the 1983 Synod.

Having returned home from the Synod, I wrote a letter on March 14, 1983 to Dr. Wasyl Lew, a philologist and my teacher of Church-Slavonic language at the Seminary in Hirschberg, Germany. He likewise was a member of the Interparchial Liturgical Committee. I sent him the "Archierarticon" and asked him to make a Ukrainian translation for the Synod, eliminating archaic words. He agreed to make a translation, but asked for time since he had other important tasks at hand.

In the meantime His Beatitude Josyf Cardinal Slipyj died September 7, 1984. His Coadjutor, Myroslav Ivan Lubachivsky, became the next Major Archbishop. He called a Synod to meet in Rome from September 22 to October 5, 1985.

The Basilian Fathers at that time were actively working on a translation from the Church Slavonic into Ukrainian of the first

Ukrainian clerical breviary. They wished to coordinate their translation with the Synodal one so as to have harmony. For this reason, their Protoarchimandrite (General) came to the Synod and asked to be heard. He brought with him a list of archaic words used in the 1968 translation, with a proposal of literary words in their stead. He gave a copy of his list to each bishop and departed.

The Synod had to decide whether to accept the Basilian proposal and to use it in our translations or not. The great majority of the Synodal Fathers were in favor of the proposal. They asked not to hold a debate on each proposed word since we are not philologists. The Basilian Fathers' proposal would be very beneficial for the Church so that our priest and the faithful would have the same translation of all liturgical services. This proposition was voted upon, and a large majority accepted it. Among those who voted for the proposition and supported it wholeheartedly was Major Archbishop Lubachivsky. There was one bishop who abstained from voting, and two others voted against the proposition. However, when the moderator announced that the Basilian Fathers' proposal as it is written on their list was accepted by the majority vote, then one of those who voted against it got up and stated, "His Beatitude Patriarch Josyf is not cold yet, and you dare to start correcting him!"

This angry public protest of one of our senior bishops against the decision of the Synod disturbed me very much. I wholeheartedly wished for harmony, and fraternal cooperation among brother bishops. So I went to Major Archbishop Lubachivsky and asked him, "Should we not ask the Synod to change its decision concerning the archaic words so as not to divide the Synod into two factions? His reply was, "Do not pay any attention to N.N. You cannot please everyone. Let it be as it was decided by the majority vote."

Afterward I tried privately to discuss the matter with several bishops in order to get their opinion. I tried very hard to avoid any possible impression that the Synod or I would appear to be in opposition to the authority or respect due to the late Josyf Cardinal Slipyj. I would never have the audacity to offend in the slightest way the great person, the loftiness and the exalted name of Josyf Slipyj. I always held him in highest esteem, and proof of this is the fact that, after receiving my nomination, I asked him to ordain me to the episcopacy. This is why I asked so many of our bishops for their opinion in this matter. Each one of them was shocked by the public opposition of Bishop N.N. and asked, "What kind of logic is there in his statement? How can one connect the elimination of archaic words from the liturgical texts with an offense against our great Confessor of the Faith? One has nothing to do with the other," was the general opinion of the bishops.

All of us admitted that to ease the passage from the Church-Slavonic language to the contemporary Ukrainian, a pastoral approach demanded the retention of some archaic expressions. But twenty years have already passed since we began to use the translation of the Intereparchial Committee, headed by Josyf Cardinal Slipyj. "But now these archaic expressions irritate the ear of anyone who knows and loves his native language," was a general opinion and agreement among the bishops.

However, when some weeks after the Synod, the official minutes of the last Synod were delivered to each of our bishops from the office of the Major Archbishop in Rome, to our great surprise the decision of the Synod of 1985 with the list with the archaic expressions prepared by the Basilian Fathers was missing. If the decision to eliminate archaic words from our liturgical texts is not in the official minutes of the Synod, then legally the decision does not exist. It exists only in the memory of the Fathers of the Synod. This fact disturbed me considerably. I was certain that Major Archbishop Lubachivsky, who was enthusiastic about eliminating archaic expressions, had nothing to do with this omission. One could only surmise that it must have been the one who typed the minutes on a computer who purposely and maliciously made the omission. His Beatitude Lubachivsky probably did not read the minutes or if he did, he did not notice the omission.

I shared my concern about this matter with several of my brother bishops and a few priests in Rome. I was personally certain, and my friends in Rome supported my conviction, that this "omission" was only the beginning of an impertinent and underhanded sub-versive rebellion against the person of the Major Archbishop and the whole Synod of Bishops, which would last for many years and introduce chaos into the liturgical life of our Church. This was a tragedy that could not have been foreseen or avoided by any of the Synodal Fathers.

The Archierarticon and the Liturgicon

The Archierarticon is a service book for bishops, while the
Liturgicon is for priests. Wasyl Lew worked for two years
on the translation of the Archierarticon from the Church
Slavonic to the Ukrainian language. He called me several times,
asking how this or that word or expression should be translated.
Actually I was astonished by his questions. They revealed to me
his great shortcomings in this field. With his letter to me dated
March 10, 1985, he enclosed the translated text and returned the
book, writing: "Thanks be to God, I finally completed the translation of the Archierarticon and marked the accents . . . I would be
happy to hear the appraisal of my work by the bishops . . . ."

At that time I had a very good priest scholar working as the
Spiritual Director at St. Josaphat Seminary in Washington, D.C.,
Father Athanasius Pekar, OSBM. I sent the translation to him, asking him to please verify the correctness of the translation. Father
Pekar, OSBM, was not only a great scholar and author of many
books and articles, but likewise a specialist in the Church Slavonic
and the Ukrainian languages as well as liturgics.

At the same time, work was underway on the English translation of the Liturgicon, i.e., a book containing the Divine Liturgies
of St. John Chrysostom, St. Basil the Great, and of the Presanctified

Gifts. At the organizational meeting of this Committee present were, Bishop Robert M. Moskal of Parma, Ohio; Rev. Joseph Shary of Chicago, Il; Msgr. Leon Mosko and Msgr. Peter Skrinkosky, both from Stamford, Ct; and Msgr. Roman Danylak of Toronto, Canada. They selected Msgr. Shary to be the chairman of this Committee. Somehow their cooperation with Bishop Moskal did not go too well, and later on they would meet without inviting him to the meetings. I did not know that since I let them work on their own without my interference. Bishop Moskal was deeply offended by their actions, and when the translation of the Liturgicon was completed and verified, approved by the Major Archbishop and the Congregation for the Eastern Churches, Bishop Moskal refused to accept it in his Eparchy. With the cooperation and help of his permanent personal secretary, Msgr. Thomas Sayuk, he published his own translation, using inclusive language. In the Calendar of Saints of his book, entitled, "The Sacrifice of Praise" he included most of the saints from the Orthodox calendar. Thus we have on February 6, the feast of our father among the saints Photius, archbishop of Constantinople! His Liturgicon, however, was not presented to the Synod for canonical approval or to the Congregation for the Eastern Churches as prescribed by the Code of Canons for the Eastern Churches, and thus its use in our churches became illegal. It is used only in the Parma Eparchy.

The English translation of the Liturgicon was sent to me in January of 1983. I sent a copy of it to each English speaking Bishop as well as to the Major Archbishop in Rome and to the Congregation for the Eastern Church in the Vatican with a request for approval. I had to wait long for the Congregation's approval. The Congregation was making an effort to have one common English translation for all the English speaking countries for the Byzantine Catholic churches and, if possible, also for the Orthodox. This plan was not successful, but not due to our fault. The Congregation issued a decree dated August 10, 1984, #353/67, granting permission to publish this translation and to use it in our churches. His Beatitude Lubachivsky made considerable effort to obtain this decree.

In his letter to me dated August 10, 1984, #287/84, His Beatitude wrote, "Enclosed please find a decree of the Eastern Congregation permitting the publication of the Liturgicon but with certain conditions. What these conditions are spelled out in a copy of my letter to the Eastern Congregation in which I gave a short history of the English translation . . ."

Father Pekar did an immense and solid job in correcting the Ukrainian translation of the Archierarticon of Dr. Lew. He sent the ready copy of the translation to me on November 8, 1986. Immediately I sent a copy to His Beatitude Lubachivsky with a reminder that he send a copy to each bishop for his input. I likewise sent a copy to the Eastern Congregation with a request for approval.

The Congregation gave a copy of the translation to their consultants, Rev. Porphirius Pidruchny, OSBM, and Rev. Rodion Holowacky, OSBM, for their opinion. Finally, the Congregation wrote to me a letter dated May 4, 1987, #111/81, saying:

> We have arrived to a state when we can answer Your Excellency on the "remarks" concerning the Ukrainian translation of the Archierarticon. The consultants of this Congregation studied carefully the text of this work and may assure Your Excellency that the translation is faithful and correct.
>
> This Congregation with this letter grants *nihil obstat* for the publication of this translation of the Archierarticon for the use of the bishops of the Ukrainian Catholic Church under the condition that the enclosed observations be included in the text.
>
> With our best wishes for the successful publication of this work, I remain with respect to Your Excellency, (signatures): D. Simon Cardinal Lourdusamy, Prefect, and + M. Marusyn, Secretary."

I sent to Father Pekar the approved text with the observations and a request to include them in the text. He compiled the text expediently and I received from him the corrected text with a recommendation, "To send the approved and corrected text to His Beatitude Lubachivsky with a request for his approval."

I wrote a letter to His Beatitude and enclosed the approved text with the observations of Rev. Porphirius Pidruchny, OSBM, and Rev. Rodion Holowacky, OSBM, and with the list of archaic expressions approved by the Synod. I asked that he engage a specialist, if he deems it proper, to once more check the text for correctness and then to mail a copy to each bishop for his observations. I even suggested that it might be better for this Archierarticon to be published in Rome and be distributed from there.

As a result of my last letter, His Beatitude Lubachivsky sent me a copy of his introductory letter to be published in the Liturgicon. Below is a summary of his letter:

Synod of Bishops of the Ukrainian Catholic Church
Peace in the Lord and my Episcopal Blessing!

The Synodal Liturgical Subcommittee for the translations of our liturgical books into the English language according to the decision of the First Synod of the Ukrainian Catholic Bishops which took place in 1980 in Rome, made a translation of the Divine Liturgy of St. John Chrysostom into the English language. This translation was approved by the Second Synod of Bishops in 1982 and the Congregation for Eastern Churches approved it August 10, 1984, #353/57, and gave permission to publish the same.

We convey this official translation for the use in our Ukrainian Catholic Church . . .

We also like to inform all of our Very Reverend and Reverend Pastors as well as all Religious priests of our Ukrainian Catholic Church to discard all privately made translations of the Divine Liturgy of St. John Chrysostom and to acquire this official translation. . . . Only this official text approved by the Apostolic See may be used in our churches or chapels.

We likewise give our approval to the Ukrainian text of the Divine Liturgy of St. John Chrysostom, including the linguistic corrections approved by the Synod of the Ukrainian Catholic Church in 1985.

Given in Rome, May 19, 1987

+ Myroslav Cardinal Lubachivsky
Major Archbishop."

His Beatitude Lubachivsky approved all of the remarks to the text of the Archierarticon and gave me a commission to go to print. He likewise sent me a letter dated December 9 (22) 1987, which was to be published as an introduction to the Archierarticon:

Myroslav Ivan Lubachivsky
Major Archbishop and Cardinal
Metropolitan of Lviv for Ukrainians

Peace in the Lord and my Episcopal Blessing!

In accordance with the decision of the Synod of the Ukrainian Catholic Bishops, we are publishing this translation from the Church Slavonic to the Ukrainian language.

The translation was made by the Intereparchial Liturgical Committee. In reference to the language it has preserved the accurate Ukrainian language with the omission of any archaic expressions or any innovations, as it was stated in the decisions of the Synod and in the approval of the Holy See. In this translation every possible effort was made for it to be exact and faithful translation of the "archierarticon," published in Rome 1973 with the blessing of the Holy Roman Apostolic See at the Typography of the Grottaferrata Monastery. All the linguistic attributes add to the Ukrainian translation a Pan-Ukrainian character so that each Ukrainian may easily understand, and in the event of his presence at a Hierarchical service, he may easily follow it.

We hope that this translation will favor the understanding of the Mystery of Priesthood which should give rise to the curiosity among the young in the priestly life and become a stimulus to follow it. May the Sacrifice of Christ, offered in our nation and in our language, be the prayer which will be heard and bring down all the necessary graces so much needed in today's sad times and become a pledge of a better future.

May the Blessing of the Lord be with you!

Given in Rome, December 9 (22) 1987 A.D.

In the composition of the above letter there were some statements that were less than correct. The 1983 Synod was not even mentioned. Yes, His Beatitude did sign this letter but it was not his style of writing or reasoning. The one who typed the Synodal Minutes of 1983 and made the glaring omission of the decision of eliminating archaic words, most probably composed this letter.

Without questioning the procedures agreed upon in the 1983 Synod concerning the opinion of each bishop, I obediently sent the two texts (the Archierarticon and the Liturgicon) to the Basilian Press in Toronto for publication. I was able to reach with them a good and favorable agreement. They would publish and sell the Liturgicon, and the Synod would get any excess money after the cost of the publication was covered. Some years later I received from them a check for in sum of $11,000.00 Canadian dollars, which I deposited in the Synod Beatification Account. The cost of publishing the Archierarticon had to be covered by the Philadelphia Archeparchy, since only a limited amount of books were printed and the book is to be used almost exclusively by bishops.

I was truly happy when Father Pekar agreed to do the proof reading for I knew the work would be done properly. The work was progressing in a very satisfactory fashion. The Liturgicon was ready by the summer of 1988. It was printed in three editions: The Ukrainian edition for the altar, the combined English and Ukrainian edition for the altar, and the small pew edition for the faithful. So in the Millennium Year of Baptism of Ukraine, all our churches had the new Liturgicon on their altars and in their pews for the faithful. The reaction to the new Liturgicon of our priests was very positive. They all liked the fluency of the language, the form and the appearance of the book, and clear and large print.

Yet I would not be truthful if I did not mention here the opposition to this Liturgicon. The one elderly bishop who publicly rebelled at the Synod of 1983 for eliminating the archaic expression in our liturgical texts was only a front. Behind him were a few priests in Rome who formed a conspiracy against the decision of the Synod in this matter. They were able to convince a few bishops who refused to buy the Liturgicon themselves and forbade their priests to do so. But thanks be to God, they were in a minority. It was the Toronto Eparchy, the Parma Eparchy, and the Eparchy in Australia that refused the new Liturgicon and thus officially rebelled against their own Synod of Bishops.

A great surprise awaited our bishops as they gathered for the following Synod in Rome, September 24 to October 8, 1989. During the first session on September 25, 1989 during a discussion on the new Liturgicon, His Beatitude Lubachivsky stood up and made this statement: "I withdraw my approval of the new Liturgicon and ask the secretary of the Synod to mark this in the minutes."

At that moment, most of the bishops raised their hands asking for the floor. Their statements could be summarized in this way: "Your Beatitude, the Liturgicon was published over one year ago. It was sold to most of our churches and is in use. It is simply impossible to recall it now. The priests and the faithful will have us bishops for fools who do not know what they are doing. This will cause a great scandal in our Church. The bishops will lose their respect and good name before their priests and their faithful. This action of Your Beatitude will mostly hurt you. It will present you to the world as a leader who does not know what he is doing. As the head of our Church, you cannot do this. Besides, it was published in accordance with the decision of our Synod, your approval, as well as the approval of the Apostolic See. Remember that your action alone without the consent of the Synod is canonically invalid and non-existent. For you to be able to withdraw your approval of the Liturgicon, you need two-thirds vote of the entire Synod."

He, who forced His Beatitude to change his mind from an enthusiast of the new Liturgicon to an opponent, wanted to actually destroy his personality, his dignity, and his good name. Someone wanted to make a fool out of our good, humble, and pious Major Archbishop, to expose him before our faithful and history as a man who does not know what he is doing. This was a cruel and malicious joke that someone was perpetrating not only on the head, but also on our whole Church.

As various bishops made their statements, I was sitting overwhelmed by what was happening. My heart was aching for His Beatitude and for what was being done to destroy him. I then raised my hand and asked to speak:

In the new Liturgicon there are no other changes except those which were approved by this Synod in 1985, i.e., only those archaic words were eliminated which were approved by the Synod. There are no other changes in it. The Congregation had this text studied by their consultants and found that it was a true and correct translation from the Church Slavonic original. I sent the text to Your Beatitude many times of both the Liturgicon and the Archierarticon together with the enclosures, the remarks of other people. I asked you to proof read it or to give it to some specialist to do so. Why then did you write to me to go to print and send me the introductory letters? Why did you not tell me at that time: I do not approve and do not permit this work to be published? Why did you lead me into error so that after one year after the sale of the books, you now withdraw your approval?

His Beatitude answered: "I did not read these texts!"

I just sat down and felt so sorry for the old, good and humble man, our Major Archbishop. I asked myself, what happened to him? Did someone use some kind of force so that he contradicts himself publicly before all of his brother bishops? I had no answer. Yet I knew he is in a need of help, a friendly and brotherly help. So I made one decision, to pray daily for him, asking God to guide and protect him, to give him the light from heaven to see the truth.

Soon after the Synod, I received a letter from a good friend of mine in Rome. He wrote about the events at the Synod pertaining the Liturgicon. He stated that the protest against the Liturgicon is a result of "a conspiracy." This conspiracy used all kinds of methods to convert Cardinal Lubachivsky to their "truth." Bishop N.N. came to Rome and lived with Cardinal Lubachivsky for a month. Day after day he tried to persuade him to change his mind. "Here in Rome," wrote my friend, "the Krylos made a decision not to permit the use of the Liturgicon in all our eparchies. There exists already a plan to publish their own Liturgicon."

The center of the conspiracy was the so-called "Krylos," composed of several of our priests permanently residing in Rome at that time. By means of telephone calls they tried to convince the bishops not to permit the new Liturgicon in their eparchies, because it was "offensive" to the memory of our Patriarch, Josyf Cardinal Slipyj.

One of our bishops told one of his priests N.N. to write a critique of the new Liturgicon. He did so by using a comparative tablet of the archaic words with those in the new Liturgicon. He did not write as a scholar, but as a propagandist, in a tendentious manner for his like-minded friends in order to sway them against the Liturgicon. Some time later Father N.N. wrote me a letter of apology, saying, "I did it only out of obedience to my Bishop." His critique was not a solid work at all and contained serious deficiencies and wrong conclusions. The conspiracy publicized the critique very widely in all the countries where our people live. Some might have accepted this critique as valid and true.

The conspirators were able to convert His Beatitude Lubachivsky to their side and with it to denigrate and humiliate him so that he probably did not know what was happening to him. Since that time he would not receive anyone without the consent of his secretary or without his presence. He also stopped associating with others. By manipulating the Synodal Minutes and using false propaganda, the conspirators were able to bring the liturgical life of our Church into chaos. When Ukraine became free in 1991, the chaos was transferred there. We had reached a point that we could not recite even the "Our Father" in common as the wording differed in the Liturgicons.

The Synodal Minutes of the 1989 Synod were being taken and typed by Rev. Klym Korchaguine, OSBM. Each morning he would read the minutes of the previous day's sessions and the bishops were able to make their corrections or approve them. At the end of the Synod each bishop would place his signature on the last page of the Minutes. Thus the Synodal Minutes became historical document. On my request, Father Korchaguine gave me a copy of the original Minutes.

The Presidium of the Synod was composed of His Beatitude Lubachivsky, Metropolitan Hermaniuk, CSsR, myself, Bishop Michael Hrynchyshyn, CSsR as Synodal Secretary and Rev. Klym Korchaguine, OSBM as the Recording Secretary. A meeting of the Presidium took place in Rome November 16, 1989. At that time the Synodal Minutes of the 1989 Synod, retyped on a computer, were distributed. Having read this 64-page-long document, I immediately noticed changes in the decisions of the Synod concerning liturgical questions. I had a copy of the original Synodal Minutes of 1989 with me and after comparing both, I recognize that the Minutes were falsified by adding decisions which were not made at the Synod. The following decisions were added: "The text of the Liturgicon, published by the Major Archbishop Josyf Slipyj remains legal, i.e., obligatory" (Page 7). "The new text of the Liturgicon will be used *ad experimentum*, i.e., it can be used when the eparch or the exarch permits its use" (Ibid). "The new text may not be sent to Ukraine since there the Church Slavonic text is used, and there are objections to the new text in Ukraine. In Ukraine there are over five millions faithful, who are under the jurisdiction of the Major Archbishop" (Ibid).

The Synodal Minutes of the 1989 Synod retyped on a computer eliminated the decisions of the Synod pertaining to the new Liturgicon which contradicted the above three decisions. In addition, another decision was eliminated, namely, "The Synod approved "*The Ordo of the Hierarchical Divine Liturgy of St. John Chrysostom and of St. Basil the Great,*" prepared by Metropolitan Sulyk in accordance with the rubrics of the Archieraticon, published by the Apostolic See in 1973, and the "*Ordo Celebrationis,*" published likewise by the Apostolic See in 1941" (Page 24).

To the computer-falsified Synodal Minutes on pages 56–58 were added: "Remarks of His Beatitude Major Archbishop Myroslav Ivan Lubachivsky concerning the new Liturgicon, published in Toronto 1988." His Beatitude did not make the two-pages-long "Remarks" at the Synod; they are not in the original Minutes since no Synodal Father heard them. This is another gross falsification of an official, historical Church document. The style and the language of the "Remarks" witness to the fact that they were not written by His Beatitude. Such falsification of official and historical Church documents is a criminal action that should be subject to Church penalties.

At the November 16, 1989, meeting of the Presidium I brought up the matter of the gross falsification of the 1989 Synodal Minutes, and gave sufficient proofs for that. His Beatitude replied that he did not read those Minutes and does not know anything about the matter. Metropolitan Hermaniuk proposed that Father Korchaguine, who had the entire proceedings of the Synod recorded on tape recorder, compare the recording with the computer-typed-Minutes and then give a report of the Presidium. Father Korchaguine did not do it, and never again did he participate in any of our Synods.

I asked Father Pekar to write a reply to the "Critique" of the Liturgicon and to the "Remarks" falsely included in the Synodal Minutes. He gave a detailed and full reply to each questioned word or expression, quoting the eleven-volume Official Ukrainian Dictionary and other scholarly sources. In his 27-page-long reply he proved beyond any doubt that all critiques were without basis. This work I sent to each Synodal Fathers.

The Extraordinary Synod of 1991

The Holy Father, John Paul II, unexpectedly invited the ten bishops from the Underground Ukrainian Catholic Church in Soviet Union to the Vatican, as well as all of our bishops from the free world for the June 25–26, 1990, Synod. The bishops from Ukraine just recently emerged from their modern catacombs. With the intervention of the Holy Father, they received permission from the Soviet Union to travel abroad. They traveled by train with all the controls and inspections and other difficulties.

First visit to the Holy Father of the Ukrainian Catholic bishops from the catacomb Church in Ukraine, June 26, 1990. (l. to r.): Michael Sabryha, CSsR, Ivan Marghitych, Julian Voronowsky, Pavlo Vasylyk, Philemon Kurchaba, CSsR, Major Archbishop Myroslav Ivan Lubachivsky, Pope John Paul II, Joseph Holovach, Volodymyr Sterniuk, CSsR, Ivan Semedij, Sophronius Dmyterko, OSBM, Irynej Bilyk, OSBM, Archbishop Angelo Sodano - Vatican.

The bishops from the Free World arrived earlier so as to welcome their brothers and to express our gratitude for their heroic profession of faith by which they astonished the world. I was fortunate to have met them in March of 1990 in Lviv during my participation in the work of the Catholic-Orthodox Commission.

On June 25, 1990, twenty-nine Ukrainian Catholic Bishops assembled in the Old Synodal Hall in the Vatican at 9:00 A.M. Soon afterward the Holy Father arrived, accompanied by Cardinal Agostino Casaroli, the Secretary of State; Cardinal Simon Lourdusamy, Prefect of the Congregation for the Eastern Churches; Archbishop Edward Cassidy; Archbishop Myroslav Marusyn, and other Vatican dignitaries. Each of our bishops approached the Holy Father and greeted him personally.

His Beatitude Lubachivsky opened the session with a prayer to the Holy Spirit. Archbishop Marusyn read a well-prepared paper, entitled "Ukrainian Catholic Church Yesterday and Today." He spoke Ukrainian, and Father George Dzudzar gave a simultaneous translation into Italian. Earphones were available for whoever wanted to use them.

I was the next speaker, likewise in Ukrainian. Father George asked me to speak very slowly so that he might have time to translate it into Italian.

In the Acts of the Apostles we read that when Herod started a campaign of persecuting Christ's Church, he had St. Peter arrested, bound him in chains and cast him into prison, intending to destroy him after Passover. But then the entire Church prayed for him unceasingly to God. The Lord heard their prayer and sent his angel to rescue Peter from prison. Thus St. Peter returned to his faithful amid great joy.

Forty-five years ago a modern Herod, who was bent on obliterating every trace of the Ukrainian Catholic Church, appeared. First of all he attacked the hierarchy, thinking to "strike the shepherd and the sheep of the flock will be dispersed" (*Matthew 26:31*). But the sheep did not scatter; other dedicated shepherds appeared who led their flocks to the catacombs to continue life there in hiding. The faithful prayed fervently, often in bloody agony, that God would save their Church. The Lord heard their ardent prayers and sent them His angel, in the person of Your Holiness, to lead our Ukrainian Catholic Church to freedom after long years of suffering.

Your Holiness thoroughly understood this providential mission as early as the Spring of 1979, when you notified His Beatitude Josyf (Slipyj) with these words: "I consider that it is of the utmost importance at this time to guarantee the right of Ukrainian Catholics to exist and to be citizens in their own native land, and, at the same time, to establish a stable, canonical form of unity within the hierarchy of your Church which would serve as a transitional stage on the way to a complete solution" of your problems. (cf. "Letter of the Pope to His Beatitude Josyf, 19 March 1979" Blahovisnyk Blazennishoho, Rome 1986–87, Vol.1–4, p. 11)

Thanks to the paternal solicitude of the Holy Father concerning the fate of the Ukrainian Catholic Church, and at his invitation, all of the Ukrainian Catholic Bishops from the Homeland and from the Diaspora have gathered together for the first time here in Rome at the grave of the priest-martyr St. Josaphat, so that, having greeted one another "with a holy kiss" (2 *Corinthians 13:12*), in fraternal accord and "with one mind" we might chart a course of further renewal for the Suffering Church in our native land, which is arising anew and awakening to a new flowering of life. In God is our hope that the prophetic words of our great Metropolitan, the Servant of God Andrew, will be fulfilled in truth; he had foreseen the terrible ruin of our Ukrainian Catholic Church under the regime of the "hammer and sickle," yet at the same time he assured us that our Church, "shall rise to new life and shall flourish." Your presence in Rome, dear Bishops from Ukraine, is a visible sign of the resurrection of our Suffering Church in our native lands.

But today a difficult task weighs upon our shoulders, on the shoulders of the Bishops at home and on those abroad—not only to renew and reinforce our Church, weakened to the limits of exhaustion, but also to lead it on the path to its full and luxuriant flowering. This is why we need the complete support and expert direction of the Apostolic See, under the leadership of the successor to St. Peter, who has taken to heart as the principal objective of his illustrious pontificate the words of Christ: "strengthen your brothers," that is the bishops (*Luke 22:32*). It is for this reason that His Holiness has summoned us here to the

Tomb of Peter (with the relics of St. Josaphat reposing safely nearby), to affirm our faith in God, our help, to bolster our hope that our Suffering Church will soon be free, and to unite our hearts by charity and mutual trust in the union of "brotherly love."

We must remember that we Ukrainians, unfortunately, are a stateless nation. Therefore, in the diplomatic or international forum we have no authoritative voice. As do other subjugated people, we must depend on the interventions of the Holy See, whose prestige has grown phenomenally during the reign of the Holy Father, Pope John Paul II. Even socialist and non-Christian nations seek to establish diplomatic relations with the Apostolic See, which never refuses to stand up in defense of the oppressed and, even more so, of those loyal and dedicated children of the Catholic Church, among whom are Ukrainian Catholics. We must acknowledge the fact that the only authoritative voice speaking in behalf of our Ukrainian Catholic Church at this time in the international diplomatic arena is the voice of the Holy See.

It is impossible for me to enumerate each and every diplomatic move and intervention that the Holy Father has made during his eleven-year pontificate to defend our Suffering Church. Nor can I number his powerful prayers, through the intercession of the Holy Mother of God, which finally led to the victory of Vatican diplomacy when the president of a mighty communist empire asked for an audience with the successor of St. Peter. Such a meeting took place on December 1, 1989, and a solemn promise was made that the Ukrainian Catholic Church would have legal recognition in the Soviet Union.

Therefore, it was not mere oratory, but rather a sincere paternal declaration of the Holy Father when, during his visit to our Cathedral in Philadelphia (October 4, 1979), he said: For many years now I have had a great respect for the Ukrainian people. I am aware of the countless sufferings and injustices you have undergone in recent times. They are for me still a cause of extraordinary concern, for I cannot forget the innumerable Ukrainian martyrs, of past and present times, who preferred to lose their lives rather than to betray their Faith. I recall this only so that you may understand my great respect for the Ukrainian Catholic Church and for its fidelity, despite trials and sufferings, to the Apostolic See (cf. Blahovisnyk, Rome 1986–87, Vol.1–4, p. 13).

In his first Apostolic Letter to the late Josyf Cardinal Slipyj dated March 19, 1979, a letter with historic significance, the Holy Father clearly stated that he does not recognize the forced liquidation of the Ukrainian Catholic Church at the 1946 Pseudo-Synod of Lviv, and that in the view of the Apostolic See the Union of Brest retains its canonical force, and therefore the Apostolic See will continue to defend the rights and interests of the Ukrainian Catholic Church. For this reason, during the episcopal ordination of Msgr. Myroslav I. Lubachivsky as Metropolitan of Philadelphia, which took place in the Sistine Chapel on the Feast of St. Josaphat in 1979, the Holy Father publicly declared (and his message was broadcast by Vatican Radio to Ukraine as well):

I wish to avail myself of today's celebration to acknowledge the great respect that the Holy See and the entire Catholic Church has for your Church. The fidelity you have demonstrated to Peter and his successors obliges us also to a special gratitude and a mutual fidelity to those who have so nobly maintained it. Therefore as a sign of our sincere love we wish to ease the pains of those who suffer because of their loyalty to the Holy See. We desire, with all our heart, to guarantee the union of your Church with the See of Peter (ibid., p. 17).

This is why the Holy Father united the Ukrainian Catholic bishops in the diaspora by establishing a synodal structure for the
Ukrainian Catholic Church (cf. Blahovisnyk, Rome 1988, pp.
9–11), assured a successor to the Major Archbishop of Lviv in
the person of Most Reverend Myroslav I. Lubachivsky, then Archbishop of Philadelphia (cf. Blahovisnyk, op.cit. p. 31), whom he
then raised to the dignity of a Cardinal, with St. Sophia in Rome
as his titular church (*ibid., pp. 51–52*), and named a Ukrainian
Catholic bishop for Poland. Furthermore, the personal participation of the Holy Father in the jubilee celebrations in Rome of
the Millennium of Rus-Ukraine's Baptism made the world aware
of the persecution and subjugation of the Ukrainian Catholic
Church in the Soviet Union (cf. Blahoviskyk, op.sit. pp. 15–17).

Because of the Holy Father's efforts and the diplomacy of the
Vatican (so often harshly criticized even by our own), the Holy
See was at last able to begin talks between the Ukrainian Catholic and the Russian Orthodox churches by establishing the so
called Quadripartite Commission, in an attempt to ameliorate
relations between the two churches until such time as the Ukrainian Catholic Church is formally legalized. Even though the first
sessions of this Commission were not very successful, nevertheless, after 45 years of persecution, imprisonment, deporta-
tion to Siberia, and the martyrdom of many of our bishops,
priests, and faithful, it was a great step forward.

I am certain that the Holy Father will have the greatest understanding for our wishes and propositions, especially those of
our bishops from Ukraine, so as to bring to a successful conclusion the matter of achieving full freedom for our Ukrainian
Catholic Church in Soviet Union. But we all must admit the
reality of the present situation in Western Ukraine. Our Church
there will exist alongside the churches of our Orthodox brethren, whether they are Russian or Ukrainian Autocephalous. Not
only must we admit this reality, but also, by our labors and by

the example of a Christian-Catholic life, we must be the light of the world, the light of truth and Christian charity.

We Ukrainian Catholic bishops gathered here express to the Holy Father and the Apostolic See "with one heart and mind" our profound gratitude for all their efforts in behalf of the Ukrainian Catholic Church, both in our native lands and in the emigrant communities. We solemnly profess our loyalty, love, and obedience to the successor of St. Peter, while remaining faithful as well to the covenant of St. Volodymyr, and we shall accept humbly the decisions of the Apostolic See and of His Holiness Pope John Paul II, as befits loyal Christian Catholics. We are confident that our Slavic Pope, who understands so well the needs and the endeavors of our Church, will, at an appropriate moment, bestow upon the Ukrainian Catholic Church the hierarchical structure characteristic of the Eastern Churches according to the decree of the Second Vatican Council.

As I finished reading my talk, I heard the Holy Father turning to His Beatitude Lubachivsky who was sitting next to him, saying, "I understood every word of it!"

At that time His Beatitude got up and announced that our bishops from Ukraine had a meeting on March 17, 1990, and prepared fourteen points of their request to the Holy See. This meeting was held immediately after the Quadripartite Commission's work in Lviv. They agreed at that time to the fourteen demands to the Holy See:

1. The Ukrainian Catholic Church, according to the teaching of the Second Vatican Council is a Particular Church,— *Ecclesia Particularis sui iuris*—in the full sense of the word, and so should all Sister Churches regard her. We must not be called communities or groups of faithful of the Eastern Rite.

2. Ukrainian (Greek) Catholic Church is in a permanent union with the Bishop of Rome, the Pastor and Teacher of the Universal Church. By this she acknowledges his leadership, and his primacy throughout the world.

3. The Ukrainian (Greek) Catholic Church is one in Ukraine and in the diaspora, whose Head and Father is His Beatitude Myroslav Ivan Cardinal Lubachivsky, the Major Archbishop of Lviv in Ukraine.

4. For this reason, everything that is proposed by the Delegation of the Holy See as well as by the bishops from Ukraine must be in agreement with the Holy Father and with His Beatitude Myroslav Cardinal Lubachivsky.

5. The Ukrainian (Greek) Catholic Church wishes to live in peace and concordance in the spirit of Christian charity and reconciliation with all churches and faiths and with such feelings her leadership approaches the dialogue in order to achieve a normalization of relationships with the Orthodox Church so that she may gain full legalization in the Soviet Union.

6. The Ukrainian (Greek) Catholic Church condemns all methods of force. At the same time, our Church declares that true dialogue among churches is possible only when it is fully stabilized and when all groundless accusations of force, proselytism, discord, and religious war cease.

7. The position of the Ukrainian (Greek) Catholic Church toward the state authorities is based on the words of Sacred Scripture, "Let everyone obey the authorities that are over him, for there is no authority except from God, and all authority that exists is established by God" (Romans 13:1). For this reason, the Ukrainian (Greek) Catholic Church will re-

spect the authorities as long as they will not go against the Law of God. Ukrainian Catholics wish to be responsible citizens of the state and active participants in the reconstruction and true democracy. As far as our conscience is concerned, let it be known that the Ukrainian (Greek) Catholic Church always was a Church of the Ukrainian people and such she wishes to remain for the future.

8. Great harm was done to the Ukrainian (Greek) Catholic Church since September 17, 1939, by the Stalinists and by the succeeding regimes. For this reason, justice demands that our Church be returned to the status which existed to that date. For the same reason—

- The Cathedral Church of St. George together with the buildings belonging to the complex in Lviv should be returned to the Ukrainian (Greek) Catholic Church.

- Likewise all other Cathedral Churches that belonged in 1939 to the Ukrainian (Greek) Catholic Church should be returned.

- We demand that the Synod of Lviv of March 8–10, 1946, be declared invalid and non-existing.

- All church buildings, chapels, episcopal residences, male and female monasteries, printing shops, schools and rectories which belonged to the Ukrainian (Greek) Catholic Church in 1939 be returned.

- The seminary buildings as well as the Theological Academy buildings, which belonged to her in 1939, are returned.

- All male and female Religious Orders and Communities will have their right as juridical persons.

- The hierarchy, the priests and male and female religious as well as the faithful who suffered during persecution since 1939 due to their membership in the Ukrainian (Greek) Catholic Church be rehabilitated.

- Because the Major Archbishop and Metropolitan of Lviv is forced since 1963 to live in Rome, his return to his see in Lviv should be made possible.

9. The Ukrainian (Greek) Catholic Church is to have all the rights and privileges that other churches have in the Soviet Union in accordance with the new Soviet legislation concerning the freedom of conscience. This means that she will have the right:

   - to be acknowledged as a Church, a juridical person, having the right to own property;

   - to be able to conduct social and charitable activity;

   - to publicly teach religion; and

   - to have access to the mass media of communication.

10. In case of divergence between the Soviet legislation and the international agreements, entered into by the Soviet regime, the rights belonging to the Ukrainian (Greek) Catholic Church will have precedence, namely:

   - Complete freedom of religion;

515

- Public acknowledgement by the state authorities;

- Free admission to the places of worship;

- The right to organize proper hierarchical structure;

- The right to free contacts with the faithful, their communities in our own country as well as with those abroad;

- The right to communicate with the Holy Father, the Pope of Rome and with the Holy See as well as with the Bishops, priests and faithful in diaspora.

All the bishops of the Ukrainian (Greek) Catholic Church will have to be acknowledged by the state government and their names be published in the Vatican *Annuario Pontificio*.

The Ukrainian (Greek) Catholic Church especially demands the right to renew the central Theological Seminary in Lviv for the formation of the future priests. She will likewise have the right to freely send priests and candidates to the priesthood to study in Rome or other places in the western world.

11. After public approval and full legalization, the Ukrainian (Greek) Catholic Church will be guided by Eastern Catholic Canon Law of the Universal Church, and by her own particular law in the creation of Church structures.

12. The leadership of the Ukrainian (Greek) Catholic Church is in the hands of the Major Archbishop with the Synod of Bishops residing in Lviv. As soon as it is possible, the Ukrainian (Greek) Catholic Church will be raised to patriarchal dignity. Then the Patriarch, approved by the Ecumenical Hierarch, and by other particular churches as well as by the

state government will govern his own Church in Ukraine and in the diaspora. Lviv, March 17, 1990."

The bishops approved the "Thirteen Demands." Then His Beatitude Cardinal Lubachivsky reminded the bishops that this Synod should request of the Holy Father to make the episcopal appointment of eparchs and auxiliaries to the existing Eparchies in Ukraine. A discussion commenced among the Bishops on this topic. Some of them claimed that the Holy Father has already appointed the bishops from Ukraine, while others claimed that the Synod should present to the Holy Father the names of candidates for the eparchs and auxiliaries. Then His Beatitude Lubachivsky stated that he has a letter from the Secretary of State, Cardinal Cassaroli, with some demands to the Synod. When some bishops asked him to read the letter to the Synod, he refused to do so since it was addressed to him personally.

After this discussion, the Synodal Fathers elected the candidates as eparchs and auxiliaries of the Ivano-Frankivsk and Uzhorod Eparchies. Then the Holy Father asked that we use this opportunity when all our bishops are present, to likewise elect a terna of candidates for the Lviv Archeparchy. At that Archbishop Sterniuk got up and enthusiastically exclaimed that all of us are ready to do that right now. But someone said, "The luncheon break is coming in several minutes and there will be no time now to finish the election of a terna. We need some time to think as to whom we should elect." So the election of a terna for Lviv to replace Cardinal Lubachivsky, who had already passed the retirement age of 75, was postponed to the afternoon session.

Thus the bishops left the synod and some went to St. Josaphat Seminary and those from Ukraine to our home on Madonna dei Monti 3 Square. Here, after the luncheon, secret deliberations took place, which had decisive impact on the Holy Father's plans for our Church. When at 4:00 P.M. our bishops gathered again in the Old Synodal Hall at the Vatican to continue the work of the Synod, Archbishop Sterniuk stood up and said:

"Your Holiness, we have discussed the matter of the election of a new Major Archbishop and came to the conclusion that right now we cannot approach this very important task for the good of our Church. We need more time to consider this matter more seriously and determine who would be the best for this all-important position. We do not know each other. We are strangers to one another. The special reason for the delay is the fact that our Church in Ukraine is very weakened and ruined by the half-century-long persecution. We cannot hurry this decision."

His Beatitude got up and asked the Holy Father to kindly postpone the elections till September of this year when he will call another Synod for this election only. The Holy Father, not saying anything, just nodded his head as a sign of agreement. With this the Extraordinary Synod called by the Holy Father himself was closed.

The following day all our bishops left Rome to travel back to their homes; only the members of the Presidium remained for their meeting. During the meeting, some of us asked His Beatitude to kindly read to us the letter he received from Cardinal Cassaroli. He did so. The letter stated that it was the request of the Holy Father that the Synod use the occasion when all of the bishops were present including those from Ukraine to elect ternas for the Major Archbishop, for the eparchies of Ivano-Frankivsk and Uzhorod.

His Beatitude proposed that such a Synod be called for the fall of this year. After some exchange of ideas on this topic, it was decided that the Synod be called for September 21–28, 1990, in Rome.

The Elective Synod

His Beatitude Cardinal Lubachivsky did not call the Elective Synod for September 21–28, 1990, as it was decided at the Presidium meeting on June 27, 1990, because he did not wish to retire. The above date of the Synod was proposed by His Beatitude himself to the Holy Father during the session of the Extraordinary Synod June 25–26, 1990, in the Vatican.

Meanwhile, His Beatitude was making plans to return to Lviv, Ukraine, before Easter of 1991. He wrote a letter to the Holy Father on October 16, 1990, asking his blessing for his plans. One of our hierarchs was given a copy of the reply of the Secretary of State to His Beatitude Cardinal Lubachivsky. He gave me the copy of this historical document, which said, in effect, that Cardinal Lubachivsky was to call a Synod of the Ukrainian Catholic Bishops to prepare a list of candidates for the Major Archbishopric of Lviv for the Holy Father.

Before my departure for Rome to take part in this Elective Synod, called by His Beatitude Cardinal Lubachivsky for February 2, 1991, I received from Msgr. Stephen Hrynuck of Olyphant, Pa., a check for the sum of $10,000.00 with a request to give each bishop from Ukraine one-thousand dollars, as an expression of his love for our Suffering Church and her bishops. I cashed the check, wrote separate letters to each bishop, explaining the purpose of the gift and the name and address of the giver. I addressed separate envelopes for each bishop and placed there the letter and $1,000.00 in cash. In my letter I asked each to write a thank-you note to the donor.

In Rome all our bishops resided at a building belonging to our church, located at Madonna dei Monti, 3 Square. In my private conversations with each bishop I tried to sound out as to whom they would prefer as candidates to the terna for Lviv. My effort to make the election easier so as to find some agreement before the Synod was futile. Not one bishop would give me an answer or a suggestion. I insisted that we should come to some kind of consensus before the Synod to secure a success. Then I tried to talk to the bishops from Ukraine. I asked each to come to my room because I had an envelope for him. So I asked one of them, "Who would you prefer as a candidate to the terna for Lviv?" His reply was, "Oh, we have a terna already! Father N.N. from Rome was in Lviv, Ukraine, about a week or so ago, called all of our bishops to a meeting, explained to us the qualifications needed for a major archbishop. We then elected a terna."

My reaction to this news was a shock, but I did not show it. I said, "That is very nice. At least you have done something; you came prepared." Then I made a mistake by telling him what I was thinking. "You know that we have here at the Synod twenty-seven bishops. To be able to elect a terna we need two-thirds of the twenty-seven, which comes to eighteen votes. Each of these eighteen bishops would have to consider him and his brother bishops unworthy or unqualified for him to cast his vote for a priest. Do you think that this is possible?" He thought for a while and said, "I really do not know if it is possible." Then I told him that the bishops from Ukraine acted illegally by electing a terna outside of the Synod. "Your meeting in Lviv without the presence of His Beatitude Lubachivsky and the rest of our Ukrainian Catholic Bishops not being invited, cannot be called a Synod." This bishop left my room and went straight to Father N.N. telling all about our conversation with most probably some exaggeration.

The following day the work of the Synod commenced. One after another candidate was presented for the terna. When discussion started concerning a candidate, he was asked to leave the room, which I think was improper. We went on and on, and no one was able to gain the needed two-thirds vote because the ten bishops from Ukraine comprised more than one-third of all the votes, and without their vote no one could receive the needed amount of votes. Their candidates in turn could not receive the needed amount of votes without the votes of the bishops from outside of Ukraine.

Thus this Elective Synod did not fulfill the will of the Holy Father and did not elect a terna of candidates for the Major Archbishop as a successor to His Beatitude Cardinal Lubachivsky. This failure caused joy to some, but sadness to the rest of us. At that time all the bishops understood why the cardinals, when they assemble to elect a new pope, are locked up in a conclave chapel and kept there until they elect someone. If we, the Ukrainian Bishops, were so locked up, then we would have certainly elected someone.

One priest, situated in a right place with enough intelligence and skills, was able to torpedo not only the plans of all of the Bishops of the Synod, but likewise the plans of the Holy Father himself. The Synodal Fathers went back home with heads bowed, humbled and helpless, not being able to fulfill the mission laid upon them by the Holy Father himself.

My Propositions Pertaining to Liturgical Books

W hen Ukraine became a free and independent nation, we transferred our Synod of Bishops from Rome to Ukraine. The first Synod in Ukraine was held inside the Cathedral of St. George in the city of Lviv from May 16 to 31, 1992, while the bishops resided in the Hotel Dnister nearby. During the second session on May 19, 1992, I presented the following propositions concerning the translation and publication of future liturgical books:

1. "In the present conditions of life our Church in and out of its Homeland must have only one liturgical text. This will serve as a means of unity within our Mother Church.

2. These texts must be full and faithful translations into the living Ukrainian literary language of all liturgical books, published for our Church by the Apostolic See of Rome.

3. In the translation of the liturgical books, published by the Apostolic See from the Church Slavonic to the Ukrainian, no one has the right to make any kind of changes, correc-

tions, or omissions without written permission from the Apostolic See (cf. Circular Letter to the Ukrainian Ordinaries from the Congregation for the Eastern Churches, prot. # 1219/28, Rome September 10, 1941) *The Code of Canons of the Eastern Churches* prescribes the following: "The approval of the liturgical texts, after prior review of the Apostolic See, is reserved in patriarchal Churches to the patriarch with the consent of the synod of bishops of the patriarchal Church." (*Canon 657.1*) Another canon (668.2) states that outside of the patriarch and the synod of bishops "no other person can add to, remove, or modify (in the liturgical texts) that which was established by this authority." Canon 656.1 decrees: "Only books with ecclesiastical approval may be used in liturgical celebrations."

4.   The Ukrainian translation of the liturgical books, published by the Apostolic See, after prior review of the Apostolic See, should be approved by the Major Archbishop with the consent of the Synod of Bishops."

After some discussion on the above propositions, the Synodal Fathers unanimously voted their approval.

But all my efforts to bring harmony and order into the liturgical life of our Church were made in vain. My propositions, although based on the law of the Church, will remain only in the Minute Books of the Synod. In order for them to have legal power they have to be promulgated by the Major Archbishop, according to the prescriptions of the Code, canon 112.1. Without such promulgation, all the decisions of the Synod are legally non-existing and non-obligatory. At the time of the 1992 Synod, we already had five Synods, whose decisions had not been promulgated. For this reason, all ecclesiastical legal power of the Synod of Bishops was practically paralyzed, as though we had no Synod at all. All that was left to our Synod was the power to elect candidates for the episcopacy.

Contrary to all the prescriptions of the Church law, the curia of His Beatitude, with his consent or without it, published in Lviv a new Ukrainian translation of the Liturgy of St. John Chrysostom in 1996 without the consent of the Synod of Bishops and ordered the priests of the Lviv Archeparchy to use it.

Unfortunately this situation is not new in our Church. In the 1920s there was a similar situation. Metropolitan Andrew Sheptytsky tried to eliminate from our liturgical texts Latin elements that in the past were adopted to prove that "we, too, are Catholics." He could not reach the consent of his brother bishops. After long debates, one bishop left the meeting. Then Metropolitan Sheptytsky gave the whole matter over to the Congregation for the Eastern Churches in the Vatican, requesting that they form a liturgical commission for this purpose. They did so, and as a result the Holy See published a whole set of our liturgical books in the Church Slavonic language early in the 1940s together with an "*Ordo Celebrationis.*"

Synod of Bishops 1995

In order to mark the 400th Anniversary of our Church's union with the Apostolic See of Rome, a Synod of Bishops took place in Rome. It was Pope Clement VIII who received two bishops-delegates of the Kievan Metropolitan on December 23, 1595, and accepted our Church into the full union with the Western Church. Because the date of December 23 was too close to Christmas, the Synod was planned one month ahead so as to open the Jubilee Year of the Brest Union.

The Synod was held in the quarters next to the church of Saints Sergius and Bacchus on Madonna dei Monti, 3 Square. Pope Urban VIII gave these buildings and the church itself to our Church on May 12, 1639. It later became a sort of an Embassy of our Church in Rome, and later on the Seminary of St. Josaphat.

The Major Archbishop, Cardinal Myroslav Ivan Lubachivsky on Thursday, November 16, 1995, with a hierarchial Divine Liturgy, opened the Synod. There were thirty-one bishops as concelebrants with several priests and a deacon. Absent were: Metropolitan-emeritus Hermaniuk of Winnipeg; Archbishop Sterniuk of Lviv; Bishop-emeritus Prasko from Australia; and Joseph Holovach, the auxiliary of Uzhorod.

In his homily after the reading of the Gospel, His Beatitude Cardinal Lubachivsky gave an outline of the goals of the Synod.

After a half century of the underground existence, our Church stands over a great ruin, caused by the atheistic Soviet government. Our priests have to face spiritual and moral poverty, deficiency of respect for human beings and for life itself, a disjointed and sick society. It is our duty to give our priests and the religious a fundamental formation so that they may become faithful and genuine preachers. Our people have to be trained in an ecumenical spirit so they may fulfill the will of God and achieve unity with our Orthodox brothers.

After his homily, he waved to me to take his place as the main celebrant at the altar, while he went behind the altar and sat down. He came back for the Consecration, for Holy Communion, and for the dismissal. One could observe that the 81-year-old Cardinal Lubachivsky was failing and was pale.

The first session of this Synod began at 4:00 P.M. of that day. Following a prayer to the Holy Spirit, His Beatitude welcomed the bishops and read his introductory talk. Afterward he asked me to conduct the session. I thanked him for the honor and, having established that we had the required quorum, I asked for the approval of the agenda of the Synod. There were only a few minor remarks and the agenda was approved.

The first one who asked for the floor was Bishop Basil Losten. I asked him whether he wanted to address the Synod on anything concerning the agenda. He said, "No!" Then we needed a vote of at least one-third of the present to assent for him to talk on something that does not pertain to the agenda. By raising their hands the bishops gave him their consent. Bishop Basil then stood up and read his talk clearly and slowly.

Your Beatitude, Your incessant labors, your peaceful lovingness, suffering, and your deep prayer life always were and will remain for us as examples of service of a true Good Shepherd.

In this decisive moment, enlightened by the Holy Spirit, we must with all responsibility, direct our Church to a hopeful way of her future. There is no doubt that the problems and the dangers, which jeopardize the very existence and the natural development of our Church, have reached such forms that they demand from the leadership dynamic and planned decisions.

With fear we observe that there is always deeper loss of contact among us in the diaspora with the Church in Ukraine and her head. It is his duty to maintain unity and living contacts among the entire membership of the Church.

We are deeply troubled likewise with the fact that our Church is not responsive to many needs and duties which are placed before her by the contemporary conditions in Ukraine.

Your Beatitude, looking realistically at your advanced age, at the state of your health, and, having before our eyes exclusively the good of our Church and of the souls entrusted into our care, we implore you to consider the highest good of our Church, having behind you the great and illustrious leaders, the blood of the martyrs and of confessors and the expectations as well as the needs of the future generations. You hear the opinions of all of us, bishops, gathered here, and request from His Holiness, the Pope, to relieve you from your duties, and at the same time to open a door that our Church be led according to the will of God by your worthy successor.

We hope that you, conscious of the seriousness of this historic moment, having accepted our petition, will give a chance to our Church to respond to the challenges which our present time placed before her.

At the same time, we wish to express to you our sincere recognition and gratitude for all you have done, our filial love for you, and a pledge of our prayers for you.

As a result of this appeal, some bishops asked that by the raising of our hands we might express our opinion as to whether His Beatitude should resign. I did stress that this was not a vote. It would not be obligatory to anyone. It's only a poll—a method of consideration of an option. An absolute majority raised their hands signifying that he should resign.

His Beatitude Lubachivsky then stated that he would not resign so as not to establish a precedent. "My predecessor, Metropolitan Andrew Sheptytsky, even though he was in a wheelchair for fourteen years, did not resign. Likewise Patriarch Josyf Cardinal Slipyj, even though he was very old and ailing, did not resign."

At that time I asked the bishops for permission to talk outside of the agenda:

> "The interpretation of canon 210 of our Code presently is such that the patriarchs and major archbishops have no obligation to resign when they reach the age of 75. The Code likewise does not permit the appointment of a vicar to a patriarch or a major archbishop. Yet in one case recently the Apostolic See has introduced a position of a *patriarchal auxiliary* with delegated faculties. Such an auxiliary is a bishop, elected by the Synod of Bishops. He cooperates with a major archbishop, represents him and acts in his name.

I proposed that His Beatitude, not wishing to resign, ask the Holy See for permission for this Synod to elect such a patriarchal auxiliary with delegated faculties. Since such an office is not in the present Code of Law, we need permission of the Apostolic See.

His Beatitude was silent, and the bishops asked again for a vote by raising of hands whether he should accept such an auxiliary. An absolute majority was for it. Then His Beatitude gave consent to accept such a patriarchal auxiliary and stated that he would ask the Apostolic See later for permission in this case. Then he said that his wishes were that Bishop N.N. be elected to this post. The Synod by secret ballot did elect said Bishop. The following day, however, His Beatitude revoked his consent to have Bishop N.N., elected by the Synod, as his auxiliary. Then Bishop N.N. humbly resigned from his elected post, and I asked the bishops to vote whether they accepted his resignation. They did accept it. I then gave the following proposition:

"With your permission, Your Beatitude, I propose that each of the Synodal Fathers write on a voting ballot the name of him whom he considers before God as the most worthy candidate for the post of a patriarchal auxiliary. In the second balloting we will vote only on the two names that have received the most votes. I ask that you do not vote for me, because I will not accept the position due to my age."

His Beatitude agreed to my proposition and a secret ballot commenced. Then, in the second balloting, to elect one of the two with highest votes. This was done. Now, His Beatitude had to have an approval from the Apostolic See for the election of his auxiliary with delegated faculties. This never happened and the election became null and void.

A Usurpation of the Major Archbishop's Powers

During the 1995 Synod in Rome, the so-called "Statutes of the Patriarchal Curia of the Ukrainian Greek-Catholic Church" was presented for the approval by the Synod. On the title page of these "Statutes" under an inscription, "Approved" by the Patriarch—Major Archbishop of the Ukrainian Greek-Catholic Church, was the hand-written signature by +*Myroslav I. Cardinal Lubachivsky,* Lviv 1995. Above the signature was impressed a personal seal of His Beatitude. We were told that these Statutes were prepared on the demand of the Government of Ukraine for the official registration of our Church.

Each bishop took these Statutes with him to get acquainted with them before the scheduled time for discussion came. I was asked to give a commentary on these Statutes. As a matter of fact, I received a copy of these Statutes about two weeks earlier in Philadelphia and had plenty of time to study them and prepare a commentary.

"The introduction to the Statutes may be characterized as follows: "The Statutes" contradict the law of the Church in many of its articles. And so, e.g., art. 49 states, "Curia is a juridical person . . . ." The Patriarchal or the Major Archbishop's Church or each Eparchy—is a juridical person, but never the workers of the Patriarch's office. (Cf. canons 920–930) The Code of Canons of the Eastern Churches does not know an instrument such as "The Statutes" of Episcopal, Metropolitan, or Major Archbishop's Curia. (cf. canon 114) But e.g. a tribunal should have its own statutes. (cf. canon 1070) This is because a Curia is not a juridical person, independent from a patriarch, major archbishop or the Church. This is why these "Statutes" represent a document that has no basis in the Church law, i.e., in the CCEC, and as such contradicts the Church law and gives a wrong concept of our Church to the Government of Ukraine.

If, according to the Church law, a curia is not a juridical person, then consequently the actions of such a curia have no valid juridical value. The power of a patriarch or a major archbishop is ordinary, *potestas ordinaria,* i.e., united to the person and to his office from the moment of his installation. (cf. canon 77.1) This ordinary power of a patriarch is his own—"*potestas propria,*" (cf. canon 78.1) i.e., it is performed by his own right and not as a vicar, a representative of the Pope of Rome or of the Bishops of the Patriarchal Church. This power is also personal in a sense that it is united to the person of a patriarch. He cannot delegate his power to anyone else for the whole Church or for all the cases—*ad universitatem causarum.* This is why a patriarch may not appoint his vicar for the whole Church. He may, however, appoint a vicar for his own eparchy (cf. canon 101) in order to help him with the administration of his eparchy. This canonical prohibition to appoint a vicar with full powers is based on a principle, which maintains that it is not in the spirit of the law that someone who was not elected by the Synod of Bishops of a patriarchal Church had full patriarchal powers. Thus, the above-named "Statutes," which delegates to the Chancellor all administrative powers of the Major Archbishop, contradicts the above quoted norms of canon 71.1, and therefore it is invalid.

In art. 32.2 of the Statutes it is written, "The Chancellor may act without authorization in the name of the Curia, to represent her in all organizations and offices." To act without authorization in the name of the Curia is wrong, because the Curia is not a juridical person, and therefore may never act in its own name, but only in the name of the patriarch or major archbishop. If so, then the term "without authorization" is a non-canonical term because the power of a patriarch is personal (cf. canon 78.1) which cannot be delegated.

I, therefore, propose that this Synod by secret ballot reject these Statutes and ask His Beatitude Myroslav I. Cardinal Lubachivsky that, for the good of the Church, he recall these Statutes from the Government of Ukraine and appoint a commission, comprised of two bishops with canonical degrees, two priests—canonists, two laymen—civil lawyers, that they prepare Statutes of the Major Archbishop's Curia."

The Synod rejected the Statutes by unanimous vote. These same Statutes reached the Congregation for the Eastern Churches in the Vatican. They, in turn, gave them to their canonical consultants who wrote a commentary. Their commentary was comparable to mine in all points. The Congregation wrote a letter to Cardinal Lubachivsky through the Papal Nuncio in Kiev, Archbishop Antonio Franco. I received a copy of this letter from a priest friend of mine in Lviv:

"Kiev, December 14, 1995. A copy of "The Statutes of the Patriarchal Curia" was given to the Congregation for the Eastern Churches for its consideration.

"The Congregation has given it to an expert for an examination. The expert gave his remarks, which I enclose here. He gave his opinion concerning the Statutes and declared that these Statues contain serious deviations from the canonical norms.

"The Congregation for the Eastern Churches has asked me to inform you that there is a need of making a new project, which should be prepared by a commission, comprised of Bishops and experts in law of your Major Archbishop's Church. The new project is to be given to the Synod of Bishops for discussion and approval, and then given to the Apostolic See for verification.

"In my former letter pertaining to the "Statutes of the Greek-Catholic Church," which should be given to the Government in Kiev for a juridical recognition of Church properties, I wrote that such Statutes should not contain norms, which would contradict the canons of the CCEC. Should such Statutes be already registered, they should be exchanged with a new corrected text.

"On this occasion I send Your Eminence my deep respect. +Antonio Franco."

No commission was ever appointed pertaining to the new draft of the Statutes and the Synod of Bishops never received a copy of the new draft. The Chancellor would not permit that, and it seems he thought he did not have to obey the Apostolic See nor the Synod of Bishops. Some time later, when Bishop Husar was elected an auxiliary with delegated faculties, I asked him for a copy of the new Statutes. He did send a copy to me. The new Statutes are called, "The Statutes of the Directive Center of the Patriarchal Curia of the Ukrainian Greek-Catholic Church." On the cover page there is a seal and a signature of His Beatitude as well as a seal of the "State Committee on the Religious Matters," registered # 4/3 dated May 5, 1996, chairman of the Committee A. Kowal. The content of these Statutes is in no way like its predecessor.

Jubilee of the Union of Brest

When the Ukrainian Catholic Bishops had an audience with the Holy Father on August 24, 1995, he expressed his desire to participate in the celebration of the Jubilee of the Brest Union by celebrating a Hierarchical Divine Liturgy with our bishops at the Basilica of St. Peter in the Vatican the next year in order to thank God not only for the grace of the Jubilee, but also for all the graces that God had showered upon the Ukrainian people in the last 400 years.

The Jubilee celebrations took place in Rome July 6–7, 1996. The program of the celebrations lasted four days. I arrived in Rome with Bishop Paska Friday, July 5, 1996. This same day at 5:00 P.M. on the grounds before St. Sophia Church, a Moleben to the Blessed Mother took place. The three Metropolitans were at a small altar, placed on a platform before the entrance to the church, while the rest of the bishops and priests, standing in two rows, concelebrated. Father Ivan Muzychka gave a well-prepared and historically based homily. This same day at 11:00 A.M. a press conference was held in the Vatican led by Bishop Lubomyr Husar and Father Athanasius Pekar, OSBM.

Saturday morning, July 6, 1996, I visited the Congregation for Eastern Churches, paying my respects to the prefect, Achille Cardinal Silvestrini, the Secretary Archbishop Myroslav Marusyn and Msgr. George Dzudzar. In the evening of the same day we celebrated another Moleben to the Blessed Mother in the Basilica of St. Peter before the side altar dedicated to the Mother of God. The Holy Father presided. His Beatitude Lubachivsky welcomed the Holy Father in Ukrainian while Bishop Sophronius Mudry, OSBM, translated his talk into Italian. There was an unusually joyful and prayerful atmosphere during the Moleben. To the male choir from Lviv, whose prayerful music, due at least in part, added much to the ambience.

I was standing close to the Holy Father and was thus able to observe the impression the Moleben made on him. His entire being was submerged in prayer, and his prayerful concentration was passed to others who were there. One could not help but pray, and for me this one Moleben was an unforgettable prayerful union with God through Mary. After the Moleben, when the Holy Father left, we stayed for a rehearsal with the Pontifical Master of Ceremonies for the following day's Liturgy.

Sunday, July 7, 1996. We were in the famous Basilica of St. Peter, the largest church in Christendom, which was filled that day to capacity. At 9:00 A.M. the procession commenced, led by cross and candle bearers, followed by about 200 priests in full liturgical vestments. Then followed the bishops, the metropolitans— all in like liturgical vestments. Behind the bishops was His Beatitude Myroslav Ivan Cardinal Lubachivsky in a wheelchair pushed by Father Ivan Dacko. At the end walked His Holiness Pope John Paul II. The priests were stationed to the left of the main altar, while the Holy Father sat on his throne in the center in front of the altar, His Beatitude next to him, and the bishops to the right and the left of him in a semi-circle.

I was chosen to commence the celebration of the Liturgy by blessing the four sides of the world with lighted candles on double and triple candelabras. Standing on the platform in front of the main altar that is over the grave of St. Peter, with trembling voice and a heart full of emotions, I sang the verse, *"O, Lord, O Lord, look down from heaven and see . . ."* I was deeply moved by this honor given me as the senior Metropolitan, due to the health of His Beatitude.

There were thirty-three of our bishops concelebrating the Liturgy, standing on both sides of the altar, while His Beatitude and the three Metropolitans were in front of the altar with the Holy Father. In attendance were fifteen cardinals, many bishops, and the diplomatic corps of the Vatican, and the Ukrainian ambassador to Italy, Anatol Orel. There were about three thousand faithful from Ukraine and the diaspora.

The Holy Father gave a homily, speaking in Ukrainian and in Italian. Fifty of our priests distributed Holy Communion. A combined choir from Lviv sang the responses in a professional manner, filling the huge Basilica with Ukrainian music and Church hymns. Thus the Ukrainian Catholic Church gloriously celebrated its Jubilee, thanking God together with the successor to St. Peter for all the blessings and graces that the Union with Rome gave our people throughout the centuries.

All could notice that the Holy Father paid special attention to His Beatitude Cardinal Lubachivsky. Although the cardinal could not walk anymore, he could stand, holding onto the altar. On one occasion when he had to turn to face the congregation, he almost fell, but the Holy Father supported him.

In the evening of the same memorable day, there was a concert in the Paul VI Aula. In the middle of the concert, the Holy Father came in unexpectedly. All present welcomed him warmly with standing applause.

A Solution to the Leadership Problem

rchbishop Antonio Franco, Apostolic Nuncio to Kiev, was working hard to find a solution to the leadership problem of our Church. During our 1995 Synod in Rome, he was able to convince Pope John Paul II, to validate the illegally conferred episcopal ordinations of Lubomyr Husar and Ivan Choma seventeen years earlier by Cardinal Slipyj. The Holy Father lifted the suspension which both of them had incurred. For all these many years he had refused to validate their ordinations, because their ordination took place without the canonically required permission of the Pope. The Synod of 1995 was asked by the Holy See for its consent to have the two bishops' ordination validated. There was no problem in that. The bishops had no objections against either one. Thus the Synod did give such consent by secret ballot.

The next step of the Nuncio was a letter to all the Ukrainian Catholic Bishops, dated August 8, 1996:

"On the request of His Eminence Cardinal Angelo Sodano, the Secretary of State, I am enclosing a letter, addressed to the Synodal Fathers of the Ukrainian Catholic Church. Enclosed likewise is an official translation (into Ukrainian) of the above-named letter. The original of this letter will be given to the Synodal assembly for the Synodal archives.

"I wish also to inform you that His Eminence Cardinal Sodano, simultaneously with the above named letter, is sending another letter to Cardinal Lubachivsky, the Major Archbishop of Lviv . In that letter he asks the Major Archbishop to present to the Synod two or three candidates from among whom the Synod may elect one, who will be accepted by him and the majority of the bishops.

"I assure you of my prayers during the period of preparations for the Synod, asking the good Lord to aid each one of you to make a right decision for the good of the Greek-Catholic Church in possibly the best way under present circumstances.

"I remain with deep respect and warm greetings, yours in Christ, + Antonio Franco."

The letter of Cardinal Sodano:

The Secretariat of State, Vatican, August 18, 1996, # 6009/96 RS. To the Archbishops and Bishops, members of the Synod of the Ukrainian Church.

Your Excellency, the recent celebrations of the 400th Jubilee of the Union of Brest have filled the heart of His Holiness with joy. Once again through me he expresses his kinship with your Church, thanking the Lord for the gift of faithfulness to the Throne of St. Peter and for the witness of love to the Church, which Christ wished to see one, holy, catholic, and apostolic.

The presence in Rome on that occasion of the majority of the bishops permitted His Holiness to learn more deeply of the present conditions of your Church and of her needs for the future.

In this regard the Holy Father noted as the first indispensable priority for His Beatitude Myroslav Ivan Cardinal Lubachivsky to have the help of a bishop for more effective execution of his episcopal ministry. With this purpose the Holy Father asked me to hear the opinion of the Congregation for the Eastern Churches and to ask all of the Most Reverend Synodal Fathers to elect at the next Synod in the month of October a bishop who could give a suitable help to the Major Archbishop in the administration of the Lviv Archeparchy and in the execution of his responsibilities for the Ukrainian Church.

The above named bishop has to be elected from among the candidates presented by His Beatitude Cardinal Lubachivsky. This will assure a better coordination of their activity.

The elected bishop could be appointed by this Synod an Auxiliary of the Major Archbishop and likewise an Executive Secretary of the Synod of the Ukrainian Church. This will make it possible for him to coordinate in the name of the Major Archbishop and with the delegated powers the pastoral as well as the administrative work concerning the questions pertaining to Ukrainian Catholic Church.

I am certain that the Bishops, who will meet at the next Synod, will accept this fraternal appeal of the Roman Pontiff, which is dictated by the solicitude for the good of the beloved Ukrainian Church.

On this day I also wrote to the Major Archbishop, asking him in the name of the Holy Father to present to the next Synod the names of the candidates, who would be able to help him in the future.

Grateful for the attention, which you gave this letter, I send you my greetings and wishes for everything best in your pastoral endeavors. With deep respect I remain sincerely yours in the Lord, +*Angelo Cardinal Sodano.*

From all the above I was satisfied that my proposition at the Synod in November of 1995, to give His Beatitude an auxiliary with delegated faculties, was accepted by the Apostolic See as the only solution. In all the plans as presented in the above letters I saw someone's cunning hand. That person must have gained the confidence of the Nuncio and with him planned the whole scheme.

All our bishops were in agreement that His Beatitude needed someone to help him. Due to his age and illness, many things were neglected. The decisions of so many Synods had not been promulgated. While the chancellor of the Major Archbishop could have done that very easily, most probably he did not agree with the decisions of the Synod and therefore would not cooperate. The minutes of the Synods were falsified. "The Statutes of the Patriarchal Curia" by means of which the chancellor usurped all of the powers of the Major Archbishop were not at that time corrected.

But most of the bishops were very much disturbed by the letter of Cardinal Sodano dated August 18, 1996, by which the canonical rights of the Synod to present candidates for the elections were illegally curtailed. If the Synodal Fathers are forbidden to present candidates, then they are not a Synod anymore but just a seal; they are not a governing body, but only tools in someone's hands. Cardinal Sodano contradicts the Code of Canons and gives the right to present candidates to only the Major Archbishop. In the Nuncio's letter this right has been further limited to only "two or three" candidates.

Bishops Synod in Lviv 1996

The first session of a Major Episcopal Asssembly took place in Lviv from October 6–10, 1996. Then October 12–13, 1996, was dedicated to the closing of the Jubilee Year of the Union of Brest celebrations. Saturday, October 12th a special Jubilee Concert was held at the Opera Theatre. Sunday a Hierarchical Divine Liturgy was celebrated on the grounds before the Opera Theatre. A high platform was built before the entrance to the Theatre to serve as a sanctuary. The main celebrant of the Liturgy was Metropolitan Michael Bzdel, CSsR of Winnipeg, while the rest of the bishops concelebrated, standing to the right and the left of the platform, away from the altar. Present were also Cardinal Silvestrini as a Papal Legate, Nuncio Antonio Franco, and five Latin Bishops from Ukraine. They were vested in full liturgical Latin Vestments. The Master of Ceremonies asked the Latin Hierarchs to stand behind the altar. This created an impression they were the celebrants, although they could not even concelebrate since they did not know the Ukrainian language of the Liturgy. The huge grounds, as well as the streets on both sides of the grounds, were filled with the faithful. The official count was nearly fifteen thousand people.

After the Liturgy a festive banquet took place at the Dnister Hotel. Following the banquet, Cardinal Silvestrini invited the three Metropolitans to his hotel room. The Nuncio, Antonio Franco, was there also. The Cardinal welcomed us and told us the Nuncio wished to speak to us.

The Nuncio apparently had a copy of a letter of the Metropolitans addressed to the Congregation dated September 10, 1996. He tried to convince us that the proposition of Cardinal Sodano, contained in his letter addressed to all of our bishops, was the only proper solution to the problem. To the protests of the Metropolitans that it contradicted the Code of Canons to deny the Fathers of the Synod the right to present candidates, he did not reply, but rather changed the subject. In speaking to us, he raised his voice as though talking to little children and stubbornly maintained that Bishop Husar was the only capable candidate for this position. All three of us stated that we had no objection to Husar's candidacy, but we seriously objected to the illegal methods used, which contradict the norms of the Code of Canon Law. Such a vociferous tirade lasted well beyond an hour. All three of us were exhausted, left the room, and tried to rest a bit.

The following day all our bishops concelebrated a Divine Liturgy at St. George's Cathedral. His Beatitude did not celebrate public Liturgies anymore. He asked me to be the main celebrant and to read his homily.

In the afternoon at 4:00 P.M. the first session took place in the spacious dining room of the Metropolitan's residence of St. George. His Beatitude invited Cardinal Silvestrini, Nuncio Antonio Franco, and Msgr. George Dzudzar, who acted as a translator from Italian to Ukrainian.

After an opening prayer to the Holy Spirit, His Beatitude read his remarks. He welcomed Cardinal Silvestrini and Nuncio Franco. He then tried to explain the letter of Cardinal Sodano dated August 18, 1996. He concluded with the following statement:

> With the election of my auxiliary with delegated faculties, all my collaborators and helpers will be released of their duties.

This concerns all those who worked here for the Lviv Archeparchy as well as those who worked for the Patriarchal Curia. For a peaceful conduct of current matters all persons holding positions such as auxiliary bishops, priests, religious sisters and lay persons in the offices of the Lviv Archeparchy and in the Patriarchal Curia will continue to perform their duties until the elected auxiliary with delegated faculties will appoint with my approval new persons.

At that moment the metropolitans looked at each other and understood that these last remarks of His Beatitude were elicited by the letter of the metropolitans dated September 10, 1996, to the Congregation for the Eastern Churches.

After an introductory word by Cardinal Silvestrini, Nuncio Antonio Franco took the floor. Before he could speak, some bishops demanded a reply from him as to why are we denied our canonical rights to present candidates at this election? On what canonical grounds is this being done? This is simple lawlessness, which should never take place in the Catholic Church. This made him very angry, and with a raised voice he maintained that Cardinal Sodano, as the Secretary of State, has the right to make such a legal adjustment in this case. This is why in his letter he clearly states that only His Beatitude Lubachivsky has a right to propose candidates.

Being angry and upset, the Nuncio gave a thunderous speech, waving his hands. He spoke down to us as though we were some rambunctious children and not his brother bishops. He declared our Synod of 1995 illegal, without explaining why. Unfamiliar with the Ukrainian language, he spoke in Italian while Msgr. George Dzudzar translated it into Ukrainian. All our bishops were under the impression that he had been consistent with one-sided half truths. Someone had to continuously misinform him, giving him one-sided and half-true information.

In his passionate speech, the Nuncio, it seemed, not only wanted to convince us, but also to frighten us so that we would vote the way he wanted us to vote. He spoke so much nonsense that it is not worthy of commentary. But when he stated, "Our Church is deeply divided, filled with gossip, because it bears the wounds of the past," it was already too much. I then felt pain in my heart. With such offensive and false statements, he offended all of us who love our Church and gave our lives to serve the Church.

Do the accusations by the Nuncio that "our Church is deeply divided, filled with gossip" refer to the Synod of Bishops or also to other clergy and the faithful? If he refers to the bishops only, then he is very mistaken. I participated in five World Synods of Bishops in which bishops from all over the world participated. I likewise participated in the semi-annual conferences of US Catholic Bishops. On the basis of this vast experience, I am convinced that among our Ukrainian Catholic Bishops there is more unanimity, harmony, agreement, cooperation, and fraternal charity than among the Latin bishops. There is no division among our bishops as to the conservatives and liberals or those who quietly demand the ordination of women as priests, or those who prefer "inclusive language" in the Liturgy and the Scriptures so as to please the feminists. Such generalized accusations represent grievous calumny and deep injury to the good name of our bishops as well as to the whole Church.

Should his accusation refer to our clergy and the faithful, then it is unfounded and, therefore, even more injurious. Are there among the clergy and the faithful of the Italian, German, or American Church fewer divisions and less gossip than among the Ukrainians? Should they have lived through a half-century of a liquidation of their Church, imprisonments, oppression, and persecution for their Catholic faith, the catacomb existence and martyrdom, I doubt if they would have retained their Catholic faith and the loyalty to the Apostolic See better than did the Ukrainians.

This is why such a generalized accusation of our martyred Church made by a high ranking member of the Roman Curia is a grievous insult, a deep injury, and an abasement of our Church and national dignity deeply felt by all of our bishops.

That this false and deeply injurious accusation made by the Apostolic Nuncio in order to confuse and frighten our bishops so that they would not demand any longer their right to present their candidates, achieved its goal. The bishops gave up their demands. Cardinal Silvestrini, the Nuncio and Msgr. George Dzudzar left the meeting room. Cardinal Lubachivsky presented Bishop Lubomyr Husar and Bishop Julian Voronowsky as his candidates for the post of his auxiliary with delegated faculties. Actually there was only one qualified candidate, Bishop Husar. Voronowsky refused to accept the candidacy, but on the insistence of Lubachivsky and his friends, he agreed to it. He knew well that his candidacy was placed only to have an appearance of an election. Actually there was no election as such, because there was only one qualified candidate—Husar. When there is only one candidate, there is no selection, therefore no election, but only an imposition or an appointment of a candidate.

A Memorandum

During and after the Synod, the bishops exchanged their ideas and impressions. Each one of them felt a certain pain in his heart, a degradation, and a feeling of anger caused by an offence. All considered the Nuncio's address as a cruel attack and a brutal rape of the will of the Synod. The Metropolitans and some others suggested that we must react to the Nuncio's behavior. For preservation of the historical truth it is imperative that a memorandum be prepared, signed by the three Metropolitans, and mailed directly to the Holy Father and to the Prefect of the Congregation for the Eastern Churches.

Such a memorandum was prepared and signed by the Metropolitans Michael Bzdel and Stephen Sulyk; Metropolitan Ivan Martyniak was not home at that time. The full text of the memorandum was mailed to him, and after his return he gave his consent to it.

A Memorandum

Previously we expressed our concerns and apprehensions concerning the Synod of the Ukrainian Catholic Bishops in a memorandum dated 10 September 1996, addressed to Your Eminence.

Now that the Synod has been held, we feel we should submit for your gracious consideration a follow-up memorandum concerning this Synod. Your Eminence, since you yourself were present at the first part of the Synod, 14 October 1996, certainly you were able to draw your own conclusions. However, we would like to provide you with some reflections of the bishops as they were expressed during the days that followed.

A major handicap was the total lack of preparation for the Synod.

Since September 1995 there was only one meeting of the Permanent Synod, which was held in July 1996. And since all authority has been usurped by the protégés of the Major Archbishop, no one else was able to prepare matters for the Synod. The program and agenda of the Synod was determined from day to day by the Synod itself. The Code of Canons of the Eastern Churches requires, *After hearing the members of the synod of bishops of the patriarchal Church, the patriarch is also to prepare the agenda to be observed in examining questions as well as to submit it for approval at the opening session of the synod. During the synod of bishops of the patriarchal Church, individual bishops can add other questions to those on the agenda if at least one-third of the members present at the synod consent.* (Canon 108,2.3) This procedure was not followed. Consequently, the results are less than desirable.

However the most distressing part of the Synod was the role played by the Apostolic Nuncio, Archbishop Antonio Franco. First, his presence would be only required if, *"To expedite certain matters, according to the norm of particular law or with the consent of the permanent synod, others can be invited by the patriarch ..."* (Canon 102,3 CCEC) We are not certain that the canonical procedure for inviting Archbishop Antonio Franco was followed unless his attendance was by the express order of the Apostolic See.

Archbishop Franco high-handedly railroaded the election of an auxiliary bishop with special powers for the ailing Major Archbishop. He talked down at the bishops—those who are responsible before God for this particular *ecclesia sui iuris*. His demeanor was condescending and his remarks were insulting to us as brother bishops.

Our bishops were not opposed to the candidacy of Bishop Lubomyr Husar. They were, however, in opposition to the very methods of conducting the election. The election itself was canonically questionable since it was not a free election, but was rather an "imposition," as one of the bishops publicly stated. Since only one serious candidate was presented, there was no choice, therefore, no election. Yes, there was a second candidate. However, the "so-called" second candidate, i.e., Bishop Julian Voronowsky, could not be considered a serious candidate for this position since he has no seminary formation and no theological schooling. To present him to the Synod as a candidate equaled an offense to the intelligence of the Synodal Fathers. His candidacy was symbolic and a blatant example of tokenism to give an appearance of an election. The remarks are in no way meant to be derogatory of Bishop Julian or to impugn his character in any way, but his name was used solely to create the appearance of an election.

Thus, the so-called "election" was at best only a ratification, and at worse an extortion. How in the world can this election be justified canonically? The consciences of the bishops were violated. One the younger bishops charitably labeled it as "Vatican paternalism." Most of the bishops did not look upon it as kindly. We feel that a case could be made about the canonical validity of the election in question. The bishops were not allowed to submit candidates. They were forced to vote for the only candidate. This kind of election was practiced only in the former Soviet Union.

The Code of Canons for the Eastern Churches is very clear about the procedures for the election of bishops. There are several canons concerning election procedures that are applicable and were specifically violated in this case.

First, there is no provision in the Code of Canons for an 'appointment' of an auxiliary to a Major Archbishop. Since the Synod was convoked for the purpose of 'electing' an auxiliary, it would be logical and canonical for the procedures for synodal election to be followed.

Concerning the election of bishops, the following canon summarizes the guiding principle each bishop is commanded in conscience to follow in the election: "*The bishops are freely to elect the one whom before all others they consider worthy and suitable before the Lord.*" (Canon 183.2)

This principle should be the guiding principle in the election of an auxiliary to the Major Archbishop. However, if the "one whom before all others they consider worthy and suitable before the Lord" cannot be nominated for election, how, in good conscience before Almighty God, can a bishop follow this guiding principle?

Canon 181.1 CCEC provides *bishops inside the territorial boundaries of the patriarchal Church are nominated to a vacant see or to fulfill another function by canonical election according to the norms of cann. 947–957, unless otherwise provided in common law.* Therefore, for valid and canonical election the provisions of canons 947–957 must be followed.

In the procedures for the election of an auxiliary with special powers during the October 1996 Synod of the Ukrainian Catholic bishops, the bishops were prevented from nominating candidates during the election. By what canonical right can a bishop be prevented from nominating a candidate during a Synodal election? Such a restriction is uncanonical and raises doubt about the validity of an election. Canon 952 CCEC clearly states this fact: *If the freedom in an election was impaired in any way whatever, the election is invalid by the law itself.*

There is also the question of the entreaties of others to us bishops to violate our conscience and "go along" with this "pseudo-election."

"A vote is null, unless it is fee. Therefore, a vote is invalid if an elector has been coerced directly or indirectly by grave fear or by fraud to vote for a certain person or persons adjunctively." (canon 954.1 CCEC) If we could not propose candidates, how "free" is our vote? If we are entreated by the Vatican nuncio to act and vote in a certain manner, how "free" is our vote? And, if our vote was not "free," it is null and void.

If and when our Orthodox brethren find out about this election, what will be their reaction? Will they once again ridicule our *sui iuris* Church, as really not self-governing, and that our Synod of Bishops is controlled and manipulated by the nuncio, contrary to ecclesiastical law and our status as a Major Archbishops Church? They will ask themselves, if they ever consider union with Rome: "Will they receive the same treatment?" Should we consider this contemptible and unjust treatment and paternalism from Rome as a reward for the loyalty and martyrdom of our Church?"

It is our humble opinions; it was a preposterous performance by the Apostolic Nuncio in the presence of a Papal Legate, Your Eminence, and the entire episcopacy of the Ukrainian Catholic Church.

The Nuncio spoke about the wounds and divisions in our Church. His ill-conceived intervention only heightened the divisions and put salt on the wounds.

The outrageous statement, claims, or promises were insulting to say the least. They contained half-truths and misrepresentations. His words were demoralizing. They left a sense of hurt and bitterness in the hearts of the bishops. There is a feeling of dismay and bewilderment and a justified questioning of whether the See of Peter sincerely understands the rights of our Ukrainian Catholic Church and the Synod of Bishops have as a *sui iuris* Church.

Consequently, doubts and anxiety remain in the hearts of those who are responsible for the welfare of the Ukrainian Catholic Church. What transpired was the result of machination and a premeditated coup that was imposed in a fashion that was hurtful to a part of the Body of Christ. It was neither honest nor transparent. It has undermined confidence towards the Apostolic See. It betrayed our expectations.

We now ask the question: *How can this be repaired?*

It is imperative that such uncanonical, ad hoc, and improvisational methods of electing bishops in our Ukrainian Catholic Church never again be imposed upon us by the Vatican emissaries. Such procedures undermine the relationship our Church has with the See of Peter—a unique relationship that was formalized at the Union of Brest four hundred years ago. Furthermore, we are writing this Memorandum so that the historical record will be complete with these observations to guide those who follow, that they may never err in following the path imposed on us at the October 1996 Synod, when we as bishops, successors of the Holy Apostles, were enjoined from exercising our free choice before Almighty God in the election of a bishop to serve our Lord Jesus Christ, His Church, and our brothers and sisters in the Lord.

In conclusion, because of the lack of fraternal good will and harm his words and actions have caused our Ukrainian Catholic Church, we humbly request that at any future Synod of the Ukrainian Catholic Church, the presence of Archbishop Antonio Franco be excluded.

November 25, 1996.

Cardinal Silvestrini did not acknowledge our Memorandum. But to my pleasant surprise the Holy Father's personal secretary Msgr. Stanislaw Dziwisz did so by a letter dated December 12, 1996, addressed to me:

I received your letter with the Memorandum addressed to His Eminence Cardinal Silvestrini. The Holy Father got acquainted with its context. (The word "<u>acquainted</u>" was underlined).

Sending you my heartfelt greetings for the forthcoming Feast of the Nativity of Christ and the New Year, I remain very sincerely yours, *Stanislaw Dziwisz*.

The above letter of Msgr. Stanislaw Dziwisz was most certainly written with the knowledge and consent of the Holy Father himself. This was his way of telling the authors of the Memorandum of his compassion and his approval of their courage to speak up in defense of the Ukrainian Catholic Church and the lawful rights of our bishops.

Walter Paska—My Third Auxiliary Bishop

Since July 11, 1989, when the Holy See transferred Bishop Michael Kuchmiak to be the Exarch of the Ukrainian Catholic Church in Great Britain, I had no auxiliary. I made the necessary efforts through our Synod of bishops, but there was no nomination for a long time. On February 4, 1992, the Apostolic Nuncio in Washington, Archbishop Augustine Caccavillian, announced that the Holy Father John Paul II had appointed Msgr. Walter Paska an auxiliary Bishop to the Metropolitan Archbishop Stephen Sulyk.

Walter Paska was born November 29, 1923 in Elizabeth, New Jersey to Wasyl and Rosalia Paska. After grammar school, he entered St. Basil's Prep School and afterward St. Basil's College in Stamford, Ct, and St. Mary's College in Maryland. He took his theological studies at the Catholic University of America while living at St. Josaphat Seminary in Washington, DC. Bishop Constantine Bohachevsky ordained him to the priesthood June 2, 1947.

He was appointed an instructor at St. Basil Prep School in Stamford while continuing his studies, specializing in English literature at Fordham University, N.Y. His next assignment was a parochial vicar at the Holy Ghost Parish, Chester, PA. The following assignment was parochial administrator at his home parish, St. Vladimir, Elizabeth, NJ. And then he was a pastor of St. Vladimir,

Hempstead, NY. From 1961 to 1971 he performed the duties of the Chancellor and Vicar General to Bishop Jaroslav Gabro, Chicago, IL. From there he returned to the Philadelphia Archeparchy and was appointed a Director of Vocations. He traveled many miles visiting each parish, conducting youth gatherings and encouraging them to follow Christ as His priests or religious sisters. In 1975 he took up canon law studies at the Catholic University of America in Washington, DC, achieving a doctoral degree. In 1979 he was appointed Rector of St. Josaphat Seminary, Washington, DC, while being an instructor of Eastern Canon Law at the Catholic University. Since 1975 he has been the Judicial Vicar. In 1984 he was appointed pastor of St. Michael's Church, Cherry Hill, NJ.

His episcopal ordination took place Thursday, March 19, 1992, at Immaculate Conception Cathedral, Philadelphia, PA. I was the consecrating bishop while Bishops Losten and Lotocky were co-consecrators.[10]

In my homily I said:

I am convinced that the newly ordained Bishop Walter is fully aware of his teaching office as well as of the other episcopal duties to which by the decision of the Holy Father and by the laying of our hands, the Holy Spirit made him a hierarch so that he may "bring glad tidings to the poor, to proclaim liberty to captives, recovery of sight to the blind" (*Luke 4:18*). From this day on, to him belong all the duties of a Good Shepherd whose image and likeness he bears by the imposition of the episcopal omophorion on his shoulders as it is said in the prayer of vest-

---

[10] Concelebrating were Metropolitan Archbishop Maxim Hermaniuk, CSsR of Winnipeg; Bishop Isidore Borecky of Toronto; Bishop Jerome Chimy, OSBM of New Westminster; Bishop Michael Dudick of Passaic; Bishop Robert Moskal of St. Josaphat in Parma; Bishop Andrew Pataki of Parma; Bishop Michael Hrynchyshyn CSsR of Paris, France; and Bishop Michael Kuchmiak, CSsR of London, England. Present were likewise Anthony Cardinal Bevilacqua of Philadelphia, Metropolitan Stephen Kochisko of Pittsburgh, and some others.

ing: "This is the image of the Son of God, who left the ninety-nine sheep on the mountains and went in search of the one which was lost. Having found her, he put her on his shoulders and brought her to the Father, according to his wishes . . .

This is why "I have a solemn charge to give you," my brother Walter. That "you may fight the good fight, and holding fast to faith and a good conscience . . ." (1 Timothy 1:18–19) "Be a continuing example of love, faith, and purity to believers." (ibid. 4:12)

Dear Bishop, at the beginning of your Rite of Episcopal Ordination I handed over to you a pastoral staff, which represents a traditional symbol of your pastoral ministry in the Vineyard of Christ. Let it be for you a continual reminder of your loving care and readiness to serve your spiritual flock. Let it remind you that following the example of Christ, the Good Shepherd, you may always be ready to even lay down your life for your sheep, (comp. John 10:15) as did some fifty years ago your blood brothers the Bishops of our Ukrainian Catholic Church in Ukraine. Not one of them broke down and defected; not one of them renounced his Catholic Faith and his loyalty to the successor of St. Peter.

For this reason we all pray warmly that, being filled with the Holy Spirit, (Acts 2:1–4) and being under the constant protection of the Most Holy Mother of God, the Patroness of this Church, you may worthily fulfill your pastoral ministry in all humility and zeal so as to build up the Body of Christ in this branch of the Ukrainian Catholic Church . . ."

After the Liturgy, a festive banquet took place in the school auditorium. During the banquet there were several speeches. Bishop Kuchmiak had a very inspiring talk. Then Vsevolod, a Ukrainian Orthodox bishop, volunteered to say a few words:

You share our concerns together with us, the bishops, the priests, and the faithful of our suffering Kievan Church. All of us are trying to do everything possible to achieve unity of our divided-for-centuries Church. In Ukraine as well as here our division is a scandal and a cause of loss of faith among many people. This should stop. We should implore the Holy Spirit to unite us. We should be united in the Holy Spirit so that His divine mercy may direct our efforts.

During my episcopal ordination, Archbishop Jacovos officially charged me to search for all kinds of ways in order to achieve unity in the Ukrainian Church. I gladly accepted this obligation. Archbishop Jacovos emphasized this obligation, which rests upon all of us. I, then, appeal to you, dear Bishop, who today became our youngest brother in the family of bishops, to energetically search for ways of full unity in our Church, so that we truly may become "orthodox in faith and catholic in love" as is frequently said by the Fathers of the Church and often repeated by Pope John Paul II. Fifty years ago, Metropolitan Andrew Sheptytsky wrote a letter to all Ukrainian Bishops in which he spoke of the question of our spiritual unity. I would like today to ask all of you to remember the words of Metropolitan Andrew. He wrote: "We should remove from among us all discord and get rid of everything that divides us and with full energy search for true unity."

There are some even today who think that we cannot achieve such a goal. We, however, with the help of the Lord should accept the view of Metropolitan Andrew, who continued in the quoted letter: "I do not see any reason why we, the clergy of the various Ukrainian faiths, should continue the spiritual discord." And Metropolitan Andrew was right. There was no and there is not now any reason why we should not search for ways to achieve true unity in our Church. How should this be done? Again Metropolitan Andrew speaks to us from his letter written fifty years ago: "I know that to do this work will not be easy. I would like to make one indispensable condition. First of all, I think that for all of us, the clergy and the faithful of all of our eparchies, it is very imperative to want reconciliation. We should pray for this. We should offer Divine Liturgies with our priests and the faithful and implore the mercy of the Lord. At last all of us must be ready to give in where it is needed. The Holy Gospel impels us to renounce one's self and even to sacrifice one's life. As much as our conscience permits us, we should renounce everything, which would stand in our way to reconciliation. This is why it is absolutely imperative that we express our thoughts to one another, and sincerely deliberating the secular and the religious questions pertaining to reconciliation of Churches, we should search for the ways to such a reconciliation.

These words of Metropolitan Andrew are today addressed to us. Metropolitan Andrew surpassed his time. Today, while the Holy See and the Great Church of Constantinople for thirty years already conduct a' very fruitful dialogue, we should follow the spiritual directions of Metropolitan Andrew, attentively listen to his words and use them in our pastoral work . . .

All listeners were pleasantly surprised by such a warm appeal for Church unity coming from an Orthodox bishop. One thing he forgot to mention, namely that the quoted letter of Metropolitan Andrew Sheptytsky was addressed to all Ukrainian Orthodox Bishops. And all of them in unison rejected his propositions to Church unity. God grant that all Orthodox Bishops as well as their priests and the lay people may soon think the same way. Ukrainian Catholic Bishops, the clergy, and the lay people avidly desire unity of "God's holy churches."

Since November 16, 1992 Bishop Paska was Cathedral Parish Rector in Philadelphia until his retirement in February of 2001.

Vocations to the Priesthood and the Religious Life

My constant concern from the first day of my episcopal ministry was the shortage of vocations to the diocesan and religious priesthood and the male and female religious life. But the crisis of vocations does not exist in the Ukrainian Catholic Church in the United States of America only. This crisis is prevalent all over the western world. Our Latin brothers comparatively are much more affected by this crisis.

According to some statistics, one priest is needed to serve the needs of one thousand people. This statistic, however, concerns more the Latin faithful who live in more compact communities and form large parishes, which in many cases number several thousand souls. There are no such parishes in our Church in the United States of America. Our largest parish numbers only one-and-a-half thousand souls. Most of our parishes number only several hundred people, while there are so many that number barely one hundred. Because our parishes are usually located far from one another, one priest could never serve one thousand people.

Before the Second World War, 85% of all the Catholic missionaries in Africa and Asia hailed from Europe. Today the western European countries are in great need of more vocations. According to some press reports in France there are fifteen thousand priestless parishes. In Rome one priest serves three thousand people. Similar situations exist likewise in Austria, Germany, Great Britain, and other countries of Western Europe. In North America one priests serves seven or more thousand people.

In the United States, especially in large urban centers, to the crisis of vocations is added another problem, namely the mobility of the population from the cities to suburbia. More and more ethnic minorities populate the cities. When some of them move into a district or a street, the market value of other homes is decreased. Some homeowners panic, sell their homes, and move to the suburbs, especially the young married couples. Through the shortage of vocations, the Latin Rite Bishops are frequently forced to either close or combine city parishes, especially those belonging to small ethnic groups. All of this causes displeasure, complaints, and protests among the faithful.

Vocational crisis causes ruin in the Church. Priests are indispensable to the life of the Church, because just as without the faithful there could be no Church, likewise no Church could exist without a priest. Without a priest, even the most beautiful church structures, or the monumental episcopal cathedrals will not help us for they will remain lifeless walls, witnesses of a dead faith. Without a priest there would be no renewal of the New Testament Sacrifice of Jesus Christ—the Eucharistic Divine Liturgy, no sacraments, no preaching of the Gospel, no teaching of the faith, and no spiritual life in the parishes.

The vocational crisis has had an extremely negative impact in the life of the Religious orders and communities, which are the form—the heart of the Church. When the heart is weak and feeble, then the spiritual life of the Church becomes weak and feeble. After Vatican Council II, in the Latin Church in the United States, the number of vocations fell more than 68% in the diocesan and religious seminaries. In 1965 in the United States there were 17,494 diocesan and 22,230 religious seminarians. In 2001 there are 3,400 diocesan and 1,517 religious seminarians. In 1965 there were in the United States 117 diocesan and 479 religious seminaries. In 2001 there are 77 diocesan and 141 religious seminaries. In 1965 in the United States there were 58,632 priests, and 179,954 religious sisters. In 2001 the United States has 30,655 diocesan priests, 15,386 religious priests, and 79,462 religious sisters. In that period of time the number of Catholics in the United State of America grew from 45,640,119 in 1965, to 63,683,030 in 2001.

In 1981 in the Philadelphia Archeparchy, when I took over, had 96 eparchial, 12 religious and 26 retired priests, a total of 134 priests. In the Archeparchy in 2001 there are 47 eparchial, 6 religious priests and 12 retired priests. In this number are included 12 priests from Ukraine. In the twenty years of my episcopal ministry, I ordained fourteen priests, while in the same time period sixty-six priests died.

The above is a very sad statistic and a picture of the tragedy of the shortage of vocations, as wells as a crisis of faith itself.

Why Is There a Shortage of Vocations?

There are many and diverse reasons that cause such a shortage of vocations. The reasons, although diverse, are connected to one another. The main reasons in my perception are secularism and materialism. Secularism is a philosophy of life, based on purely natural principles with total negation of the supernatural truths and laws revealed by God. This is a concept of life seen not with the eyes of faith, not with the eyes of God, but purely with natural eyes, with the eyes of the world, with senses. It is not with a point of view of eternity, but only of temporality. Practically, this means a removal of all the teachings of Christian religion, which demand a sacrifice or causes inconvenience. Secularism casts away God, His Church, His commandments, and the Gospel as things which are not needed nor profitable. Secularism is the spirit of the world, a disdain and a deprecation of everything that is holy or belongs to God.

Materialism considers matter as the only reality. This is why it renounces spirituality and supernatural revelation. Where materialism prevails, there can be no vocations to the priesthood or religious life; there is no spirit of sacrifice or self-dedication. There, however, exists a yearning for gain, wealth, well being, comfort, the treasures of the world, and luxury. Such a life is idealized and systematically propagated by the secular press, modern electronic media, and especially television, which by means of commercial ads glorify material comforts, an easy life, fast money, and immoral life style. This is why the TV is often called "the sin box."

This morally poisonous atmosphere subtly draws Christians away from the traditional Christian religious and moral principles. Everything that pertains to the Church or religion is presented in such negative forms so as to incite disgust and hopelessness in church people, especially the priests and the bishops.

The greed and the pursuit for ever more wealth and comforts in life become the goal and the purpose of life. Such an attitude fears any kind of sacrifice and self-dedication, while idealism is considered as stupidity. Therefore, wherever there exists materialism, there will be no sacrifice for God, for neighbor, for the Church, or the nation. Materialism does not know and cannot suffer the idea of vocation, of service to God and the people.

Parents live in the midst of this materialized world, which influences them to hope that their children would be better off than they. Thus almost involuntarily they dread the very thought of vocation for their children. When I was a young priest and a pastor of St. Michael's Church in Frackville, PA, a fourteen-year-old girl, a parishioner, came to see me one day. With tears in her eyes she said: "I want to be a religious sister, but my parents have forbidden me to even think about such matters. If you mention this once more, we will throw you out of this house." Yet God's ways are not our ways. This young lady did not become a nun. She achieved higher education and became a university professor, yet to this day she did not get married. In another case the mother told her daughter: "I would prefer to see you in a casket rather then a nun." These are the effects of the hardness of heart caused by secularism and materialism.

Many Ukrainian immigrants who came to the United States of America after the Second World War became victims of materialism. Because of the war, they lost all their earthly possessions in Europe. Having arrived at the shores of America, they became immersed in the pursuit of wealth, of comfort in life, and neglected a religious education of their children.

It happened in 1956. At that time I was working at the Archbishop's Chancery when my friends from the Boy Scouts invited me to attend one of their meetings. They asked me to elaborate a question for them: "How can we preserve the Ukrainian language in our churches?" They were complaining that our young priests prefer to speak in English with their children. This was my reply to them:

> You would have to be good strategist like the generals are in a war. You have to plan ahead of time and not just complain. Remember that some 75,000 new Ukrainian immigrants came to the United States of America after the Second World War. Most of them are people with at least a high school education, and many are university graduates, unlike the first immigrants who came before the First World War. If out of the 75,000 you would send only ten well-brought-up young boys to our seminary and ten young girls to one of our female religious communities per year, in ten years after they graduate you would have one hundred priests, and one hundred new religious sisters who would speak perfect Ukrainian. In fifteen to twenty years, from among them you would have them as your pastors and maybe even a bishop. This is the only solution to your problem.

No one said, "Well done, a good talk, or even thank you." Never again was I invited to one of their meetings.

Sad to say, the spirit of materialism is like the thorns in our Lord's parable about the seed (Matthew 13:1–23), as it choked God's call to priesthood or the religious life in the hearts of our young people.

Is There a Solution?

At first it seems that there is no solution. It seems that the situation is hopeless. Pessimism like a dark cloud crawls into my mind and tortures me with the question: Is this the end of our Church in the United States of America? Crises of vocations are actually a slow death of the Church. The very thought is very painful to any priest who dedicated his whole life to the Church. It is natural for a person to want to live, to see success and growth. I tried very hard not to let such pessimistic thoughts enter my mind. When it happened, I prayed with the Psalmist:

"Restore us, O God our savior, and abandon your displeasure against us.

Will you be ever angry with us, prolonging your anger to all generations?

Will you not instead give us life; and shall not your people rejoice in you?

Show us, O Lord, your kindness, And grant us your salvation" (Psalms 85:5–8).

Contemporary secularism and materialism steal away the virtue of faith from the hearts of the people; often they throw a person into fire of sinful life or into water of diabolical deception, killing even the smallest seed of vocation. It personifies that "mute and deaf spirit" (Mark 9:25) that is of the kind "you can drive out only by prayer and fasting" (ibid 29). The solution then is in prayer and fasting. These two form a key that opens the floodgate of God's graces from heaven. I shared this idea with my faithful during parish visitations and in my pastoral letters:

> Prayer and fasting are mighty forces, overcoming even the strongest enemies. They open to us the doors of heavenly treasures. In our Archdiocese, one of the greatest treasures we can petition from the Lord is this special grace: the increase of vocations to the priesthood and religious life. We have come to realize the great need of priests and religious in our Church. This Lent, therefore, should become a time of renewing our efforts at prayer and fasting, seeking from God the incomparable blessing and gift of the priesthood. This gift is generously given to people who seek it sincerely, and who, with devotion, "Beg the harvest master to send laborers to gather his harvest." (Matthew 9:38)

All of us, young and old alike, must implore the Lord for this grace with our most fervent daily prayers. Every family should pray together daily for this intention. Such petitions should come from the depths of our hearts, with firm faith in God and His almighty power, for "Everything is possible to a man who believes" (*Matthew 19:26*). John the Baptist describes this power of God: "God can raise up children of Abraham from these stones" (*Luke 3:8*). So, too, the Lord may grant us candidates to the priesthood and call them to His service. This Prayer Campaign must be shared by all of us: fathers and mothers, laity, clergy, religious Sisters, young and old, all storming heaven for the grace of vocations from the Lord. No one should be indifferent to this sacred and all-important cause, for it touches our lives so closely. During this period of Lent we have the occasion to unite our generous and most sincere prayers, our fasting, our sacrifices for the vocations we need. In addition to private prayers, fasting, and sacrifices, we request that our faithful, as they attend the Divine Liturgy on Sundays and Holy Days, arrive earlier to recite the rosary in common before the beginning of the Liturgy. Let all our faithful offer to God the Divine Liturgy itself in which they participate as well as the reception of the Holy Communion for the intention of vocations to the holy priesthood and religious life. Let all our parish organizations and associations, at the beginning and closing of their meetings and gatherings, offer the opening and the closing prayer for this intention. We turn to the children of our parochial and catechetical schools, that, with the encouragement and direction of their teachers, they open and close each day's classes with a prayer for vocations in our Church. A special form of offering should also be made by the aged, the infirm, and those confined because of illness. Their sufferings have a particular merit before God if offered daily to Him in union with the suffering Lord for holy vocations . . .

Our diocesan-wide Prayer Campaign, performed with living faith, must be confirmed by our godly and virtuous lives, and especially by our individual acts of mortification, sacrifice, and fasting, for Our Lord reminds us that certain kinds of evil can be overcome "only by prayer and fasting." (Matthew 17:21)

Such obstacles and sins are legion in number, and our contemporary society reflects only too clearly the extent of their harm. Our youth face an unprecedented array of distractions and temptations in such an antichristian atmosphere, and the effect on possible vocations is clearly evident. All these factors require us to unite our prayers in ever-increasing fervor in a campaign of petition, asking Our Lord to bless our aspirations and strengthen those whom He has called to His service, who also have to struggle against the secular and anti-religious influences that surround us. Our prayers must be unceasing, for Christ has solemnly assured us: "Ask and it will be given to you; seek and you will find; knock and the door will be opened to you . . . Which one of you will hand his son a stone when he asks for a loaf of bread, or a snake when he asks for a fish? If you then, who are wicked, know how to give good gifts to your children, how much more will your heavenly Father give good things to those who ask him." (Matthew 7:7–11) Let us then with magnanimity and constancy every day fervently implore our Heavenly Father, asking for vocations for our archdiocese, the entire Ukrainian Catholic Church throughout the world, and in our Homeland . . ."

Such and similar homilies I gave on many and various occasions. Special liturgical petitions for vocations I sent to our priests, asking them to include them in each Divine Liturgy they offer.

God did hear the fervent prayers of our good faithful, of our priests and religious, but not in a way that we expected. In 1989 the Lord stretched out His mighty right hand and freed our homeland from the centuries-long captivity. Our persecuted and liquidated Ukrainian Catholic Church was able to come out into the world from the modern catacombs with her heroic faithful, her priests, religious, and her bishops. They all came out with their Catholic faith strengthened and confirmed by their great sufferings.

The graces earned before God by the blood of numerous martyrs and confessors during the persecution of the Ukrainian Catholic Church in Ukraine was and still is the source of many vocations to the priesthood and the religious life. The seminaries could hardly contain all the applicants. Each year so many candidates apply for admission to our seminaries in Ukraine that at least one half of them cannot be admitted due to the lack of space in the seminary buildings. They are sending seminarians out from Ukraine to the seminaries in Western Europe. Thus St. Josaphat Pontifical College in Rome has 48 individual rooms, and all are filled. Recently the Eastern Congregation closed the minor seminary in Rome on

Via Boccea, renovated the building, and opened it as the Protection of the Mother of God Pontifical Ukrainian Catholic Seminary for graduate studies. In the United States, bishop Basil Losten accepts annually a number of students to his St. Basil's Minor Seminary in Stamford, CT. I, too, have been accepting seminarians from the Seminaries in Ukraine to our St. Josaphat Seminary in Washington, D.C. True, some of them will fall away, mostly because of mandatory celibacy, but some will remain and will be of great help to our Church.

Synod of Ukrainian Catholic Bishops in 1997

Bishop Lubomyr Husar invited the bishops to come to Lviv two days before the commencement of the Synod so as to have time for the Synodal commissions to coordinate their reports and to plan the work given them by the previous Synod.

Saturday, September 13, 1997, was a day set aside for a Spiritual Retreat for the Synodal Fathers. Father Dionisius Lachowych, the Protoarchimandrite of the Basilian Fathers was the retreat master. He gave three homilies of a highly philosophical and theological nature.

The day began at 6:30 A.M. with common morning prayers in the chapel of Transfiguration Monastery Church in Krechiw. At 7:00 A.M. the Matins Service was started. Following Matins, a concelebrated Divine Liturgy took place at which I was the main celebrant. A young Basilian deacon served in that role at the Liturgy. Thirty bishops surrounded the altar and "with one voice and one heart" they praised the Lord by offering to God the Mystery of the New Testament. At 11:00 A.M. the bishops went back to the church, recited part of the Office of the Hours, which was followed by a homily by Father Lachowych, OSBM. The theme of the homily was, "Unity of the Ukrainian Catholic Episcopacy." Each bishop is called to have his own determination and to share with others his spiritual treasures for the building up of the Church. His second conclusion was: Love comes from on high and is given as a grace to him who asks for it. Thus every one who is given a charge over the goods of others, with a spiritual flock, and—the sheep belong to the Father,—is called to have an intimate connection with the One who gave him the charge.

At 1:00 P.M. the bishops went back to the church for another common recitation of the Office of the Hours and a homily on a theme: "Unity in the name of the Church." He reminded the bishops that one love unites the three Persons of the Holy Trinity. God is Love. This is why a profession of the Holy Trinity demands a progress towards the perfection of love: "You must be made perfect as your heavenly Father is perfect" (Matthew 5:48). He then made the following conclusion: This spiritual renewal requires us to ask: are we united as is demanded by the very nature of the Church, which is a communion in love? Do we desire the unity demanded from us by the Church?

At 5:00 P.M. the bishops sang Vespers in the church, followed by the third homily of the retreat master on the theme: "Unity in the name of the People of God." Here he stressed the necessity of unity among the Bishops in their relationships with the People of God and the personal ministry of unity of the individual bishop in his eparchy.

Sunday, September 14, 1997, after the Matins Service, the bishops traveled on a bus to St. George's Cathedral in Lviv for a concelebrated Hierarchical Divine Liturgy. There were thirty-three bishops present and concelebrating. I had the honor of giving the homily:

> Today we gather in this historic church of St. George, in the ancient city of Leo. We, the shepherds of our Church—modern successors of the Apostles—come from all the corners of the world to raise our voices together with you, our dear faithful to give praise, glory, and thanksgiving to Almighty God.

As we celebrate this Divine Liturgy here, let us recall the moment, the celebration of another Divine Liturgy over 1,000 years ago in the city of Constantinople.

According to the Chronicle of Nestor, Prince Wolodymyr of Kievan Rus' sent his emissaries around the world to help him decide his state religion. Visiting the Hagia Sophia in Constantinople, the emperor and patriarch welcomed the representatives of St. Wolodymyr. In their report back to Wolodymyr, they wrote: "We went to Constantinople and the Greeks led us to the edifice where they worship their God and we knew not whether we were in heaven or on earth. For on earth there is no such splendor or such beauty, and we are at a loss how to describe it. We only know that God dwells there among men."

From that spiritual experience, our nation received the great gift of Almighty God, Christianity, and in 988 our ancestors were baptized in the Most Holy Trinity, in the Name of the Father, and of the Son, and of the Holy Spirit.

From that moment forward, God made our homeland part of his sacred vineyard, and today we stand here as the direct descendants of this spiritual heritage, this precious treasure, our faith, and our Ukrainian Catholic Church.

The Gospel message of today recalls the parable of the property owner who planted a vineyard. Every time he sent messengers to harvest his fruit, they were met with cruel treatment—beating, stoning and killing. After they killed the property owner's son, our Lord asked: "What do you suppose the owner of the vineyard will do to those tenants when he comes?"

581

They replied: "He will bring that wicked crowd to a bad end and lease his vineyard out to others who will see to it that he has grapes at vintage time."

My dear brothers and sisters in Christ, for many centuries our ancestors, who were sent to harvest fruit for the Master from His vineyard in Ukraine were also treated harshly. From the Mongol invasions to the Tsarist persecution, to atheistic Communistic atrocities of this century, our spiritual leaders, our priests, religious and our faithful were stoned, tortured, and put to death. They tried to kill the Vine of Christ in our beautiful vineyard, our Ukrainian Catholic Church.

But instead of killing the Vine and its Spirit, the Vine continued to live underground. The world was told the vine is dead; our Ukrainian Catholic Church no longer exists in our beloved Ukraine. But in the catacomb church, the dormant vine was alive and waiting for the long night of persecution to end, ready to blossom forth in the warm rays of the bright sun of dawn of a new day.

Once the "wicked crowd was brought to a bad end," the vine miraculously grew forth, inspired by the sacrifice and faithfulness of the thousands of martyrs—bishops, priests, religious, and faithful, who sustained its roots during the long nightmare of persecution. Through the rays of grace of the Son and the Holy Spirit, Almighty God has blessed our Church with the opportunity for a glorious new life.

Throughout history our vine has been severely pruned and often, to many, appeared dead. Today, we are alive; today we are thriving; today, we have the opportunity of yielding fruit a hundredfold. We have been entrusted with the task of bringing forth the fruit for the harvest.

To do so, we must heed the advice of St. Paul. In today's Epistle, just as he advised the Corinthians in the first century, he also advises us: "Be on your guard, stand firm in faith, and act like men. In a word, be strong." (1 Corinthians 16:13–24)

For our Church to flourish, each of us who has been blessed by God to be baptized into this flock of Christ must always be on guard; we must stand firm in the faith, and we must act like men. Simply, we must always be strong.

As we your bishops gather here in this Holy Synod, the world is on the threshold of a new millennium. We ask all of you to pray that the Holy Spirit may inspire our deliberations and guide us as we lead our Church into the twenty-first century.

We, as people of God, are called upon to build on the legacy of faith that has been entrusted to us through St. Wolodymyr and our ancestors, through the blood of our martyred Church of the catacombs, through the witness of generations of our faithful for over 1,000 years.

"As we approach this new century, let us be filled with renewed hope, confidence, and the eternal optimism we share as Christians. To us, our task is great; our cause is noble. At this moment in history, Almighty God has placed into our hands the awesome responsibility as guardians of our Church for this and future generations.

Ten centuries ago, the emissaries of St. Wolodymyr were overwhelmed with the treasure they found in the Church of Constantinople. Our Church, part of the Vine of Christ that survived for over 1,000 years through the onslaught of innumerable attacks, continues to be the repository of this spiritual treasure. May this and future generations who experience the beauty and receive the supernatural grace of the Liturgy of our

Ukrainian Catholic Church—a foretaste of the glorious heavenly celebration in the Kingdom of God—always exclaim: "We knew not where we were in heaven or on earth; we only knew that God dwells there among men." In our Church and among our people, may Almighty God always dwell among us.

Concelebrating this Liturgy were likewise guest bishops: Archbishop Antonio Franco, Apostolic Nuncio to Kiev; Bishop Szilard Keresztes of Hajdudorog, Hungary; Metropolitan Marian Jaworski of Lviv of the Latin Church; Bishop Markian Trofymiak, Auxiliary Latin Bishop of Lviv; and a priest guest—Father Blahovist Nikolov, Vicar General of the Greek Catholic Church in Bulgaria.

Following the Liturgy an official opening of the Synod took place at the St. George's Metropolitan's residence. Besides those who participated in the Liturgy there was a representative of the Ukrainian Orthodox Church. Bishop Husar opened the Synod by reading an opening talk of His Beatitude Myroslav Cardinal Lubachivsky, and by his own personal address. Most of the guests greeted the Synod by short speeches wishing our Church success, growth and progress.[11]

When Bishop Robert Moskal read his report at the Synod, he stated that he was given a task to coordinate the two Ukrainian texts of the Liturgy, i.e., of 1968 Cardinal Slipyj's translation, and the 1988 Synodal text. But the work had not yet been done. It was given to a renowned linguistic scholar, a Ukrainian Catholic from the Carpathian region. At that time I asked for the floor and said the following:

> Our Synodal text of the Liturgy of St. John Chrysostom is not a new translation. It is the 1968 translation of the commission headed by His Beatitude Cardinal Slipyj. All we did was elimi-

---

[11] Absent from the Synod were: His Beatitude Myroslav Ivan Cardinal Lubachivsky; Archbishop Volodymyr Sterniuk; Bishops Theodore Majkowycz; Platon Kornylyak; Augustine Horniak, OSBM; Andrew Sapelak; Basil Filewych; Innocent Lotocky, OSBM; and Ivan Prasko.

nate archaic words and expressions. These archaic words might have been useful in the transitional period from the Church Slavonic to the living Ukrainian language so that the faithful might easily accept the change. But after the span of twenty years the faithful themselves demanded the elimination of archaic expressions. This is why our Synod made the decision to eliminate them.

There was one bishop at that Synod who protested the decision, saying: 'His Beatitude Patriarch Joseph is not cold yet, and you are already correcting him.' Two or three more bishops openly joined him in the protest, while secretly one more might have joined. This is how discord began in our Synod. This discord was supported by some priests, members of the so-called "Krylos" in Rome. They did everything possible to persuade our priests and the faithful not to use the Synodal Liturgicon, published in 1988. The bishop who was the first to express his opposition to the Liturgicon, was able in more that a month's stay in Rome to persuade His Beatitude Cardinal Lubachivsky to reject the Synodal Liturgicon. When the Liturgicon was already published, sold and used in our churches, at the 1989 Synod His Beatitude Myroslav Ivan Cardinal Lubachivsky recalled his approval of the 1988 Liturgical text. Yet, without the consent of the two-thirds of the Synodal Fathers, such a recall was uncanonical and not binding, but it introduced and confirmed the discord existing in our Church.

Such discord in our Synod became a reality. It became more and more firm, and when Ukraine became free, it was transferred there, too. In one eparchy in Ukraine the Synodal Liturgicon is prohibited while the others use it. So as to make the discord even more firm and lasting, a great number of popular prayer books were published with the use of archaic words in the Liturgy.

Our discord brought us to the point that we, the bishops of our Church, are not able anymore to pray in common "with one voice and one heart" even the Lord's Prayer or the "Hail Mary," because there are variances in the text of these prayers. Our faithful, as well as our young people, look at us and ask themselves: When will our bishops achieve some accord and unity on the liturgical life of our Church?

One has to congratulate our enemies. What they could not achieve by the forceful liquidation of our Church, by the martyrdom of our bishops, priests and faithful, this same was accomplished by our own lovers of archaic words and expressions in our liturgical texts. They have gone so far in their opposition to the legitimate and canonical decision of the Synod as to split our Church in half, and with it they abased our Synod and all its decisions. The Synod of Bishops is the highest moral authority in our Church and among our people. To ruin the authority of the Synod matches a ruination of the authority of the Church.

And so, my dear brother bishops, all of us will someday stand on Judgment Day to give an account of our decision pertaining to the Vineyard of Christ among our people. Most probably we will never be able to return unity to our Church since we Ukrainians have a tendency to split and divide. Our Orthodox brothers and sisters already have three Patriarchates. In our Ukrainian Catholic Church it seems that we will have at least two, unless at this Synod we shall once and for all liquidate the rebellion against the canonical decisions of our Synod.

You may ask why could we not have unity? Since it was possible for some bishops to oppose the canonical decisions of our Synod and to refuse to accept the approved text of the Liturgy, then, logically, I and all other bishops are free to opt for any other text to our liking. Once we set a precedent that a bishop may be in good standing in our Synod while he refuses to abide by the canonical decisions of the majority of the Synodal Fathers, we then have actually confirmed the division of our Church.

The only solution to this sad and very dangerous situation is to liquidate the precedent of rebellion and decide that from now on all our bishops will abide by the canonical decision of the Synod, accept and use the Liturgicon which this Synod as well as the Apostolic See of Rome has approved. All our priests and religious are bound by this decision.

After a brief discussion, all of the Synodal Fathers voted to accept my proposition. Then Bishop Husar asked about the Lord's Prayer. Here there was no need for any further discussion. Since we accepted the Liturgicon we likewise accepted the Lord's Prayer contained in the Liturgy.

Bishop Husar then formed a commission to study the "Hail Mary" prayer. Which of the texts of this prayer is a correct one? When this commission presented its report and the opinion of a linguist, a very confused discussion commenced. In the Ukrainian language there are two words for the term "womb"—an old one— "utroba," or a newer one—"lono." The discussion concentrated on which of these two words is more proper.

I then asked to speak. "As long as we have not made a decision to revise all our liturgical texts, let us not introduce more confusion in the prayer life of our faithful. Besides, the approved text of our Book of the Gospels gives us a solution to our discussion—in Luke 1:42. As long we read in our churches the Gospel lessons from this book, we must use the same word in our prayer." Thus the prayer "Hail Mary" was approved.

At an appropriate time I spoke up on the subject of the promulgation of the Synodal decisions.

From time immemorial the Church, especially the Eastern Church, used a collegial system to make important decisions. The bishops were called to assemble for deliberations, and, having called upon the Holy Spirit, they made decisions in common. Such deliberations of bishops, the Church called the Synod of Bishops. This tradition was practiced in our Ukrainian Church. The new Code of Canons for the Eastern Churches legalized this tradition and prescribed: "The synod of bishops of the patriarchal Church must be convened whenever:

1. matters are to be decided which belong to the exclusive competence of the synod of bishops of the patriarchal Church which, in order to be done, require the consent of the bishops;

2. the patriarch, with the consent of the permanent synod, judges it necessary;

3. at least one third of the members request it for a given matter . . ." (c. 106). "The synod of bishops of the patriarchal Church is exclusively competent to make laws for the entire patriarchal Church . . ." (c. 110).

My brother bishops, my conscience and sense of duty impels me to remind you that already six previous Synods of Bishops were not yet promulgated, which is demanded by Church law.

Canon 112 of the Code of Canons prescribes: "The promulgation of laws and the decisions of the synod of bishops of the patriarchal Church is the competence of the patriarch." Thus the patriarch has the authority as well as the duty and the obligation to promulgate the laws and the decisions, which were decided at the synods of bishops.

Canon 111,3 prescribes likewise the following: "Acts regarding the laws and decisions are to be sent to the Roman Pontiff as soon as possible . . ." We do not know whether this was done. All we know is that our Major Archbishop did not do his duty since he did not promulgate the decisions of six synods already and did not inform us why this was not done.

The following synods were not promulgated:

1. Synod which was held from Sept. 24 to October 8, 1989 at the Vatican;

2. Synod which was held from June 25 to 26, 1990 at the Vatican;

3. Synod which was held from Feb. 3 to 10, 1991 in Rome;

4. Synod which was held from June 16 to 30, 1992 in Lviv;

5. Synod which was held from Feb. 20 to 27, 1994 in Lviv;

6. Synod which was held from February 16 to 25, 1995 in Rome.

During the 1995 Synod in Rome, His Beatitude Myroslav Cardinal Lubachivsky in the presence of Bishop Hrynchyshyn asked me: "Help me prepare the decisions of our several past synods so that I may promulgate them." It took me almost a month of my spare time to search in the documents, mostly in the official minutes of these past synods, and to prepare the decisions ready for publication. Bishop Hrynchyshyn was kind enough to take them with him as he was going to Lviv for a Permanent Synod meeting. He gave them to His Beatitude. Yet to this day they were not promulgated.

My proposition is canon 111,1, which gives the Synod of Bishops the power to decide the manner and the time of the promulgation of laws and decisions of the Synod. The canon reads: "The synod of the bishops of the patriarchal Church designates the manner and the time of promulgation of laws and the publication of decisions." I, therefore, present the following proposition: 'The promulgation of laws and the publication of decisions of the Synods, which were held in 1989, 1990, 1991, 1992, 1994 and 1995 is to be made not later than November 30, 1997 in each eparchy's or exarchate's official publication.'

For the approval of this proposition a simple majority of votes is required. The vote was unanimous. Bishop Husar promised to publish it in a separate brochure or in a new issue of the *Blahovisnyk* before the end of November of the year, i.e. 1997.

All the bishops were happy with the results of the peaceful ending of these old, neglected matters. Some of them were congratulating me while Metropolitan Michael Bzdel of Winnipeg joked privately with me, saying:" This Synod should be called, "Sulyk's Synod." Indeed, I was really happy and grateful to God for helping us resolve the old painful matters that had disturbed me for a long time. The next morning my intention for the Liturgy was a thank you to God.

Bishop Losten and I volunteered to donate one thousand dollars each to the Provincial of the Basilian Fathers, Theodosius Jankiv, to have them print one thousand Liturgicon books of St. John Chrysostom Liturgy, which were to be distributed among the priests in Ukraine. Father Jankiw accepted the money from both bishops and promised to do as we requested.

The five-year term for three of the five members of the permanent synod expired that year, so the next point on the agenda was the election. Bishop Husar was a member of the permanent synod *ex officio*. Major Archbishop Lubachivsky appointed Bishop Michael Koltun. By a secret balloting Bishop Hrynchyshyn, Bishop Mudryj, and Archbishop Sulyk were elected. I tried to refuse the election due to great distances for traveling, but my brother bishops said, "You are needed here!" I had no heart to say "no" to such firm demands and fraternal expression of trust.

An Extraordinary Synod of Americas

In the recent past the Holy Father convoked the World Synod of Bishops every three years. Now he began to convoke regional Synods of Bishops also in preparation for the Great Jubilee, the 2000th year since the birth of Jesus Christ. So far there were the following regional synods: two Synods of Europe, one of Africa, and in 1998 a Synod of Asia was planned. From November 16 to December 12, 1997, a Synod of Americas was held in the Vatican. Each continent has its own characteristics and separate difficulties as well as separate problems in the building of the Kingdom of Heaven on earth. It is easier to learn and find solutions to problems when one considers the conditions of life, cultural and social influences in a certain part of the world in which the Church of Christ exists and lives. The American continent is very large. In it live one-half of all Catholics of the world. This is why special attention was to be paid to the Church in the Americas.

The problems intrinsic to the American continent are various, but in my humble opinion the one that is common to all in this continent is widespread secularism and extreme materialism. As a result of these two maladies, there exists in the Americas a certain coolness or weakness in faith, an indifference to prayer, and poor image of the Church and her authority. This is followed by the consequent neglect of Christian practices and virtues. This condition is easily recognized by the low attendance in Church services on Sundays and Holy Days, by the break-up of families, and by the number of abortions. Together with these follows also the decrease in the number of vocations to the priesthood and the religious life, the ever-greater shortage of priests, and the increase of immorality and crime. Such a morally negative situation creates a sort of vacuum, which becomes a field for the spread of all kinds of sects and atheistic organizations.

For this Synod the Holy Father selected a theme: *"Encounter with Jesus Christ on a way to conversion, unity and solidarity in America."* It was the task of the Synodal Fathers by way of a thorough analysis of the theme to present a series of propositions, which would show how conversion, unity, and solidarity with the living Christ might be achieved in America. The Holy Father, by his supreme power as the successor of St. Peter, convokes regional synods and gives the local bishops the task that they in common seek solutions to the problems in their part of the world.

When the Holy Father some time after the synod prepares his Apostolic Letter to the Americas, based on the propositions that were agreed upon by the bishops themselves, all will know that he does not impose on them something new, but puts forward only what they themselves proposed at the synod.

At that time the metropolitans of the Eastern Churches were *ex officio* members of the world or regional synods. Now this rule was changed. In the Latin Church the local bishops' conference elects the prescribed number of delegates to such synods. The United States delegation to the Synod of Americas held a meeting on September 12, 1997, where they assigned a theme for each delegate's intervention at the synod. Since at that time I was attending our Ukrainian synod, I asked them to assign a theme for me as well. They selected the following theme for me: *"Relationships between the Eastern Catholic Churches and the Latin Church in the Americas."*

Patriarch Bartholomew I Visits Unites States of America

In the fall of 1997, the Patriarch of Constantinople was on an official visit to the United States. The Ukrainian Orthodox Bishops, the priests, and the faithful were to welcome him at their center in South Bound Brook, N.J. on Monday October 27, 1997. I was invited to attend this celebration. The Patriarch with his entourage arrived, after a delay, by helicopter from New York City. The Ukrainian Orthodox Bishops from the United States and Canada welcomed him and escorted him to his throne situated in front of their church under a canopy. Present were also Bishops Losten and Moskal.

An altar was placed under a canopy. The guest bishops were seated on chairs to the side of the canopy under the open skies. It was 7:20 P.M. and a very cold wind blew, flapping the canopy. I had no topcoat. Our wait for the Patriarch and the Moleben that was to follow lasted over two hours. I was very cold. Metropolitan Constantine (Buhhan) welcomed the Patriarch. After the Moleben service the Patriarch spoke briefly.

At about 8:00 P.M. all were invited to attend a banquet. I was to welcome the Patriarch in the name of the Ukrainian Catholics, but due to the chill I had lost my voice completely. So I asked Bishop Moskal to read my welcome speech. The Patriarch asked for a copy of my talk, to which I gladly agreed. I left for home at 10 o'clock, before the banquet ended.

The following day one of my friends sent me a copy of Bartholomew's speech, which he had given on October 25, 1997 at Georgetown University in Washington, D.C. on the occasion of receiving an honorary doctoral degree. Having read this speech very carefully I could not believe my eyes. So I read it again to be sure that I was not mistaken. This speech was the Patriarch's reply to the Holy Father's apostolic letter *Orientale lumen*. The Patriarch's speech gave me an idea for my intervention at the Synod of Americas.

I left for the Synod on Friday, November 14, 1997, arriving in Rome Saturday morning. I stayed at St. Josaphat's Seminary on the Gianicolo. On Sunday, November 16, at 9:30 A.M. the Holy Father presided at a solemn Eucharistic Liturgy at the Basilica of St. Peter with all the Synodal Fathers as concelebrants. Before the Liturgy, approximately two hundred bishops assembled at the Constantine corridor, vested and then began a very imposing procession into the Basilica. This was the first time the master of ceremonies placed the four Eastern Bishops in front of the cardinals. They were: Metropolitan Michael Bzdel of Winnipeg; Metropolitan Judson Procyk of Pittsburgh; myself; and Pier Moallema, a Melkite Bishop from Sao Paulo, Brazil.

My Intervention at the Synod

Your Holiness, and esteemed Brothers and Sisters in the Lord, We are gathered together in response to the call of our Supreme Pontiff, His Holiness Pope John Paul II, as the whole Church is preparing to celebrate the advent of the Third Millennium of the Saving Passover of our Lord Jesus Christ. The approach of this milestone should arouse profound joy within Christian hearts as we reflect on the amazing spiritual harvest, which has been gathered over the course of two millennia. At the same time we are not afraid nor do we shrink from honestly assessing our culpability for the woeful division which developed among the Lord's flock so as to scatter multitudes, and damage the bond of ecclesial communion, divisions which are yet painfully apparent to this day which we are committed to overcoming with the help of the Holy Spirit.

In his address 25 October 1997, at the Jesuit Georgetown University in Washington, D.C., the Ecumenical Patriarch Bartholomew I, speaking of the "diversity" between the Orthodox and Catholic churches said: *"We confirm not with unexpected astonishment, but neither with indifference, that indeed the divergence between us continually increases and the end points to which*

our courses are taking us, foreseeably, are indeed different . . . Un-
less our ontological transfiguration and transformation toward one
common model of life is achieved, not in form but also in substance,
unity and its accompanying realization become impossible."

These are words that should grieve us deeply. Since that memorable Kiss of Peace, exchanged thirty-three years ago between
Pope Paul VI and Patriarch Athenagoras in Jerusalem and so
many other gestures of love mutually given subsequently, and
mindful of the many dialogical accords achieved so painfully till
now, I assess that everything has justified spiritual confidence
so as to finally begin to envision the approach of the day of full
Communion in the Lord. Most assuredly, no one who has so
hoped, I may boldly so state, need fear that he has been a victim
of self-delusion. We Eastern Catholics, at once in communion
with Rome and sharing fully in the heritage of the Orthodox
Faith, experience this wound of *"divergence"* in an intimate way
because we, more than anyone, find ourselves suspended over
the gap, and even in some sense bisected by it. And so we, from
the depth of our soul declare with His Holiness John Paul II:
"there can be no second thought about pursuing the path of unity,
which is irreversible and the Lord's appeal for unity is irreversible."
(Orientale lumen, Preface sec. 3)

In making the charge that a difference of *ontological proportions*
lies at the root of any such divergence, the Patriarch pronounces
a certain sentence of death upon the ecumenical dialogue. He
implies that one Church, the Orthodox Church, remains the
true Church, founded by Christ, while the *path of divergence*
pursued by the Latin Church has changed the basic ontological
nature of it. In essence, the end point to which the Latin Church
is leading is different from that intended by Christ himself. By
implication, one can infer the Patriarch's perceived *ontological*
change in the essential nature of the Latin Church, he no longer
considers it the true Church of Christ. For this reason, unless

"our ontological transfiguration and transformation toward one common model of life is achieved, not only in form but also in substance, unity and its accompanying realization become impossible."

In the same statement, the Patriarch succinctly states: "concerning those that have freely chosen to shun the correct glory of God, the Orthodox Church follows the Apostle Paul's recommendation which is,' A man that is a heretic after the first and second admonition, reject' . . ." (Titus 3:10)

These are harsh words. Contrast them with the words of the Fathers of Vatican II. In *Lumen Gentium*, after describing the foundation by Christ of the Church and its nature, they state: *"This is the sole Church of Christ which in the Creed we profess to be one, holy, Catholic and apostolic, which our Savior after his resurrection entrusted to Peter's pastoral care, (John 21:17) commissioning him and the other apostles to extend and rule it (cf. Matthew 28:18 etc.) and which he raised up for all ages as 'the pillar and mainstay of the truth.' (1 Timothy 3:15) This church, constituted and organized as a society in the present world, subsists in the Catholic Church, which is governed by the successor of Peter and by the bishops in communion with him. Nevertheless, many elements of sanctification and of truth are found outside its visible confines. Since these are gifts belonging to the Church of Christ, they are forces impelling towards Catholic unity."* (L.G.8)

The wounds of the division between East and West are keenly felt by Catholics of the Eastern churches who, for the sake of communion with the Apostolic See of Rome, have suffered consequent separation from major portions of their native local churches. Now, as the Church looks to the future, and its recognized mission to evangelize anew throughout the world, we might seek to learn from the lessons of the past so as not to repeat them.

Since the Second Vatican Council a renewed respect for the traditional diversity of authentic ecclesiastical traditions, rites, and way of life has been manifestly insisted upon by the Apostolic See of Rome. *"Between these churches there is such a wonderful communion that this variety, so far from diminishing the Church's unity, rather serves to emphasize it."* (Orientalium Ecclesiarum 2). Our Eastern churches have been constantly reminded of our unique responsibility to give evidence of that essential *"diversity within unity"* for the sake of advancing the prospect for restored ecclesial communion with the Orthodox churches. Especially in more recent years, we have been encouraged—and even directed—to undertake every effort to perfect the formularies of our liturgical rites, restoring them where necessary and aligning them where appropriate, with the texts utilized by our respective counterpart within the Orthodox churches. Such efforts for an informed renewal require an understanding and acceptance of the spirituality of Eastern churches which is necessary to remove the practices we adopted *"to prove we are Catholic"* in light of the historical rejection we once painfully experienced.

Why have I pursued the line I have thus presented, considering my topic is the relationship between the Eastern and Latin churches in America, especially the United States? It is because the history of relations between Catholics of Eastern and Latin churches has not always represented an ideal example of respect and solidarity. If Latin Catholics reflect upon the suspicion and hostility, which they once experienced from the non-Catholic majority in the United States, we Eastern Catholics find more distressing the uninviting reception we were accorded by the predominant Latin hierarchy when we arrived at the shores of the Americas.

While notable examples of fraternal goodwill and practical assistance to fledgling Eastern Catholic communities can be identified, our clergy and faithful can all too easily recall incidents of inequitable and repressive administrative measures imposed upon them which in turn fostered underlying feelings of inferiority and reflexive defensiveness.

Picture the scene of a young Eastern Catholic priest, Father John Wolansky, newly arrived in Shenandoah, Pennsylvania in 1884 from Ukraine to serve the Greek Catholic faithful, being denied the use of the local Catholic Church by the Latin pastor, or having to bury his faithful in the local Odd Fellows cemetery because permission to bury in the Catholic cemetery was refused.

Imagine the feelings Father Wolansky felt when the Latin Archbishop of Philadelphia not only refused to meet with him, but forbade him to exercise his priestly ministry and denied him any jurisdiction to serve the Ukrainian Catholic faithful within the confines of the Archdiocese.

Listen to the words, in a declaration of the Archbishops of the United States, meeting in Chicago in 1893, concerning the different disciplinary practices: "*It is the solemn judgment of the Archbishops of the United States that the presence of married priests of the Greek rite in our midst is a constant menace to the chastity of our unmarried clergy, a source of scandal to the laity and therefore the sooner this discipline is abolished before these evils attain larger proportions, the better for religion, because the loss of a few souls of the Greek rite, bears no proportion to the blessings resulting from uniformity of discipline.*"

The hostile attitude and uncharitable behavior of the Latin hierarchy directed against Eastern rite faithful had a negative impact on Eastern Catholic churches in the U.S., effects which are felt to this day. This hostility resulted in the growth of the Orthodox Church in the Eastern and Midwest U.S. and the eventual loss of hundreds of thousands of Catholic faithful to these Orthodox churches. Indeed, even at this very moment, voices all throughout international Orthodox churches cite this history, in all its effects, as evidence as to why they might rightfully fear drawing so near to Rome. Convincing them that the Catholic Church is truly sincere, as our Holy Father has recently said in his Apostolic Letter *Orientale Lumen*, "*the experience of the individual churches of the East . . . as an authoritative example of successful enculturation,*" is an endeavor, which requires the utmost cooperation between Catholics of all particular churches, including the predominant Latin *sui iuris* Church. To the extent that this intention manifests itself in particular pastoral applications on the level where clergy and laity of different sister churches interact in specific instances, only then will the Church project a genuine paradigm of collegiality and communion.

In this vein I would like to request your consideration of several such practical matters, which have been of constant concern to Eastern Catholic churches.

Some 33 years ago, November 21, 1964, the Council Fathers of Vatican II declared "*Provision must be made therefore everywhere in the world to protect and advance all these individual churches . . . All clerics and those who are to receive sacred orders should be well-instructed concerning rites and particularly rules for inter-ritual questions. Lay people also should receive instruction concerning rites and their rules in their catechetical formation.*" (OE 4). This concern was incorporated in the Code of Canons for Eastern Churches, which reads: "*The Christian faithful of any Church sui iuris, even the Latin Church, who have frequent relations with the Christian faithful of another Church sui iuris by reason of their office, ministry, or function are to be accurately instructed in the knowledge and practice of the rite of that Church in keeping with the seriousness of the office, ministry, or function which they fulfill.* (CCEO #41)

In all candor, let us ask ourselves, a third of a century later, have the words of this decree of the Council Fathers been truly implemented, especially where different churches *sui iuris* exist side by side in the same areas?

Cases still occur when Eastern Catholic children, having received all three sacraments of initiation at baptism according to the ancient custom of the universal church, are made to repeat them at the time their classmates are first receiving them. This does violence to the nature of the sacraments themselves, instills a suggestion of incompleteness of the Eastern tradition, and demonstrates a thorough lack of knowledge concerning the Eastern Church on behalf of the pastor, religious sisters, or lay catechetical director.

We have also found that in seminary courses of instruction, candidates for priesthood are often led to believe that Eastern churches present an outmoded model of ecclesial life not in keeping with the renewal set in motion by the Second Vatican Council. This is especially true in matters of liturgical comparison.

On January 6, 1987, the Congregation for Catholic Education, by its Cardinal Prefect Cardinal William Baum, issued a Circular Letter concerning instructions in the liturgy, law, discipline and spiritual patrimony of the Eastern Churches for Latin Catholics. Let us review the recommendations of the Circular Letter and sincerely ask ourselves if they have been implemented?

In that Circular Letter addressed to the hierarchy, seminary rectors, and heads of ecclesiastical faculties in the United States, Cardinal Baum said, as a result of the *"Massive migration to the American continents from Eastern Europe . . . in the early part of this century . . . further reinforced by new migrations following the Second World War"* Eastern Catholics *"are no longer people who* are distant cousins. They are the brothers and sisters who now live beside Catholics of western tradition throughout the world."

At that time he asked, "how much is known of the liturgical and spiritual life of the ancient Christian tradition of these new neighbors? Are serious efforts being made to acquire and spread this knowledge and to draw suitable conclusions of a pastoral nature?" How far are the theological, liturgical, and ascetical writings of the Fathers and spiritual teachers of the Christian East "becoming properly understood and assimilated by Catholics . . ." ?

In that same document, the Congregation urged "Bishops and Religious Superiors to encourage clergy and lay people who are particularly qualified, to undertake higher studies at the Pontifical Oriental Institute, to support them in these studies, and once trained, to use them effectively in diocesan and religious institutions."

In seminaries and theological faculties, courses should be made available to students on the fundamental notions regarding the Eastern churches, their theological ideas, their liturgical and spiritual traditions. In all seminaries, in accordance with Optatum totius n. 16 . . . there must be a full and proper knowledge of the Fathers of the Church, both East and West. . . . In faculties of Canon Law, adequate attention should be given to disciplines governing Eastern Catholics and to the principal elements of current Orthodox discipline."

In Catholic colleges and universities, attention should be given to including some treatment of Eastern Christianity in the general curriculum of studies. Where there is a significant number of Eastern Christians among the teachers and students, particular care should be given not only to their pastoral needs, but also to making a sufficient academic formation in their religious and cultural traditions."

Ten years ago, Cardinal Baum concluded his Letter by acknowledging *"that, despite progress in this area, there is still need among Catholics of the Latin tradition for a great deal of knowledge of the people, traditions, and churches of the Christian East."*

Sadly, the recommendations of the Congregation for Catholic Education were seemingly ignored, and Cardinal Baum's noble efforts among the Latin Catholics in the United States to increase their knowledge of Eastern Catholics were less than successful.

In matters pertaining to marriage between parties of different *sui iuris* churches, admission of candidates into Latin religious congregations and seminaries, and of Eastern students into Latin parochial schools, Latin authorities often ignore existing canonical legislation. Particularly distressing is the proselytism that often occurs, where a family is informed that the parochial school tuition will be lower simply if the parents would abandon their church and join the Latin parish.

Contrast this disturbing practice with the norm expressed in the Latin Code of Canon Law. *If he (the diocesan bishop) has faithful of a different rite within his diocese, he is to provide for their spiritual needs either by means of priests or parishes of that rite or by means of an episcopal vicar.* (CIC 383.2)

It seems so ironic that in many instances there is a greater emphasis and opportunity provided by the Latin Catholic Church for their clergy, religious, and faithful to learn about the separated Reformation churches of the western tradition, with no corresponding emphasis to teach Latin Catholics about their fellow Catholics of the Eastern churches in union with the See of Peter.

Dear brothers, as we approach the sunset years of the second millennium, we must strive to heal the divisions to the Body of Christ, His Church that characterized the last thousand years. During this, the twentieth century, the Ukrainian Catholic Church has experienced much pain and distress in the United States from these wounds of division, from both our brothers and sisters of the Latin tradition, often through ignorance or pride, and from our brothers and sisters of the Orthodox Churches, because of our fidelity to the See of Peter, which they viewed as a betrayal of our authentic spiritual patrimony. Nevertheless, despite innumerable obstacles, through Divine Providence and the grace of the Holy Spirit, we have managed to survive.

As we approach the Third Millennium, we pray that the Holy Spirit will inspire in all our hearts and souls the grace and grant each of us the wisdom to fulfill the prayer of our Lord, *"so that they may all be one . . . that the world may believe that you sent me."* (John 19:21)

Then the hope and desire of His Holiness, John Paul II, in his Apostolic Letter *Orientale Lumen,* will be fulfilled: *"The words of the West need the words of the East, so that God's Word may ever more clearly reveal its unfathomable riches. Our words will meet forever in the heavenly Jerusalem, but we ask and wish that this meeting be anticipated in the holy Church, which is still on her way towards the fullness of the Kingdom. May God shorten the time and distance. May Christ, the Orientale Lumen, soon very soon, grant us to discover that in fact, despite so many centuries of distance we were very close, because together, perhaps without knowing it, we were walking towards the one Lord, and thus towards one another.*

The text of my intervention had to be given in advance to the office of the Secretary of the Synod. The time assigned for each speaker was eight minutes. When someone tried to speak longer, his microphone was disconnected. Of course I could not finish reading my intervention in eight minutes, but I was not the only one. Many Synodal Fathers had pages and pages of undelivered speeches. The Secretariat assured us that their reporters would read the entire speech and take into consideration their context.

Before the daily session, and especially during the coffee breaks, many of the Synodal Fathers would approach me, congratulate me on my intervention, and express their astonishment on Patriarch Bartholomew's negative position on the unity of churches. Somehow they were of the conviction that unity between the Catholic and the Orthodox churches is very close and might happen any time soon.

This topic was a theme of daily conversations and discussions among many of the Synodal Fathers. They asked me: "What do the other Orthodox Bishops think about a possible unity with the Catholic Church?" To such and similar questions I had this response: "The Orthodox bishops as well as their priests and religious in general do not trust the Catholic ecumenical movement. They shun their own bishops who are involved in any kind of dealings or ecumenical meetings with Catholics. They have a suspicion that the Catholic ecumenical movement is only a method of enticing them to the Catholic Church. This they do not want. They consider the Orthodox Church as the only true Church, while the Pope and the Catholic Church are heretics. They do not want any kind of unity not even between the Orthodox themselves. They have no one as the head of their church. The Patriarch of Constantinople is only the first among equals. For over one thousand years they were not able to convoke a single "Ecumenical Orthodox Synod." Thus the possibility of union with the Orthodox churches is far in the distant future. All of us should pray fervently for the Holy Spirit to come upon the Orthodox and us to enkindle in our and their hearts and souls a fervent desire for unity among Christians so that the Orthodox, too, would desire the unity.

The Holy Father was present at all the sessions of the Synod and attentively listened to the interventions, except on Wednesday morning when he held a general audience. He would invite ten to twelve bishops for lunch and the same number for dinner to his private apartment. On Monday, November 24, I had the honor of being invited to a dinner with the Holy Father. He recognized me immediately since it was not the first time that I had the honor of being with him.

For the duration of the Synod there were 250 interventions. Some 62% of these were given in Spanish, 20% in English, 10% in Portuguese, while the others were in French or Italian. Each intervention was translated simultaneously into any of the above named languages.

In all the interventions, and especially in the discussion of the small language groups, one could easily discern that each delegate was trying to give his best for the good of the Church. In all the interventions it was clear that the Holy Spirit was present among us and aided us in achieving common understanding and agreed-upon resolutions. On Friday, November 12th the Holy Father celebrated a solemn Eucharistic Liturgy of thanksgiving with all the Synodal Fathers as concelebrants at the Basilica of St. Peter. I offered this Liturgy as my private thanksgiving to God for the grace of being able to be a participant in this historic Synod.

Following the Liturgy, the Holy Father invited all the Synodal Fathers to the Santa Marta House in the Vatican for a lunch. I departed from Rome the following day, Saturday, November 13th. I took a flight to Lviv through Warsaw for a meeting of the Permanent Synod.

Pope's Visit to Ukraine

I had the great and unique pleasure, as well as the unforgettable experience, of being able to take part in this historic first visit of Pope John Paul II to Ukraine, from Saturday, June 23, to Wednesday, June 27, 2001. I arrived in Kiev at the Boryspol Airport Thursday, June 21, 2001, and was met by two young ladies from the Coordinating Committee. They drove me to the Rus' Hotel, a fairly modern structure, well-furnished and structured, with American prices. There I met some of our bishops who had arrived before me and was able to exchange some impressions concerning the city itself and the tense preparations for welcoming the Pope. Soon our local bishop, Vasyl Medwit, OSBM, came to visit us and gave us written instructions and the schedule of our activities.

Watching television, I saw a demonstration composed of some fifty Orthodox monks and nuns from the Monastery of the Caves, under the jurisdiction of the Moscow Patriarchate. The demonstrators were marching with banners and carrying icons, protesting the visit of the Pope. Some of them called the Pope the Antichrist and the Devil. The Russian Orthodox Church had already been opposing the Pope's visit to Ukraine for many months. The press was full of these protests for a long time before the actual visit.

Later on I was able to contact Rev. Theodosius Jankiw, OSBM, former Provincial Superior of the Basilian Fathers in Ukraine, by phone. He was able to secure a building lot and erect a new church and a monastery building in Kiev, close to the Dnipro River. He invited me to concelebrate a Divine Liturgy on Friday, June 22, 2001, which marked the official opening of the new church and monastery. The church structure is of a more modern architectural design with a great deal of glass and outdoor light. Bishop Medwit was the main celebrant with other bishops and several priests as concelebrants. The buildings were not quite complete. There was a lot of work yet to be done before an official dedication. Yet it was a colossal achievement of this very capable and talented priest, especially in Kiev, the capital city where Catholics are a very small minority with very few friends.

Saturday, June 23, 2001, was the day of the Pope's arrival at the Kiev airport. The arrival was scheduled for 12:30 P.M. The bishops were transported from the hotel by a bus and arrived at the airport at approximately 11:00 A.M. On the bus each of us received an I.D. tag. As we assembled in one of the rooms, an official escorted us outside to the chairs set up in rows. I was fortunate to sit in the front row and thus had a good view of everything.

The Al Italia airplane landed minutes before schedule, taxied slowly so that at 12:30 P.M. the plane was close to the welcoming platform. The Holy Father walked slowly down the stairway from the plane, waving his hand in reply to the loud applause. Behind him came his entourage consisting of a few cardinals, archbishops, and bishops. The press people came out of the plane by the rear doors.

As soon as the Holy Father stepped on the ground, Mr. Leonid Kuchma, the President of Ukraine, welcomed him, and three girls, dressed in Ukrainian national costumes welcomed him with bread and salt. Another girl had some Ukrainian soil on a platter. The Holy Father kissed the soil. As the Pope stepped on the platform, the military band began playing the Ukrainian and then the Vatican anthems. Afterward a 21-gun salute was given. Then President Kuchma approached the microphone and gave his welcoming speech:

On behalf of the Ukrainian people and myself I heartily welcome the Head of the Vatican State His Holiness John Paul II onto the Ukrainian soil.

This day will certainly become a milestone in our nation's history. We welcome His Holiness not only as the Head of the Church uniting more than one billion people worldwide. We welcome, first of all, a prominent figure of the present, a person who was in the epicenter of great events that changed the character of our world. Today Ukraine welcomes the unbending champion of human rights and dignity, inflexible enemy of totalitarianism, intolerance, discrimination, and fratricidal conflicts . . ."

Afterward the Holy Father gave a very moving talk in Ukrainian:

I have long awaited this visit and have prayed fervently that it might take place. Finally, with deep joy, I have been able to kiss the beloved soil of Ukraine. I thank God for the gift, which today he has given me . . . I come among you, dear citizens of Ukraine, as a friend of your noble nation. I come as a brother in the faith to embrace all the Christians who, amid the severest tribulations, have persevered in their fidelity to Christ. I come in love, to express to all the sons and daughters of this nation, to Ukrainians of every culture and religious background, my esteem and my cordial friendship.

I greet you, Ukraine, brave and determined witness of adherence to the values of faith. How much you suffered in order to vindicate, in difficult times, the freedom to profess this faith . . .

As a pilgrim of peace and brotherhood, I am sure that I shall be welcomed with friendship also by those who, although they are not Catholic, have hearts open to dialogue and cooperation. I wish to assure them that I have not come here with the intention of proselytizing, but to bear witness to Christ together with all Christians of every Church and Ecclesial Community, and to invite all the sons and daughters of this noble Land to turn their eyes to Him who gave His life for the salvation of the world . . .

These are the thoughts that fill my heart as I take my first steps on this visit, eagerly awaited and today happily begun. God bless you, dear people of Ukraine, and may He always protect your beloved Homeland!"

After the Holy Father's speech, the military units paraded in front of the platform on which the great guest and the President were sitting, while the military band played some beautiful marching music. It was all so very beautiful that tears of joy filled my eyes.

A long caravan of automobiles and buses began to roll from the airport into the city. On each side of the road about every hundred yards or so there was an armed soldier standing and facing away from the road. Then we noticed that some distance from the road there were another two rows of soldiers, likewise armed and facing away from the road. Entering the city of Kiev we noticed that the armed soldiers were standing closer to each other and were more numerous. We were informed that the people of the city were told not to stand on the sidewalks, not to look through the windows and not to carry an umbrella. During the Pope's visit, workers were not given a day off from work, so they could not attend the Pope's Liturgies.

On his way from the airport, the Holy Father stopped before a Ukrainian Catholic Church (or rather a chapel) of St. Nicholas where the miraculous icon of the Most Holy Mother Mary from Zarvanycia, was purposely brought from Western Ukraine. The Holy Father knelt before this icon, and prayed thus:

"O Blessed Virgin Mary, Our Lady of Zarvanycia, I thank you for the gift of my visit to the Kievan Rus' From where the light of the Gospel spread through this whole region.

Here before your miraculous icon, Kept in this church of Saint Nicholas, I entrust to you, Mother of God and Mother of the Church, My apostolic journey to Ukraine.

Holy Mother of God, Spread your maternal mantle over all Christians and over all people of good will who live in this great nation.

Lead them to your Son, Jesus, Who is for everyone the way, the truth and the life."

The Holy Father stayed at the Apostolic Nunciature in Kiev. This same day he paid a visit to the President of Ukraine and his family at 6:00 P.M. And at 6:30 P.M. he had a meeting with the representatives of culture, science, and politics at the Mariansky Palace.

The following day was a Sunday. June 24, 2001. The main event for that day was the Latin Eucharistic Liturgy held at the Chayka Airport. A high platform was erected for the altar so the great masses of people could see the Pope and the bishops with him. Ukrainian Catholic bishops concelebrated this Liturgy. The Liturgy was mostly in Ukrainian. This is the first time I heard the Latin Mass said in Ukrainian. The attendance was impressive. Present were several hundred thousand pilgrims on the huge field. There were some people from Poland waving Polish flags. But the great majority must have been local Ukrainian Orthodox people who came to see the Holy Father and hear him speak, in spite of the difficulties they had to overcome to get there. The weather was good and since it was a Sunday, free from work, it made it easier for the people to attend this Liturgy.

Following this Liturgy, all the bishops were bused to the Apostolic Nunciature for a luncheon with the Holy Father. The dining room was not large enough to accommodate all the invited guests, so some were seated in other rooms. But the bishops were all in the dining room. The Holy Father spoke to us thus:

> The joy of today's meeting will grow still stronger in the days to come. When together we shall take part in the solemn beatification of your brother bishops, who exercised their episcopal ministry in the most dangerous of circumstances. We will pay them the homage of our gratitude for having persevered intact, by their sacrifice, the heritage of Christian faith among the members of their Churches. In raising them to the honor of the altar, I wish to recall with gratitude other Pastors, too, who also paid dearly for their faithfulness to Christ and for their decision to remain in union with the Successor of Peter.

> How can we fail to recall, among them, the Servant of God Metropolitan Andrew Sheptytsky? My revered predecessor, Pope Pius XII, declared that his noble life was cut short "not so much by his advanced age, but by the sufferings of his soul as Pastor, struck down with his flock" (AAS XLIV [1955], p. 877). Together with him, I recall Cardinal Joseph Slipyj, first Rector of the Greek Catholic Theological Academy of Lviv, happily reopened in recent times. This heroic confessor of faith suffered the hardship of imprisonment for eighteen long years.

> Among you are still priests and Bishops who were imprisoned and persecuted. I embrace you with deep emotion, dear Brothers, I give praise for your faithful witness. It encourages me to accomplish my own service to the universal Church with ever more courageous dedication. I make my own the words, which you say when you celebrate the Liturgy of Saint John Chrysostom: *'Let us commend ourselves and one another and our whole life to Christ our God.'* This is what the martyrs and confessors of the faith teach us. It is a lesson which we too must learn and live as Pastors of the flock which God has entrusted to us."

Following the luncheon, the Pope's attendees distributed to each of the Bishops present there a package, containing a pectoral cross with a chain, a number of rosaries, medallions, and other religious souvenirs.

At 5:15 P.M. that day the Holy Father took part in the meeting of the representatives of the Ukrainian Council of Churches and religious organizations, held at the Palace of the National Philharmonic. Represented were Ukrainian Orthodox of the Kievan Patriarchate, the Ukrainian Orthodox Autocephalous Church, Protestants, as well as Jews and Muslims. No one came from the Ukrainian Orthodox Church of the Moscow Patriarchate. Patriarch Filaret of the Kievan Patriarchate greeted the Pope with these words:

For the first time in history a peaceful foot of the Head of the Roman Catholic Church stepped upon the Ukrainian soil where in the past a war between the Catholics and the Orthodox was waged. The world respects you as the peace-making Pope, who tries to heal the wounds upon the body of the churches and of all mankind. You try to appease what from a mere human viewpoint seems to be unappeasable.

We hope that your visit to Ukraine will help the development of a dialogue between the Orthodox and the Catholics and not what the Moscow Patriarchate prophesies—a deepening of the division. We will gladly witness that the Orthodox and the Catholics can and should live as brothers and sisters in the spirit in Christian charity. Your visit will aid this cause . . ."

The next day, Monday, June 25, 2001, a Byzantine Liturgy was celebrated at the Chayka sports complex. Cardinal Husar was the main celebrant with all the bishops as concelebrants. Hundreds of priest vested in Liturgical vestments concelebrated and distributed Holy Communion. The attendance was likewise very good. Even though it was a working day, many thousands of people came, and most of them must have been local Ukrainian Orthodox. In his homily the Holy Father among other things said this:

> With your independence renewed again, a new period, rich in promises, has been opened. This obliges the citizens to follow the goal of "building your own house"—Ukraine as Metropolitan Andrew Sheptytsky used to say. Ukraine is a free and independent state for ten years already. These ten years have shown that, in spite of lawlessness and corruption, her spiritual roots are strong. I express my sincere wish that Ukraine would continue to be nourished by the personal, communal, and Church morality, serving the common good, human dignity and self-dedication, not forgetting the gift of the Ten Commandments of God. The vitality of her faith and the power of her revitalized Church are worthy of admiration. The roots of her past became a pledge of hope for her future.

In the afternoon all the bishops, along with some dignitaries, left Kiev on a chartered plane for Lviv to be there before the Holy Father arrived so as to be able to welcome him there.

Pope's Visit to Lviv

The bishops were taken to a hotel "Hetman," located on Vladimir the Great Street in Lviv and were assigned rooms. Soon afterward a bus took us back to the airport for the arrival of the Holy Father. The airport was full of people eagerly awaiting the Pope. There were a lot of young people dressed in national costumes, President Kuchma, representatives of state and local governments, and the city fathers. The sidewalks were full of people stretching from the airport to the center of the city. There were also armed military men, but not as many as there were in Kiev. On his way from the airport the Holy Father was welcomed warmly and enthusiastically by the crowds of people from the sidewalks and windows of homes with small papal and Ukrainian flags and shouts: "Welcome, Holy Father!" "John Paul II, we love you!" The joy and the enthusiasm of this Catholic city were plain and visible to the world through the mass media. It was something like a triumphant entry of a conqueror of old that the Holy Father received when coming from the airport to center city and then to St. George's Ukrainian Catholic Cathedral. He resided at the Metropolitan's Residence at St. George's, which was especially renovated and refurbished for this purpose.

The following day, Tuesday, June 26, 2001, the Latin Liturgy on the huge Hippodrome field was the main event of the day. Several hundred thousand people were present. Almost half of the field was filled with faithful. There were many pilgrims from nearby Poland who came by bus and displayed their Polish flags. Yet the majority were local Ukrainian Catholics.

The Holy Father was the main celebrant of this Liturgy while the Latin and the Ukrainian Byzantine Bishops concelebrated. The highlight of this Liturgy was the beatification of two Polish clerics, Josef Bilczewski (1860–1923), a Latin Archbishop of Lviv, and Zygmund Gorazdowski (1845–1920), a Latin priest of the Lviv Archdiocese. Following this Liturgy our bishops were invited by Cardinal Marian Jaworski to a luncheon held in their seminary located in the section of the city called Briuchowychi.

The Pope's meeting with the Ukrainian youth took place that day in the afternoon on a large meadow-like field in front of the Nativity of the Mother of God Church in the section of Lviv called Sykhiv. Some estimated that between five and six hundred thousand young people were present there. The throne for the Pope was erected on an elevated platform before the entrance to the church with a canopy overhead.

On his way from St. George's cathedral to the Church in Sykhiv, the Pope's mobile stopped at the site where the future Ukrainian Catholic University is to be erected. Father Borys Gudziak, Rector of the Lviv Theological Academy, addressed the Pope:

Holy Father! The Lviv Theological Academy, the future Ukrainian Catholic University, greets you with these holy images. We ask you, Holy Father: bless our Academy, the future Ukrainian Catholic University, its professors, workers, students and their families; bless the ground of the Ukrainian Catholic University, its building, and its future.

As a memento of this act we ask you to accept from us this portable altar with cup and discos, on which confessors of the faith during the time of the catacomb existence of our Church celebrated the Liturgy. From Ukrainian catacombs to the Roman catacombs!

In response, the Holy Father blessed the grounds and building of the future Ukrainian Catholic University with holy water, saying: "May the Almighty God, Father, Son, and Holy Spirit bless you, now and always and unto ages of ages. Amen."
The arrival of the Holy Father to the place of his meeting with the youth was met by thunderous chants and yells of "Veetayemo! Veetayemo!"—Welcome! Welcome! As the Holy Father sat on his throne, a young man, named Oleh Horodetsky from the Ternopil Eparchy, addressed him:

"On behalf of millions of Ukrainian youth, together with the whole Ukrainian Catholic Church, with great joy and expectation we, the young generation of our country, greet Your Holiness.

We are the descendants of Volodymyr the Great, the baptizer of Ukraine, and Danylo, who received his crown from the Apostolic See. We have grown up with the experience of many generations, strengthened by the blood of the martyrs and the persecuted. Today we have a special grace from God, the grace, together with Your Holiness and in union with the Universal Church, to praise God's holy name at this significant time for Ukraine. Your service, as well as your whole life, is an example for us of love of Christ and neighbor, to which we also aspire.

We hope and sincerely believe that Your Holiness' visit to Ukraine, blessed by God, will begin a new stage in development of our Church, nation, and state. We trust that your great mission will confirm the truth of the Christian faith among Ukrainians and that the evil, which comes from our recent past, will disappear, never to return . . .

We hear you, we listen to you, we look into your shining eyes, and we follow the word of your teaching. We have come today to show our love for you and our faithfulness to the Apostle Peter of our day.

Holy Father, bless today Ukrainian youth and through them the future of our people, so that resurrected Ukraine will follow Christ, for He is the Way, the Truth, and the Life."

The meeting was opened with a Prayer Service during which the Holy Father addressed the youth:

Dear young people, Christ has the "words of eternal life." His words last forever, and above all they open for us the gates of eternal life. When God speaks, His words give life, they call things into existence, they direct our journey, and they restore disappointed and broken hearts and pour fresh hope into them . . .

Your country is going through a difficult and complex transition form the totalitarian regime that oppressed it for so many years to a society at last free and democratic. Freedom, however, needs strong, responsible, and mature consciences. Freedom is demanding, and in a sense is more costly than slavery.

For this reason, as I embrace you like a father, I say to you: choose the narrow path that the Lord is showing you through His commandments. They are words of truth and life. The path that often seems wide and easy later shows itself to be deceptive and false. Do not go from the slavery of the communist regime to the slavery of consumerism, another form of materialism, which, without explicitly rejecting God, actually does deny Him by excluding Him from life.

Without God you will not be able to do anything good. With His help, however, you will be able to face all the challenges of the present moment. You will succeed in making demanding decisions against the current, as for example the decision to stay confidently in your own country, without giving in to the illusions of an easy life abroad. You are needed here, young people, ready to make your contribution to improving the social, cultural, economic, and political situation of your own country. Here the talents in which you are rich are needed for the future of your country, which has such a glorious history behind it . . .

As the Holy Father began his talk, a torrential rain began to fall. The umbrellas opened up, and some people, who were prepared, put on their raincoats with hoods. However, no one left. I had no raincoat or an umbrella. Someone behind me noticed that, and gave me his umbrella, saying: "Father, please take it, I have a rain coat." I was very grateful to this unknown person. The Holy Father observed carefully the determined behavior of his audience. He interrupted his talk and joked with the youth, saying in Polish: "Let it rain—the children will grow!" He continued his talk, and as the rain did not let up, he repeated his joke. When he finally finished his talk, jokingly he then sang a Polish folk song to the youth:

"Set, sun, as you have to set, because our legs hurt from walking in the field. Because our legs hurt from walking in the field.

If you were a day laborer, sun, then you, sun, would set more quickly. Then you, sun, would set more quickly."

As soon as he finished singing, the rain stopped, and the setting sun came out again!

The Greatest Day in History

ednesday, June 27, 2001 I consider the greatest day in
the history of the Ukrainian Catholic Church. Even
though a torrential rain fell the whole night through, it
stopped in the morning and the sun came out. The field where the
people gathered became one huge mass of mud. Yet nothing de-
terred the people. They came from all over Western Ukraine. Some
made it a pilgrimage and walked barefoot, making it a penitential
action. They came from other neighboring countries as well. The
field was partitioned into sections by ropes with wide walks between them. Each section was numbered. When the Bishops processed from the lower level of the huge platform to the upper level
where the altar was, I could see the huge field completely filled
with the people. There was nowhere an empty spot as far as the
eye could see.

The approximate count was two million or more. I was told
that about half a million people could not be admitted to the field
because they had no admission tickets. The admission was closed
at 8:00 A.M. even when one had an admission ticket. So they were
outside, filling the streets and the wide sides of the field. This was
the largest attendance at a Divine Liturgy in the history of Ukraine.
When the choir sang the responses to the Liturgy, the whole huge

congregation sang along with them. Thus this again was the largest choir ever to sing the Liturgy.

In front of the altar platform, on the ground, several hundred priests, vested in especially made-for-this-occasion liturgical vestments, concelebrated the Liturgy. In front of them many tables were set up, covered with white cloths, upon which were set hundreds of chalices to be used by the priests to distribute Holy Communion.

Before the Liturgy began, His Beatitude Cardinal Lubomyr Husar, welcomed the Holy Father with these words:

> The grace of the Holy Spirit has today brought us together with you, Most Holy Father, in common prayer at this Divine Liturgy . . . The masses of people present here today—and I am their spokesman—bear witness directly that our Church has survived the persecution successfully, and has returned as soon as it was possible to a normal public existence. We are very proud of this, but do not consider it to be our own accomplishment. Indeed, we are aware that the divine grace has sustained us, revealing to the world a true miracle: the rebirth of our Church. Divine grace has been particularly present in these brothers and sisters of ours, many of whom are present today: bishops, priests, monks, sisters, and lay people who received the overflowing gift from God and with his help witnessed to the whole world their faithfulness to God and his Church. Some of them, as the first fruits of countless martyrs and confessors that this land has given, you, Most Holy Father, will proclaim blessed before those present and all those who follow this Liturgy. For this we are profoundly grateful.

> We extend to you our most sincere acknowledgment, Most Holy Father, for the gift of your personal care for our Church, and in your person we thank also your predecessors who sustained us during the seemingly endless years of persecution. Unity with

the Apostolic See of Rome became a spiritual treasure for our Church and an unshakable support . . ."

The main celebrant of this Liturgy was Cardinal Husar with the bishops as concelebrants while the Holy Father was presiding at a throne on the right side of the altar. The Rite of the Beatification took place after the little entrance of the Liturgy. The diocesan bishops, from whose dioceses the candidates for the beatification came, were asked to approach the Holy Father and ask him to proclaim as Blessed their candidates. Thus Cardinal Husar spoke in their name: "Holy Father, the Major Archbishop of Lviv for Ukrainians, the Bishop of Mukachiv of the Byzantine Rite, the Bishop of Ivano-Frankivsk (Stanyslaviv) for Ukrainians and the Bishop of Sokal for Ukrainians ask Your Holiness to add to the ranks of the Blessed the Servants of God: Mykola Charnetsky and 24 fellow martyrs, Theodore Romzha, Emilian Kovch and Josaphata Hordashevska." Then each of the bishops there present read aloud the biography of his candidate.

The Servants of God to Be Beatified

Mykola Charnetsky was born December 14, 1884 in the village of Semakivtsi, Ivano-Frankivsk District. In 1903 he entered the seminary in Stanyslaviv. He continued his theological studies in Rome, where he defended his doctorate and in 1909 he was ordained to the priesthood. After returning to his homeland he became a spiritual director and teacher at the seminary in Stanyslaviv. In 1919 he entered the novitiate of the Redemptorist Fathers in Lviv. In 1926 he began work in Volyn, where the Tsarist regime had destroyed the structures of the Greek Catholic Church in the 19th century. In 1931 he became Apostolic Visitor for Catholics of the Byzantine-Slavonic Rite in Poland. The Servant of God was ordained bishop in Rome February 2, 1931. He was arrested with the other Ukrainian Catholic bishops by the NKVD (KGB) April 11, 1945. At first he was sentenced to six years of hard labor in Siberia and he spent 11 years in prison. He suffered terrible tortures and interrogations. He bore all with patience, finding the strength to pray for his persecutors and to comfort his fellow prisoners, for whom he was a spiritual leader. In 1956 the Servant of God Mykola Charnetsky, debilitated and terminally ill, was released from prison. In Lviv he became a pastor for the catacomb church. He died April 2, 1959. From the very start, the people considered him a saint and a martyr for the faith. There are faithful constantly praying at his grave.

The group of 24 servants of God, martyrs of the Ukrainian Catholic Church from the World War Two period who witnessed to their faith in God during persecution for the faith by the Communist regime is composed of: seven bishops, seven eparchial priests, seven hieromonks, three nuns, and one layman:

1. **Hryhorij Khomyshyn**, bishop of Stanyslaviv (1867–1945).

2. **Josaphat Kocylovskyj, OSBM, bishop** of Peremyshl (1876–1947).

3. **Symeon Lukach**, bishop of the catacomb Church (1893–1964).

4. **Vasyl Velychkovskyj**, bishop of the catacomb Church (1903–1973).

5. **Ivan Sleziuk**, bishop of the catacomb Church (1896–1973).

6. **Mykyta Budka**, auxiliary bishop of Lviv, the first bishop of Canada for Ukrainians (1877–1949).

7. **Hryhorij Lakota**, auxiliary bishop of Peremyshl (1883–1950).

8. **Leonid Fiodorov**, studite monk, Exarch for Eastern Catholics in Russia (1879–1935).

9. **Mykola Konrad**, a priest of the Lviv Archeparchy (1876–1941).

10. **Andrij Ishchak**, a priest of the Lviv Archeparchy (1887–1941).

11. **Roman Lysko**, a priest of the Lviv Archeparchy (1914–1949).

12. **Mykola Cehelskyj**, a priest of the Lviv Archeparchy (1896–1951).

13. **Petro Verhun**, a priest of the Lviv Archeparchy, Apostolic Visitator for Ukrainian Catholics in Germany (1890–1957).

14. **Oleksa Zaryckyj**, a priest of the Lviv Archeparchy (1912–1963).

15. **Klymentij Sheptytsky**, a hieromonk, an Archimandrite of the Univ Monastery (1869–1951).

16. **Severijan Baranyk**, OSBM, a priest (1889–1941).

17. **Jakym Senkivskyj**, OSBM, a priest (1896–1941)

18. **Zynovij Kovalyk**, CSsR a priest (1903–1941).

19. **Vitalij Bajrak**, OSBM, a priest (1907–1946).

20. **Ivan Ziatyk**, CSsR, a priest (1899–1952).

21. **Tarsykia (Olha Mackiw)**, a sister of the SSMI (1919–1944).

22. **Olympia (Olha Bida)**, a sister of St. Joseph (1903–1952).

23. **Laurentia (Leukadia Harasymiv)**, a sister of St. Joseph (1911–1952).

24. **Volodymyr Pryjma**, a layman, cantor (1906–1941).

Bishop Theodore Romzha was born April 14, 1911 in the village of Velykyj Bychkiv, Transcarpathia into a railroad worker's family. His theological studies were conducted at the Papal Gregorian University in Rome. In 1936 he was ordained to the priesthood. In 1938 he became pastor in the village of Berezovo and Nyzhnij Bystryi, Khust District. Beginning with the fall of 1939 he taught philosophy and was spiritual director at the Uzhorod Spiritual Academy. On September 24, 1944 he was ordained to the episcopacy. In accordance with plans drawn up from Stalin's directives in 1945, the subjugation and the total destruction of the Greek Catholic Church were foreseen. The clergy and laity would be assimilated into the Russian Orthodox Church. Because Bishop Theodore Romzha bravely refused to cooperate with the authorities and leave the unity of the Catholic Church, and because he called his clergy and faithful to join him, he became an obstacle to the liquidation of the Greek Catholic Church. The officials could not find Bishop Theodore guilty of any charges, even fabricated ones. Therefore authorities at the highest level made the decision to destroy the bishop. They took advantage of a trip the bishop was taking: a large truck collided with the horse-drawn carriage in which he was riding. The bishop and his companions were wounded and taken to the hospital. But the General of the Security Service was already waiting there. He organized the bishop's poisoning, which was successfully carried out on November 1, 1947.

Father Emilian Kovch, a victim of the Nazis, was a priest of the Stanyslaviv eparchy, married, the father of six children. He was born on August 20, 1884, in Kosmach near Kosiv into a priest's family. He prepared for the priesthood at the Roman College of Saints Sergius and Bacchus, studying theology at the Urbanum University. In 1911 he was ordained to the priesthood. At first he worked in western Ukraine, later in Bosnia, where he volunteered to minister to Ukrainian settlers. In 1919 he became field chaplain for the Ukrainian Galician Army. In these stormy years in the life of the Servant of God Emilian there were many situations, which, on first glance, seemed hopeless. One might say that only a miracle rescued Father Kovch at these times. In 1922 Father Kovch was appointed pastor in Peremyshliany. He began actively organizing the religious, social, and cultural life of his parishioners. His house was a refuge for orphans, a shelter for the poor. "Angels fly over this house." Thus spoke the parishioners in Peremyshliany about the humble building in which the Kovch family lived. During the German occupation Father Emilian bravely fought anti-Semitism. He baptized those Jews who requested it. On December 30, 1942 he was arrested for this activity. At first he was a prisoner in Lviv, but in August 1943 he was taken to the Majdanek concentration camp. Learning that his family was trying to have him freed, he wrote: "I am asking you not to do anything. Yesterday they killed 50 persons here. If I were not here, who would help them to endure these sufferings?" About his experience of suffering with the prison community he said: "Except heaven, this is the only place I would want to be. Poles, Jews, Ukrainians, Russians, Latvians, and Estonians. Here I see God who is the same for all of us, regardless of the religious differences which exist among us." The Servant of God Emilian Kovch died on March 25, 1944 in the concentration camp's infirmary. In one of his letters to his family he wrote: "Pray for those who created this concentration camp and this system. They are the ones who need prayers. . . . May God have mercy on them . . ."

The Servant of God **Sister Josaphata Hordashevska** was born in Lviv 1869 into a poor family. From a young age Josaphata manifested piety and clear signs of virtue. At the age of 18 she participated in a retreat conducted by Father Lomnytsky, OSBM, who became her spiritual director. In 1892 Josaphata, together with Father Lomnytsky and Father Kyryl Seletsky, established the Sisters Servants of Mary Immaculate, the first female religious congregation called to an active apostolate among the people. Josaphata wanted this congregation to become a light for her poor fellow countrymen, who at that time were spiritually and socially neglected. The Sisters Servants had a great field for the apostolate: they took care of the sick, established shelters for children, taught catechism to young and old, looked after the cleanliness of village churches, sewed ecclesiastical vestments and took an active part in parish life. The growth of the congregation was unprecedented. In 10 years there were 123 sisters in 23 centers. In those years the Sisters traveled to Canada, Yugoslavia and Brazil. Now the Sisters Servants work in 16 countries and the newest mission is in Kazakhstan. Sister Josaphata's holiness showed itself in her total dedication to her calling, in constant embodying in her life Christ's command to love God and neighbor. Calling Christ to mind every day gave her the strength to accept all the hardships of life peacefully. The Servant of God speaks to modern humanity about the beauty of radical evangelical life and about the need for compassion and active love towards the needy.

After the short biographies of the Servants of God had been read, all were asked to rise. The Holy Father, sitting, ceremoniously pronounced:

"Carrying out the request of our brothers, Lubomyr Husar, Major Archbishop of Lviv for Ukrainians, His Excellency Ivan Semedij of Mukachiv of the Byzantine Rite, His Excellency Sofron Mudryj, Bishop of Ivano-Frankivsk (Stanyslaviv) for Ukrainians, His Excellency Mykhail Koltun, Bishop of Sokal for Ukrainians, and many other episcopal brothers and many faithful, after hearing the opinion of the Congregation for the Causes of Saints, **by our apostolic authority we allow from this moment on the most honored Servants of God:**

Mykola Charnetsky and 24 fellow martyrs, Theodore Romzha, Emilian Kovch and Josaphata Hordashevska, to be honored as Blessed and their feast to be celebrated every year in the month and according to the following designated rule, namely:

Mykola Charnetsky and 24 fellow martyrs on 27 June;
Theodore Romzha on 1 November;
Emilian Kovch on 27 June
And Josaphata Hordashevska on 20 November.

In the name of the Father and the Son and the Holy Spirit."

The choir and all the people sang: Amen. Amen. Amen.

Now the icons of the newly proclaimed Blessed were brought from the lower level up the stairs to the platform. Cardinal Husar then thanked the Holy Father:

"We thank Your Holiness for today proclaiming Blessed those honored Servants of God: Mykola Charnetsky and 24 fellow martyrs, Theodore Romzha, Emilian Kovch and Josaphata Hordashevska.

Then the bishops present for the beatification exchanged a kiss of peace with the Holy Father.

After the Gospel reading the Holy Father in his homily said:

"Greater love has no man than this, that a man lay down his life for his friends (John 15:13). This solemn statement of Christ echoes among us today with particular eloquence, as we proclaim Blessed a group of sons and daughters of this glorious Church of Lviv of the Ukrainians. Most of them were killed in hatred of the Christian faith. Some underwent martyrdom in times close to us, and among those present at today's Divine Liturgy there are some who knew them personally. This land of Halychyna, which in the course of history has witnessed the growth of the Ukrainian Catholic Church, has been covered, as the unforgettable Metropolitan Josyf Slipyj used to say, "with mountains of corpses and rivers of blood."

Yours is a living and fruitful community, which goes back to the preaching of the holy brothers Cyril and Methodius, to Saint Vladimir and Olga. The example of the martyrs from different periods of history, but especially from the past century, testifies to the fact that martyrdom is the highest measure of service of

God and of the Church. With this celebration we wish to pay homage to the martyrs and to thank the Lord for their fidelity.

With this evocative rite of beatification, it is likewise my desire to express the whole Church's gratitude to the People of God in Ukraine for Mykola Charnetsky and his 24 companion Martyrs, as well as for Martyrs Theodore Romzha and Omelian Kovch, and for the Servant of God Josaphata Mychajlyna Hordashevska. Just as the grain of wheat falls into the ground and dies in order to give life to the new plant (*cf. John 12:24*), so, too, did the Blessed offer their lives so that the field of God would bear fruit in a new and more abundant harvest . . ."

The visit of Pope John Paul II to Ukraine can and must be called historic, unique, highly significant, and epoch-making. This unequaled gathering of the faithful of the Ukrainian Catholic Church to worship together with their beloved Pope was about the greatest manifestation of their faith ever in this country. It was a public profession of their Catholic faith for the whole world to see. It was also a public thanksgiving to God for the freedom of their Church and their country.

What will be the long-ranging effects of this visit, only history will be able to judge. How much good this successor of St. Peter has done with his visit to the Ukrainian people and their Church is incomparable. The Pope's homilies were so excellent that they were much more than we had hoped for. Each word was well prepared and analyzed. In my lifetime I read hundreds of papal letters, encyclicals, and speeches. Yet his homilies and speeches in Ukraine were so well and thoroughly prepared, dogmatically balanced, politically and diplomatically weighted, that they will remain for a long time as this Pope's deep respect to our nation and his love of our Church. I hold deep conviction that by words and deeds of this seemingly feeble old man, the Holy Spirit descended from above with His almighty graces and blessings of life and joy becharmed Ukraine. His white stature became like the sailboat, which shows clearly which way the winds of the future blow.

The Pope's visit had an immediate effect on all citizens. People would walk with their heads up and with smiles on their faces, which before was unusual or very rare. Even the government officials became kinder and gentler. It was evident that the Pope has returned hope to Ukrainians as a nation. In their souls for most of them, for the first time in their lives, there arose feelings of moral "good" and "evil." Their consciousness was awakened; it became alive and the curative action of their conscience became legitimate and normal.

One thing remains clear, evident, and most certain—John Paul II is a great friend of Ukraine and the Ukrainian people. He loves our Church, the ritual, and wholeheartedly has supported us from the very first day of his pontificate.

My Retirement

In the new "Code of Canons of the Eastern Churches" in canon 210.1–2, the law reads: *"An eparchial bishop who has completed his seventy-fifth year of age or who, due to ill health or another serious reason, has become less able to fulfill his office, is requested to present his resignation from office. This resignation from office by the eparchial bishop is to be submitted to the patriarch if it is the case of an eparchial bishop exercising authority inside the territorial boundaries of a patriarchal Church; in other cases, it is submitted to the Roman Pontiff; further, if the bishop belongs to a patriarchal Church, the patriarch is to be notified as soon as possible."*

Some of my brother bishops and some canonists interpret this law as not strictly obligatory since it states that a bishop "is requested," not that he should or must. I personally know some bishops who delayed writing their letter of resignation for years and the Holy See did not admonish them. My whole priestly life I lived by the letter of the law, and now, when by the grace of God I was able to reach 75 years of age, I decided not to change my way of life, but to continue to be faithful to the law of the Church.

In preparation for this, two years before my 75th birthday, while in Rome, I asked Cardinal Silvestrini, the Prefect of the Eastern Congregation, if I should ask for a coadjutor bishop. He was very affirmative, encouraged me, and even stated that this is the time to do so. To follow his advice means that I would know who is going to succeed me. Bishop Paska, my auxiliary, and some of my trusted priests were consulted and we thoroughly discussed this case. All of them were of the opinion that coadjutor is the preferred way to go. I had three candidates for bishop's office submitted previously and approved by the Synod. So now I prepared a petition to the Holy Father for a coadjutor and sent it through the Apostolic Nunciature in Washington, DC. In such cases, the Congregation for the Eastern Churches normally asks the opinion of the bishops of our province and of the Major Archbishop in Lviv, Ukraine. Apparently one or more of our bishops were not happy with my candidates and they opposed them. Instead of just refusing my request, which would have been in accordance with the Code, the Congregation turned it to our Synod of Bishops for a decision.

In our 1998 Synod of Bishops, Lubomyr Husar, then an auxiliary bishop with delegated powers to the Major Archbishop Lubachivsky, introduced the case to the Synodal Fathers. His introduction lasted for some 50 to 60 minutes and it was all negative. He was trying very hard to explain that according to his thinking great harm would be caused to the Church if I would choose my own successor. I would then perpetuate my own manner and style of work and administration. Actually his introduction was a sort of a political campaign talk trying to persuade the Synodal Fathers to vote against my coadjutor. Actually he was telling the bishops how to vote. In my opinion this was wrong. As the presiding Bishop, he should be neutral. He should have simply introduced the case without his comments.

I got up and thanked my brother bishops for their trust and stated that from the introductory talk of Bishop Husar I learned the bitter truth for the first time that I am actually a bad bishop. If I would choose my own successor, I would perpetuate my disastrous episcopal ministry. I was not aware in what way my episcopal ministry was or is disastrous. But I rely on God and ask Him to be my judge and let Him direct the choice of my successor.

On the day of my seventy-fifth birthday, I wrote this letter to the Holy Father:

663-99-CB
2 October 1999

His Holiness
John Paul II
The Pope of Rome
The Apostolic Palace
00120 Vatican City State

Your Holiness,

I, Stephen Sulyk, Archbishop of Philadelphia for Ukrainians and Metropolitan of Ukrainian Catholic Church in the United States, with the grace of God have now reached the age of 75 years. Today, on my 75th birthday, in obedience to the prescriptions of canon 210 of the Code of Canons for the Eastern Churches, do submit my resignation from the above named offices I hold.

At the feet of Your Holiness, as the successor to St. Peter, I lay my heartfelt thanksgiving to God for the great privilege of being able to serve the Lord God and my people to the best of my ability as a bishop of the Catholic Church.

I am also most grateful to Almighty God that He has blessed me with good health, and in humble obedience to Your Holiness I will continue to shepherd my faithful until Your Holiness determines the will of our Lord and Savior Jesus Christ for me.

I ask Your Holiness for your blessing for me so that I may spend the rest of my earthly life doing the will of God in serving Him in His people.

+ Stephen Sulyk

About three months later I received a note from the Apostolic Nuncio in Washington, informing me that my resignation had been accepted by the Holy Father and that my status now is *nunc pro tunc*, meaning that I must continue my service to the Church until my successor is appointed. At the July 2000 Synod of Bishops, a terna of candidates for my successor was elected and submitted to the Holy Father.

On November 29, 2000, the Apostolic Nuncio announced that the Holy Father appointed Stefan Soroka, Auxiliary Bishop of Winnipeg, as the new Metropolitan Archbishop of Philadelphia for Ukrainians and instructed me to call a meeting of the Archieparchial Consultors for them to elect an administrator of the Archeparchy. On that day I published the following letter, which was mailed to all the priests and the Religious of the Archeparchy and published in the Archieparchial newspaper, *The Way*:

To our Reverend Clergy, our Venerable Religious and our God-loving Faithful, all brothers and sisters in the Lord, Glory be to Jesus Christ!

I am pleased to share the wonderful news that our Holy Father Pope John Paul II has appointed the Most Reverend Stefan Soroka, 49, presently auxiliary bishop of the Archeparchy of Winnipeg, Canada, my successor as Metropolitan-Archbishop of the Ukrainian Catholic Archeparchy of Philadelphia. Archbishop Stefan will serve as the seventh spiritual head of the Ukrainian Catholic Church in the United States. In making this appointment, the Holy Father accepted my resignation, which was submitted to him pursuant to the provisions of canon law when I attained the age of 75 in October 1999. Until the installation of Metropolitan Soroka next year (the date is not determined), I will continue to serve as Administrator of the Archeparchy. The Holy Father also accepted the resignation of my auxiliary Bishop Walter Paska, 77, who submitted his resignation to the Holy See in November 29, 1998, upon reaching the canonical age of 75 for retirement.

The Synod of Bishops of the Ukrainian Catholic Church, which met in Ukraine in July, made its recommendation to the Holy See for the selection of the Metropolitan-Archbishop of Philadelphia.

I have known Bishop Soroka since 1981, when he was a seminarian and a priest student at our St. Josaphat Ukrainian Catholic Seminary in Washington, D.C. from 1979 to 1985, where he earned both his STB and a doctorate in social work from The Catholic University of America. During this time, he became known and a friend of many of our priests, and became most familiar with our Archeparchy and many of our parishes.

Since he was named auxiliary bishop of the Archeparchy of Winnipeg in 1996, he has been a colleague and good friend, especially as we gathered in Synodal meetings of our Ukrainian Catholic Church. His youth, his enthusiasm, and his dedication will enable him to bring a new vitality to our Church as we journey into the twenty-first century.

In the coming weeks, as we prepare to welcome our new spiritual shepherd, I would ask all to pray for him and to remember Bishop Walter and me in your prayers. St. Ignatius of Antioch reminds us how we should welcome our new Metropolitan, *"Whoever is sent by the Master to run his house, we ought to receive him as we would receive the Master himself. It is obvious, therefore, that we ought to regard the bishop as we would the Lord himself."*

Finally, I wish to thank all of you personally for your support, cooperation and prayers throughout the years since I became your Metropolitan almost two decades ago, in 1981. May God bless you all.

The same day I called a meeting of the consultors, and they elected me as the administrator of the archeparchy until the installation of the new archbishop. I called Archbishop-elect Soroka in Winnipeg and congratulated him. I invited him to come to Philadelphia and help us with organizing his installation. I likewise advised him to join the Catholic Bishops of Region III, at their Annual Spiritual Retreat in Jacksonville, FL. the second week of January, so that he may get acquainted with them. I called the Apostolic Nuncio, Archbishop Gabriel Montalvo, and asked him when would he be able to come to Philadelphia for the installation of the new Archbishop. He checked his calendar of appointments and gave me the date of February 27, 2002, asking me to write him a letter on this matter.

In the meantime I was making plans for my retirement. I spoke to Sister Thomas Hrynewich, my chancellor, if she would go with me and another sister and help me keep our house. She agreed to it. With the help of my good friend, Archpriest John Fields, we toured several housing developments to see where we could find a good location for my retirement home. We finally located one in Montgomeryville, Pa. Father Fields hails from Frackville, Pa. As his pastor, I prepared him for his first Holy Communion. He received his First Holy Communion from my hands on Sunday, May 11, 1958, and on the same day, May 11, 1986, I ordained him into the sacred priesthood.

We selected a suitable building lot and made a down payment on it. Then we chose from among several home projects one that would be best suited for our purpose. The downstairs would be a common place for both the nuns and myself. There were two sets of stairs leading to the second floor, one on each side of the house. So the second floor would be divided by a permanent partition across the corridor. The right side would have two bedrooms and a common room, while the left side would have only one bedroom for myself. Next I took Sister Thomas with me for a ride to show her the location with the plans of the house in our hands. She liked the location and I did not expect any changes in my plans. I asked her several times to please talk to her Provincial Superior to approve my and her plans. So next I had a company prepare a contract for the construction of my new home. I signed it and gave them the required $8,000.00 deposit. The date of completion of the construction was to be July of 2001.

Now I was trying to envision my life in retirement. Until my home is built I will have to stay in the present residence. I will move to the apartment on the first floor and Archbishop Soroka will occupy the second floor. I hope that he will agree to this plan. Then I can get one small office or at least a desk in the chancery building and do my work there and help him with whatever he wants me to do. I could, e.g., type his Ukrainian letters, translate his sermons into Ukrainian, I could serve him with my 20-years of experience, give him my opinion on whatever matters come along, substitute for him if needed, etc. But I will never interfere with his business. I will be out of the administration or any other matters that are in his competence. These were my thoughts and plans.

Archbishop-elect Stefan Soroka informed us that he would visit us the third week of December 2001. Sister Thomas and I picked him up on the airport and brought him to my residence. It was evening already. So we set down in my upstairs parlor and had a very friendly, fraternal talk.

Next morning going to the chapel for the 6:30 A.M. Liturgy I found a note on the floor by his door: "I will not concelebrate the Liturgy with you this morning since I did not sleep the whole night." After breakfast both of us went to the chancery building for a 10:00 A.M. meeting with Msgr. James Melnic, Archpriest John Fields and Sister Thomas to start planning his installation. He started the meeting with a statement: "I know of difficulties during the transitional period when a new bishop is appointed. In Winnipeg we had our experience when Metropolitan Michael Bzdel was appointed, even though the retired Metropolitan Maxim Hermaniuk was a gentle and mild man. This is why I would prefer that you, Metropolitan Sulyk, would live somewhere else, but not here to avoid difficulties and clashes."

I then asked:" Could I get a small office in the chancery building where I could work?" He replied: "No! You have to stay in the residence!"

This was a heavy blow for me, a shock that I found difficult initially to overcome. To hear that from my brother bishop in front of my priestly friends and Sister Thomas was very humiliating and depressing. He could have told me all of that privately, but not in front of priests and Sister Thomas. But after some reflection I came to understand his position. He was a stranger, not a member of the clergy of this Archeparchy. For him to have me, who had spent all of my forty-nine years of priestly life in this Archeparchy, including my twenty years as a Metropolitan-Archbishop around, would be too big a challenge. Simply put, he must have been afraid of my personality. So he just had to try to convince me to move away from Philadelphia. In addition to this blow, Sister Thomas told me a few days later that her Provincial Superior refused her request to go with me on my retirement. They have no vocations and not enough sisters to be able to give me two of them. Besides, her Provincial likes to have one of her sisters as a chancellor, a position of authority and influence.

This now placed me in a completely different situation. Not being able to get two sisters to be with me, I would not need a big house all for myself. So I talked it over with Archpriest John Fields, and he promised to look for a decent apartment for me. A few days later he called and said that there is a development of apartment houses near his church called "Jacob's Woods" in Lansdale. Right now they have no vacancies but should have one in early February. So we went there to see a model apartment, and I liked it. Since the installation of my successor would be on February 27, and the vacancy will occur in early February, I agreed to the proposition and signed the lease for one year. Now I had to cancel the construction contract for my house. The company was generous enough and returned to me one-half of the deposit I made—$4,000.00.

Pursuant to the demand of Archbishop-elect Soroka that I should vacate the residence not later than February 10, 2001, I started getting ready to pack my belongings and to move on February 9, 2001. I ordered the furnishings for my new apartment from the store of Michael Hashin in Minersville, Pa.

This was emotionally a very depressing and physically a very tiresome task. I called my friend, Msgr. Myron Grabowsky, a pastor of St. Mary's Church in Bristol, Pa., my former altar boy in Phoenixville parish, whom I sent to the seminary. He agreed to come and help me pack. We got a large number of Quill boxes and began the task of clearing one room after another. In the process I had to discard, give away, or leave behind a great number of things, which could not fit into my small apartment. Out of my large library I gave to the chancery library about 85 percent of my books. Most of my episcopal liturgical vestments went to the cathedral sacristy.

Slowly we were making progress. It took about a week or so to do the job. On February 9, 2001, I rented a Ryder covered truck and asked Tarcisio Calvarho, the janitor at the cathedral church, to help me move. Before we left I went into the chapel, the place where I had spent daily time in prayer, meditation, reciting the Office of the Hours, and celebrating the Divine Liturgy. I loved that chapel so much. It was like a jewel, covered with colorful icons, a precious iconostasis and decorations. I said goodbye to this dear place and asked the Lord to be with me in my new residence, an exile from the home I built.

My apartment is on the second floor. Tarcisio had to carry all the boxes up stairs and pile them up in the office section of the apartment since there were no furnishings there yet. I thanked him and paid him for his help. He left, and I was left alone with the huge task of unpacking, finding room for things, arranging them properly, etc. Feelings of depression suddenly came upon me. All my adult life I was working, and by the help of God achieved success. Now, suddenly I am nothing, I am not needed, a hindrance and an obstacle for others. What is the reason for my present life? What am I now going to do with my time? I have to do something or else I will lose my mind.

Before, when I felt low, I just went to the chapel and prayed to the Eucharistic Lord and He lifted me up. Now I had no chapel as yet, no altar, no tabernacle. I just had to place myself in the presence of God and talk to Him. The Most Holy Mother of God interceded for me. After a while, the Lord came to my aid, gave one consolation, peace, and joy into my heart. Such feelings of depression would come again and again, but each time I was able with the help of God to overcome them.

Slowly I unpacked. Each day I did only so much so as to not to overtire myself. I placed my computer on boxes with books and began slowly to work on it between the unpacking job. Archpriest John Fields ordered office furniture for me and found a man who built an altar and an offertory table for my chapel, which I located in the second bedroom. I ordered a tabernacle in Ukraine from the Studite Fathers. It took eight weeks for my office furniture to arrive. I was slowly getting used to the apartment. There was one difficulty, however, with me living away from our community. I never mastered the culinary arts. I always had someone doing the cooking for me. Now I resolved this problem by going to the nearby Boston Market and buying prepared meals.

Preparations for the installation of Archbishop Soroka were going well. Soon the day arrived. I concelebrated the Installation Divine Liturgy with the other guest-bishops. After the Liturgy the bishops were bused to the hotel for the reception. At the reception I was invited to give an invocation:

Heavenly Father, today we gather as church, to break bread together, as we celebrate with joy and thanksgiving your gift to us, our new spiritual shepherd and my successor, Metropolitan Stefan.

Grant us the grace to be always faithful to your Son, our Lord and Savior Jesus Christ, and may the Holy Spirit be ever present, bestowing His treasury of blessings upon us, Your children, as we journey to the promise of eternal salvation in Your heavenly kingdom.

In a special way, we ask the Holy Spirit to shower his special gifts of holiness, teaching, sanctifying, and shepherding, upon your servant and our brother in the Lord, Metropolitan Stefan, as today he begins his new ministry in your vineyard. As he walks in the footsteps of the Apostles, guide him with your holy wisdom as he leads our Church into the twenty-first century, the Third Millennium since the incarnation of our Lord and Savior Jesus Christ. '

May Christ, our God, bless this food and drink of your servants, for you are holy always, now and forever and ever. Amen.

I used this occasion to say a few words:

My brothers bishops and priests, venerable religious, dear seminarians, dear faithful, all brothers and sisters in the Lord, Glory be to Jesus Christ!

Today, I welcome you to this Testimonial Luncheon in honor of my brother bishop and successor, Metropolitan Stefan, and I am most pleased that you have joined us in this celebration. First, I must admit to you, I really like the first name of my successor, Stefan; it has a familiar ring to it. His last name Soroka begins with the letter "S" so does Sulyk. Guess what? We do not have to change any monograms and all of our priests in commemorating their diocesan bishop in the Liturgy do not have to learn another name.

But really, it is truly an historical day in the life of our Church in the Archeparchy of Philadelphia and throughout our Ukrainian Catholic Church in the United States. And it is unprecedented. All of my predecessors died in office, with the exception of the late Cardinal Lubachivsky, who left Philadelphia to eventually become the Major Archbishop of the Ukrainian Catholic Church.

Today, I thank Almighty God, for blessing me with the grace of priesthood and for the gift of good health and longevity. I also thank all of you, my friends, for your support, cooperation, and prayers throughout the years since I became your Metropolitan some twenty years ago, in 1981. Please continue to remember me in your prayers.

Our Church has been truly blessed with the appointment of Metropolitan Stefan by His Holiness, Pope John Paul II, upon the recommendation of our synod through the power and guidance of the Holy Spirit. His youth, enthusiasm, and his dedication will enable him to bring a new vitality to our Church as we journey into the twenty-first century and face the challenges of contemporary society. With his appointment, my prayers of the last few years for a worthy successor have been answered by Almighty God and *"now, O Lord, you may dismiss me, your servant in peace.* (Luke 2:29)

When the festivities of the installation of my successor were over, the guests went home and so did I. In time, my office furniture came in and so did my chapel altar and the tabernacle. Our good Missionary Sister Yosaphata from Perth Amboy is a good seamstress. She made my altar covers. My life began to take some semblance of normal existence. I had to force myself to follow some kind of daily schedule, i.e., time for rising and going to bed, time for morning and evening prayers, meditation, the Office of the Hours, then Divine Liturgy, thanksgiving, and breakfast. After breakfast I dedicated some forty minutes for reading of the daily newspaper. By 9:00 A.M. I was in my office behind my computer.

I was asked to substitute for Msgr. Theodore Boholnick at Simpson, Pa., on Easter Sunday, since he was ill. I took two of our seminarians with me who helped me drive and sing the responses at the church services. I stopped in Olyphant to see Msgr. Stephen Hrynuck and remained there for the night. After the services in Simpson on Easter Sunday, I returned to Olyphant and celebrated the 12 Noon Liturgy there. Father Roman Dubitsky invited me to come to Perth Amboy to bless a new chapel in the vestibule of his church and to celebrate Divine Liturgy and give a homily. The following Sunday he invited me to his second parish—Toms River, N.J. to bless an icon in the shrine and to celebrate a Divine Liturgy.

On one occasion Archpriest John Fields asked me to substitute for him Sunday morning in his church in Lansdale. So far these are all my substitutions.

I was working in my spare time for several years on my memoirs, written in Ukrainian. Now I was able to complete them. Lucy Vnukova, who works in our chancery, proofread the book, and her husband, Serge, made the layout on Page Maker and inserted thirty-four photos in their proper places. I prepared an alphabetical index of names, and the book came to have 691 pages. I gave it a title: "How Stephen Became a Metropolitan." My long-time friend, Father Dmytro Blazejowskyj from Rome, Italy, volunteered to have the book published in Ukraine and will take care of its sales.

To occupy my time with something of interest, I began to write my memoirs in English, giving then another title, "I am With You Always" (Matthew 28:20). In it I followed the layout in the Ukrainian book, but did not make it a strict translation. I did skip some parts that would not be of interest to an English reader and added many others that were not in the Ukrainian book. The Ukrainian text ends with the year 1997, while the English one continues to 2002. Now I pray that after my English book is done, and I find a good editor for it, that the Lord God will give me an idea what I should do next. Pray for me!

Epilogue

I entrust these my memoirs to print and then to my beloved brothers in the episcopacy, to my brother priests, religious, and to all the dear to my heart faithful as my witness before God of my love of the one, holy catholic and apostolic Church of Christ. To her I have dedicated all my life, my labors, and endeavors for the increase of the Kingdom of God on earth, for God's greater glory and for the salvation of the souls committed to my care.

From my life's journey, it is very evident that God was leading me and coming to my aid in all circumstances. He guided my steps constantly, and He was with me always. He poured into my heart the grace of vocation to the holy priesthood and blessed all my endeavors. When in January of 1981, I was informed of the Holy Father's intention to appoint me to the position of a Metropolitan-Archbishop, before I could give my consent, I prayed for more than an hour before our Lord in the Blessed Sacrament. I was trying hard to find an excuse as to why I should not accept this nomination. My biggest excuse was that I was not capable of such an exalted office; not strong enough and, therefore, liable to fall and cause scandal.

But the Lord, in my case, did exactly what He did long ago. When a vast throng of people followed Him, He was moved with pity, and He cured their sick. *"As the evening drew on, his disciples* came to him with the suggestion: 'This is a deserted place and it is already late. Dismiss the crowds so that they may go to the villages and buy some food for themselves.' Jesus said to them: 'There is no need for them to disperse. Give them something to eat yourselves.' 'We have nothing here,' they replied, 'but five loaves and a couple of fish.' 'Bring them here,' he said. Then he ordered the crowds to sit down on the grass. He took the five loaves and the two fish, looked up to heaven. Blessed and broke them and gave the loaves to the disciples, who in turn gave them to the people. All those present ate their fill. The fragments remaining, when gathered up, filled twelve baskets. Those who ate were about five thousand . . ." (Matthew 14:15–21). The Lord God used their insufficiency, and with His divine power made it more than sufficient. He did the same in my case. He used my little talents, my small loaves of energy, blessed and multiplied them so they became more than sufficient for my episcopal ministry.

The love of His Church alone prompted me to put down on paper not only my personal experiences in life, not only my successes and mistakes, but also the events pertaining to the life of the Church, since they always were so very closely tied to my life, my plans and dreams.

I firmly believe that the faithful should always be well informed as to the work of our bishops in their Synods. The bishop is the leader of the Church. When the faithful get to know better the labors of the bishop, the difficulties he has to overcome, they will appreciate more the efforts that had to be sacrificed on their behalf. Then they will more readily support the bishop with their prayers and cooperation. This is why in my memoirs I included some of the aspects of the work of our bishops in their Synods, avoiding always what by the Church law is to be kept a secret.

I am very much aware that there will be critics of this my work. I will be judged not only as a hierarch, but likewise all of my life, my work, achievements or failures, all will be scrutinized. But I do not write about these events or happenings to please someone or to be praised. I cannot please everyone. I write out of love for my Church for the history's sake so that the future generations would not repeat our mistakes.

Our Lord commanded his apostles: *"You will receive power when the Holy Spirit comes down on you; then you are to be my witnesses in Jerusalem, throughout Judea and Samaria, yes even to the ends of the earth"* (Acts 1:8). This is why, being always conscious of my sacred duty to be a witness of Christ, in these my memoirs I tried to the best of my ability to give a true and faithful testimony concerning events, persons, or things as God made me to see and to understand them. I am very much aware that these, my memoirs, are not a complete description of the events or happenings contained here. Even though I knew about the things or events omitted here, yet I did not write about them out of respect for persons or because I personally did not see or hear them. Hearsay witness was not used in this book. I always tried to base my testimony on proven facts as it is fitting a reliable witness.

Looking back on my life's journey with a critical eye, I have to say that I enjoyed being a priest of Christ and then a bishop. Priesthood is the most wonderful and most enjoyable life if one has faith in God, love of God and of one's neighbor. With God in my heart, if I had a chance to choose my life's vocation again, I would without hesitation choose priesthood. Priestly life for me was so wonderful and enjoyable due to the quality of our priests who always were good to me, always brother like, helpful, and cooperative. It is most of all due to the quality of our faithful. To them I owe a great debt of gratitude and love for their goodness, cooperation, and generosity, and above all for their love for me. I think that the Ukrainian Catholic faithful in the United States of America are about the best people in the world. To serve them was the greatest joy of my life.

In my earthly life's journey it is already nearly evening; the day is practically over. This is why, as long as my memory serves me well, I collected and recorded the events and happenings in my life to witness before the world that *"God was with me always"* (Matthew 28:20). With His guidance and help I was able to go through life and am leaving for the future generations true facts and experiences so as to share them with others and to hand over to history some of the important events in the life of our Church which no one else recorded.

I impart my episcopal blessing to each and every reader of these my memoirs and ask for their prayers. May the blessing of the Father, the Son, and the Holy Spirit descend upon you, keep you in good health, peace and happiness, and remain with you always!

+ Stephen Sulyk
Metropolitan-Archbishop *emeritus*

February 2003 A.D.

To order additional copies of

I am with you

ALWAYS

Have your credit card ready and call:

1-877-421-READ (7323)

or please visit our web site at
www.pleasantword.com

Also available at: www.amazon.com

Printed in the United States
15674LVS00003B/19